W9-DEQ-889

Autonomy and Order

Rights and Responsibilities:
Communitarian Perspectives
Series Editor: Amitai Etzioni

National Parks: Rights and the Common Good
edited by Francis N. Lovett

Community Justice: An Emerging Field
edited by David R. Karp

Civic Repentance
edited by Amitai Etzioni

Marriage in America: A Communitarian Perspective
edited by Martin King Whyte

Autonomy and Order: A Communitarian Anthology
edited by Edward W. Lehman

Between Consent and Dissent: Democracy and Peace in the Israeli Mind
by Ephraim Yuchtman-Ya'ar and Yochanan Peres

Autonomy and Order

A Communitarian Anthology

Edited by
Edward W. Lehman

CABRINI COLLEGE LIBRARY
610 KING OF PRUSSIA ROAD
RADNOR, PA 19087

ROWMAN & LITTLEFIELD PUBLISHERS, INC.
Lanham • Boulder • New York • Oxford

HM
758
.A87
2000

#43701770

ROWMAN & LITTLEFIELD PUBLISHERS, INC.

Published in the United States of America
by Rowman & Littlefield Publishers, Inc.
4720 Boston Way, Lanham, Maryland 20706
http://www.rowmanlittlefield.com

12 Hid's Copse Road
Cumnor Hill, Oxford OX2 9JJ, England

Copyright © 2000 by Rowman & Littlefield Publishers, Inc.

All rights reserved. No part of this publication may be reproduced,
stored in a retrieval system, or transmitted in any form or by any
means, electronic, mechanical, photocopying, recording, or otherwise,
without the prior permission of the publisher.

British Library Cataloguing in Publication Information Available

Library of Congress Cataloging-in-Publication Data

Autonomy and order : a communitarian anthology / edited by Edward W. Lehman.
    p.   cm. — (Rights and responsibilities)
    ISBN 0-8476-9702-9 (cloth : alk. paper)—ISBN 0-8476-9703-7 (pbk. : alk. paper)
    1. Communitarianism.   I. Rights and responsibilities (Lanham, Md.)

    HM758 .A87   2000
    303.3′72—dc21   00-035382

∞™ The paper used in this publication meets the minimum requirements of American
National Standard for Information Sciences—Permanence of
Paper for Printed Library Materials, ANSI/NISO Z39.48-1992.
Manufactured in the United States of America.

For Jennifer O'Neil Lehman,

The Newest Member of Our Family "Community"

Contents

Acknowledgments   ix

Introduction: Autonomy and Order   xi

Prologue: From Compliance to Community in the Works of Amitai Etzioni   xvii
Edward W. Lehman

1   Autonomy, Functionalism, and the Common Good:
Some Liberal Doubts about *The New Golden Rule*   1
William R. Lund

2   Communitarianism, Human Nature, and the Spirit of the Times   23
Dennis H. Wrong

3   Procedure and Conviction: On Moral Dialogues   37
Hans Joas

4   The Integrity of Unrestricted Desire: Community, Values, and
the Problem of Personhood   57
Thomas C. Kohler

5   What Can the Study of Communities Teach Us about Community?   71
Benjamin D. Zablocki

6   Defining Community: A Psychological Perspective   89
Tom R. Tyler and Robert Boeckmann

7   Community and Its Discontents: Politics and Etzioni's
The New Golden Rule   111
Wilson Carey McWilliams

8 Integrating Diversity: Boundaries, Bonds, and the Greater Community
   in *The New Golden Rule*   125
   Paul Lichterman

9 Communitarianism: The Issue of Relativism   143
   Nicos Mouzelis

10 Moral Dialogue across Cultures: An Empirical Perspective   155
    Shalom H. Schwartz and Anat Bardi

11 The Cycles of Moral Dialogue   185
    Joel H. Rosenthal

12 Accounting for Order   193
    J. Russell Muirhead

13 Toward an International Human Rights (and Responsibilities) Regime:
    Some Obstacles   211
    Daniel A. Bell

Epilogue   219
    Amitai Etzioni

Index   237

About the Contributors   245

Acknowledgments

The idea for this anthology grew from a conference I organized at New York University on February 20 and 21, 1997. It was titled "Community and Morality in a Democratic Society" and was occasioned by the publication of Amitai Etzioni's *The New Golden Rule*. Given the considerable success of that conference, Amitai and I agreed that the larger question of the theoretical strength of communitarian thought in the 1990s deserved further scrutiny. I decided to begin such an examination using the themes in *The New Golden Rule* as a springboard. *Autonomy and Order: A Communitarian Anthology* is the result. However, I also felt strongly that to keep this volume as tightly focused as possible I would commission an entirely new set of papers rather than to use any of the many commendable ones given at the conference.

An acknowledgment section for a collection of essays should begin with a salute to the contributors. I am deeply indebted to these authors, not just for the quality of what they have produced but for the patience and perseverance they have shown throughout the process. I peppered them with demands to focus on specific questions and to adhere to demanding timetables. But that's not all. They were asked to respond to comments from a review committee as well. Frankly, some very promising, potential contributions fell by the wayside as the enterprise went on. Those authors who did stay the course have contributed significantly to how we will view communitarianism at the dawn of a new millennium.

I also want to express my appreciation to Amitai Etzioni for his unwavering support and suggestions throughout this project. Amitai has managed to be consistently helpful without ever being interfering. In particular, I wish to acknowledge the grant he assisted me in obtaining from the Center for Policy Research of the George Washington University (GW project AA39600), which made the completion of this volume possible.

Without Ethna Lehman's wisdom, intelligence, encouragement, and common sense this project would not have been completed. She has been a steadfast colleague at every stage. I also wish to acknowledge the advice of the three-person internal review committee who made detailed comments and recommendations for every draft submitted to me. They have asked me to continue to respect my pledge of anonymity.

The prologue is reprinted (with minor revisions) with permission from: Edward W. Lehman, "From Compliance to Community in the Works of Amitai Etzioni," *The Responsive Community* 9(1): 38–47. The chapter by Daniel A. Bell is a revised and enlarged version of a paper from the same journal and is reprinted with permission from: Daniel A. Bell, "Toward an International Human Rights (and Responsibilities) Regime: Some Obstacles," *The Responsive Community* 9(1): 72–8.

Introduction:
Autonomy and Order

The communitarian movement asserts that a specter is haunting the United States and other Western societies: the specter of overemphasis on individual rights and underemphasis on social responsibilities. Its proponents challenge prevailing individualist and social-conservative paradigms in public life and social policy as well as in the theoretical arena. This volume's central concern is with the latter realm: the *intellectual merit* of communitarian thinking as developed in the 1990s. As debate swirls over the robustness of contemporary communitarian theory, *The New Golden Rule* by Amitai Etzioni, one of the movement's founders, has emerged at the intellectual cutting edge of what he has termed the New (or Responsive) Communitarianism.

This anthology of essays by prominent philosophers, political scientists, and sociologists allows us to systematically ask how theoretically comprehensive and empirically open the communitarian paradigm is. This volume is not about Etzioni's book per se. Rather, since it is the paradigm's most complete articulation to date, I regard it as an excellent basis from which one can launch an assessment of the overall approach. With *The New Golden Rule* as the guidepost for organizing "conversations," essays are structured around key questions that spring from the New Communitarianism's basic theoretical assumptions. Contributors have criticized, modified, augmented, or supported these positions as they saw fit. The chapters offer diverse intellectual points of view; some deal primarily with the theoretical completeness of communitarianism, while others address the theory's empirical strength. The only mandate given the authors was to engage pivotal issues in a way that would guarantee the volume's integrated and comprehensive thrust.

Contributors were asked to confront one or more of the following themes raised by Etzioni:

1. A "good society" springs from shared core values that privilege neither individual self-interest (*autonomy*) nor the common good (*order*) but seek a judicious balance of the two.
2. "Moral dialogues," in the face of seemingly divergent values, are the most effective means for defining the "good" without lapsing into "culture wars." These exchanges are not just rational deliberations but must be complemented by dialogues that engage values.
3. A good society cannot rely merely on families, schools, or communities to bring up persons of conscience and good character. It must also be able to draw continuously on the "moral voice" of the community. Under most circumstances, informal, persuasive communal voices are preferred to the law to foster morally responsible behavior.
4. The idea that each community or society is its own moral arbiter and not accountable to others is rejected. Given this rejection of moral relativism, one must ask: Which standards are the most appropriate for judging the moral soundness of the values that various communities and societies underwrite?

In my prologue I situate the "communitarian Etzioni" in the context of his earlier scholarly works. I do this to stress that not only is there no necessary discontinuity between the "young Etzioni" and the "more mature" one but that appreciation of his original focus on power, alienation, and compliance can enrich our understanding of the New Communitarianism. Chapters one through thirteen cluster around four overriding themes of the communitarian paradigm as articulated in *The New Golden Rule*. Chapters one and two address the thorny theoretical problem of what exactly constitutes a judicious balancing of autonomy and order. Specifically, William R. Lund and Dennis H. Wrong examine whether Etzioni has taken the value of individual autonomy seriously enough given the tenor of our times. Lund, a self-proclaimed "egalitarian liberal," sees Etzioni's formulation as a significant advance beyond the claims of individualistic liberals and social conservatives because it assigns a legitimate place to both individual rights and social responsibilities. But Lund also points to tensions in Etzioni's approach to autonomy, which he attributes to a "teleological core" built on functional and moral-sense analyses. These tensions, he insists, may inadvertently provide a justification for unwarranted hierarchies and coercive measures that undermine individual rights.

Wrong finds Etzioni's framing of the need to balance autonomy and order far more theoretically nuanced and empirically grounded than the formulations of most other contemporary communitarian thinkers. He praises Etzioni for avoiding an "over-socialized" conceptualization of this balance, although he questions the interpretation of the 1950s as an era of consensus and the 1960s as the root of the erosion of moral order. Wrong declares himself closer to the liberal-individualist end of the autonomy/order continuum than is Etzioni and hints that the New Communitarianism might do well to follow this lead.

Chapters three and four focus on the nature of moral dialogues and their capacities to transcend "culture wars." Hans Joas (chapter three) contrasts a "discourse in ethics," which he associates with Jurgen Habermas, with (what he calls) Etzioni's "dialogue of convictions," and he sketches a possible combination of the two. Such a linkage, Joas argues, demonstrates that the apparently insurmountable breach between "value pluralism" and "moral universalism" is, in fact, not so irreconcilable as it first seems.

Thomas C. Kohler (chapter four) endorses Etzioni's ambitious attempt "to identify a basis for values and community that goes beyond some forms of mere consensus or nose-counting." But he argues that Etzioni tends to relapse into "expressive individualism" because he has not provided an adequate justification for truly authoritative norms. Kohler suggests that such a justification demands an understanding of human personhood that more fully appreciates the intentional operations of an individual's consciousness. Kohler also proposes that "issues raised by Etzioni are in a most profound sense religious." However, he suggests that Etzioni fails to give sufficient credence to the inevitable religious grounding of community, values, and the common good.

Chapters five through eight zero in on Etzioni's perspective on communities and the prospects for "megalogues" as the grounding for a "community of communities." In chapter five, Benjamin D. Zablocki not only disputes Etzioni's meaning of "community," but, more pivotally, he argues that this formulation may be neither empirically feasible nor morally desirable, even for those seeking "new communal forms with teeth." In the process, Zablocki reviews four historical cases as well as data on five contemporary U.S. community experiments to point out pitfalls that may face current attempts at communal regeneration.

Tom R. Tyler and Robert Boeckmann (chapter six) follow with a quantitative chapter based on a survey of 166 citizens conducted in the East Bay area of northern California to consider the psychological foundations of communities. Their findings deepen our knowledge of factors that motivate citizens to voluntarily participate in their communities: namely, "views about morality in society, status judgments that define people's relationships with the community, and views about social bonds in the community." They also inform us that community members are less concerned with moral consensus (than they believe is implied in Etzioni's perspective) while being more committed to having their own views respected and having at least some others in the community who share their values.

Wilson Carey McWilliams and Paul Lichterman both explicitly extend the analysis of communities to the broader social and cultural contexts in which they are embedded. In chapter seven, McWilliams applauds the idea of a community of communities as a "mosaic" that must be framed by defining values and glued by attachments and procedures. But he believes that Etzioni underestimates the tenacity of American individualism and does not sufficiently accentuate the need for politics (although it also contributes to the problems of community) and authoritative decisions to strengthen the common good and the building of layered loyalties. In making this case, however, McWilliams reinforces Etzioni's emphasis on the importance of democratic norms and agrees that societal transformation rests, in the final analysis, on moral foundations.

In chapter eight, Lichterman commends Etzioni's advocacy of "thick" social order over mere "thin" agreement on procedures as a surer basis for promoting both shared values and diversity. However, drawing on his own fieldwork among community activists, he concludes that Etzioni's community of communities is not communitarian enough because it lacks a sufficiently nuanced vision of bonds and boundaries. In the process, Lichterman sketches a picture of communities as mutually constitutive and marked by permeable boundaries and evolving and interpenetrating loyalties. The more these traits occur among (what he terms) "specific greater communities," the greater are the prospects for "creating unity in diversity."

Finally, in one way or another, "postrelativism" (viz., communitarianism's rejection of the notion that each community or society is its own final moral arbiter) is the theoretical theme that informs chapters nine through thirteen. Nicos Mouzelis (in chapter nine) asserts that Etzioni's call for balance between autonomy and order and for megalogues is more theoretically compelling than his critique of relativism. To overcome this lacuna Mouzelis proposes that communitarianism adopt a "more historically oriented, macrocomparative, evolutionist perspective," which transcends relativism, not by arguing that values are universally self-evident, but by emphasizing what Talcott Parsons called "evolutionary universals."

In chapter ten, Shalom H. Schwartz and Anat Bardi report on a sixty-two-nation survey that examines Etzioni's claim that a small set of core values exists that both are self-evident and speak to people cross-culturally. They compared the ratings of ten "value types" across nations and report that indeed there are universally shared core values, although cultures vary according to the priority they give to particular values. Their chapter concludes with a consideration of why some values enjoy widespread endorsement whereas others are assigned lesser importance.

In chapter eleven, Joel H. Rosenthal examines the lessons of Mahatma Gandhi and Martin Luther King and applauds an emphasis on moral dialogues because it highlights the "power of principle" and its ability to transcend purely local and particularistic interests. But he believes that a fully satisfying postrelativist program for building shared and binding values must also account for the limitations of moral dialogues and include a recognition of history, memory, and the exigencies of political power.

J. Russell Muirhead's chapter (twelve) continues the focus on the role of political power in achieving consensus within a community of communities. He concurs with Etzioni that we must give an account of value that does not rest content with conventions. But moral sense, he argues, is the wrong place to look for such an account of value. Taking up the social value of order, Muirhead contrasts two fundamentally different accounts for justifying order: one looking to the community, and the other looking to individual interest. While the language of individual interest is more dominant and familiar today, Muirhead argues that some element of the organic account is necessary, both for the sake of deepening the liberal commitment to equal respect and for better addressing social and economic inequalities.

In chapter thirteen, Daniel A. Bell examines Etzioni's proposals for improving international human rights so that they better reflect fundamental agreements on global values. He spotlights three possible complications in this approach: the more inclusive the megalogues, the more difficult it is to achieve politically meaningful resolutions; the greater the appeal to foundational values, the greater risk of undermining trust among members of different societies; and the greater the recourse to a language of responsibilities, the higher the danger of abuses by those who want to curtail individual rights.

This volume concludes with an epilogue by Amitai Etzioni. His reflections on the preceding essays mirror this collection's primary agenda. His remarks are intended to incorporate our contributors' comments into a more theoretically comprehensive and empirically open communitarian paradigm rather than to provide a personal defense of particular theoretical positions.

As the editor, I believe I'm entitled to some modest boasting. Among these essays' many commendable features is the fact that they actually defy the neat conceptual compartmentalization that I have tried to impose. Each essay raises theoretical questions for all the others. These are authentic scholarly "conversations" about the communitarian paradigm's theoretical robustness. For example, Kohler's chapter could easily have been put alongside Lund's and Wrong's in order to contrast more sharply his claim that Etzioni is still too individualistic with Lund's and Wrong's worries that at times he is not individualistic enough. Or, I might well have grouped the chapter by Lund with those by McWilliams, Rosenthal, and Muirhead in light of their common concerns with political power. Moreover, the line between the Joas and Kohler chapters and the five I've categorized under "postrelativism" is highly permeable. Anyone interested in a more complete theoretical grasp of the roles (and interaction) of inter- and intracommunity consensus would do well to look at all seven at the same time.

Readers no doubt will find other ways to "shuffle the deck," given their own special intellectual foci. But, in the final analysis, this only testifies to the internal coherence and cogency of the volume. Although the New Communitarianism raises a range of questions, it is unified by a shared core of theoretical problematics. Confronting this core, I hope, helps advance our understanding of its intellectual challenge to the twenty-first-century world.

Prologue:
From Compliance to Community
in the Works of Amitai Etzioni

Edward W. Lehman

In assessing Amitai Etzioni's contributions to the "New Communitarianism" it is important to recall that he did not start out as a communitarian thinker. Indeed, his immense body of work, covering the last five decades of the twentieth century, may tempt observers to exaggerate differences between the "young" and the more "mature" Etzioni.[1] Yet, despite seemingly abrupt shifts in subject matter, his accomplishments are marked far more by continuity than by disjuncture.

In this chapter, I highlight this continuity by pointing out the common threads that link his first major book, *A Comparative Analysis of Complex Organizations*, to *The New Golden Rule*. On the surface these two books appear to come from entirely dissimilar theoretical universes. The former, published in 1961, is an academic, apparently "value free," tour de force that extends Weberian and Mertonian analyses of bureaucracies by contrasting their social structures via such "hardheaded" factors as power and compliance; the latter, published in 1996, is a bold exercise in "normative" (viz., prescriptive) theory that advocates greater individual and collective responsibilities by underscoring the availability of shared moral understandings. Closer inspection, however, reveals complementary "moral" concerns and reliance on similar theoretical tools. Such inspection also rebuts the criticism that Etzioni's communitarianism represents a soberly high-minded but basically unrealistic strategy for a world riven by economic exploitation and irreducible social conflicts.[2]

When *Comparative Analysis* was published, the study of complex organizations (or bureaucracies or institutions, in other scholars' parlance) was at the cutting edge of sociological analysis, even more so than today. An explanation of why this was so is beyond this chapter's scope; but, in light of my objective here, let me stress that the factors transcend the disciplinary exigencies of sociology in the early 1960s. Organizations were (and are) seen as essential ingredients of modernity. (Max Weber, for instance, believed that bureaucratization defined the contemporary world and that its manifestations in premodern times were extremely rare, e.g., in pharaonic Egypt, the medieval papacy, and the mandarin administration of imperial China.) Since organizations permeate virtually every aspect of our lives, sociologists—heady with post–World War II optimism—puzzled over how these "social machines with human parts" could be made not only more effective and efficient but also more responsive to staff and "clients" and more congenial with a democratic culture.

By the late 1950s, Etzioni and a younger generation of organizational sociologists believed the time had come to confront these questions by bringing together case studies and ambitious theorizing to zero in on the systematic differences among the diverse range of units classified as complex organizations. Theoretically informed comparisons were seen as essential because commonsense labels, such as, for instance, hospital, mental health facility, prison, and labor unions, cannot do the job of rendering what is going on in such social units. "Comparative analysis" became the order of the day, and no formulation has had a more abiding impact than Etzioni's organizational sociology. Theoretical rigor alone does not account for the success of his "compliance model." Its influence also stems from the fact that it is not a "parochial" exercise in organizational theory but embodies pivotal *societal* concerns of (those whom today we call) classic sociological theorists, particularly Karl Marx, Émile Durkheim, Max Weber, and Talcott Parsons.[3]

Like them, Etzioni assigns a key place to *social structures* (patterns of relationships produced and reproduced by individual and collective actors who are members of a social unit). And, especially following Weber, he grasps that a nuanced understanding of *power* (the ability of an actor in a relationship to attain goals despite resistance) is fundamental to understanding organizational and societal structures. Power is central, for Etzioni, because it shapes both: (1) the means by which a social unit is able to advance its goals and hence to maintain or transform itself; and (2) the extent to which participants can be mobilized to perform and contribute creatively. In Etzioni's communitarian theory these two dimensions are to be formally christened as the linked problems of *order* and *autonomy.*

A TYPOLOGY OF COMPLIANCE

The decisive basis of comparison in Etzioni's *compliance* model is how organizational needs and wants are reconciled with what participants would prefer to do. Specifically, it directs our attention to: (1) the kinds of *power* exercised primarily by elites as they pursue organizational goals (and, in his later terminology, *order* more generally); and (2) the kinds of *involvement* different forms of power elicit from lower participants (who try to retain some *autonomy*). Etzioni argues that organizational arrangements that may foster effectiveness and efficiency (and implicitly, responsiveness and democracy as well) in one compliance structure will not do so in all others. Economic incentives, for example, may successfully induce workers to make greater contributions in a typical U.S. business organization but fall flat when mobilizing community activists, Trappist monks, or prisoners of war.

Etzioni assumes that power is more than simple "coercion" (conceived broadly as compelling people to do what they would not do otherwise). He posits three analytically distinct types of power: (1) *coercive power* (conceived more narrowly), which rests on the control of physical sanctions that can do violence to people's bodies or psyches; (2) *remunerative power,* which springs from control over material rewards such as goods, services, property, and income; and (3) *normative power,* which derives from the command of symbolic rewards and deprivations, the most universal of which are prestige, esteem, acceptance, and love.

Etzioni posits that compliance's other dimension, involvement, similarly contains three analytical types. Lower participants' actions are marked by *alienative, calculative,* or *moral* involvements. "Alienative involvement," he notes, "designates an intense negative orientation. . . . Inmates in prisons, prisoners of war, people in concentration camps, enlisted men in basic training, all tend to be alienated from their respective organizations."[4] He defines calculative involvement as "either a negative or positive orientation of low intensity"[5] and views the prevailing mood as "what's in it for me." Etzioni suggests that calculative involvement characterizes not only the dispositions of workers under advanced capitalism but that of most managers, traders, and entrepreneurs too. Finally, he states: "Moral involvement designates a positive orientation of high intensity"[6] and points to the commitment of parishioners to their church and activists to their party as typical examples.

While the combination of power and involvement logically yields nine possible compliance structures, Etzioni rivets attention on three "congruent" types: (1) *coercive compliance,* the joining of coercive power and alienative involvement; (2) *utilitarian compliance,* the combination of remunerative power and calculative involvement; and (3) *normative compliance,* the linking of normative power with moral involvement. Etzioni's spotlighting of these three is not the gimmicky heuristic device other theorists sometimes resort to when reasserting command over a conceptual apparatus that threatens to run amok. Rather his "reduction" is premised on a "dynamic hypothesis" regarding the interplay of power and involvement that anchors not only his comparison of organizations but informs his subsequent work. The "dynamic hypothesis" states:

> Congruent types are more effective than incongruent types. Organizations are under pressure to be effective. Hence, . . . *organizations tend to shift their* compliance structures from incongruent to congruent types and organizations which have congruent compliance structures tend to resist factors pushing them *toward incongruent compliance structures* [italics in original].[7]

Congruence is achieved by a shift in either the power wielded by elites or the involvement of lower participants. Coercive power to implement *order goals*[8] (controlling "deviants" by segregating them from the rest of society) is most effective when dealing with lower participants who are highly alienated (e.g., inmates of traditional prisons or custodial mental hospitals); remunerative power to achieve *production goals* (creating goods and services that are supplied to "outsiders") works best in the context of calculative involvement by lower participants (e.g., assembly-line workers); and normative power to obtain *cultural goals* (creating, preserving, and transmitting cultural objects like beliefs, values, and expressive symbols) operates most smoothly when lower participants are morally involved (e.g., graduate students, members of social-movement organizations, patients in intensive psychotherapy).

TO COERCE OR NOT TO COERCE

A surface reading of *Comparative Analysis* may leave the erroneous impression that Etzioni (at this stage) feels that coercive, utilitarian, and normative compliance are moral equivalents and that no one of them is superior to the others; our organizational society, after all, depends on all three and which one organizations should implement depends on what they want to accomplish. Closer reading, however, discloses normative compliance's privileged position.

To begin with, this unstated preference for normative compliance is rooted in the very logic of Etzioni's comparative analysis. Since organizations' compliance structures do not coincide with their taken-for-granted identities (and may contradict them), he goes to particularly great lengths to emphasize that mental hospitals and prisons can be either coercive or normative and labor unions occur in all three categories. Even what such organizations claim to do often is not corroborated by study of their actual compliance structures. Prison systems that advertise themselves as being in the rehabilitation business often operate as coercive organizations whose real goal is to incarcerate "social undesirables." Some mental hospitals that trumpet a therapeutic agenda are in reality closer to prisons pursuing order goals. And many labor unions officially advocating workers' rights (and normative compliance) are either really built around "delivering the goods" (and hence utilitarian compliance) or are linked to "organized crime" (and thus coercive compliance).

These pivotal examples are an implicit acknowledgment (which actually runs throughout the book) that ceteris paribus normative compliance represents the most humane way to control and to build commitments. Normative compliance is essential for organizations whose intent is to buttress or transform participants' inner selves. These organizations see lower participants as *ends* and not just means. In such circumstances, normative power is most effective because it alone is capable of penetrating people's interior dispositions; the efficacy of the other forms of power rests merely on the successful manipulation of external, "objective" rewards and punishments. Moral involvement is essential when treating people as subjects whose capacities for thinking, evaluating, feeling, and choosing are at the core of an organization's agenda.

In short, Etzioni implicitly advocates the superiority of normative compliance. In effect, he is not saying that only organizations such as prisons, mental hospitals, and labor unions ought to be marked by normative compliance. His book indicates that schools, churches, and voluntary associations should also adopt such structures. Moreover, by extension, he is suggesting that *all* social units (and not just organizations) that strive to treat their members as the ends of action and not merely as cogs in a social machine should adopt normative compliance. (The view that people must *always* be treated as more than means to others' ends, of course, becomes a defining feature of Etzioni's communitarianism.) Normative compliance is the best structure, not only for satisfying the highest collective goals and needs but also for displaying the greatest respect for participants as authentic subjects of I-Thou versus I-It relations (to use the language of Etzioni's first mentor, Martin Buber).

Comparative Analysis contains brief discussions of a subtype of normative compliance, the *social normative*, which is less pivotal to that inquiry because it occurs most commonly in "horizontal" primary groups (rather than "hierarchical" secondary units); hence it was largely overlooked by commentators at the time. Based on *social power* and *social involvement*, it tends to occur more in peer relations than does "pure" normative compliance. Social power rests on the ability to reward and punish by wielding acceptance and positive responses; and social involvement depends on participants' commitments to primary groups and their members. Social normative compliance is organizationally important, however, in accounting for the "collegial" relations among the professional staffs of professional organizations.[9] It assumes strategic significance later in clarifying the role of "moral dialogue" and the "moral voice" in Etzioni's communitarianism.

FROM ORGANIZATIONS TO SOCIETY

This privileged position of both types of normative compliance, however, does not become an integral feature of his theorizing until *The Active Society*.[10] Published amidst the tumult of the late 1960s, that book is as relentlessly social structural as *Comparative Analysis* and employs many of the same categories. It raises the level of analysis, however, from organizations to society. Organizations like the state, political parties, labor unions, business corporations, churches, and so forth are still pivotal actors, but Etzioni's concern shifts to how they foster or impair the prospects for "*societal* transformation." More significantly, *The Active Society* assumes an overtly normative (i.e., prescriptive) stance with its focus on how to move societies to ever higher levels of activation.

The Active Society is perhaps Etzioni's most notable *scholarly* attainment, but it is not at the hub of this chapter. I fix on it because it illuminates the transition from his earlier compliance model and his later concerns with the "moral dimension" and especially "moral dialogue" and "moral voice." It shares a core problematic with

Comparative Analysis: the relationship between governing elites and the commitments of those they govern (and implicitly the theme of balancing order and autonomy). But it broadens our understanding of both elite power and lower participant involvement. Elite capacities must be weighed by more than their ability to constrain, induce, or persuade the governed. There are now rich analyses of how the knowledge, consciousness, and commitment capacities of societal elites also affect their ability to transform and guide. Moreover, the problem of involvement is translated into the question of consensus-formation structures. Lower participants' contributions are now explicitly no longer just reactions to elite power. Consensus-formation structures must be "responsive" and nonelites must have a share of power, a sense of efficacy, and reduced alienation. In short, consensus formation is normative compliance on a societal, more fully developed, and realistic scale. When societies rely too heavily on utilitarian or coercive compliance the grounding for a more "active society" erodes.

THE MORAL VOICE EMERGES

In *The Moral Dimension*,[11] Etzioni, in a stinging critique of neoclassical economics, concentrates on the relevance of normative compliance in molding both individual actions and societal order. While not abandoning social-structural considerations, Etzioni now gives cultural factors equal weight. Moral evaluations are irreducible features of both action and order, he argues, and cannot be conflated with the pleasure principle or self-interest. Action "in line with one's moral values" he argues, "produces a kind of satisfaction, a sense of moral worth . . . of *affirmation* of having done what is required."[12] Along with affective elements, morals are the most important bases for individual choices; "logical/empirical considerations" play only a secondary role. Indeed, Etzioni rejects neoclassical economics' assertion that market principles are a sufficient basis for social order. Market competition, unless "encapsulated," will "escalate into destructive, all out conflict."[13] The final section of *The Moral Dimension* explores the normative, social, and governmental ingredients of a societal "capsule" that is strong enough to contain competition without undermining its positive contributions.

This heightened emphasis on the moral bases of autonomous actions and social order has led Etzioni to communitarianism and reflects his deepening appreciation of normative compliance. While *The Moral Dimension* still visibly displays the influence of *The Active Society* (most notably in its detailed discussion of the positive role of government power), by the time one gets to *The New Golden Rule* the transition is complete.[14] The focus is now more on the content of moral principles and less on formal hierarchic mechanisms of compliance. Etzioni argues that a "good society," in its search for shared core values, privileges neither individual predilections (*autonomy*) nor the common good (*order*) but seeks a judicious balance of rights and responsibilities. Moreover, he believes that we are capable of "moral dialogues" in the face of seemingly divergent values. These dialogues are the most effective means for locating shared values because they are not just rational deliberations, that is, based on "ground rules" that allow social life to go on. But they are capable of defining the "good," Etzioni says, without lapsing into "culture wars" only when certain moral rules are followed.[15]

"Moral dialogue" as the preferred source of shared values is complemented by the "moral voice" as the most effective foundation for compliance. The moral voice is a type of normative compliance and springs not from the pleasure principle or self-interest but from the quest for *affirmation*, originally identified in *The Moral Dimension*. The moral voice has two sources: the inner, personal voice—"what the person believes the shared values ought to be, based on education, experience, and internal development,"[16] and the communal voice—"the moral voice of others [these persons] care about, those to whom they are affectively attached—members of their community."[17] In short, it is *social normative compliance*, which is only lightly touched on in *Comparative Analysis*. Now it has moved to center stage. Although not rejected, the relative efficacy of the hierarchical formal (coercive, utilitarian, and "pure" normative) compliance structures of Etzioni's organizational theory is now in the background, eclipsed by the unique advantages of horizontal communal (viz., social normative) compliance.

The communitarian Etzioni is unequivocal in touting the superiority of the moral voice over more alienating forms of compliance. Informal, persuasive control is a surer guide to identifying and complying with shared values than officially sanctioned measures, whether they are coercive, utilitarian, or even "pure" normative. The same logic must apply to the intracommunal, national, and international spheres because he rejects the notion that each community is its own final moral arbiter and not accountable to others. Of course, on these macro levels, the forms the moral dialogues assume (dubbed "megalogues") and how moral voices are raised inevitably take on a more formalized character; but their substances are unaltered.

The call for moral dialogues and voices undoubtedly has contributed to the aforementioned criticism that Etzioni's communitarianism is sober and high-minded but basically unrealistic. A case can be made that *The New Golden Rule* has stressed social normative compliance too much and that all three forms of hierarchic compliance warrant more emphasis in complex, modern societies if one truly wants to balance order and autonomy effectively. But this charge does appear a touch ironic in light of the interests in power and alienation that run from *Comparative Analysis* through *The Active Society* to *The Moral Dimension* and remain implicit subtexts in *The New Golden Rule*. Nevertheless, the more "hardheaded" foci of earlier, less "cultural" writings do receive more muted expression in the latest book. Perhaps no relatively slim volume can be expected to balance all of a thinker's agendas. Fortunately, the more one follows the unifying thread of compliance, the more one appreciates that not only is there no inherent contradiction between the early and more recent works but there are solid reasons for claiming that the latter builds on the former. It may be too much to ask Etzioni to provide such an explicit synthesis in light of all his current projects. It is more realistic to urge that other scholars explore these linkages. And it is most appropriate to suggest that Etzioni's critics should ponder the full body of his work and how concerns with power, alienation, and compliance have led him, perhaps ineluctably, to communitarianism.

NOTES

1. His first book was published in Israel before he came to the United States for graduate work in sociology. See: Amitai Etzioni, *Befrotz Haportzim* [A Diary of a Commando Soldier] (Jerusalem: Achiasaf, 1952).

2. This position has been taken most recently in Steven Lukes, "The Responsive Community," *Dissent* (Spring 1998): 87–9.

3. Three of Etzioni's teachers at Berkeley—Reinhard Bendix, Seymour Martin Lipset, and Philip Selznick—have had related concerns about the embeddedness of organizations in larger societal and historical contexts. Lipset's work has been primarily in political sociology, while Bendix and Selznick are known more for their organizational sociology. Moreover, Philip Selznick has followed a route similar to (although independent of) Etzioni's from organizational studies to communitarianism.

4. Amitai Etzioni, *A Comparative Analysis of Complex Organizations*. Revised and enlarged edition (New York: Free Press, 1975), 10.

5. Etzioni, *Comparative Analysis*, 10.

6. Etzioni, *Comparative Analysis*, 10.

7. Etzioni, *Comparative Analysis*, 14.

8. The *order goals* of coercive organizations should not be confused with the *problem of order* in Etzioni's subsequent communitarianism. The latter formulation, influenced by the works of Talcott Parsons and Dennis Wrong, deals with a far more inclusive issue. See especially: Talcott Parsons, *The Structure of Social Action* (New York: McGraw-Hill, 1937) and Dennis H. Wrong, *The Problem of Order: What Divides and What Unites* (New York: Free Press, 1994). The order-goals formulation refers to one possible, albeit highly alienative (and relatively unsatisfactory), solution to the problem of order.

9. Etzioni, *Comparative Analysis*, 303, passim.

10. Amitai Etzioni, *The Active Society: A Theory of Societal and Political Processes* (New York: Free Press, 1968).

11. Amitai Etzioni, *The Moral Dimension: Toward a New Economics* (New York: Free Press, 1988).

12. Etzioni, *Moral Dimension*, 45.

13. Etzioni, *Moral Dimension*, 182.

14. Amitai Etzioni, *The New Golden Rule: Community and Morality in a Democratic Society* (New York: Basic Books, 1996).

15. Etzioni, *New Golden Rule*, 104–6.

16. Etzioni, *New Golden Rule*, 120.

17. Etzioni, *New Golden Rule*, 125.

1

Autonomy, Functionalism, and the Common Good: Some Liberal Doubts about *The New Golden Rule*

William R. Lund

The New Golden Rule is a most welcome addition to our public conversation on the nature of the good society and its political and sociological prerequisites. The book's theoretical claims and policy suggestions reflect and refine Professor Amitai Etzioni's prior efforts to synthesize truths from competing positions into a sensible and morally plausible communitarianism. As a leading voice in a loose family of communitarians, "strong democrats," and classical republicans, he has long been criticizing liberal theory and our public practices on the grounds of their excessive individualism, while defending alternative arrangements and understandings more conducive to a renewed emphasis on community and the common good. He continues that project in his newest work, but also takes great pains to distinguish his communitarianism from harsher forms of social conservatism by arguing that a defensible search for the common good ought not to rely on coercion and unreflective traditionalism. The core of that argument rests on a powerful and attractive idea: a "good society" is one that seeks an "equilibrium between universal individual rights and the common good" or, more particularly, "a balance between autonomy and order."[1]

However, a fundamental aspect of Etzioni's good society is the presence of ongoing "moral dialogues," which he defines as "communications about value, about the normative standing of one suggested course as compared to another." While honoring various "rules of engagement" to prevent deterioration into "culture war," participants in such dialogues should engage "substantive convictions" and "strong commitments" rather than limiting themselves to a wishy-washy search for compromise reflecting an inability to take one's own side in an argument.[2] In that spirit, I shall argue that the power and many attractions of *The New Golden Rule* are ultimately vitiated by a few weaknesses that warrant further exploration. From the perspective of what he has called "moderate liberalism," and what, for reasons that should soon

1

become clear, I call egalitarian liberalism, most of those weaknesses stem from certain ambiguities and tensions in his conception and justifications of autonomy.[3] To preview, I shall argue that his account of autonomy and its value rests on a teleological core of functional or ethical goods. That core, in turn, tends to support particular conceptions of public authority and equality, the implications of which yield some significant doubts about the real meaning and status of autonomy in his good society. Ultimately then, there are still serious questions about whether his moves away from harder-edged conservatism are sufficient to mollify concerns for individual freedom and equality that have been brought to bear against other communitarian arguments.

THE GOOD NEWS IN *THE NEW GOLDEN RULE*

In laying out his communitarian gospel, Etzioni seeks to spread the "good news" that we can reduce, in theory and practice, the ineliminable tension between citizens' self-interest and their duties to others. To accomplish that, he urges a "new golden rule": citizens ought to make it a social and political imperative to "[r]espect and uphold society's moral order as you would have society respect and uphold your autonomy."[4] Both his analysis of that rule and his account of its concrete policy implications are broadly informed and acute, and for me at least, his general position is attractive from several different perspectives.

As a citizen, one cannot help but to applaud the depth and obvious sincerity of his concern for the moral health of our polity. While anxious to avoid simplistic and hyperbolic assertions of "moral crisis," he nonetheless makes it clear that all is not well in our contemporary moral landscape and that some focus on the "regeneration" of values is essential. Compared with his "baseline" of "American society in the 1950s," the cultural changes of the last forty years have been a complex story that defies easy analysis: individuals may well have more autonomy today, but such gains must be balanced against significant evidence of social dis-order and the presence of more anarchic and ethically dubious behavior.[5] High crime and divorce rates, low family formation and voting rates, increased alienation from and distrust of government, absurdly solipsistic pop psychology, decreased economic stability, and more are for Etzioni evidence that clear improvements in the status of women and racial minorities as well as a general increase in freedom from oppressive communal customs and coercive regulations cannot be taken as unalloyed progress. Moreover, he takes pains to indicate that the recent "*curl back*" expressed in policies seeking greater social order and responsibility has included some measures that are "misdirected" in their tendency toward overly dramatic reductions in personal freedom. As citizens then, we face a defining moment as we confront several key questions: Do we really need moral "regeneration"? If so, should it take the form of a turn back to "traditional, especially religious, values" or rely on more secular and inclusive core commitments? Should efforts to promote such "regeneration" be grounded on moral "suasion" or legal coercion?[6]

In confronting individualistic liberals and moralistic conservatives on such questions, Etzioni is willing to move beyond theoretical abstraction to risk a range of concrete policy proposals. They include some moderation in the rights to free speech and against self-incrimination, various options for reducing the economic insecurity citizens face in unchecked markets, alternative means of conducting and financing our elections, and city planning. His proposals are not intended to be deep or thorough; instead, they are offered merely as suggestions to illustrate the implications of his communitarianism and to provide a starting place as we deliberate and struggle to define our public relationships. From a citizen's perspective then, we should welcome both his continued faith in the capacity of average persons to think through and manage their own affairs and his refusal to cave in before mounting evidence of public apathy and cynicism regarding politics. Decreasing trust of government and politics may simply be an exacerbation of our culture's traditional distaste for authority, or it may be a product of glacial increases in "postmaterialist" values, increased ideological polarization of political elites, or the media's focus on scandal and "gottcha" journalism.[7] Whatever its ultimate explanation, Etzioni wisely rejects the notion that such distrust, and its corollary in lowered expectations of citizens' potential for reasonable self-government, are permanent and acceptable aspects of our politics.

From the perspective of a political theorist, Etzioni's more sociological and empirical approach is also a welcome addition to debates about the good society. While well informed by moral and political philosophy, he seeks other grounds for his value and policy prescriptions and tends to sidestep abstract normative argument in favor of cross-cultural and historical comparisons. This adds fresh insights to the debate between liberals, communitarians, and various sorts of conservatives, a debate that many see as having reached a point of diminishing returns when carried on in terms of metaethical disputes about teleological goods and deontological rights. If the cottage industry spawned by, say, the debate between John Rawls and Michael J. Sandel has become overly "polemical" and overly reliant on a "common conceptual binary" in which abstract liberalism is pitted against abstract communitarianism, then Etzioni's approach may stimulate a greater sense of realism regarding the problems we actually confront.[8] Fortunately or unfortunately, my argument here does rely on normative abstractions and does recur to the problems in teleological approaches, but there is little doubt that the fruits of his general effort to work a little closer to the empirical and cultural ground enhances the substance of political theory and lends some urgency to more cross-disciplinary engagements.

From the narrower perspective of a "moderate" liberal theorist, *The New Golden Rule* is also welcome news in modulating some of the more troubling aspects in other communitarian literature. In the first place, Etzioni makes it perfectly clear that a good society is one that has "faith in faith," which means that its efforts to promote order and virtue will rely on "the moral voice of the community, education, persuasion, and exhortation" rather than on coercive legislation.[9] While this view was embodied in the initial communitarian platform, it has not always been a clear and consistent part of communitarian analyses, and that has led to some rather nervous reactions by liberals.[10] In confronting such reactions, he is on sound footing in arguing that social order should be maximally voluntary and in assuming that it makes some real difference if the behavior that instantiates value in the world stems from persuasion and inner conviction rather than being merely a hypocritical response to threats of punishment.

As a corollary of the preference for persuasion over legislation, his views on majority rule and individual rights are also more carefully tempered than those expressed by some other communitarians and should, as such, be less troubling to liberals. On his view, a sound democracy is not and cannot be achieved by aggregating the current preferences of individuals and acting on those expressed by the greater number. The prospect of a politics that simply sums up the brute preferences of the majority frightened James Madison, it frightens contemporary liberals such as Ronald Dworkin, and it rightfully worries Etzioni as well. In suggesting the necessity of certain procedural restraints to provide time for deliberation, reflection, and the transformation of initial preferences, he eschews the ideal of "democracy as a voting machine" with its attendant dangers to individual liberty and the value of action based on inner conviction.[11]

With regard to individual rights, Etzioni argues that they can be neither analyzed nor defended without contextualizing them in terms of the rights-bearers' social responsibilities, and he goes on to note that an excessively broad array of rights may threaten society's ethical health and viability. However, he is careful to emphasize that these facts should lead us to seek only "a *temporary* moratorium on the minting of *new* rights" rather than "a *total* suspension of *all* rights." As valuable instruments for protecting individual autonomy and sound democracy, any downward adjustments regarding rights must be carefully "notched" in order to avoid slippery slopes toward authoritarian or even just more conservative impositions. There is room to quibble with the content and application of some of his "notches," but the idea that limitations on rights should be allowed only if there is a *"clear and present danger"* to social order, if all less intrusive means have been exhausted, and if the proposed regulations are *"minimally intrusive"* and as careful as possible of autonomy-reducing side effects should comfort those worried by rather overheated remarks about the dangers of rights in other communitarian arguments.[12]

Beyond their relation to autonomy, Etzioni's views on majority rule and individual rights also reflect a desire to transcend the threat of cultural ethical relativism. In chastising liberals for their supposed Enlightenment universalism, some communitarians have argued as if the values and traditions of a particular community were justified simply by virtue of having been adopted and promoted over time. To paraphrase Plato's *Euthyphro*, they appear to have sided with the view that values and practices are good because a particular community loves them, thereby denying the view that individuals (or a community) ought to love and follow them because they are rationally defensible as good or true or just without regard to their effects on attitudes. On the former, collectively voluntaristic view, particular substantive values are morally compelling by virtue of community acceptance and support, and there is no external fulcrum to use in checking the validity of such support. As Etzioni notes, various liberal critics have had "a field day with such community-based relativism," or the idea that currently shared conventions are justified simply by virtue of their acceptance.[13]

Etzioni treats such criticisms as worthy of serious consideration, and he devotes a chapter of *The New Golden Rule* to laying out a hierarchical framework of increasingly external criteria that can be used to evaluate the legitimacy and moral validity of particularistic conventions and shared understandings. If they have been derived from a sound democratic process, including means of refining brute preferences and extending societal consensus, then we have an obvious improvement on elite or autocratic imposition and a sign of necessary but not "sufficient normative accountability." Such conventions will be further legitimized if they comport well with higher level but still internal understandings, with more general community commitments of the sort often embodied in written and unwritten constitutions. While those background commitments can provide a check on particular decisions, he goes on to argue that we need "a still higher framing criterion" in order to evaluate constitutions and societal traditions themselves. Such a criterion, he thinks, may emerge from properly constructed moral dialogues among citizens of a particular nation or citizens of the world. Such deliberations might yield a consensus on a list of universal values that could ground claims for human rights and be used to check particular decisions and the background values of various societies. While admitting that the idea of a "core . . . of globally shared values" is still "largely a gleam in the eyes of a small number of visionaries," he urges the rejection of relativism in the name of cross-cultural criticism and dialogue aimed at discovering such a core to be used in checking communitarian particularism.[14]

Short of having such a list finalized and in hand, he urges that we seek the ultimate antidote to communal relativism in certain "primary" moral concepts that *"present themselves to us as morally compelling in and of themselves."* In other words, Etzioni accepts the idea that wherever and whoever we might be, we have an operative "moral sense" that renders the value of certain virtues and goods as "self-evident." While aware that this view is "controversial" and subject to significant ambiguities, some of which will be discussed below, he nonetheless argues that the products of sound democratic procedures, general societal values, and even a thin core of global values must all ultimately be tested against the need for "moral order and autonomy." Those "basic social virtues" provide a "final substantive normative criterion" with the same self-evident and universal appeal as the nonmoral values of "life and health." As the peak of his ethical hierarchy then, order and autonomy provide the ultimate constraint on the relativism implicit in emphases on community and locally shared values.[15]

Thus, while noting potential problems in the unalloyed view that "more freedom is better than less,"[16] Etzioni does defend individual autonomy as a core normative commitment of any good society. When coupled with his preference for persuasion over coercion, his tempered views on majoritarianism and rights, and his counters to relativism, his emphasis on autonomy should provide some comfort for liberals otherwise exercised by fears of a gemeinschaft community swallowing individual freedom and creativity in the name of order and local traditions. Some critics see communitarians as only "soft" antiliberals who barely move away from standard liberal views on concrete policy questions,[17] but others have seen just enough extremism in communitarian criticisms of rights, individualism, and privacy to warrant such fears. That, it seems to me, has for too long foreclosed meaningful dialogue between egalitarian liberals and communitarians, and it has precluded potential coalitions aimed at certain shared goals, especially that of reducing the crippling economic inequalities that are inconsistent with both liberal justice and responsible civic action by too many of our fellow citizens. There are recent efforts at a similar synthesis coming from the other direction,[18] and insofar as *The New Golden Rule* can contribute to softening liberal concerns and enhancing such dialogues, it is welcome news indeed for all progressives.

THE WHAT AND WHY OF AUTONOMY IN *THE NEW GOLDEN RULE*

Despite all that good news, there are still several reasons for a moderate liberal to be concerned about the status of individual rights and freedom in Etzioni's good society. Many of those emerge from a closer analysis of various tensions and ambiguities in his conception and justifications of autonomy, as well as from attending to his account of its relationship to societal order. I shall pay particular attention to unpacking the implicitly teleological aspects of his justifications of autonomy and to drawing out the implications of that reliance on a substantive conception of the good for thinking about the best conception of political equality and authority.

Part of the problem here is definitional or conceptual. As Gerald Dworkin points out, there are any number of often-conflicting definitions of autonomy, and the concept has been "used in an exceedingly broad fashion." While typically sharing the view that autonomy is valuable and good, theorists have gone on to offer accounts that closely relate it to political concerns for liberty, ethical concerns for a particular substantive way of life thought to realize human "perfection," or metaphysical concerns for freedom of the will. As such, we are not likely to arrive at a "core meaning" for the concept simply by analyzing ordinary language, and it is thus always necessary to "construct" a conception of autonomy "given various theoretical purposes and some constraints from normal usage."[19] Etzioni's purposes yield a rather unstable blend, which refers at various times to the political, ethical, and metaphysical elements of autonomy. Moreover, while recognizing it as a self-evident value of individual lives, his purposes also lead him beyond standard concerns with individual capacities or achievements to focus on autonomy as a "social virtue" rather than a "personal attribute." On that view, questions of autonomy relate to whether or not a given society "provides structured opportunities and legitimation for individual and subgroup expression of their particular values, needs, and preferences." In responding to potential charges of vagueness, he goes on to add that autonomy also includes both "negative and positive liberties" and that it "must be socially bounded," or balanced against competing concerns for order and valuable traditions.[20]

Now that is not an especially vague definition, but the reference to both "negative and positive liberties" does yield a certain troubling equivocation. By referring to positive liberties, he opens a door to defining autonomy in terms of a particular substance for the "values, needs, and preferences" the good society is to respect. In other words, he may be hanging the question of whether one is really autonomous or not on the moral substance of her judgments and actions, thereby implicitly adopting a substantive approach such that "only certain decisions count as retaining autonomy whereas others count as forfeiting it."[21] This aspect is most clearly displayed in his chapter on human nature. There, he takes up Harry Frankfurt's justly influential argument that the defining criterion of personhood is the "capacity for reflective self-evaluation" and the freedom to will action based not only on brute desires but also on "second-order desires," or desires "to have (or not to have) certain desires and motives."[22] For Etzioni, that philosophical analysis mirrors both psychological findings and religious insights regarding the internally divided nature of human beings. While we are, he says, simply animals and "barbarians" at birth, we are also capable of being socialized to virtue. Thus we are "continuously conflicted" between natural, animal desires and a checking "moral voice," and each of us is naturally "'doomed' to a struggle between a lower and a higher (a debased and a nobler) self."[23]

The potential problem here stems from the inherently moralized content of Etzioni's second-order desires and their definitional connection to autonomy. That goes well beyond Frankfurt, who emphasizes that "second-order volitions" need not reflect "a moral stance" since the evaluations used in forming such desires can be "capricious and irresponsible" as well as morally informed.[24] In other words, there is no real conceptual or empirical necessity that the capacity to will what we reflectively want to will is synonymous with the triumph of morally "higher" over "lower" and "debased" selves. Treating it as if it were simply defines autonomy as a matter of achieving a particular and variously defined notion of the good. That may take a classic teleological form, in which "real" autonomy is a matter of acting on desires that accord with Aristotelian, Thomistic, or Marxian views of the development of innate human potentials to their full perfection; alternatively, it may reflect a Kantian view in which autonomy is the rational and fully self-determined construction of laws to control heteronomous desires. While I argue below that Etzioni plumps for the first approach, the point for now is that either option yields clear threats to negative liberty. If autonomy is a particular substantive content for, or a particular way of arriving at, second-order desires, and if the state is supposed to promote such autonomy, then we confront Isaiah Berlin's (and others') nightmares about citizens being "forced to be free" through policies that override individual judgments about desirable lives in the name of "genuine" freedom and a particular content for such lives.[25]

If, on the other hand, we take as primary his linkage between autonomy and "negative liberties," or being free from intentional external restrictions, we face yet other problems. As a conceptual matter, we ought not to draw too close a connection between negative liberty and autonomy. Both deception, which might restrict autonomy while leaving the deceived individual at full liberty, and self-generated restrictions on one's liberty of the sort associated with the example of Ulysses and the Sirens call that connection into doubt.[26] However, I want to put that issue aside for now and, instead, focus on his justifications of autonomy and their potential for undermining the place of such negative liberty in his good society.

If asked why we should worry about autonomy, Etzioni offers two apparently distinct lines of reply. The first grows out of his long-standing commitment to a "functionalist" methodology, in which "certain *needs*" are universal "requirements" of societal viability. There may be a variety of more and less effective ways of meeting those functional requirements, but they must be met in one way or another if the society is to survive over time. On that view, the "social virtue" of autonomy is simply one such requirement, the presence of which enables societies to avoid long-run, destructive problems. In the first place, he argues, providing "opportunities and legitimation" for the expression of individual preferences and values "enhances the ability of the society to adapt to change, to be metastable," by countering the tendency of governments to ignore or be unaware of the problems created by their current policies. Second, a reasonable amount of autonomy enables societies to make use of citizens' "different capacities and their specific environmental circumstances," thereby avoiding the sort of inefficiencies that result from one-size-fits-all rules and regulations. Finally, autonomy is socially functional in allowing religious and ethnic "subgroup differences" to be expressed and accommodated rather than having them collapse into the sort of bloody intranational conflicts so much in the news recently.[27]

Importantly, the functionalist approach forces us to attend to an ironic reality: if pushed too far, even "social virtues" can become dysfunctional. Here, while autonomy is essential for a society's adaptability, efficiency, and peace, it can also become a vice if not bounded by the alternative functional need for, and the alternative "social virtue" of, "order." He relates the two virtues in an "inverting symbiosis," which he defines as a "*blending of two basic formations that—up to a point—enhance one another . . . ; but if either element intensifies beyond a given level, it begins to diminish the other: the same two formations become antagonistic.*" Thus societies that lack or severely restrain autonomy will become dysfunctional, but equally or even more important in our current context is the fact that policies that tilt toward too much autonomy will pose significant threats to order and the very autonomy they seek to enhance. In recognizing the mutual relationship between order and autonomy, a good society takes steps to find "the balanced middle" between them rather than adopting policies that pull it to "*the opposite extreme.*" The search for an enhancing rather than antagonistic balance is then a contingent matter of judgments regarding the current tilt of the society; and Etzioni's view is that we should now be more worried about the dysfunctional results of excessive individualism, excessive rights claims, and excessive economic deregulation. Such moves may appear to have enhanced autonomy, but in reality, by ignoring the alternative claims of community, responsibility, and the common good, they have actually undermined the "inverting symbiosis" and threatened both sound order and autonomy by inviting harsher and more authoritarian responses.[28]

As I indicated previously, Etzioni's defense of the "social virtues" is not exhausted by his functionalist and instrumental account of their goodness. Referring to that approach as "secondary," he also seeks to justify order and autonomy as self-evident goods that "speak compellingly for themselves" and ought to be valued in and of themselves. Drawing on recent work by Robert Wright and James Q. Wilson, he traces the source of this ethical compulsion to a universal "moral sense" of the sort often associated with Lord Shaftsbury, Francis Hutcheson, and others in and around the eighteenth-century "Scottish Enlightenment." Motivated to defend traditional Christian morality against both the corrosions of Hobbesian skepticism and the rigidities of radical Protestantism's divine command ethics, early moral sense theorists emphasized an analogy between the perception of aesthetic beauty and a developed sense of moral right and wrong. They also emphasized equality by arguing that all normally functioning humans, whether high or low, well or ill educated, had similar capacities to perceive and act on moral truth in order to fulfill their telos as social beings. As Charles Taylor describes it, Hutcheson and others simply assumed that God had arranged the world so that "(1) our moral sense pushes us to benevolence and (2) benevolence is what works most for our happiness." These days, as Etzioni notes, the theological grounds of original moral sense arguments have been replaced by more secular appeals, often emphasizing biological claims about "moral genes" or arguments about the "universal socialization experiences" of creatures who have our particular developmental needs.[29]

In his own appeal to the moral sense, Etzioni is not especially interested in answering questions about its precise origins; nor does he seek to determine whether it refers to a special human faculty analogous to other senses or simply stands for common values stemming from a common human nature. His point, rather, is to provide a defense of autonomy and order that goes beyond the vagaries of consequentialist (functionalist) considerations. Of course we might make the same point via Immanuel Kant's search for rationally grounded and absolutely binding duties, but Etzioni prefers the moral sense view because it comes without the "individualistic" and rationalistic baggage he associates with the "deontological" tradition.[30] In grounding binding norms on reason alone, that tradition neglects the community's role in mediating between individuals and their conduct through primary and secondary socialization processes and too quickly takes our focus away from the social. Moreover, as with the original moral sense theorists' emphasis on sentiment, Etzioni wants to downplay moral reasoning in order to highlight the apparent immediacy of our perceptions of right and wrong, good and bad. Eschewing the subjectivist view that his commitment to autonomy and order is "merely a statement of preference," he nonetheless argues that they are values that "present themselves to us as compelling" in a way analogous to religious "*revelation.*" Impersonal reason may add elements of "accountability" and articulation for such values, but their "essence" and universal appeal are better understood in more emotive and intuitive terms.[31]

THREATS TO AUTONOMY IN *THE NEW GOLDEN RULE*

For Etzioni then, autonomy should be a core societal value because of both its functions and its immediate appeal to our moral sense. While novel and insightful, there are several problems with this justificatory strategy. I will leave aside the complaints of various sorts of libertarians, who would reject outright the functionalist justification on the grounds that it puts the collective cart before the individual horse. Similarly, I ignore the doubts of those whose moral sense might lead to a more conservative view entailing a complete rejection of all sorts of autonomy in the name of collectivist, traditionalist, or theocratic visions. Unfortunately, however, even for those whose initial reaction to his general approach might be more friendly, there are still two other problems, problems that, when combined with the definitional ambiguities discussed above, yield some doubts as to just how fundamental autonomy as equal negative liberty will be in his good society.

The first focuses on tensions between the functionalist and the nonconsequentialist moral sense justifications of autonomy and asks whether the latter doesn't ultimately collapse into the former. If we say that lots of societies and even many of our own fellow citizens don't accept the value of autonomy, Etzioni's response is that they ought to see it as an "ultimate" value for the following reason: without it "all other virtues lack standing because they presume a measure of free will, i.e., of autonomy as well as socially structured opportunities to exercise it."[32] Now that is, on the one hand, heartening to liberal sensibilities because it restates the linkage between voluntary endorsement and genuine value and makes autonomy a constitutive and noninstrumental good. Yet, to the extent that those "other virtues" are viewed as character traits that promote the good, defined as either order and the functional health of society or, as I will discuss below, a substantive picture of the ethical "health" of the individual, the intuitive moral sense appeal of autonomy may ultimately be linked in a circular fashion to its functionalism.

While game theoreticians and others have argued that morality can be functional to the satisfaction of subjective interests, Etzioni's view is of course quite different. In starting from the perspective of society as a whole (or from a substantive picture of an objectively good life), he invites doubts as to whether there can be moral sense support for acts that are inconsistent with the proper functioning of either societies or individuals. If not, if that is conceptually impossible, then the moral sense justification loses its independent standing and autonomy is defined and valuable only as a metaphysical base for behavior that meets the functional test. With that, the apparently independent moral sense support for the negative liberty aspects of autonomy drops out, and we are left with more conservative and autonomy-denying implications than he admits.

The second and more troubling problem emerges when we are forced to apply his general framework to particular cases. If, despite my suggestion above, we grant that functionalism and the moral sense are both basic, but distinct, justifications for autonomy, then it must be possible for them occasionally to come into conflict. Moreover, we will also confront lower-level conflicts between the demands of order and autonomy themselves as well as conflicts between those "basic communitarian virtues" and such "corollary and secondary values" as equality, peace, *"some feminist values,"* and a "commitment to the environment as a common good."[33] As noted above, he seeks to counter relativism by including a hierarchy of external criteria to be used in evaluating locally shared values, and the same criteria could perhaps be applied to evaluating particular trade-offs in such conflict cases. Ultimately, however, it seems to me that, since his "final substantive normative criterion" itself includes the potentially conflicting values of order and autonomy, and since those values are justified by the potentially conflicting findings of functionalism and the moral sense, his strategy here may not be much help. For example, it is one thing to say that functional needs and humanity's moral sense both condemn killing the innocent or failing to care for one's children. But matters break down when we ask if abortion is murder or seek consensus regarding optimal trade-offs between spending time with children and providing for their well-being by devotion to one's career.

Thus, in the absence of some more general principle, Etzioni leaves us to engage in ad hoc balancing of competing values and justifications in such cases, and for those of us who accept ethical pluralism, that is not a completely wrongheaded portrait of our public and private dilemmas. However, his justificatory strategy for his core values means that in our balancing, and in asking whether greater or lesser autonomy is warranted in a particular case, the answer will eventually hang on community dialogues rooted in conflicting products of the moral sense and/or contested empirical claims about the functional nature of actions expressing such autonomy—is it divorce per se or the facts of predivorce conflict and postdivorce poverty that create emotional and behavioral problems for children? Is pornography a causal agent or merely a symptom of underlying problems in relation to rape and other physical abuse of women?

In confronting the prospect and outcomes of such public balancing, we are naturally enough led to questions of political authority. While Etzioni doesn't specifically address that concept, both his general theory and his justifications for autonomy do have some relatively clear implications for how we should think about it. At the very least, his critique of excessive individualism rules out a radical view in which any sort of authority and any sort of nonvoluntary obligations are so inconsistent with moral autonomy that anarchism becomes the only legitimate politics.[34] With regard to less uncompromising positions, we might get some help in characterizing his implicit view by drawing on Richard Flathman's distinction between two different conceptions of authority.

In the first, a "formal-procedural" model typically associated with liberalism, the practice of authority aims at solving problems created by deep and intractable conflicts between free and equal persons. Where there is no right-for-all substantive answer to such disputes, the best solution lies in the voluntary creation of rules and offices whose occupants will be merely "in authority," and whose judgments will be obligatory only in virtue of their holding office and ruling according to specified procedures rather than because of their special moral or religious insight. Their authoritative status "is an attribute of offices and rules and commands issued by offices, never of persons," and the limits imposed on individual freedom by specific instances of such authority will be justified only in virtue of the overall acceptability of the background rules to equal individuals and their freely chosen purposes. The second model is a "substantive-purposive" conception of authority, famously displayed in Plato's *Republic*, present in our own early Puritan communities, and for Flathman at least, associated with functionalist social science. On that view, authority reflects and aims at instantiating a consensus on facts and values, and it is understood as "an attribute of a person or persons" who, in virtue of superior knowledge or insight, are particularly well placed to understand the shared goods of an activity or a community. Given that consensus on ends, there should also be a correct substantive answer to the best balance of means in particular cases. Authority is then a matter of certain persons issuing such answers as claims about the world and "statements to be believed" in a process that "presupposes inequality" between those who are "an authority" on such questions and those who are not.[35]

Now if our balancing grants pride of place to Etzioni's functionalism, then in principle we are left with an open door to the latter model of authority and its presumption of inequality regarding capacities to determine which questions should be matters of public concern and how they should be resolved. Assuming a general consensus on society's functional prerequisites and core values, there should be empirically correct answers as to the proper balance of conflicting means in particular cases. In considering the questions surrounding the divorce and pornography examples mentioned above, authority is then a matter of finding a factual and functionally proper balance between order and autonomy and of offering such answers as "statements to be believed." In that case, there are obvious dangers for negative liberty as Etzioni invites public rules that override supposedly inferior individual judgments about the best balance of conflicting values on the basis of authoritative functional claims.

This is not to suggest that he is promoting government by a "bevy of Platonic guardians," even if drawn from the ranks of top-notch functionalist academics. After all, democracy is a key element in his conception of a good community. Moreover, he shares with liberals the notion that democracy itself must be constrained by some higher level criteria and that those criteria should be applied through fixed procedures to check majoritarian excesses. However, there are still two important questions here. First, how broad a scope do those criteria and procedures leave for democratic decision making? And second, what is the nature of those criteria—are they relatively substantive or more formal and abstract? Are they a matter of achieving particular states of affairs or a more open-ended commitment to, say, individual agency and choice?

On those questions, Etzioni's criteria (order and autonomy) appear rather more substantive than formal, and his functionalist justification tends to invite citizens to engage a broader range of behaviors and questions as appropriate matters for public decision. Thus, even with his requirements for greater public deliberation and reflection, the necessity of drawing democratic balances in particular cases assumes that majoritarian nose counting will kick in at some point. The danger here is that determining proper balances by an aggregative procedure can and often will be tainted by a lack of public impartiality. As citizens struggle over public resolutions of contested empirical claims, they will naturally enough be tempted to discount one side on the grounds that they are highly unlikely ever to suffer from authoritative regulations based on its denial. That is, if I think there is little or no chance that I will ever seek divorce or abortion, read dirty books, or devote myself to a career at the expense of family activities, then engaging in a kind of "probabilistic" balancing will ease my way to being convinced by claims that such conduct is dysfunctional and should be restricted. Certain formal constraints, often embodied in notions of rights, due process, or a rigid boundary between public and private, reflect the principle that we ought to judge such cases *as if* we were considering whether we would accept such restrictions if they were *actually* to occur in our lives. But in the absence of such constraints, Etzioni's functionalism takes in too many questions, makes it too easy to discount contrary evidence, and subverts the equality of those whose liberty will be denied in the name of authoritative balancing.[36]

While less obvious than in the functionalist case, the moral sense justification of autonomy also tends toward a "substantive-purposive" account of authority. Assuming a consensus on the facts and values relevant to a theological, sociobiological, or ethical conception of a good human life, such views will treat conflicts between autonomy and other values as requiring a resolution based on a public ranking of differing and unequally valid intuitions regarding our innate telos. The point here can be drawn out by analyzing Etzioni's application of the concept of virtue to societal wholes. Although somewhat idiosyncratic, talk of "social virtues" is plausible enough if the goal is the ethical evaluation of societies as such, but just as with recent efforts to revive "virtue ethics" for evaluating individual decisions and character, it does carry with it some heavy baggage. In the first place, if "a virtue of a thing is any respect in which the thing is good or exemplary of its kind," then the concept is "most at home in the case of things with identifiable functions" like knives, racehorses, or hearts, and it is less easy to apply when things such as individuals or societies lack clearly identifiable and agreed-upon functions.[37] Thus, in order to make sense of the notion of "social virtues," we need some argument that renders the functions of society itself less obscure, some argument about, not what societies need to be functional, but what functions they themselves are meant to perform. Only then can we proceed to evaluate whether a particular society "is good or exemplary of its kind."

Of course, specifying the very general purposes of a social order is notoriously difficult and contentious: Is the goal of society per se to amass military power and territorial conquest, glorify a particular conception of divinity, make possible the creation of great cultural artifacts, create the largest possible economic pie, or help individuals to realize and experience good lives somehow defined? While there are passages in *The New Golden Rule* suggesting that the function of a society is simply to maintain itself as an end in itself, Etzioni's critique of unreflective tradition, his efforts to distinguish his approach from earlier versions of functionalism that were criticized as inherently biased against change, and the general idea of evaluating types of stability as better or worse lead away from such a notion.[38] Remembering that he seeks a "responsive community," the overall spirit of his work leans toward a tighter connection between such stability and the goodness of individual lives. Thus his argument for attributing the notion of virtue to social wholes looks something like this: a society's function is to enhance the prospects for individuals to achieve the good; a proper balance of order and autonomy, derived from a proper moral sense, yields "metastability" and other conditions that enable the successful performance of that function; therefore, that balance constitutes the virtue of societies, making them good or exemplary of their kind, and is also best for individuals in enabling them to lead good lives.

Ultimately, of course, such arguments must specify the content of the human good that marks the proper moral sense and constitutes the purpose or function of society as such. In sorting through and characterizing the dizzying array of such views presented in even the limited contest of Western philosophy, we can always ask both a metaethical and a closely related political question. First, is the relevant notion of the good one that can be realized simply (?) by instantiating certain conduct and behavior as part of the world's state of affairs, or does it also require that its value be accepted by the individual? That is, is the presence of particular behavior sufficient for the goodness of a life in realizing an agent-neutral "value for the universe at large," or is it also a necessary condition of its value that it flow out of the inner convictions and beliefs of those who experience it?[39] Second, does the theory assume that the law and other public action can directly promote the good, or does it see the role of politics as more indirect and properly limited to providing formal rules and procedures under which citizens can then determine their own conception of the good? Depending on the answers, we will have an Aristotelian, Lockean, Utilitarian, Kantian, Marxian, or other theory of society, politics, and the good.

While his imaginative synthesizing complicates any such judgment, it seems to me that Etzioni leans toward the first option on each of those questions. On the first, his view of a good human life might be described as a matter of the sound integration of competing values into a coherent whole. Rummaging quickly but, I hope, not unfairly through some of his earlier work, we come across various formulations of this notion. A good life (and, hence, a good society) is one that eschews complete devotion to the charms of materialism and consumption in favor of integrating and attending to *"'inner space,'* that is, the search for greater insight into self and better relations with others," as well as education, artistic creation, and public engagement. Elsewhere, he has suggested that the good life is a matter of living out Buber's "I-We view," so that individuals live well to the extent that their lives embody the following ideals: *"Individuals and community are both completely essential, and hence have the same fundamental standing,"* and *"The individual and the community make each other and require each other."*[40] As discussed previously, *The New Golden Rule* argues that we are continuously torn between our animal and human natures, implying that the good life requires perfecting the latter and enacting the agent-neutral value of integrating bounded autonomy and the virtues that contribute to social order in the name of efforts to move from our "lower" to our "higher" and "nobler" selves.

Insofar as this is accurate, then we may have to take his explicit rejection of ethical consequentialism as actually limited only to rejecting the substantive conception of the good at work in utilitarianism and welfare economics.[41] As an ethical approach, consequentialism involves both a theory of value, or a substantive account of a teleological or other agent-neutral good that can be used in ranking states of affairs, and the ethical prescription that right action or policy is the maximization of that value in the world.[42] Thus Etzioni may (rightly in my mind) reject the hedonistic or preference satisfaction views of the good at work in much economistic thinking, but he maintains the maximization formula and simply plugs in a substitute conception of the good whose incidence is to be increased. Replacing preference satisfaction with his moral sense of a good life (or society's functional health) may well improve things, but it still leaves him working very closely to the more explicit teleologies of some of his communitarian allies and his conservative opponents. Such views ride rather roughly with both negative liberty and the inner endorsement aspects of autonomy since, if we can increase the incidence of an agent-neutral good by coercion or manipulation, we will still be maximizing value whether or not it is accepted as such by those who will have to enact it.

On the question of the proper role of politics, Etzioni defends the view that law and public policy should be aimed directly at promoting the good. Despite his criticisms of conservatism and his preference for the internalization of values, a major goal of his communitarian agenda would seem to be to enhance the role of society and representative democracy in bringing about good lives. Since the "I-We view" treats community and the individual as an interdependent whole, the goodness of individual lives is clearly dependent on the goodness of the community and its shared values. Political attention to (and support for) those values is seen as a necessary correction to the overly individualistic and procedural approach offered by much of recent liberalism. That approach tends to limit the public's role here by arguing that the state should be neutral on the good life and should provide public, if not private, tolerance of ethical differences. With others, Etzioni treats the neutrality requirement as the source of many of our current problems, arguing that the "long- and short-term neglect of shared values led to a thinning of the moral order and to the expected dysfunctional consequences."[43] Thus, despite his modulations and criticisms of coercive approaches, the moral sense justification of autonomy still tends to front-load public balancing of value conflicts by granting authoritative status to intuitions that promote or enforce a particular substantive conception of the good life even at the expense of negative liberty.

The chief problem here lies in the fact that public and probabilistic balancing on either of his justifications of autonomy will tend to undermine the best understanding of citizens' moral equality. In expanding the scope of politics and in denying room for principled constraints on the authoritative imposition of either functionalist or moral sense conceptions of the good, Etzioni risks outcomes that could reasonably be rejected by those who will have to live under them. Of course, teleological and virtue-oriented theories are consistent with at least one conception of equal concern and respect. As Ronald Dworkin notes, their proponents can always say that equal concern requires treating the individual "as the truly good or wise person would wish to be treated,"[44] and Etzioni's appeal to our "higher" rather than our "lower" selves seems to mirror that view. If that "higher" self and some particular content for it is the good life, and if it should be made available to all equally, then, whatever citizens' current interests and desires might be, paternalistic and moralistic legislation can be seen as actually enhancing, rather than subverting, their equality since it is necessary to treating them as they would wish to be treated if they were "truly good or wise."

In contrast, egalitarian liberals assume that genuine value and virtue depend on inner persuasion and that politics has a limited role in their production. In turn, they emphasize a "formal-procedural" view of authority and argue that the best conception of equal respect requires the public's role to be limited to the provision of a minimal framework of rules enforcing justice and reciprocal rights. Within that framework, citizens should be free to act on and alter their own convictions on the good life and on the best balance of competing goods, virtues, and obligations. Thus any public balancing must be constrained by the neutrality requirement and the idea that equal respect is due to individuals as they are or might be persuaded to be through their voluntary relationships. That does not completely cripple public authority: we can still prohibit actions that violate second party rights, regulate the exercise of even harmless liberties, and otherwise seek to persuade citizens to ethically responsible exercises of their freedom and rights. But it does provide a more secure foundation for equal negative liberty than Etzioni's thicker and more teleological conception and justifications of autonomy.

CONCLUDING THOUGHTS

Given his general framework, Etzioni has done about as much as possible to ward off his perspective's inherent threats to equality and the dangers of "substantive-purposive" authority. His critique of social conservative excesses and the pains he has taken to elevate autonomy itself to a core status cannot but help to mitigate those dangers and protect individual freedom against tradition- and community-based impositions. He provides similar mitigating features by treating rights as universal values rather than a Eurocentric bias and by rejecting arguments that "base individual rights only on community needs." That strategy leaves rights and the autonomy they protect "without normative accounting if community needs . . . can be shown to conflict with" them. Thus, while doubting the need for new rights, his various "notches" discussed above do create significant hurdles to be jumped before restrictions on existing rights can be seen as legitimate. In concrete cases, that leads him both to reject legal policies or campus codes aimed at stifling "hate speech" and to leave other proposed limits on speech and privacy rights as very open questions, questions that require further public deliberation about where to draw the line "between individual rights and community needs."[45]

However, insofar as those deliberations reflect the teleological core of Etzioni's functional and moral sense analyses, they will open up space for hierarchical and inevitably coercive rankings of citizens' characters and ways of life. In simple terms, ways of life and judgments about the good will be publicly ranked as better and worse in terms of their contribution to the well functioning of the community or the realization of a particular conception of "higher" and "nobler" selves. From a moderate liberal perspective, the problems here do not lie in claiming that some lives are intrinsically better than others or that what individuals really want are lives that *are* good rather than ones that might merely be thought to be good. As Ronald Dworkin argues, the skeptical denial of such claims must itself be rejected given the fact of "critical well-being," or the idea that there are certain elements of a life that we ought to want, elements that are good independently of our current preferences and about which we might be mistaken.[46] Rather, the real threat lies in the notion that such judgments (and such lives) ought to be politicized so that legal enforcement and other public efforts to manipulate individual behavior are seen as proper methods to secure that agent-neutral well-being.

Etzioni seeks to limit the imposition of those inegalitarian appraisals by grounding the value of autonomy and individual rights on something other than "community needs," but in doing so he still assumes that those values are always to be balanced against the functional needs of the community and the true good of individuals. If such balancing is characterized as a matter of weighing the community's good or the individual's achievement of a "higher" self against only losses imposed on "lower" and "animal" desires, it seems easier than he imagines to roll through concerns for a clear and present danger and the other "notches" he provides to protect against a tilt away from autonomy. And since he treats the law in a good society as *"first and foremost the continuation of morality by other means,"* expressing such publicly determined balances will be its chief business. Recognizing that laws cannot be effective or fair if they run too far ahead of, or fall too far behind, societal consensus on enforced values, he nonetheless argues that, for those functional or moral sense goods that are generally shared, the law should function as the moral voice of the community.[47] Thus, rather than treating the law as a resource whose opportunities and restrictions ought to be distributed on the basis of equal concern and respect, he invites us to think of it as a reflection of community sentiments and inegalitarian rankings of citizens and their conceptions of the good life.

In practice, that leads him to calls for various restrictions on individual autonomy, such as requiring garbage to be put out in transparent bags, welfare recipients to be fingerprinted, and juries to be instructed that they may draw inferences of guilt from a defendant's refusal to testify. Etzioni also argues for bans on certain kinds of expression, including those aimed at informing people how best to shoot federal agents or seduce young children. While I would oppose such measures, I'm not suggesting that the republic would fall or that the worst sort of Puritanism would reign if we adopted them in the name of greater recycling, the elimination of fraud in public benefit programs, the reduction of crime, or the gagging of G. Gordon Liddy. Nor am I suggesting that Etzioni's call for greater reliance on the mechanism of nonviolent public shaming, aimed at adding a measure of "psychic discomfort" to the calculations of those who might otherwise violate "the community's values," would mock our rights or reduce us to Orwellian nightmares.[48] However, I am suggesting that, at the end of the day, his stated preference for autonomy and the internalization of norms rides rather roughly with some of his other views and can more easily than he suspects give way to harsher and more freedom-denying approaches. When efforts to persuade to voluntarily change fail, there is the law and less coercive, but still heavily manipulative, mechanisms such as shame that will undermine the equal autonomy of many of our fellow citizens in the name of supposedly authoritative functional or moral sense goods.

Etzioni defines community as "a set of attributes, not a concrete place," and those attributes include "a web of affect-laden relationships . . . , and second, a measure of commitment to a set of shared valued, norms, and meanings."[49] For anyone impressed by the inherently conflictual nature of social relations among individuals seeking good lives amidst a plurality of often incommensurable ethical values, the chief problem here should be protecting those who find themselves falling outside those "affect-laden relationships" or at odds with "the shared values, norms, and meanings" of a particular community. Some principled commitment to conceptions of equality and authority that prohibit the state from coercive and manipulative treatment of those minorities, ensuring at least public respect for their autonomy, seems the better course here. As Etzioni himself recognizes, "communitarian societies are much more prone to a centripetal breakdown than a centrifugal one."[50] They are, in other words, prone to continual efforts to expand their sphere of influence by encroaching on judgments and decisions that individuals need to make for themselves if we are to continue to treat them as responsible and rational agents. If that is so, the inevitable tensions between the common good and autonomy, and the inevitable strains against the latter, need a resolution resting on something more than functionalism and the moral sense. However dubious it might be on other grounds, the liberalism of equal respect for negative liberty, stringent individual rights, and public neutrality on the proper balance between conflicting ethical requirements may still be the best course for those who want to take autonomy seriously.

NOTES

1. Amitai Etzioni, *The New Golden Rule: Community and Morality in a Democratic Society* (New York: Basic Books, 1996), xviii, 28.

2. Etzioni, *New Golden Rule*, 102–5.

3. See Amitai Etzioni, "Contemporary Liberals, Communitarians, and Individual Choice," in *Socio-Economics: Toward a New Synthesis,* ed. Amitai Etzioni and Paul R. Lawrence (Armonk, N.Y.: M. E. Sharpe, 1991), 61–2, where he distinguishes, largely on the grounds of the room the latter leave for consideration of a common good, between libertarians and "moderate" liberals such as John Rawls and Ronald Dworkin. I assume rough familiarity with the latter theorists, who not only reject libertarianism's crude atomistic ontology and its defense of market outcomes as the best standard for justice but also go on to argue that individual flourishing is best promoted when government honors equal concern and respect for varying conceptions of the good life available in an ethically pluralistic and democratic society. For further analysis and defense of that view, see my "Egalitarian Liberalism and the Fact of Pluralism," *Journal of Social Philosophy* 27(3) (Winter 1996): 51–80.

4. Etzioni, *New Golden Rule*, xviii.

5. Etzioni, *New Golden Rule*, 59–60.

6. Etzioni, *New Golden Rule*, 73, 76. All emphases in quotations are in the original.

7. For empirical support for, and various explanations of, the declining trust in government, see *Why People Don't Trust Government*, ed. Joseph Nye Jr., Philip D. Zelikow, and David King (Cambridge, Mass.: Harvard University Press, 1997), esp. Gary Orren, "Fall from Grace: The Public's Loss of Faith in Government," 77–107.

8. See the somewhat jaundiced view of the liberal-communitarian debate in Mary Dietz, "Merely Combating the Phrases of This World: Recent Democratic Theory," *Political Theory* 26(1) (February 1998): esp. 116.

9. Etzioni, *New Golden Rule*, 16.

10. See Amitai Etzioni, "The Responsive Communitarian Platform: Rights and Responsibilities," in *Rights and the Common Good: The Communitarian Perspective*, ed. Amitai Etzioni (New York: St. Martin's Press, 1995), esp. 22. In reacting to vague and potentially threatening

generalizations, as well as some harsh policy prescriptions, critics have urged that communitarianism is a "dangerous and anachronistic ideal" (H. N. Hirsch, "The Threnody of Liberalism: Constitutional Liberty and the Renewal of Community," *Political Theory* 14[3] [August 1986]: 441), that it is built on claims, the full implication of which might present "a frightful countenance" to unpopular minorities (Carlos Nino, "The Communitarian Challenge to Liberal Rights," *Law and Philosophy* 8[1] [April 1989]: 41–2), and that it is at least loosely associated with authoritarianism (Steven Holmes, *The Anatomy of Antiliberalism* (Cambridge, Mass.: Harvard University Press, 1993).

11. Etzioni, *New Golden Rule*, 115, also 221.

12. Etzioni, *New Golden Rule*, 42, 52.

13. Etzioni, *New Golden Rule*, 223. For the critics' case, see Ronald Dworkin, *A Matter of Principle* (Cambridge, Mass.: Harvard University Press, 1985), 219, where he attacks Michael Walzer's attempt to derive justice (or the true and the good) from locally shared conventions as ultimately "incoherent" because it turns justice into a "mirror" rather than a "critic" of our social arrangements, thus denying the central importance of "worrying about what justice really is."

14. Etzioni, *New Golden Rule*, 220, 227, 236–7.

15. Etzioni, *New Golden Rule*, 241–5.

16. Etzioni, *New Golden Rule*, xv.

17. Holmes, *Antiliberalism*, 88, 176.

18. See, e.g., Richard Dagger, *Civic Virtues: Rights, Citizenship, and Republican Liberalism* (New York: Oxford University Press, 1997), who begins from the liberal premise of a fundamental right to autonomy, but sees that capacity as sufficiently situated in communal relations to warrant more concern for ascribing republican and virtue-oriented responsibilities to citizens. From the communitarian side, Philip Selznick, "Social Justice: A Communitarian Perspective," *The Responsive Community* 6(4) (Fall 1996): 13–25, argues that communitarians must not let their concerns for individual responsibility lead them to neglect communal responsibility for the weak and impoverished.

19. Gerald Dworkin, *The Theory and Practice of Autonomy* (Cambridge: Cambridge University Press, 1988), 6.

20. Etzioni, *New Golden Rule*, 23, 243.

21. Gerald Dworkin, *Autonomy*, 12, contrasts "substantive" conceptions of autonomy with an alternative, "formal" model, in which "what one decides for oneself can have any particular content."

22. Harry Frankfurt, "Freedom of the Will and the Concept of a Person," in *The Inner Citadel: Essays on Individual Autonomy*, ed. John Christman (New York: Oxford University Press, 1989), 64.

23. Etzioni, *New Golden Rule*, 167–71.

24. Frankfurt, "Freedom of the Will," 75, n. 6.

25. Isaiah Berlin, *Four Essays on Liberty* (Oxford: Oxford University Press, 1969), ch. 3; see also, Richard Flathman, *The Philosophy and Politics of Freedom* (Chicago: University of Chicago Press, 1987), 58–62 and ch. 4. Egalitarian liberals tend to reject as a public project the promotion of either Kantian self-determination or classical perfectionisms insofar as they require political support for particular and contested conceptions of the self or the good life; see John Rawls, *Political Liberalism* (New York: Columbia University Press, 1996), xliv–xlv.

26. Gerald Dworkin, *Autonomy*, 14–18.

27. Etzioni, *New Golden Rule*, 6–7, 23–4.

28. Etzioni, *New Golden Rule*, 36–47.

29. Etzioni, *New Golden Rule*, 244, 234. See also Charles Taylor, *Sources of the Self: The Making of the Modern Identity* (Cambridge, Mass.: Harvard University Press, 1989), ch. 15, with the quote at 261. For the influence of the moral sense school, and especially its egalitarianism, on early American thinkers such as James Wilson and Thomas Jefferson, see respectively, Jennifer Nedelsky, *Private Property and the Limits of American Constitutionalism* (Chicago: University of Chicago Press, 1990), ch. 4, and Garry Wills, *Inventing America: Jefferson's Declaration of Independence* (New York: Vintage, 1979), ch. 3. For a critique of at least James Q. Wilson's theory of the moral sense, see Peter Singer, "Is There a Universal Moral Sense?" *Critical Review* 9(3) (Summer 1995): 325–39.

30. Etzioni, *New Golden Rule*, 303, n. 82.

31. Etzioni, *New Golden Rule*, 243–4.

32. Etzioni, *New Golden Rule*, 266, n. 86.

33. Etzioni, *New Golden Rule*, 251–2.

34. The most famous version of this argument is probably Robert Paul Wolff, *In Defense of Anarchism* (New York: Harper and Row, 1970).

35. Richard Flathman, *The Practice of Political Authority: Authority and the Authoritative* (Chicago: University of Chicago Press, 1980), 14–16. For Flathman, "formal-procedural" theories and rigid distinctions between "in authority" and "an authority" must be moderated by the recognition that shared values and beliefs about the authoritative are common to all such relationships. His aversion to "substantive-purposive" conceptions is nonetheless clear.

36. Thomas Scanlon, "Due Process," in *Due Process: Nomos XVIII*, ed. J. Roland Pennock and John W. Chapman (New York: New York University Press, 1977), 118–21.

37. L. W. Sumner, "Is Virtue Its Own Reward?" *Social Philosophy & Policy* 15(1) (Winter 1998): 18.

38. Etzioni, *New Golden Rule*, 6; on his desire to ward off the charge that functionalism is inherently biased against change, see also Amitai Etzioni, *The Active Society: A Theory of Societal and Political Processes* (New York: Free Press, 1968), 79–80.

39. Eric Mack, "Deontic Restrictions Are Not Agent-Relative Restrictions," *Social Philosophy & Policy* 15(2) (Summer 1998): 62. On the debate about the conditions of goodness and for an argument in favor of a "constitutive" view in which individual "endorsement" is a condition of having a good life, see Ronald Dworkin, "Foundations of Liberal Equality," in *The Tanner Lectures on Human Values*, vol. 11, ed. Grethe Peterson (Salt Lake City: University of Utah Press, 1990), 53–8. The alternative view, which Dworkin calls an "impact" model of value and which figures in various teleological theories, is defended in whole or in part by Thomas Hurka, "Indirect Perfectionism: Kymlicka on Liberal Neutrality," *Journal of Political Philosophy* 3(1) (March 1995): 36–57, and William Galston, *Liberal Purposes: Goods, Virtues, and Diversity in the Liberal State* (Cambridge: Cambridge University Press, 1991), 86–7.

40. Amitai Etzioni, *Social Problems* (Englewood Cliffs, N.J.: Prentice-Hall, 1976), 171–2, and Amitai Etzioni, *The Moral Dimension: Toward a New Economics* (New York: Free Press, 1988), 8–9.

41. See Etzioni, *Moral Dimension*, ch. 1, where he rejects the hedonistic view of human behavior laid out in utilitarianism and neoclassical economics and urges, besides the "I-We

view," the notion that we often act out of duty and motives unrelated to narrow, self-interested calculations of preference satisfaction.

42. Samuel Scheffler, "Introduction," in *Consequentialism and Its Critics*, ed. Samuel Scheffler (Oxford: Oxford University Press, 1988), 1. See David Norton, "On Recovering the Telos in Teleology, or, 'Where's the Beef'?" *The Monist* 75(1) (January 1992): 3, arguing that teleological theories are a particular species of the wider genus of consequentialisms and that the former are distinguished by their reliance on the notion of "an innate end whose actualization through a process of development constitutes the 'flourishing' or 'fulfillment' of the entity whose end it is."

43. Etzioni, *New Golden Rule*, 89. For a more sustained critique of the public neutrality doctrine, see Michael Sandel, *Democracy's Discontent: America In Search of a Public Philosophy* (Cambridge, Mass.: Harvard University Press, 1996), ch. 1 and 321–4. I have tried to respond to some of the criticisms of neutrality in my "Egalitarian Liberalism and Social Pathology: A Defense of Public Neutrality," *Social Theory and Practice* 23(3) (Fall 1997): 449–78.

44. Ronald Dworkin, *Matter of Principle*, 191–2; see also my "Communitarian Politics and the Problem of Equality," *Political Research Quarterly* 46(3) (September 1993): 577–600.

45. Etzioni, *New Golden Rule*, 240, 248; and Amitai Etzioni, "Introduction to Part II," in *Rights and the Common Good*, 73–4. For his more recent and sustained thoughts on line drawing in the area of informational privacy, see Amitai Etzioni, *The Limits of Privacy* (New York: Basic Books, 1999).

46. Ronald Dworkin, "Foundations of Liberal Equality," 43–4.

47. Etzioni, *New Golden Rule*, 143–4; for further argument that the law should be the moral voice of society, see William Galston, "Social Mores Are Not Enough," *Responsive Community* 7(4) (Fall 1997): 16–20.

48. Etzioni, *New Golden Rule*, 32, 54–6, and Amitai Etzioni, "The Virtues of Humiliation," *The American Prospect* (November-December 1997): 74–5.

49. Etzioni, *New Golden Rule*, 6, 127.

50. Etzioni, *New Golden Rule*, 50.

2

Communitarianism, Human Nature, and the Spirit of the Times

Dennis H. Wrong

The communitarians articulate in thoroughly convincing fashion many sociological home truths that have often been ignored in current discussions. In Amitai Etzioni's books, most notably in *The New Golden Rule*,[1] he insists that *society* as a partially independent realm needs to be added to the state and the market in all considerations of social policy and collective goals. Recognition of the autonomy of society as against state and economy, which had become subjects of systematic study a few decades earlier, was a primary mandate for the very birth of sociology as a distinctive academic field in the late nineteenth century. Etzioni's argument for a voluntary moral order independent of state coercion and market exchange is central to his case for communitarianism and makes it both more and less than a political movement in the conventional sense. Communitarian insistence that human nature is a social product through and through is unexceptionable.

Occasionally, however, communitarians, including Etzioni, seem to be attacking a familiar straw man in imputing to liberals a belief in individuals with fully formed attributes that are independent of any social influence or shaping. There are vestiges here of the polemics against psychologism and biologism that were favored by the founders of sociology, especially Émile Durkheim, in addition to their rejection of the too exclusive emphasis on force and self-interest of classical political theory and economics. A "revolt against individualism"[2] whether conceived of in economistic or biopsychologistic terms, animated both the fathers of the field, such as Auguste Comte and Karl Marx, and its founders as an academic discipline. Echoes of this continue to resound in sociology at large: I have been listening to attacks on "atomistic individualism" ever since I first studied sociology half a century ago. Yet I don't believe that even Thomas Hobbes, John Locke, and Adam Smith, the original targets of this polemic, were really guilty of seeing human beings as asocial or antisocial animals. They rather, out of the normative political and legal concerns with which they were primarily preoccupied, failed to *problematize,* to use a fashionable term, the natural and/or social sources and determinants of human nature. Jean Jacques Rousseau is a more complicated case: he believed that human beings had once lived in a largely asocial state of nature in which they lacked all the distinctively human qualities of language, foresight, and morality that later social thinkers have regarded as products of socialization.[3] Since under these conditions human beings possessed no moral sense at all, they were not subject to internal conflict between right and wrong, between the beast and angel in their natures. Indeed, they *were* no more than beasts, but amiable, peaceable beasts equipped with natural sympathy for one another's pain rather than the ferociously aggressive and competitive creatures of Hobbes, the Social Darwinists, and Rousseau himself in his negative conception of the stage *after* men had become more dependent on one another in society.

The neoclassical economists' conception of individuals as rational egoists continuously engaged in "utility-maximizing" calculations that dictate their behavior is another matter. In this view, although the very capacity for calculation, or "rational choice," is the result of the acquisition through socialization of language, which makes possible action guided by foresight in pursuit of desired ends, objects of desire are simply taken as given "preferences," and moral restraints on the choice of both ends and means, also results of socialization, are ignored.[4] Contemporary neoclassical economists make plain that these are heuristic assumptions: human mental processes are deliberately treated as a "black box" that need not be opened for accurate predictions—the goal of science—to be made. Predictability and the construction of mathematically refined "modeling" of economic behavior are regarded as sufficient justification for the assumptions, incomplete or unrealistic as they may be from a psychological or sociological standpoint. Etzioni's *The Moral Dimension: Toward a New Economics* is a book-length critical examination of this utilitarian paradigm in which "individuals are assumed to be the effective actors, able to act independently and to be psychologically complete unto themselves."[5] It led to his creation of a new academic association, the Society for the Advancement of Social Economics, which has attracted leading scholars from several nations and all of the social sciences—including economics—who are critical of the narrow free-market economism of neoclassical economic theory.

In the debate between liberals and communitarians, the communitarian political theorists have deployed fairly commonplace sociological considerations against their adversaries. I find it quite remarkable how frequently these days writers in other disciplines aggressively reinvent the wheel in propounding ideas, often in oversimplified versions, that are utterly familiar to sociologists. This may reflect the recent decline in influence of sociology, although the field has never ranked high in the university or come close to matching political science, economics, psychology, or the major fields of the humanities in the numbers of its practitioners.

The communitarian political theorists have insisted that there is no such thing as an "unencumbered self"—the phrase is Michael Sandel's.[6] A fundamental tenet of sociology, primarily based on the work of George Herbert Mead, is that the very existence of the "self" derives from social interaction involving the exchange of symbolic gestures. *Self* here means the reflexive awareness by individuals of their own thoughts, actions, and feelings. Yet it does not necessarily follow from this that one owes a primary moral debt to the "encumbrances" with which one is burdened, as some communitarians seem to imply. The very notion of encumbrances suggests hindrances one might want to rid oneself of, even while admitting that one can never do so completely and that the formation of one's own nature was much influenced by them. We are all, for instance, most powerfully shaped by our parents—without them we would be different people altogether. But it does not follow that we owe an immeasurable lifelong debt to them and should therefore devote much of our lives to serving them and honoring their memory, granting that some societies have engaged in ancestor worship.

The view that we are primarily the products of the social forces that have made us underlies the claim of postmodernists that "socialization goes all the way down."[7] That this imposes on us a moral obligation to celebrate and affirm those forces is plainly implied by the insistence of partisans of identity politics that our essence resides in social identities that we cannot and, accordingly, should not try to transcend or to subordinate to individual identities forged out of multiple and unique personal social experiences. Etzioni's argument is a more balanced one. His dictum "the me needs the we to be" certainly evokes cloying rhetoric about "togetherness," "belongingness," and "we-feelings." Yet he immediately follows the phrase with the statement "the normative implications of this ontological observation are subject to different interpretations; however, that humans are social is incontestable."[8] Moreover, he explicitly repudiates an oversocialized conception of human nature that treats people simply as mirrors of the social and cultural environment to which they have been exposed.[9] He also fully recognizes a need for and the value of individual autonomy, according it equal status with community as both need and value. Etzioni's title "the new golden rule" suggests, undoubtedly by intention, Aristotle's "golden mean," in this case the balance Etzioni recommends between autonomy and order, the two components of his "spirit of community," the title of an earlier book of his.[10] He roundly rejects libertarianism, on the one hand, and authoritarian traditionalism, on the other, the opposed extreme ideological exemplars of these values.

Communitarianism as a perspective has been assimilated into the long-standing theme in social thought of "loss of community" as a major affliction of modern life. It has, accordingly, been accused of succumbing to the often-exaggerated lamentations of the many sociologists and social critics who have made much of this proclaimed loss. Given the movement's name, it is scarcely surprising that communitarianism should have been subjected to such criticism, but it is nevertheless far from fully warranted. The familiar theme represents "community," the unfulfilled psychological need and ensuing "quest" for it, as the antidote to the "alienation of modern man," "the world we have lost," "the lonely crowd," "the need for roots," "the pursuit of loneliness," "the homeless mind"—all conceived of as constituting the virtual essence of modernity and the titles of well-known books by social scientists and philosophers.[11] Yet far from celebrating "the ecstasy of belonging"[12] and "the pleasures of social cohesion,"[13] the very title of Etzioni's most recent and major communitarian book asserts the *moral obligation* imposed by community rather than the satisfactions it provides. If the title suggests Aristotle, it more directly echoes traditional biblical morality, for "the golden rule" is, of course, "do unto others as thou wouldst thyself be done by others." Nor does Etzioni confine himself simply to affirming community and consideration for others as abstract "values": he is unfailingly concrete in specifying the kinds of actions—actions not just words—he would like to see independently undertaken by individuals or mandated by public policy or law. Examples of these are: striving to prevent littering and vandalism in public places, police checks on drunk driving, intervening to admonish a mother who is beating her child, protesting queue jumping, praising an adolescent who offers help to a disabled senior citizen, and taking legal account of the interests of children before granting a divorce. Most of these and other examples given require some individual gumption, even a minimum of moral courage, to carry out, going well beyond mere rhetorical prating about common values. Many presuppose the efficacy of *shaming* people who engage in antisocial behavior, although one critic oddly claims that Etzioni ignores shame as "a powerful instrument of moral order."[14]

If community has been "lost" under the conditions of modern life, it presumably was present in the past. This belief was dubbed "*Gemeinschaftschmerz*" by the late Christopher Lasch[15] to connote mourning over the lost world of "organic community" that allegedly prevailed before it was shattered by the great transformations of modernity. Derek Phillips wrote an entire book refuting the idealization of past social orders implied by such a view, complaining that it overlooks or minimizes the frequent oppressive conformism and authoritarianism of premodern societies. Etzioni was one of Phillips's targets, and he objected that such criticism was "misdirected" in focusing on "old or total communities, which are neither typical to modern society, nor necessary for, nor even compatible with, a communitarian society."[16] If Etzioni avoids waxing nostalgic for the distant past, he is nevertheless too inclined like a great many others, mostly social conservatives, to invoke America in the 1950s as a recent more communitarian alternative to the present. Yet the 1950s was a decade in which *both* the "quest" for the lost community[17] "eclipsed" under modern conditions[18] *and* stifling conformism imputed to American life in general and suburbia in particular, evincing an enforced and unspontaneous version of community, became major themes of social criticism.[19]

In both of his books propounding communitarianism, Etzioni included chapters entitled "the moral voice," underlining his definition of community as morally demanding rather than merely psychologically fulfilling. His insistence on such a voice as universally human (except for sociopaths) also endorses the basic assumption of sociologists that a central feature of the socialization of individuals is their *internal-*

ization of social norms. Etzioni recognizes that this view is derived from Sigmund Freud's conception of the superego and the process of its formation, although he otherwise does not dwell on psychoanalytic theory. Freud regarded an internal "moral voice" as a universal component of human nature formed out of the young child's emotionally charged identifications with its parents and the eventual self-imposition of their moral directives and prohibitions. The performance of active duties dictated by the moral voice of the superego is largely confined to the individual's microsociety of family, friends, and neighbors. Relations with strangers, on the other hand, are primarily subject to negative prohibitions against theft, violence, fraud, vulgar display, and milder forms of incivility.

Contrary to the alleged "isolation of modern man in mass society," sociologists in the immediate postwar years "rediscovered" primary group relations governed by informal social norms and sentiments of solidarity flourishing even in the interstices of large-scale organizations where impersonal bureaucratic rules and regulations prevailed.[20] More recently, alarmists decrying the nation's alleged moral decline have deplored high rates of crime, sexual abuse, unmarried motherhood, substance addiction, and divorce resulting in child neglect, as well as such lesser derelictions as "road rage" and queue jumping. To his credit, Etzioni takes note of what he calls "curl back," the recent tapering off and even decline in the rates for most of these forms of antisocial behavior that had been rising since the 1960s.[21] He thus refuses to add his voice to the more heated jeremiads of conservatives like William Bennett and Robert Bork. The communitarian movement continues to see its mission as opposition to antisocial behavior both in "private" personal relations and in more public places involving encounters with strangers, although its main concern has been with the latter and with the total society, conceiving of "community" at the macro and the intermediate level sometimes labeled "meso" rather than in micro terms.

A moral sense may be regarded as largely innate, as by some conservatives,[22] or as acquired through early socialization, as by Freudians and sociologists, but it is indeterminate whether its commandments are considered binding beyond the sphere of family and personal relations. Freud recognized this in *Civilization and Its Discontents.*[23] Are the superego's injunctions confined entirely to kin as in the "amoral familism" Edward Banfield[24] attributed to South Italian peasants; do they fail to apply beyond the boundaries of the tribe or local community; do race, gender, ethnicity, and class set important limits to them; or do they at least adumbrate in their reach the brotherhood of man, or humanity at large?[25] Etzioni insists on the need for shared and recognized "core values" underlying the "community of communities" he extols and wishes to see more fully realized. The larger society must itself become a prime object of value, reflecting a social bond extending beyond the personal and local levels. This value entails concern for a wider sense of a "common good" or "public interest" to guide "behavior in public places"[26] as well as enlisting support for enlightened public policies. But at this point communitarian rhetoric about "values" becomes abstract and often vacuously hortatory in contrast to the very concrete examples of approved individual actions toward strangers that Etzioni adduced to illustrate a proper spirit of community.

Etzioni lists "patriotism" as a "core value" of Americans in the 1950s that has since faded as part of a general deterioration of "moral order." This leads one to reflect that there is nothing about the spirit of national community that a really big threatening war or even cold war could not revive. A major depression might have the same effect: it has often been observed that the economic crisis of the 1930s created a wider and deeper sense of the American experience. It is commonly noted how at the local level group and individual differences are ignored and conflicts suppressed in response to public disasters such as floods, earthquakes, blizzards, power blackouts, terrorist bombings, mass murders, or even perceived threats to neighborhoods, as in NIMBY ("Not in My Backyard") groups. Perhaps there is a trade-off between the avoidance of actual or potential calamities facing communities and their fragmentation into individuals and groups "doing their own thing," including quarreling with each other short of civil war.

Etzioni is much too ready, I think, to accede to the argument of social conservatives that there has been a moral decline, originating in the various protest and countercultural movements of the 1960s. Like the conservatives, he overlooks that many of the trends seen as exhibiting this decline had deep roots in the fairly distant past, some of them going back to the closing decades of the previous century. Changes in the status of women, increases in sexual permissiveness, including the legalization of homosexuality, abortion, and pornography, as well as greater tolerance for nonmarital sexual relations, liberalization of divorce laws, and concern for the rights and treatment of criminals are cases in point. Some of these changes, to be sure, came about quite abruptly, lending plausibility to the notion of a "sexual revolution" bursting out in the1960s. Policies and laws, some of which dated back to the eighteenth century, were abandoned or repealed, and long-standing taboos on acceptable public discourse vanished, including protections of the "privacy" of politicians and other public figures, as has been remarked on ad nauseam in connection with the Clinton-Lewinsky sexual scandal. Right-wing politicians have made a particular issue of the vastly greater openness in the depiction of sex and violence in the mass media, especially movies and television.

There can be little doubt that the removal of legal restrictions has increased the incidence of speech and behavior that were once illegal, morally tabooed, or, in the case of divorce, subject to restrictions that required often costly subterfuges to overcome. Yet there is still a problem, familiar to researchers of crime and deviance, of the extent to which formerly banned or concealed actions have now become merely more visible rather than more frequent. The honoring of values and norms in the breach rather than in the observance has long been recognized, especially with regard to sexual behavior. Do communitarians wish for, or unrealistically think possible, an actual abandonment of the various "liberations" associated with the 1960s? Do they want no more than to reinstate public professions of values and rules to which lip service is duly paid but that no one is really expected to live up to in conduct? Some conservatives are thoroughly realistic about this: they have no objections to hypocrisy as the tribute vice pays to virtue; they want only to restore it to its past prevalence, never mind how people, including conservatives themselves, may conduct their private lives. Most of us who came of age between the 1920s and the 1960s could not help but be partly aware that the sexual morality publicly affirmed when we were young was a relic of the Victorian past that rarely guided actual behavior (and may not have done so then). The sexual revolution produced greater changes in public expression and visibility than in actual behavior and came after decades in which private sexual conduct and the norms actually governing it frequently transgressed the standards frozen in the letter of the law and upheld in the ritualized language of "official" public discourse, including the injunctions of parents and teachers. The wider diffusion and greater penetration of the media into everyday life accelerated these changes, making them seem more abrupt and far-reaching than they really were.

The notion, shared by social conservatives and communitarians, that traditional "family values" reigned in the 1950s is also contestable. The decade was the first since the 1920s in which both peace and prosperity prevailed. High rates of marriage, decreasing ages at marriage, higher fertility—the "baby boom"—reflecting, however, only modest increases in the number of children per couple as against a larger number of childbearing couples, and the mass migration to single-family homes in the suburbs that was both cause and effect of these vital trends reversed the demographic profile of the two previous decades. But this conduct to a considerable degree represented a "making up" of postponed family-building and residential choices that had been blocked by depression and war rather than either the continuation of traditional ways or a new family pattern replacing an earlier one.[27] These trends and the values affirmed in conjunction with them may have reflected a kind of "neo-traditionalism" in the wake of a devastating depression, innovative reforms to cope with it, a world war, and the threat of another war involving nuclear weapons. Most of the consensus and stability that marked the 1950s came after Joseph Stalin's death in 1953, the censure of Senator McCarthy the following year, the end of the Korean War, and the "spirit of Geneva," which ushered in for the first but not the last time what was called "détente" in relations with the Soviet Union. The baby boom was part of this neotraditionalism, and so was the "feminine mystique," later deplored by Betty Friedan, but they too came after the reversal of previous all-time lows in marriage and fertility. It is therefore questionable that the 1950s, and only the late 1950s at that, truly exhibited a stable "moral order" rooted in a national consensus on "core values." As in the specific case of the higher birthrates that produced the baby boom[28] many features of the 1950s, now mourned and idealized in retrospect, were aberrations reflecting a very particular set of conditions when viewed in the larger context of the preceding half-century or longer.

Nor did the 1960s elimination of the gap between operative and publicly proclaimed "official" norms represent merely an outbreak of antinomian hedonism inspired by the "counterculture," although there was certainly much of that. Legal reformers, psychiatrists, intellectuals, and bohemian avant-gardists had long been advocates of greater sexual permissiveness on the morally principled grounds of improving psychological health, increasing personal freedom, and ending cynically deceptive manipulations of the legal code that contributed to disrespect for the law. Opposition to restrictions on abortion, capital punishment, and the harsh treatment of criminals also had a history antedating the 1960s by many decades. Far from manifesting the breakdown into nihilism of an established moral order, the 1960s witnessed the implementation of reforms long favored for moral, largely humani-tarian, reasons: the reduction of mental suffering and social stigma, the elimination of hypocrisy, greater tolerance of individual differences, and expansion of the range of personal freedoms. It may be that, though advocated on moral grounds, this amounted in the end to a "triumph of the therapeutic"[29] that undermined moral judgment as such. Undoubtedly, the removal of restrictions on formerly proscribed or severely disapproved actions produced at first overindulgence and the testing of remaining limits. In addition to initial excesses, the new practices produced, as changes always do, some unwanted unanticipated effects, such as, most notoriously, AIDS and other epidemics of sexually transmitted diseases, and the problems asso-ciated with single-parent families. A stabilizing adjustment to the new order may account for the "curl back" Etzioni recognized in the rates for crime and extremes of hedonistic behavior, which has since become greater than when he wrote. The failure of the U.S. public to be as shocked by the Clinton-Lewinsky affair as con-servative moralists think it should have been may also reflect a realistic recognition, if not necessarily approval, of sexual practices, which, before the 1960s, were veiled in relative ignorance.

Critics of communitarianism have charged that it focuses almost exclusively on the behavior of individuals. Etzioni's emphasis is indeed on public-spirited individual conduct rather than on the actions of large organizations and the hierarchical power structures they embody. Steven Lukes, reviewing the major communitarian journal, has written: "There is very little . . . about the moral and cultural consequences of market processes, and virtually nothing about the ramifications of economic inequal-ity."[30] Protests against inequality and the effects of uncontrolled markets have been virtually definitive of socialism. Socialism is "about equality," as a British socialist leader once declared, but it has also been about *fraternity*, the third in the famous French revolutionary triad of *"liberte, egalite, fraternite."* "Community" as an ideal to be pursued and "fraternity" in the slogan clearly amount to much the same thing. *Communitarianism* belongs to an entire family of words coined since the early nine-teenth century to encapsulate social ideals opposed to the egoistic individualism imputed to laissez-faire capitalism and to the suffering caused by it during early in-dustrialization: collectivism, cooperativism, fraternalism, mutualism, solidarism, communalism, communism, socialism. The last two, of course, became the names of the ideologies and political movements that dominated the politics of so many nations in the twentieth century. Doubtless this verbal kinship to "commun-itarianism" accounts for the hostility to the present movement of some conservatives despite the similarity of communitarian complaints about moral decline to their own and the—excessive, in my view—efforts of Etzioni to enlist their support.

The United States has notoriously never possessed a major socialist movement. Nevertheless, most of the features of socialist programs and ideals that have been combined in a single party, movement, or ideology in Europe have been present here though espoused at different times by different groups and political actors. Middle-class professionals in both parties supported the Progressives in imposing regulations on big capitalists; Gompers's "business unionism" promoted the interests of workers and defined the character of the U.S. labor movement; the New Deal exhibited "a social democratic tinge," as Michael Harrington once put it, in laying the foundations of a U.S. welfare state; feminist and civil rights movements acted in different periods to extend the electoral franchise. The U.S. creed itself, as has often been pointed out, extolled most of the same egalitarian ideals that have animated socialists elsewhere. Communitarianism can be seen as another example of this parceling out of democratic, egalitarian, and collectivist objectives among a variety of groups and organizations, one that stresses the fraternalism and social responsibility inherent in the socialist appeal. It is a political movement insofar as it presses demands for certain legal restrictions on antisocial behavior, such as drunken driving, and ignoring the interests of children in divorce; it is both more and less than a political movement in proselytizing for greater sacrifice and subordination of individual interests to the common good in the contemporary United States. This clearly differentiates communitarianism from libertarianism and free market economism, although what it affirms is widely assented to, at least in the abstract, by partisans of quite different persuasions.

Unsurprisingly, I find myself, as a fellow sociologist, in complete agreement with Etzioni's basic assumptions about the relation between society and the individual. I also approve of the communitarian movement's broad summons to greater concern for the common good as well as most of its specific political demands for the curbing of various forms of antisocial behavior. Yet I confess to a certain ambivalence to communitarianism both as a theory and as a movement, even though I find Etzioni himself innocent of many things I dislike about them. I have had the frequent experience of starting to read in a sympathetic spirit communitarian polemics against the egoistic and narcissistic excesses of individualism only to find my liberal-individualist hackles rising in opposition to aspects of the case being made. This also applies to at least some of Etzioni's strictures against liberals and individualists, although most of the time he recognizes that there are many breeds of these, not all of them guilty of the sins he imputes to some. I am therefore driven to conclude that I stand closer to the liberal-individualist end of the autonomy/order continuum in political and ideological terms. The political and social thinkers I have most admired for the better part of my life have been Max Weber, Raymond Aron, Isaiah Berlin, Ernest Gellner, David Riesman, and Laszek Kolakowski—liberals all, none of them tainted with libertarianism or extreme free market economism, let alone support for what the late Brough Macpherson called "possessive individualism," that communitarians rightly reject, though Etzioni criticizes Berlin on "negative liberty" at one point.[31] These thinkers, be it noted, are mostly Europeans, and it may be, as has often been charged, that the excesses of capitalist individualism in both its acquisitive and hedonistic-narcissistic, or "expressive"[32] forms are particularly pronounced in the United States. But accusations of superficial conformism and chameleon-like other-direction have also been seen as typically American. Communitarians lack a fully comparative perspective separating what is distinctively American from what may be inherent in modernity, which embeds small groups and communities in a far-flung system of indirect and impersonal connections.

I confess to a sense of identification with Richard Ford's central character in his novel *Independence Day,* who reflects that "'Community' is actually one of those words I loathe, since all its hands-on implications are dubious." Earlier he says, "I don't think communities are continuous. . . . I think of them—and I've got a lot of proof—as isolated, contingent groups trying to improve on an illusion of perma-nence, which they fully accept as an illusion."[33] Ford's character is talking to a child-hood friend who has been describing his not entirely happy experiences living on an Israeli kibbutz. One suspects that Etzioni's enthusiasm for community may go back to his youth on a kibbutz, although in fairness to him he is by no means a supporter of any version of the "goofball utopian ideals of every stripe" that Ford's character finds in "hippie communes, Brook Farms, kibbutzes."[34] In my own case, I am unable to dissociate calls for more community from the denunciations by the authorities in high school of "three-fifteeners," students who went home after classes without participating in sports or other extracurricular activities, thereby revealing a deplorable lack of "school spirit." More significantly if rather predictably, Ford's character alludes to Hitler in rejecting model utopian communities; enthusiasm for communitarian appeals is likely to be tempered by anyone with a vivid recollection of the terrible events of the 1940s. Zygmunt Bauman has pointed to a strong simi-larity between the traditional appeals of extreme nationalism, considerably if not, alas, totally discredited by the Nazi experience, and the communitarian message.[35]

Bauman, however, thinks it paradoxical that communitarians support precisely the "natural communities of origin" based primarily on locality that earlier nation-alist ideologues (Barres is his major example) wished to transcend to create a supralocal identification with the nation-state. Bauman's argument seems more ap-plicable to proponents of muticulturalism who affirm identity politics than to communitarians, for Etzioni's "community of communities" encompasses both a pluralist appreciation of local communities and a wider loyalty to the larger society in which they are embedded. Yet there are clear affinities as well as differences among communitarians, celebrants of multicultural "diversity," and neo-Tocquevillian [36] advocates of "civil society," all of them reflecting a zeitgeist in which alarm over "the rise of selfishness in America"[37] has become as prevalent a theme of social criticism as complaints over conformism were in the 1950s and complaints over alienation and bureaucracy were in the 1960s. Alan Wolfe maintains that community as an ideal "has probably been much more frequently proclaimed in *limited* rather than in expansive form"[38] (his emphasis). Undeniably, there is tension between the two forms, but Wolfe's remarks, like Bauman's, fit multiculturalist identity politics better than the communitarian movement.

Three group or social levels are involved in these debates: primary group relations, or the micro level of friends, neighbors, and relatives; the intermediate, or meso, level of voluntary associations extolled by neo-Tocquevillian theorists of civil society; and the macrosocial level of the most comprehensive unit, usually the nation-state. The ideal relation among levels, adumbrated at least in Etzioni's "community of communities," pictures successively widening loyalties and identifications with the smaller groups "nesting" within the larger ones, or forming a set of concentric circles. Disequilibrium among levels, the overvaluing of one over the others, is the basis of a number of variants of contemporary social criticism. Complaints about the "privatization" of American life, whether in the form of gated residential enclaves of the rich or the political apathy and indifference of the poor, deplore the primacy of the micro level. Attacks on identity politics assail the vesting of ultimate value in the second level, seen as dominating the first while repudiating the "universalist" third. Fears of the totalitarian potential in the exaltation of the most inclusive level, whether sacralizing nation, race, or the solidary "toiling masses" as the major object of veneration, have only too often been justified by the terrible events of the twentieth century and inspire in some an almost reflex rejection of any appeal to "imagined communities" in Benedict Anderson's resonant phrase.[39] And just about every group beyond the micro level—and even that in one sense[40]—is an imagined community. Only small tribes or isolated villages constitute possible exceptions larger than small face-to-face groups.

There is a parallelism between Horace Kallen's image of the United States as a "nation of nations" in his famous argument for "cultural pluralism" and Etzioni's ideal of a "community of communities." But Kallen was speaking up for the meso level of the diverse cultures immigrants brought with them against an overarching Anglo-conformity, whereas Etzioni's aim in an altogether different period is to insist on obligations to the larger national community that override without superseding the diverse group identities celebrated by the partisans of multiculturalism. The emphasis on the civic duties of individuals and the lack of a substantive national reformist or state-interventionist program that has aroused critics who are descendants of the old socialist tradition, "what is left of the left," also reflects the current political mood. If Etzioni's communitarianism is not, as I have argued, oriented to the past, to what Stephen Holmes calls "deprivation history," bemoaning the world we have lost, neither is it what he calls "promissory history," projecting a vision of a glorious future establishing a new moral consensus that will redeem us all.[41] The "nebulousness" of communitarian politics about which Holmes as well as others have complained attests to its congruence with the present.

In a brilliantly perceptive article subtitled "the smallness of centrism," Nicholas Lemann observes: "The consensus right now is not to have a consensus about what the country as a whole should be or do."[42] No large national projects in domestic or foreign policy are the order of the day, not the ending of poverty; instituting universal health insurance; addressing the widening inequalities of income; intervening, except minimally, to curb local wars abroad; reconstructing Russia after winning the Cold War; or facing up to the Asian economic crisis with more than unsolicited advice.[43] As the Republicans learned after winning control of Congress in 1994, even negative objectives have failed to win public support, such as scaling down the welfare state, reversing most of the cultural changes since the 1960s, or impeaching a president of the other party. The New Deal era of forceful policy initiatives from Washington ended in the 1980s with the success of the Republicans' Southern strategy under Reagan; Clinton's accommodations and small-bore reforms ended the "counterrevolution" misperceived as having triumphed in 1994. The period is truly conservative in its literal meaning of preserving the status quo against any alteration rather than in the ideological sense the label has acquired in political rhetoric and the lucubrations of right-wing intellectuals, many of them defectors from the left. Under these conditions it is hard to see what the communitarian movement would gain by advancing a comprehensive program of reform even were it so inclined. Perhaps communitarianism can be seen as a kind of holding action keeping alive a spirit of commitment to larger goals transcending self-interest and narrow group "special interests" for the day when such a spirit is once again needed to deal with truly national opportunities and crises.

NOTES

1. Amitai Etzioni, *The New Golden Rule* (New York: Basic Books, 1996).

2. Robert Nisbet, *The Sociological Tradition* (New York: Basic Books, 1966), 7–9.

3. Jean Jacques Rousseau, *A Discourse on Inequality* (Harmondworth, England: Penguin Books, 1984).

4. Dennis H. Wrong, *The Modern Condition: Essays at Century's End* (Stanford, Calif.: Stanford University Press, 1998), 15–25.

5. Amitai Etzioni, *The Moral Dimension: Toward a New Economics* (New York: The Free Press, 1988), 6.

6. Michael Sandel, *Liberalism and the Limits of Justice* (Cambridge: Cambridge University Press, 1983).

7. Richard Rorty, *Contingency, Irony, and Solidarity* (Cambridge: Cambridge University Press, 1988), xiii.

8. Etzioni, *The New Golden Rule,* 166–7.

9. Etzioni, *The New Golden Rule,* 169–71.

10. Amitai Etzioni, *The Spirit of Community* (New York: Simon and Schuster, 1993).

11. Dennis H. Wrong, *Skeptical Sociology* (New York: Columbia University Press, 1976), 71–80; *The Modern Condition,* 140–141.

12. Derek Phillips, *Looking Backward* (Princeton, N.J.: Princeton University Press, 1993).

13. Richard Sennett, "Drowning in Syrup," *The Times Literary Supplement* (February 7, 1997): 3.

14. Sennett, "Drowning in Syrup," 3.

15. Christopher Lasch, *The True and Only Heaven* (New York: W. W. Norton, 1991), 139–43.

16. Etzioni, *The New Golden Rule,* 128.

17. Robert Nisbet, *The Quest for Community* (Oxford: Oxford University Press, 1953).

18. Maurice Stein, *The Eclipse of Community* (Princeton, N.J.: Princeton University Press, 1960).

19. David Riesman, et al., *The Lonely Crowd* (New Haven, Conn.: Yale University Press, 1950); William H. Whyte, *The Organization Man* (New York: Doubleday, 1956); William J. Newman, *The Futilitarian Society* (New York: George Braziller, 1960); Daniel Bell, *The End of Ideology* (New York: Basic Books, 1960).

20. Edward A. Shils, *The Present State of Sociology* (Glencoe, Ill.: The Free Press, 1948), 40–52.

21. Etzioni, *The New Golden Rule,* 77–8.

22. James Q. Wilson, *The Moral Sense* (New York: Free Press, 1993); for my critical discussion of this book, see Dennis H. Wrong, "Conscience and Culture," *Dissent* (Winter 1995): 127–39.

23. Sigmund Freud, *Civilization and Its Discontents* (New York: W. W. Norton, 1961).

24. Edward Banfield, *The Moral Basis of a Backward Society* (Glencoe, Ill.: Free Press, 1958).

25. Martha Nussbaum, *Cultivating Humanity* (Cambridge, Mass.: Harvard University Press, 1997).

26. Erving Goffman, *Behavior in Public Places* (Glencoe, Ill.: Free Press, 1963).

27. Dennis H. Wrong, *Population and Society* (New York: Random House, 1977), 67–71; Dennis H. Wrong, "Discussant," in Wilbur J. Cohen and Charles F. Westoff, *Demographic Dynamics in America* (New York: Free Press, 1977), 101–10.

28. Charles F. Westoff, "Fertility Decline in the United States and Its Implications," in Cohen and Westoff, *Demographic Dynamics,* 53–88.

29. Philip Rieff, *The Triumph of the Therapeutic* (New York: Harper & Row, 1966).

30. Steven Lukes, "The Responsive Community," *Dissent* (Spring 1998), 87–9.

31. Etzioni, *The New Golden Rule,* 22–3.

32. Robert Bellah, et al., *Habits of the Heart* (New York: Harper & Row, 1985).

33. Richard Ford, *Independence Day* (New York: Random House, 1995), 386.

34. Ford, *Independence Day,* 384.

35. Zygmunt Bauman, "Communitarianism, Freedom, and the Nation-State," *Critical Review* 9 (1995): 539–53.

36. Sheri Berman, "Civil Society and the Collapse of the Weimar Republic," *World Politics* 49 (1997): 401–29.

37. James Lincoln Collier, *The Rise of Selfishness in America* (Oxford: Oxford University Press, 1991).

38. Alan Wolfe, "Making Sense of Multiculturalism," *The Responsive Community* 6 (1995): 65–8.

39. Benedict Anderson, *Imagined Communities* (London, England: Verso, 1983).

40. Michael Walzer, "Only Connect," *The New Republic* (August 13, 1990): 32–4.

41. Stephen Holmes, *The Anatomy of Antiliberalism* (Cambridge, Mass.: Harvard University Press, 1995), 177–8.

42. Nicholas Lemann, "The New American Consensus," *The New York Times Magazine* (November 1, 1998): 70.

43. Fareed Zakaria, "Our Hollow Hegemony," *The New York Times Magazine* (November 1, 1998): 44–7, 74, 80.

3

Procedure and Conviction: On Moral Dialogues

Hans Joas

In his book *The New Golden Rule*, Amitai Etzioni has taken the communitarian idea forward in two important directions. On the one hand, he elaborates the political implications of an originally philosophical debate beyond what had already been achieved in his earlier *Spirit of Community* book. On the other hand, he defends communitarian thinking not only against the objection that it is nothing but con-servatism with a human face but also against the charge that it necessarily remains restricted to particularistic, antiuniversalist views. Whatever the personal intentions of individual communitarians, their moral philosophy compels them—according to the critics of communitarian thought—to overemphasize one's attachment to other members of one's own community and consequently to neglect obligations toward the vast majority of human beings. The communitarian strategy, which aims at a "recommitment to moral values," becomes problematic for these critics because they assume that it can only be successful in communities or societies that are based on a strong and consistent value system. The more fragmented and heterogeneous a society is, the less such a strategy is said to be possible. And conversely, the more integrated it is, the less such a strategy would be necessary.

The strengthening of the moral voice instead of legal or quasi-legal regulation makes sense only when we assume that such a way is open at all and that it does not cause more difficulties than it solves. Some authors in this field, most notably, perhaps, Jurgen Habermas, are well aware of the deficiencies of so-called rights talk or juridification, but they nevertheless prefer it to the dangers they see in a values talk and an increased emphasis on moral values, at least under the conditions of functionally differentiated societies. A fair evaluation here would have to balance the advantages and disadvantages of moralization *and* juridification.

In this chapter, I would like to confront Etzioni's project with Habermas's dis-course theory of morality and the law, which dominates large parts of the German and, to a certain extent, even U.S. academic discussion. Such a confrontation is all the more important since the idea of "discourse" is not Habermas's invention but is taken from Charles S. Peirce, John Dewey, and George Herbert Mead, that is, from the American pragmatist tradition. My question is: What can a radically democratic position based on the procedure of rational discourse on the one hand and communitarian thought emphasizing a recommitment to moral values on the other hand—what can Habermas and Etzioni, so to speak—learn from each other?

Such a comparison of Etzioni's contribution with Habermas's approach is certainly only one of the comparisons necessary for a full understanding of the place of Etzioni's ideas in the present range of moral philosophy. Whereas the critique of John Rawls's theory of justice had been constitutive for the formation of communitarian thinking and thus is less likely to produce new insights today, another important possibility would be to address the question of whether conversational *restraints* in public dialogue are not the most important characteristic of a liberal political culture. From such a perspective, articulated most forcefully today by Bruce Ackerman,[1] both Habermas's insistence on discursive legitimation of normative validity claims[2] and Etzioni's plea for moral dialogues look antiliberal and dangerous, because they seduce us to neglect these restraints and launch conflicts among citizens over deep-seated convictions.

This chapter is clearly selective with respect to Etzioni's more recent book. It focuses exclusively on the idea of moral dialogues, and it does not so much discuss this idea directly as it attempts to remove certain obstacles in contemporary moral philosophy that could prevent the idea from becoming as fruitful as it deserves to become. My comparison between discourse ethics and Etzioni's plea for moral dialogues takes place in four steps. The first step is a thorough examination of Habermas's own understanding of the status of discourse ethics in the wider framework of moral and political philosophy. In a second step, I will develop a critique of Habermas's self-understanding and propose a different understanding of the place of discourses in the sphere of moral and political life. On the basis of this changed understanding, I can then—in a third step—argue that the apparently insurmountable breach between "value pluralism" and "moral universalism" is, in fact, not so irreconcilable as it first seems and sketch a possible combination between the two. This combination is based on contributions from the American pragmatist tradition and on my own attempts elsewhere to make this tradition fruitful for contemporary debates. In the concluding fourth step I can then briefly defend Etzioni's idea of moral dialogues against a liberal "commandment of silence" regarding values questions.

1

Habermas's understanding of the status of discourse theory and discourse ethics has undergone considerable modification over the years. There can be no doubt that intensive substantial motives have driven him from the very beginning to empha-size the potential of public communication and symbolically mediated interaction.[3] Such motives lurk behind the theory of communicative action as a whole and dis-course ethics in particular. In the early phases, the idea of the discourse was conse-quently understood as the "foreshadowing of a way of life,"[4] as a variant of a way of life that can be experienced in communication today, but which has yet to be com-prehensively realized by social criticism and politics. Because Habermas soon rec-ognized that ways of life cannot as a whole be subordinated to a normative point of view and that hubris lay in the desire to derive the correct form of societal struc-tures from the structures of rational argumentation, he retreated to a formal-proce-dural understanding of the status of discourses. Habermas's systematic major work published in 1981, *The Theory of Communicative Action*,[5] clearly expresses this shift in his understanding. Yet in the same work, namely in the thesis of the "lin-guistification of the sacred"[6] building on Émile Durkheim, the enormous claim with which he burdens rational argumentation in the discourse becomes apparent once again. Habermas defines the "linguistification of the sacred" here as the "the trans-fer of cultural reproduction, social integration, and socialization from sacred foun-dations over to linguistic communication and action oriented to mutual understand-ing."[7] His hypothesis is that "the socially integrative and expressive functions that were at first fulfilled by ritual practice pass over to communicative action; the au-thority of the holy is gradually replaced by the authority of an achieved consensus. . . . The aura of rapture and terror that emanates from the sacred, the spellbinding power of the holy, is sublimated into the binding/bonding force of criticizable validity claims and at the same time turned into an everyday occurrence."[8] Though this thesis is developed with reference to Durkheim, it corresponds far less to his notion of the persistence of the sacred in the modern society than to Dewey's position, which one could characterize and criticize as a "secularization of democracy."[9]

After *The Theory of Communicative Action*, Habermas extends and modifies dis-course ethics and its foundation in various ways. A chronological presentation of the development of Habermas's thought, though, is of no relevance to the present context. It is therefore better to describe systematically which problems arise when we reflect on the status of discourse ethics and how Habermas reacts to them.

I propose distinguishing six problems that emerge from reflection on the status of discourse ethics. The first problem (1) consists in the question, which has already arisen while looking back at Habermas's development, as to whether or not discourses as formal procedures are really completely detachable from value-related presuppo-sitions. The other five problems are most clearly arranged according to their place in an imaginary chronology resulting from the task of the discourses, no matter how mediated and removed they are from the actual action situation, to assess and to justify proposals for solving problems of action. Thus, the following questions are entailed: Where do the candidates for the assessment procedure come from in the first place?—How, that is, do validity claims themselves originate? (2); Where does the motive to enter into a discourse and to keep to its rules come from? (3); What internal differentiation of the discourse must we accept? (4); How should the results be applied in action? (5); And by what means can discourses themselves develop a binding effect for the participants? (6).

As far as the first problem (1) is concerned, Habermas himself does not put forward new ideas—he has made and stuck by his decision regarding a formal-procedural interpretation of the discourse. New ideas have come, rather, from critics sympathetic to him, who either do not want to travel the whole way with him or who wish to exploit still further the potential of the perspective he has surrendered. Thus, Richard Bernstein, one of the leading authorities on the work of John Dewey, has held it against Habermas that, in the explanation of the discourse as procedure, he himself constantly refers to virtues, which he then denies.[10] Bernstein, following Dewey and in opposition to Habermas, stresses the indispensability of a "democratic ethos" for the success of discourses; he refuses to equate the democratic ethos with the antipluralistic characteristics of classic republicanism. Axel Honneth thinks with the earlier Habermas against the later Habermas and defends materially substantial implications of discourse ethics. He sees these in the aspect of a freedom from restrictions on the one hand, and, on the other, in the "egalitarian freedom to take a moral stance,"[11] which refers to conditions of social recognition.[12] Habermas himself is unimpressed with these objections; he remonstrates with Bernstein that he has never called into question cultural prerequisites for democracy in an empirical sense, but certainly does not "ultimately place the burden of democratically legitimating law *entirely* on the political virtues of united citizens."[13] It is exactly this withdrawal of a substantial-ethical interpretation of discourse that leaves him free to consider the significance of the law in modern societies and the realizability of democracy under such conditions.

The question of the origin of validity claims (2) is only of peripheral interest to Habermas. If the separation of genesis and validity is carried out abruptly, then a theory of assessing validity claims must not, indeed, occupy itself with the origin of these claims. They remain banished to an irrational realm, from where they are unable to escape until they appear in the examination procedure of the discourse. Now, I certainly do not want to contest this distinction itself; it is only its abruptness that I find dubious. Even in the case of empirical validity claims, the origin of a hypothesis cannot always be clearly separated from the examination of its truth content.[14] Normative validity claims in particular are not made arbitrarily. To open certain norms to discussion is morally impossible, and we can value more highly that person to whom moral actions come naturally than the one who must first be convinced of them.[15] Habermas himself concedes that the separation of genesis and validity becomes more difficult with questions of value;[16] this does not, however, lead him to pursue the question of the genesis of values. If, as he asserts, no substantial conclusions can be drawn from the formal procedure of discourses, however, and if it is only in individual discourses that an argument can be developed and a particular consensus reached on the basis of the arising validity claims,[17] then it is precisely in the case of a discourse about values that the connection of genesis and validity, of a self-reflexive explanation of the origin of certain validity claims and an assessment of their legitimacy, becomes unavoidable.

In contrast, Habermas is fully aware of the problem of discursive and moral motivation (3). After *The Theory of Communicative Action* he retracts, in his all too rare reflections on religion, his earlier unconsidered assumptions about the development of religion in modernity and the complete replacement of religious conceptions of the world with a universalistic ethics of responsibility.[18] Habermas thereby erases at least the traces of an Enlightenment or Nietzschean dogmatism of "God is dead," which were also discernible in his work. He does not, however, go beyond an agnostic declaration of openness and does not pose the question of the possibilities of a "postmetaphysical religiosity" or, to put it better, a religiosity under postmetaphysical conditions.[19] His attitude toward the question of moral motivation is thoroughly defensive. In his meditations on Max Horkheimer's religious thought,[20] as well as in his critical dialogue with Charles Taylor's *Sources of the Self*,[21] he declares postmetaphysical philosophy to be unable to take over the task of moral motivation. "Even today philosophy can explicate the moral point of view from which we can judge something impartially as just or unjust; to this extent, communicative reason is by no means equally indifferent to morality and immorality. However, it is altogether a different matter to provide a motivating response to the question of why we should follow our moral insights or why we should be moral at all."[22] The almost utopian and optimistic undertone that once clung to Habermas's thesis of the "linguistification of the sacred" has now completely vanished. Justification and consensus achieved through argumentation are now granted only the "weak force of rational motivation."[23] Once again, as with the question of the citizens' virtue, this stance pulls Habermas in the direction of the law, which intervenes when the force of these rational motivations is just too weak. "This is why, in important sectors of social life, the weak motivating force of morality must be supplemented by coercive positive law."[24]

Habermas also devotes a great deal of attention to the question of a differentiation of the idea of the discourse according to various tasks to be fulfilled (4). While *The Theory of Communicative Action* had distinguished between the validity claims of truth, correctness, and truthfulness and developed on the basis of this a typology of possible argumentation,[25] Habermas later introduces another tripartite division, whose relationship to the second and third type of the older division remains somewhat unclear. Since 1988 he has distinguished between the "pragmatic," "ethical," and "moral" employment of practical reason.[26] This means that a different type of discourse is said to be required according to the type of question. "*Pragmatic questions* pose themselves from the perspective of an actor seeking suitable means for realizing goals and preferences that are already given. . . . *Ethical-political questions* pose themselves from the perspective of members who, in the face of important life issues, want to gain clarity about their shared form of life and about the ideals they feel should shape their common life. . . . In *moral questions*, the teleological point of view from which we handle problems through goal-directed co-operation gives way entirely to the normative point of view from which we examine how we can regulate our common life in the equal interest of all."[27] This distinction is certainly a perceptive response to an important material problem. From a terminological point of view, however, it is unfortunate, since the separation of the ethical from the moral in this way corresponds neither to the prior use of these concepts in philosophy as a whole, nor even to Habermas's own use of them in his work. Habermas himself recognizes that he is pulling the rug from underneath his concept of "discourse ethics" with this shift in terminology; it would instead, he says, have to be called "a discourse theory of morality."[28] Even more important than this terminological question is the issue of content: whether Habermas's differentiation is appropriate to the matter. We shall return to this issue when determining the difference between pragmatist ethics and his understanding of discourse ethics.

Under the influence of Albrecht Wellmer and Klaus Günther, Habermas has taken account of the problem of norm-application (5), that is, of the distinction between the establishment of a norm and the justification of the application of a norm, by extending the types of discourse to include the discourse of application.[29] This is certainly a productive amendment to the original conception. However, the gap between a discourse theory oriented to justification and an ethics centered on the solution of action problems only appears to have been narrowed. Certainly, the point of view of a context-sensitive application of universalistic norms and of a consideration of the irreducible distinctiveness of each individual person[30] thereby finds a more appropriate place within the framework of discourse ethics. But, as Habermas clearly recognizes, discourses of application remain, like justificatory discourses, "a purely cognitive undertaking and as such cannot compensate for the uncoupling of moral judgment from the concrete motives that inform action."[31] Discourses of application are not the place where "applications"—new actions—are creatively devised, but where we argue about the justifiability of an application in isolation from the action situation.

Finally, the question as to the binding effect of the results of a discourse (6) develops in parallel to the question of motivation for the discourse. The clearer the recognition of the "weak force of rational motivation" appears, the more feeble becomes Habermas's faith in the binding force of consensus produced by argumentation. The difference between Dewey and Habermas is instructive at this point. While Dewey attributes to conversation—not rational argumentation as such—the potential of an experience of self-transcendence,[32] from which an affective bond with the interlocutor and the possibility of intercommunication may result as a value, Habermas ruins this possibility for himself through the increasingly ascetic tailoring of conversation to an argumentative discourse. One cannot, at least, have it both ways: if the discourse is only a formal procedure, then it cannot develop an affective binding power. Should it develop one, it is necessary to ascribe to it more than the rational exchange of arguments.

2

Both completed and uncompleted tasks begin to emerge after this cursory look at the problems involved in Habermas's discourse ethics. There are certainly unanswered questions regarding the origin of validity claims, discursive motivation, and the binding effect of the consensus. All these questions point to the theme of values. The discourse tests that which people feel themselves evaluatively drawn to. Without value commitment, they cannot feel motivated to participate in the discourse and keep to its rules, and they feel themselves bound to the result of the discourse only when this results from their value commitment or the experience of participation itself produces value commitment. Thus, in all three questions, discourse ethics and the theory of the genesis of values touch on one another. In Habermas's work itself, however, there is no fruitful contact, because he distinguishes the discourse types in such a way that this contact is prevented.

The way in which Habermas distinguishes between the ethical and the moral, the good and the right, values and norms is, in particular, deeply problematic. His explanations in this regard are not always consistent; for such a conceptually astute and self-critical thinker, this is already in itself a sign of festering problems. There are basically three characteristics that Habermas invokes to define his distinction. First of all, norms and values are distinguished from one another by their relationship to the obligatory or teleological aspect of action; secondly, they are distinguished in terms of their prescriptive validity in such a way that norms are said to aim at universality and values, on the other hand, at particularity. Thirdly, Habermas declares that norms are necessarily concerned with the regulation of interpersonal relationships, as opposed to values, which refer to the telos of each individual life and therefore "by no means call for a complete break with the egocentric perspective."[33]

If one examines these three definitions, then one recognizes that the first does indeed correspond to the usual distinction between the good and the right in philosophy, or the distinction between norms and values that has been current since Durkheim in sociology.[34] However, the other two dimensions are another story entirely. The assertion that ethics contains only maxims that formulate what is good "for me" or "for us," while it is morality that aims at what is good for all, is wrong. Habermas falls victim to the linguistic ambiguity of the expressions "for me" or "for us." Ethics does not describe what is good "for me" in the sense of my own happiness, but what is good "for me" in the sense of my honest understanding of the good, my being captivated by values. The only thing these two meanings have in common is their sound. In the one case, I myself am, or my happiness and well-being are, the standard of my judgment; in the other, I am only aware of the fact that in making a judgment I am the one who judges—the standard, however, lies outside myself. To claim that all ethics are only ever concerned with the happiness of members of a particular culture or religious denomination is—as Richard Bernstein has written with uncharacteristic acerbicness[35]—"a violently distortive fiction." It does an injustice to all universalistic ethical traditions (like the Christian one) and even to that fund of ideals of justice and value conceptions regarding conduct toward strangers that are present in every cultural ethos. The same goes for the third dimension of the distinction. It is simply inaccurate to say that ethics are not essentially directed at the formation of interpersonal and social relations and that universalistic ethics do not motivate us to break with egocentric perspectives.

I argue, therefore, that Habermas, in the development of his discourse ethics and particularly where he is concerned with the question of the primacy of the right or the good, confuses the obligatory-teleological distinction with that of universalism and particularism as well as that of egocentricity and altruism. These distinctions are definitely not different dimensions of one and the same distinction; they are different distinctions that are to a large extent variable in their relationship with one another. A universalistic value system is logically possible and empirically real. Moreover, none of these three distinctions coincides with that between an ethics centered on foundation and justification and an ethics from the perspective of action. This fourth distinction, which is essential for an understanding of pragmatist ethics, must also be taken into consideration. Values *and* norms must both arise in an ethics from the perspective of the actor; the universalization potential of the normative interacts with the contingent values and produces different ways for the motivating value systems to approach the potential universality of the norms.

If this thought is correct, then a whole sequence of theoretical and empirical conclusions that Habermas draws from his understanding of the status of discourse ethics proves to be invalid. His fear that justice would no longer be available "as a context-independent standard of impartial judgment,"[36] if it should appear only as one value among others, is then unfounded. According to the argument I am putting forward here, the standard of justice can only present itself as one point of view among others from the perspective of the actors; precisely this point of view is, however, because of its reference to the anthropological-universal problem of the coordination of action, unavoidable for all social action. While Habermas assumes that the distinction between norms and values would be invalidated if universal validity is claimed for the highest values or goods,[37] which has become untenable under postmetaphysical conditions, the argument I am advancing here asserts that the distinction between the restrictive-obligatory and the attractive-motivating is not invalidated under any conceivable conditions. At the same time, however, the universal validity claim of values is held to be formulable even under postmetaphysical conditions. Habermas also relates his distinction between the three different ways of employing practical reason to three great moral-philosophical traditions.[38] Seen in this way, the utilitarian tradition corresponds to the pragmatic, the Kantian-deontological tradition to the moral and the Aristotelian tradition to the ethical employment of practical reason. But this also has a strategic purpose for Habermas. It serves, namely, to burden all modern attempts to defend the primacy of the good over the right, or merely to contest the primacy of the right over the good, with Aristotle's metaphysical assumptions and thereby to declare them obsolete from the very outset under the conditions of postmetaphysical thought. Now, it is certainly true that there exists a contemporary neo-Aristotelianism, for which the reconstruction of the critical potential of a morality aiming at universality is anathema. But Habermas also speaks of neo-Aristotelianism where the association with Aristotle's metaphysical presuppositions is explicitly contested and new syntheses with the deontological tradition are being attempted.[39] What is even more astonishing, however, is that Habermas omits pragmatist ethics from his entire account. If he had included it, then it would have become clear that a synthesis with the Aristotelian and Kantian tradition is just as possible from the starting point of the pragmatic employment of practical reason as it is from that of the discourse—and that means an intersubjective continuation of Kantianism. Because pragmatist ethics is based on the creativity of action, it relativizes the role of the discourse, seeing its function as the justification of validity claims. But it is for this very reason that it is able to do greater justice to the dynamics of human action than a theory that, with its exclusive concentration on the discursive justification, mistakes the reality of action.[40]

What follows from Habermas's theory in an empirical regard is a profound skepticism vis-à-vis every contribution made by concrete value traditions and particular commitments to the social integration of modern societies. A universalistic morality and, where this is too weak, modern law are for him the royal road leading to the integration of modern societies. Modern law is supposed to be particularly suitable for the social integration of economic societies because these "rely on the decentralized decisions of self-interested individuals in morally neutralized spheres of action."[41] But, Habermas continues, the law must also "satisfy the precarious conditions of a social integration that ultimately takes place through the achievements of mutual understanding on the part of communicatively acting subjects."[42] This process is made possible by a legal framework that safeguards freedom of action, and which derives its own legitimacy from a legislative procedure that for its part stands under the principle of the sovereignty of the people, so that—according to this ingenious train of thought—legitimacy itself originates in the citizen's rights of freedom. To construe the arguments put forward here as contradicting this conception would be to misunderstand them. Our objections arise only when Habermas overruns his evidence and not only asserts the possibility that legitimacy originates in this way but declares this possibility to be the only acceptable one. This point is reached when he claims that a moral community constitutes itself *"solely* by way of the negative idea of abolishing discrimination and harm and of extending relations of mutual recognition to include marginalized men and women."[43] There is no doubt that community can constitute itself in this way; but we must dispute the claim that only a community constituted in this way deserves the adjective *moral!*

But Habermas is quite ambiguous in this respect. It is possible to deduce from his work another metaphorical way of speaking, which seems to me to be more appropriate; Habermas says that morality and the law are *safety nets* "for the integrative performances of all other institutional orders."[44] However, we fall back on "safety nets" only in the case of an emergency; we try to prevent recourse to them. What is hence attractive about this metaphor is that it reveals how little morality and the law should stand at the forefront of social action. Admittedly, every reliance on integration exclusively through community and value commitments would be unacceptable today; no such commitment can persist either, without constant correction against the universalization potential of the normative. But just as we require the procedural rationality of the law, so must those values themselves be reproduced that can protect us from the wrong use of "safety nets." The reproduction of these values cannot rely solely on the weak motivation of the rational consensus and the legitimating effects of civic freedoms. The powers of social solidarity can also regenerate themselves today—but, contra Habermas, not only—"in the forms of communicative practices of self-determination."[45] It would be an antitraditional effect if one denied this capacity to every traditional commitment to particular values and communities.

3

What we need, therefore, is not a dogmatic demarcation between moral universalism and a value-centered approach, but mutual understanding and a combination of both in an integrated moral philosophy. This presupposes self-revisions on both sides, a changed view of the status of discourses on the side of the proponents of discourse ethics and an acceptance of value pluralism on the side of communitarian thinkers.[46] For such an attempt to combine value pluralism and moral universalism, we need an anthropologically based understanding of moral universalism *and* of the genesis of value-commitments. And here I turn to my own proposal. American pragmatism had—in William James and John Dewey—a theory of the contingent genesis of values, but also—in Dewey and George Herbert Mead—a conception of moral universalism. How are we to envisage the combination of these two divergent theoretical components in the pragmatist spirit?

    In order to answer this question, we should recall two distinctive features of pragmatist ethics that distinguish it from several other approaches.[47] First of all, pragmatist ethics is based on an elaborate anthropological theory of human action in general, and human communication in particular. Dewey and especially Mead developed the essential features of such a theory of the biological preconditions for specifically human achievements.[48] Without going into these in detail, it can nevertheless be emphasized that even the attempt at such a theory involves the assumptions that there are universal structures of human action that distinguish it from animal behavior and that it is possible to make substantial statements about these universal human structures. Dewey and Mead have no doubt that typical functional disturbances are located in these universal structures, from which there arises a need for regulation. George Herbert Mead, above all—and subsequently, under his influence, John Dewey—interprets the universal human capacity for "role-taking," the decisive characteristic of typically human communication, as the prerequisite for overcoming these disturbances. The development of this capacity and the social conditions which make possible this development are thus of the highest empirical significance. At the same time, however, Dewey and Mead see a substantial ideal located in precisely this empirically verifiable capacity: "Universal discourse is then the formal ideal of communication."[49] Mead shows how the capacity to employ significant symbols refers every participant in communication beyond his or her immediate community to a virtual world of ideal meanings. Pragmatist ethics thus stands opposed to culturalistic moral relativism and stresses the universal need for the normative regulation of human cooperation[50] and care, as well as the possibility of seeing a substantial ideal in the solution of these problems of cooperation through communication itself.

The second distinctive feature of pragmatist ethics consists in the fact that it is an ethics from the perspective of the actor.[51] Of central interest for Dewey and Mead is not the issue of the legitimation of norms, nor even that of the justification of actions, but the issue of the solution to problems of action. What was novel in Mead's critique of Kant's ethics was his suggestion that the categorical imperative as such could only serve to subject actions to a universalization test, but not to discover which actions were adequate in the first place.[52] Action itself demands a creative design. The concept of the "application" of norms or values is hardly appropriate for this emphasis on the creative and risky performances in action. Of course, a value, as well as the "application" of a value, can be subjected to a discourse of justification, but pragmatist ethics separates the perspective of such a discourse from the existential perspective of the agent.

If we now take these two distinctive features together—pragmatism's elaborate theory of human action and its emphasis on the perspective of the actor—then it becomes apparent how the universalistic conception of morality and the theory of the contingent genesis of values can be combined to form a whole along pragmatist lines. According to this point of view, there is no higher authority for the justification of norms than discourses. From the perspective of the actor, however, it is not the justification that is uppermost, but the achievement of the good or the right. Even if we, as agents, wish to concede a clear primacy to a particular good or the right as we understand it, we do not have at our disposal certain knowledge of what we must then therefore do. We can honestly strive to increase the good or to act exclusively according to the right, but this does not furnish us with any certainty that we will actually meet with success in doing this with all the actions that we decide upon and all the direct and indirect consequences that we thus bring about. In the light of the consequences of action, every conception of the good and the right will come under the pressure of revision.[53]

Each new specification does not liberate us from this either; a clear termination cannot be envisaged, since the situations in which our action takes place are always new, and the quest for certainty remains forever unfulfilled.[54] While we can establish for certain in the abstract, that is to say, in the discourse taking place outside action situations, that certain aims of action should enjoy priority on the basis of certain presuppositions we have about points of view to be considered, in the concrete reality of the action situations we often achieve a subjective feeling of certainty but, intersubjectively, only one of plausibility.[55] In retrospect—and having become wiser after the event—we can discover more about the actual appropriateness of our action, but even here a definitive and certain judgment eludes us, because the future will yield further consequences of action and points of view, which again jeopardize our appraisal.

While some might concede that our action has the character described here, they might nevertheless dispute that an answer to the question of the relationship between the good and the right and between value pluralism and moral universalism follows from it. In which respect, then, should this emphasis on the creativity of action suggest such an answer? It might at first seem as if this emphasis were at best banal and at worst dangerous.[56] It would be dangerous if it exclusively emphasized the situation-specific nature of our decisions and thereby opened the way to arbitrariness and a lack of principles. It would be banal if it only stressed what no one, even the most ardent proponent of an ethics of conviction, has ever contested—that the right acts do not always follow from a good will. But the way in which the pragmatists present the argument for the creativity of action in ethical contexts does not open the door to unlimited arbitrariness; it declares only certain revisions and specifications to be acceptable. And it is not banal to incorporate into the concept of the good will itself the moral duty to recognize what works and what doesn't. From the pragmatists' understanding of action and from the structure of their ethics as an ethics from the perspective of the actor, it follows that, in the action situation itself, the restrictive point of view of the right *must* inevitably arise, but *can* arise only as one point of view alongside the various orientations of the good.

This double assertion requires further clarification. The viewpoint of the right *must* arise because it represents the universal requirements of the coordination of social action, and these are unavoidable in the face of the unavoidable embedding of action in social contexts. All action is unavoidably embedded in the social because the capacity for action is itself already socially constituted, and our cooperation by no means aims only at individually attributable, but also at irreducibly social, goods.[57] This point of view of the right is always present in the manifold diversity of our orientations; the situative revision of our objectives does not degenerate into arbitrariness because it must pass through the potentially universal "sieve of the norm" (Ricoeur).

The viewpoint of the right *can* only arise, according to this view, as one point of view among several in the action situation, because this potentially universal "sieve of the norm" would have nothing to test if the agent were not oriented to various conceptions of the good, of which he cannot be certain if they are acceptable from the point of view of the right. Even the self-overtaxing moralist who is thoroughly determined always to give precedence to the universalization procedure, may well want to eliminate his inclinations, but will only be able to test his conceptions of possible actions in this procedure. A decisive point in emphasizing the creativity of action is the recognition that actions cannot be derived from the universalizing point of view itself, but can only be assessed as to whether a possible action is acceptable from this point of view. Even the person who wishes to eliminate his or her inclinations does not thereby eliminate the candidates for examination that the rule of universalization represents.[58] These candidates are our conceptions of our duty, on the one hand, and our conations, on the other; they too contain a potentially universal validity claim. If with Kant and his followers it remained unclear whether the universalization test of the categorical imperative is directed at our inclinations or at the maxims of our action, then this was due to his failure to understand the interplay obtaining between our prereflective conations and our conscious intentions.[59] If one assumes a theory of action, however, which anchors intentionality in the situation-specific reflection on our prereflective conations, then it becomes clear that the right can only be an examining authority—unless it becomes itself the good, the value of justice.

In the action situation, consequently, there is no primacy of the good or the right. There is a relationship of neither superordination nor subordination, but rather one of complementariness. In the action situation, the irreducible orientations to the good, which are already contained in our conations, encounter the examining authority of the right. In these situations, we can only achieve a reflective equilibrium between our orientations. Certainly, the extent to which we subject our orientations to this test may vary. For this reason, there is in the point of view of the right a perpetual, unflagging potential to modify the good, in order to enable it to pass the universalization test. But it does not follow from the universality of the right that in action situations we should give precedence to the right as a matter of course before all other considerations—or that that we should not do this. The debate over the question whether primacy should be attributed either to the good or the right must be sharply distinguished from the debate over the universalizibility of the right. From the pragmatist perspective, the debate over the universalizibility of the right does not have to take place—not because this possibility is rejected, but because it is held to be beyond dispute, following from the premises of the anthropological theory of action. The emphasis on the situatedness and creativity of action here does not involve the slightest skepticism toward the notion of the universality of the right.[60] But in turn, this does not entail for the pragmatists that within the action situation the testing of an orientation against the universalization principle *must* self-evidently be given precedence above all other considerations.

Not only individual agents, but also collectives, entire communities, and cultures are placed in action situations. From the philosophical conceptualization of the "good" and the "right," let us switch to the sociological terminology of "values" and "norms" when we come to speak of collective actors and aggregations of action. Like individual actors, these too exist in a field of tension between their particular value systems, which have arisen contingently, and the potential of a morality, which is pressing toward universality. Universally distributed structures of morality can be ascertained entirely by empirical means. Fundamental norms of fairness, for example, can be discovered by children by merely concentrating on the internal need for the regulation of cooperation and, right up to the reflective formulation of the "golden rule," seem to be known in all cultures.[61]

An emphasis on the contingency of the genesis of values from a relativist perspective has difficulties with this phenomenon; by contrast, the universalistic-deontological tradition of moral theory has always been able to find greater confidence in these facts. We should qualify this allusion to the universal distribution of fundamental norms by immediately adding the rider that every culture fences in the potentially universal morality, by defining its areas and conditions of application. Which people (or organisms) and which situations are "set free" for this morality is a matter of interpretation and consequently varies across cultures and history. In each case, a justification is produced for excluding people of different nationalities, ethnic groups, races, or religions, people of another sex or age, or of other mentalities and moralities. Without such a justification, the right would become cultural dynamite. But in the exuberance of the plea for a universalistic morality it would again—as in the case of the individual agent—be an error to overlook the fact that no culture can manage without a definite, particular value system and a definite, particular interpretation of the world. Here, of course, *particular* does not mean *particularistic*; cultural distinctiveness does not lead to an inability to consider the universalistic point of view. On the contrary, the question is which particular cultural traditions from the point of view of the universality of the right can be most readily adhered to, and how other cultural traditions can be creatively continued and reshaped from this point of view. In the particular value systems of democratic societies we find rules that can be viewed as translations of universal moral rules into particular political institutions. These remain, nonetheless, inevitably particular and must, each time they are imported into another culture, always be examined in order to assess whether their particularity is a particularism. The notion, however, that in order to overcome particularism, particularity itself must disappear, overlooks the necessarily contingent character of values. It is condemned to remain a mere morality and, cut off from the attractiveness of values, to admit the possibility of motivation by pure morality.

4

If we can succeed in preventing an unnecessary polarization between the justification of actions and institutions from universalistic points of view and attempts to clarify the conditions necessary for the genesis and transmission of democratic values, then the goal of these observations comparing pragmatist ethics and the discourse theory of morality, the law, and the democratic constitutional state would have been realized.[62] This kind of false polarization resides in the controversies about liberalism and communitarianism. Truly, the aim cannot be to oppose undialectically the universalism of the liberal tradition with a mere particularism, the centering on the value of justice with the emphasis of particular commitments and the orientation to morality and law with the invocation of values and community. The communitarian critique of liberalism only has a chance if it can demonstrate that it represents the more reasonable version of universalism, that it exhibits the more appropriate appreciation of the place of justice in action, and that it offers a more balanced criticism of "rights talk"[63] *and* "values talk." What we seek here is neither the polarization the controversy nor growing weary of it, but the integration of both viewpoints. In reality, liberals and communitarians share the same problem: What degree of respect must the individual accord the social order from which he expects a guarantee of his individual rights?[64]

In political terms, this question removes the "commandment of silence" (Martin Seel) that individual currents of liberalism impose upon the question of values. In ethical terms, only the inclusion of the dimension of values suggested by this question prevents the ever-present threat of the reduction of justice to mere utilitarian reciprocity.[65] In sociological-empirical terms, this question refers us to the particular conditions under which the values, which are presupposed for the continuity of the democratic polity, originate and can be maintained.[66] And it is through this that a space is once again opened for the conversation about values in society. This conversation must not be allowed either to be reduced to moral or legal argumentation or to deteriorate into conflict and the distribution struggle among fixed identities.

So what is the answer to the question with which we began, namely, what Habermas and Etzioni can learn from each other? I think that Etzioni has demonstrated convincingly that there are indeed moral dialogues—distinct from rational deliberation and culture wars. Communication about values is possible, but it differs from rational argument. If this is correct, Habermas and other discourse theorists have to accept that even if discourses are the appropriate procedure for the justification of validity claims, this does not mean that a value consensus can be based on them or that communication about values has to take on the character of rational argumentation if it is not to degenerate into pure conflict. On the other hand, Etzioni has to accept the challenge to delineate more precisely what the nature of such moral dialogues is. In the fourth chapter of *The New Golden Rule,* he has demonstrated their existence on the macro level and even described some basic rules for their effective functioning, but he certainly does not give an analysis of their inner structure as elaborated as Habermas's theory of discourse is.

If we take Etzioni's claim that many values are self-evident, we can see this point very clearly. To my eyes, it is true that a feeling of self-evidence often accompanies our emotional attachment to a value. In that sense, Etzioni is right again. But I differ from his position if he assumes that we can really refer to such self-evidence in situations of value-conflict. If there is no value conflict, communication about values is probably unnecessary. But if there is a value conflict or a disagreement about values, the reference to self-evidence obviously does not help to come to an agreement or even to better mutual understanding. Hence we need a theory of "moral dialogues" that preserves the specific qualities of values—as distinct from norms—

and of the communication about values—as distinct from a rational justification of validity claims. Even if Etzioni has not fully worked out the specific character of this type of communication, his insistence on a space for moral dialogues is, in my opinion, a most important contribution to contemporary moral and political thinking.

NOTES

This chapter is an elaboration and summary of thoughts from my book *Die Entsehung der Werte* (Frankfurt: Suhrkamp, 2nd edition, 1999). An English translation is forthcoming (Cambridge: Polity Press, 2000). The title of this chapter alludes to Etzioni's distinction between procedural dialogues and dialogues of conviction.

1. Bruce Ackerman, *Social Justice in the Liberal State* (New Haven: Yale University Press, 1980).

2. For a comparison between Ackerman and Habermas, see Seyla Benhabib, "Liberal Dialogue versus a Critical Theory of Discursive Legitimation," in *Liberalism and the Moral Life*, ed. Nancy L. Rosenblum (Cambridge, Mass.: Harvard University Press, 1989), 143–56.

3. This is clearly visible in, on the one hand, his early book on the public sphere and, on the other, in his action-theoretical distinction between "work" and "interaction" taken up from Hannah Arendt and George Herbert Mead. See Jurgen Habermas, *The Structural Transformation of the Public Sphere* (Cambridge, Mass.: MIT Press, 1989); Habermas, "Arbeit und Interaktion. Bemerkungen zu Hegels Jenenser Philosophie des Geistes," in *Technik und Wissenschaft als Ideologie*, ed. Jurgen Habermas (Frankfurt: Suhrkamp, 1968), 9–47.

4. Jurgen Habermas, "Vorbereitende Bemerkungen zu einer Theorie der kommunikativen Kompetenz," in *Theorie der Gesellschaft oder Sozialtechnologie Was leistet die Systemforschung?* ed. Jurgen Habermas and Niklas Luhmann (Frankfurt: Suhrkamp, 1971), 101–41, here 141.

5. Jurgen Habermas, *The Theory of Communicative Action* (Boston: Beacon Press, 1984/1987), vol. 2, e.g., 107ff.

6. Habermas, *Communicative Action*, 77ff.

7. Habermas, *Communicative Action*, 107.

8. Habermas, *Communicative Action*, 77.

9. See the chapter on Dewey in Hans Joas, *The Genesis of Values* (Cambridge: Polity Press, 2000).

10. Richard Bernstein, "The Retrieval of the Democratic Ethos," *Cardozo Law Review* 17 (1996): 1127–46.

11. Axel Honneth, "Diskursethik und implizites Gerechtigkeitskonzept," in *Moralität und Sittlichkeit. Das Problem Hegels und die Diskursethik*, ed. Wolfgang Kuhlmann (Frankfurt: Suhrkamp, 1986), 183–93, here 191. This characterization of the direction of his thought also applies to his book *The Critique of Power: Reflective Stages in a Critical Social Theory* (Cambridge, Mass.: MIT Press, 1991). The following sentences by Habermas can perhaps be read as an implicit reply to Honneth: "The equal distribution of communicative freedoms and the requirement of truthfulness *in* discourse have the status of *argumentative* duties and rights, of *moral* duties and rights. So too, the absence of coercion refers to the process of

argumentation itself, not to interpersonal relationships *outside* of this practice." (Jurgen Habermas, *The Inclusion of the Other* [Cambridge: Polity Press, 1998]), 44–5.

12. As Honneth has since elaborated in his book *The Struggle for Recognition* (Cambridge: Polity Press, 1995), and in numerous other studies.

13. Jurgen Habermas, "Reply," *Cardozo Law Review* 17, part 2 (1996): 1477–558.

14. In Peirce's philosophy of science the discourse theory was, as Habermas well knows, accordingly combined with a logic of abduction, of the creative discovery of hypotheses worth examination.

15. With dry English humor, Bernard Williams argues for the evaluation of a mere discussion of a possibility: "One does not feel easy with the man who in the course of a discussion of how to deal with political or business rivals says, 'Of course, we could have them killed, but we should lay that aside from the beginning.' It is characteristic of morality that it tends to overlook the possibility that some concerns are best embodied in this way, in deliberative silence." *Ethics and the Limits of Philosophy* (London: Fontana, 1985), 185.

16. Jurgen Habermas, *Between Facts and Norms: Contributions to a Discourse Theory of Law* (Cambridge: Polity Press, 1996), 163.

17. Habermas, *The Inclusion of the Other*, 45.

18. Essentially, it is a matter of only two essays: Jurgen Habermas, "To Seek to Salvage an Unconditional Meaning without God Is a Futile Undertaking: Reflections on a Remark of Max Horkheimer," in *Justification and Application*, ed. Jurgen Habermas (Cambridge: Polity Press 1993), 133–46, and Habermas, "Exkurs: Transzendenz von innen, Transzendenz ins Diesseits," in *Texte und Kontexte* (Frankfurt: Suhrkamp, 1991). These were recently supplemented by the essay directly concerned with the question of moral motivation: Jurgen Habermas, "A Genealogical Analysis of the Cognitive Content of Morality," in *The Inclusion of the Other*, 3–46.

19. See the chapter on James in my book *The Genesis of Values*.

20. Habermas, "Reflections on a Remark," 146.

21. Habermas, "Remarks on Discourse Ethics," in Habermas, *Justification and Application: Remarks on Discourse Ethics* (Cambridge, Mass.: MIT Press, 1993) 19–112, particularly, 69–76, here 75.

22. Habermas, "Reflections on a Remark," 146.

23. Habermas, *Between Facts and Norms*, 5. Johannes Weiß had already argued along these lines as early as 1983. See "Verständigungsorientierung und Kritik," in *Vernunft und Vernichtung. Zur Philosophie und Soziologie der Moderne*, (Opladen: Westdeutscher Verlag, 1993), 223–37.

24. Thus says Habermas in the essay "A Genealogical Analysis of the Cognitive Content of Morality," in which he tackles this problem head-on for the first time, 274 n51.

25. Habermas, *Theory of Communicative Action*, 36ff.

26. Habermas, "On the Employments of Practical Reason," in *Justification and Application*, 1–17.

27. Habermas, *Between Facts and Norms*, 159–61.

28. Habermas, *Justification and Application*, vii. In opposition to Habermas, Thomas McCarthy emphasizes "the dialectical interdependence *in practice* of these *analytically* distinguishable aspects. . . . Thus, *in practice* political deliberation is not so much an interweaving of separate discourses as a multifaceted communication process that allows for fluid transitions among questions and arguments of different sorts." See McCarthy, "Legitimacy and

Diversity: Dialectical Reflections on Analytical Distinctions," *Cardozo Law Review* 17 (1996): 1083–125, here 1096, and 1105. Habermas accepts this in a legal-theoretical, but not in a general discourse-theoretical, regard. See Habermas, "Reply to Symposium Participants," 1497ff.

29. Albrecht Wellmer, *Ethik und Dialog. Elemente des moralischen Urteils bei Kant und in der Diskursethik* (Frankfurt: Suhrkamp, 1986); Klaus Günther, *Der Sinn für Angemessenheit: Anwendungsdiskurse in Moral und Recht* (Frankfurt: Suhrkamp, 1988).

30. As Axel Honneth has energetically demanded, under the influence of postmodern reflections on ethics. See Honneth, "The Other of Justice: Habermas and the Ethical Challenge of Post-Modernism," in *Cambridge Companion to Habermas,* ed. Stephen White (Cambridge: Cambridge University Press, 1995), 289–325.

31. Habermas, "On the Employments of Practical Reason," in Habermas, *Justification and Application,* 1–17, here 14.

32. See the chapter on Dewey in my book *The Genesis of Values.*

33. Compare these definitions with Habermas, *Between Facts and Norms,* 255 and Habermas, "On the Employments of Practical Reason," 6 (where the quotation is also to be found). I won't deal with two further determinations, the binary versus graduated coding of the validity claim and the different criteria for the coherence of "systems of norms" or "constellations of value," since these are, it seems to me, only logical properties of the first distinguishing feature.

34. Habermas, though, seems to waver as far as his precise understanding of the concept of value is concerned. While in *Between Facts and Norms* (255) he still defines values along utilitarian lines as "intersubjectively shared preferences," in *The Inclusion of the Other* (6) he writes, "What in each instance is valuable or authentic forces itself upon us, so to speak, and differs from mere preferences in its binding character, that is, in the fact that it points beyond needs and preferences." Here the feeling of captivation inherent in the experience of value, which must be central to a modern theory of value, finds appropriate expression (under Taylor's influence?).

35. Bernstein, "The Retrieval of the Democratic Ethos," 1143.

36. Habermas, *The Inclusion of the Other,* 6.

37. Habermas, *Between Facts and Norms,* 256.

38. Habermas, "On the Employments of Practical Reason," 2.

39. Charles Taylor explicitly contests this connection in "Die Motive einer Verfahrensethik," in *Moralität und Sittlichkeit,* ed. Wolfgang Kuhlmann (Frankfurt: Suhrkamp, 1986) 101–35, particularly 104 and 108. The most sophisticated argument can be found in Paul Ricoeur, *Oneself as Another* (Chicago: University of Chicago Press, 1992).

40. I am referring to my criticism of Habermas's *Theory of Communicative Action.* See Hans Joas, "The Unhappy Marriage of Hermeneutics and Functionalism," in *Pragmatism and Social Theory* (Chicago: University of Chicago Press, 1993), 125–53. I have attempted to elaborate a theory of action inspired by pragmatism in Hans Joas, *The Creativity of Action* (Chicago: University of Chicago Press, 1996). Just as Habermas uses the concept "neo-Aristotelianism" in the area of ethics, so he employs that of the "philosophy of praxis" in the sphere of action theory, in order to occlude the differences between those who describe themselves as such and the philosophy of Taylor, pragmatism, and others (see Joas, *The Creativity of Action,* 102ff). I find the use of such terminology misleading and irritating.

41. Habermas, *Between Facts and Norms,* 83.

42. Habermas, *Between Facts and Norms,* 83.

43. Habermas, *The Inclusion of the Other*, xxxvi (my emphasis, H. J.).

44. Habermas, *Between Facts and Norms*, 73–4.

45. Habermas, *Between Facts and Norms*, 445.

46. I cannot develop here why value pluralism seems to me to be so important for the further development of communitarian thinking. But see my paper on Isaiah Berlin—perhaps the greatest proponent of value pluralism—on which I draw in the following: Hans Joas, "Combining Value Pluralism and Moral Universalism: Isaiah Berlin and Beyond," *The Responsive Community* 9(4) (Fall 1999): 17–29.

47. I have already brought out these two distinctive features in two studies on George Herbert Mead. H. Joas, *G. H. Mead: A Contemporary Re-examination of His Thought* (Cambridge, Mass.: MIT Press, 1985), 121ff, esp. 127; H. Joas, "The Creativity of Action and the Intersubjectivity of Reason—Mead's Pragmatism and Social Theory," in *Pragmatism and Social Theory*, 238–61.

48. John Dewey, *Human Nature and Conduct* (London: Allen and Unwin, 1922/1925); John Dewey, *Experience and Nature*, (London: Open Court, 1958), 167ff; George Herbert Mead, *Mind, Self, and Society* (Chicago: University of Chicago Press, 1934).

49. Mead, *Mind, Self, and Society*, 327.

50. In this respect the pragmatist theory thus resembles the rational choice theory and the universal developmental psychology in the Piaget-Kohlberg tradition. For Durkheim's relationship to the notion of a universal cooperative morality, cf. Joas, *The Creativity of Action*, 90–3.

51. Joas, *Pragmatism and Social Theory*, 251–5.

52. Mead, "Fragments on Ethics," in *Mind, Self, and Society*, 379–89.

53. Following Dewey's theory of value, Henry Richardson sees this particularly clearly in "Beyond Good and Right: Toward a Constructive Ethical Pragmatism," *Philosophy and Public Affairs* (24) (1995): 108–41, here esp. 113.

54. Richardson, "Beyond Good and Right," 132.

55. Cf. Ricoeur, *Oneself as Another*, 177.

56. Richardson, 127ff.

57. For Mead's understanding of the "social act" as a complex group activity, cf. Mead, *Mind, Self, and Society*, 7, n7; for the thesis of a "primary sociality" of the capacity for action, see Joas, *The Creativity of Action*, 184–95; for the thesis of "irreducibly social goods," cf. Charles Taylor, *Philosophical Arguments* (Cambridge, Mass.: Harvard University Press, 1995), 127–45.

58. Ricoeur, *Oneself as Another*, 208ff.

59. Dewey's, in John Dewey and James H. Tufts, *Ethics*, rev. ed. (New York: H. Holt, 1932), 219–25; Dewey, *The Later Works, 1925–1953* (Carbondale: Southern Illinois University Press, 1981), vol. 7, and Mead's (in *Mind, Self, and Society*, 379–89) critiques of Kant as well as those of Max Scheler argue along similar lines to Ricoeur in his interpretation of Kant.

60. Cf. Ricoeur: "As we have repeatedly affirmed, the conflicts that give weight to the contextualist theses are encountered along the path of actualization rather than along that of justification. It is important to be clear about this difference of site so as not to confuse the arguments that stress the historical character of choices to be made along the second path with the skeptical arguments that are addressed to the foundational enterprise" (*Oneself as Another*, 283–4).

61. The classic work on this topic is Jean Piaget, *The Moral Judgement of the Child* (Harmondsworth, England: Penguin, 1977). For the question of the cultural relativity of morality, cf. the anthology edited by Traugott Schöfthaler and Dietrich Goldschmidt, *Soziale Struktur und Vernunft* (Frankfurt: Suhrkamp, 1984).

62. I should point out, if only briefly, that there have been a number of interesting attempts in the recent literature to bring together the good and the right in the sense of a balancing through the actor as well as to integrate ethics of prescription and of striving. A critical discussion of these studies must, however, be omitted here. Besides the studies already referred to in this context, the following should be mentioned: Martin Seel, *Versuch über die Form des Glücks* (Frankfurt: Suhrkamp, 1995); Hans Krämer, *Integrative Ethik* (Frankfurt: Suhrkamp, 1995); Wolfgang Schluchter, "Gesinnungsethik und Verantwortungsethik," in *Religion und Lebensführung*, vol. 1 (Frankfurt: Suhrkamp, 1988), 165–338; Christoph Menke: "Die Vernunft im Widerstreit. Über den richtigen Umgang mit praktischen Konflikten," in *Zur Verteidigung der Vernunft gegen ihre Liebhaber und Verächter*, ed. Christoph Menke and Martin Seel (Frankfurt: Suhrkamp, 1993), 197–218; Christoph Menke, *Tragödie im Sittlichen. Gerechtigkeit und Freiheit nach Hegel* (Frankfurt: Suhrkamp, 1996); as well as, of course, all the recent work by John Rawls, especially his *Political Liberalism* (New York: Columbia University Press, 1993).

63. For a critique of "rights talk," see Mary Ann Glendon, *Rights Talk: The Impoverishment of Political Discourse* (New York: The Free Press, 1991).

64. I used this formulation for the first time in my article "Angst vor der Freiheit," *Die Zeit* (April 11, 1997). It alludes, of course, to the "Golden Rule," which Amitai Etzioni has placed at the center of his communitarian program: "Respect and uphold society's moral order as you would have society respect and uphold your autonomy." See Amitai Etzioni, *The New Golden Rule: Community and Morality in a Democratic Society* (New York: Basic Books, 1996), xviii.

65. Paul Ricoeur (*Amour et Justice,* Tübingen: Mohr-Siebeck, 1990) elaborates this best of all.

66. This question was developed and pursued for the United States by the group around Robert Bellah. See especially Robert Bellah et al., *Habits of the Heart: Individualism and Commitment in American Life* (Berkeley: University of California Press, 1985). For the application of this question in a German context, see my "Communitarianism. A German Perspective," Indiana University Institute for Advanced Study, Distinguished Lecture Series No. 6, Bloomington, Indiana, 1995.

4

The Integrity of Unrestricted Desire: Community, Values, and the Problem of Personhood

Thomas C. Kohler

INTRODUCTION

Amitai Etzioni is a serious man, who is preoccupied with some extremely serious questions. Among these are the character of a good society, the conditions necessary to the maintenance of a flourishing democracy, and the circumstances that will promote the proper unfolding of human personality. These are the great themes, and in pursuing his questions, Etzioni has practiced sociology in the grand style. Consequently, in following-down his queries, he has been willing to cross the borders that artificially divide disciplines, and to chase down unaccustomed, and often not well-marked paths. His pursuit has led him to challenge many orthodoxies, including some that lie at the heart of the catechism of modernity, and to reopen some deeply unsettling questions long-proclaimed resolved. Such effrontery has not gone unnoticed. While his critique of certain forms of liberalism has gained Etzioni more than a few opponents, his crystallization of the issues concerning the nature of our ties and obligations to one another has launched a discussion that no serious observer can ignore.

In his recent book, *The New Golden Rule*,[1] Etzioni attempts to go to the heart of the tensions inherent in the modern liberal project. His now famous and important concern is that our typically one-sided emphasis on personal freedom has seriously eroded the very social foundations on which our individual liberties rest. True autonomy, he argues, can only be realized in the context of a good social order, which in turn must be anchored by a common commitment to a set of substantive values, through which the community constitutes itself. The ultimate source of these values, the manner in which the community identifies them, and the role of the "moral voice of the community" in encouraging their observance constitute a major part of the book's focus.

57

It is difficult not to admire Etzioni's undertaking or to overstate both the importance and the difficulty of the tasks he has set for himself. Having worked to identify the underlying causes of social and moral erosion, he now seeks to develop an approach to reverse this cycle of decline. Consequently, his goal is not to produce yet one more critique of the sort of expressive individualism that so characterizes the patterns of contemporary life. Rather, he wants to provide a concrete framework within which all societies can strike an appropriate balance between a good social order and personal autonomy, or between universal individual rights and the common good. In Etzioni's words, establishing this "virtuous equilibrium" between the self and the community entails "the synthesis of some elements of traditionalism with some elements of modernity," which will result in a "recasting" of both.[2] The proper blend of these appropriately reworked values, he believes, will set the foundations for a good, communitarian society.

The tension that Etzioni has attempted to resolve is one that is grounded in human character itself. Likewise, the core of my difficulties with his discussion stems directly from some of the assumptions that he holds about the character of our personhood. Etzioni has a deep concern about the consequences that flow from the various strains of expressive individualism that typically inform our contemporary self-understandings, and he subjects them to a powerful and incisive examination. In the final analysis, however, those understandings remain his own. As a result, I believe that he inadvertently undermines his crucial project of reinvigorating a public moral dialogue. Properly anxious to find an "exit from the maze of moral relativism,"[3] Etzioni wants to identify a basis for community, and the values that ground it, that is more than merely conventional. This he ultimately locates in "self-evident" propositions or concepts that "present themselves to us as morally compelling in and of themselves."[4]

The problem with this approach, oddly enough, is that it tends to neglect the very individuals for whom morals and truth count. Strictly speaking, nothing is self-evident.[5] The truth or value of a proposition is evident only to a person who already has weighed the relevant evidence, considered the appropriate questions, and in light of them, made a judgment about the proposition's accuracy or worth. For everyone else, the matter at best remains an object of reflection, an issue still pending decision. Hence, the act of judging represents a personal commitment and entails personal responsibility. When we judge, we assert or deny something about the character of reality, or the worth of a certain course of action. We thereby literally commit ourselves to a certain understanding of the world and its meaning. This is why Aristotle states that we are responsible for the way that we perceive things and that the world appears differently to the virtuous person than it does to one who is not.[6] We do not come to an understanding of reality or the good by "viewing" it, but by making correct judgments about it. At the same time, we constitute ourselves through our judgments and determine through them the sort of people we become. Human freedom and personal accountability constitute two sides of the same coin.

A matter is evident only when there is sufficient evidence to compel one to judge. In turn, sufficient evidence exists when there are no more relevant questions to be raised about the issue under consideration. Our questioning has a normative direction and heads toward a limit, which is revealed in our mastery of, and familiarity with, the data. When there are no further relevant questions to be answered, the reasonable and responsible person decides. As Søren Kierkegaard's Don Juan character illustrates, try as we might, we cannot avoid deciding, and the person who attempts to avoid the commitment it entails does so at the cost of his or her true humanity.

In sum, the good is self-evident only to one who already has made the proper judgments, who already is in a significant sense normative. This is a person who not only can make proper judgments about the authentically best thing to do in the ever-changing circumstances of real life, but who can then carry those judgments into action. We constitute ourselves not only through our knowings, but more significantly, by our doings. Indeed, we cannot long stand a contradiction between the two.

If one ascertained the morally desirable in the fashion described by Etzioni, the process of making good individuals and good societies alike would primarily be a matter of disseminating the proper information. Once confronted with the obvious, people could be expected both reliably to comprehend it and to arrive at the appropriate conclusions concerning its concrete applications. In such a world, there would be neither room nor necessity for true moral deliberation but only for moral exhortation. Similarly, personal freedom and its consequent, moral responsibility, would be largely meaningless. The chief distinction would be between the informed and those who somehow as yet hadn't gotten the word. Achieving the virtuous society would boil down to the production of a sufficient number of public-service announcements.

As will be discussed more fully, truth is independent of us, but the way we come to know it is not. The patterned set of conscious operations by which we gain some apprehension of reality is grounded in our primordial desire to know and represents the goal of our characteristically human activities of experiencing, understanding, judging, and valuing. These operations, in turn, correspond to the four levels of human consciousness.[7] They are integral to, and constitutive of, our personhood and provide the framework for our knowings, doings, and valuings.

Throughout his entire account, Etzioni strives to identify a basis for values and community that goes beyond some form of mere consensus or nose counting. This effort engages him in a discussion of human nature, moral deliberation, and related topics. What he neglects in all this, however, is the intentional operation of his own consciousness. As a result, the subjective conditions through which we come to know the good tend to get overlooked by Etzioni, as do some of the essential attributes of our personhood. There is an intrinsic normativity to the dynamic structure of our questioning and deciding, and it is through these activities that we make ourselves to be the people we are. Likewise, it is through the authentic performance of these activities that a person becomes truly autonomous and the source of his or her own norms.

Thus, Etzioni is not far off the mark in characterizing "moral order and autonomy" as representing "the twin virtues" of a good society, but I think he is mistaken when he sees a tension or an "antagonism" between them.[8] It might be more accurate to say that these two "virtues" stand in a mutually conditioning relationship and that one proceeds from the other. This point helps to explain why Etzioni is correct in his insistence that there is a social aspect to every virtue and that no virtue can be attained by individuals in some sort of splendid isolation from others.[9] To put the point slightly differently, the good is at once both individual and social. For the reasons that will be further developed, however, the social stands at a higher level of significance because it sets the conditions for the individual's achievement of his or her full personhood.

As this discussion implies, authentic human autonomy is more than a matter of the unhindered will loosed to seek the satisfaction of its own idiosyncratic and ultimately inexplicable drives. Etzioni's notion of a "bounded autonomy"[10] hedged by a set of shared values, or "republican virtues,"[11] implies some recognition of this fact. Nevertheless, his treatment of autonomy seems strongly informed by some version of expressive individualism that understands us as self-originating, self-defining, auto-teleological selves. And I do not agree with his assertion that autonomy "exists only as a social construction."[12] Autonomy has a social aspect, one that is well contextualized within the principle of subsidiarity.[13] The meanings and scale of values suggested by the cultures in which we live do condition the probabilities that we as individuals can become autonomous. In its fullest expression, however, autonomy transcends particular places and times. It represents a normative state, a way of being that is consistent with the character of our humanity and oriented by the unrestricted desire to know. It implies going beyond the narrow constraints of our private emotions, imaginings, and understandings to what actually is. Consequently, for all of us, autonomy is at best a limited achievement. To the degree that we realize it, autonomy represents the product of a slow and not necessarily steady development. It is a condition of standing in between what we already have accomplished and that toward which we still strive.

Consequently, Etzioni is right to observe that our "assumptions about human nature set an important context for the endeavor to build and sustain a good society."[14] He is also correct to note that there seems to be an inherent tension, or what he terms an "eternal struggle"[15] between the immediate and manifold desires that each of us experience as individuals and the constraints that the community imposes on them. It is completely human for each of us to prefer ourselves before others and to be tempted to see our case as the one that merits a special exception to the general rule. At the same time, as Etzioni realizes, human community is not some foreign structure that mysteriously descended on us, and it is not, as some suggest, simply the product of force, trickery, or blind convention. As humans, we are both intelligent as well as spontaneously social beings. The same intelligence that generates the rules and social systems that promote and sustain ongoing cooperation among us also requires us to submit to rules and solutions that we regard as intelligent. The tension that characterizes community is a tension inherent in us. Likewise, as will be discussed, the resolution of this tension depends on how authentically and responsibly we appropriate our own activities of deliberating, choosing, valuing, and acting.

In summary, the key to Etzioni's project does not lie, as he asserts, in some novel "synthesis" of ancient and modern ideals. The answer to the question of how we are to live together in the unprecedented conditions now facing us will not be found in some new syncretism. Instead, if it is to be successful, this undertaking requires a new appreciation of who we truly are and an unblinking reassessment of the genuine character of our personhood.

My second set of difficulties is tied closely to the first. Many of the issues raised by Etzioni are in the most profound sense religious. His work relentlessly demands that we ask who we are, why we act, and how we should live. Etzioni makes a major contribution by placing these questions at the center of the civil society debate. Consequently, Etzioni's palpable uneasiness about the topic of religion is worthy of some note. People commonly think of religion as something in the nature of a lifestyle elective, an option available on a take-it-or-leave-it basis, like power windows or heated seats on a new automobile—nice perhaps, but hardly necessary. This is a mistake. Everyone and every community has a religion: the issue is not whether but what we worship. The question of God is integral to our desire for meaning, and we cannot avoid responding to it. The topic constitutes an essential aspect of any discussion of values. Thus, despite our best efforts to wall it off from the public square, to declare it wholly private, or to declare it wholly dead, the matter of religion and the ground of our being insistently reappears. The subtle interrogator insists on an answer, and our very muteness constitutes a reply.

Etzioni's argument for grounding a good social order is a complex one that proceeds along a broad front, and only a few elements of it can be treated here. So far, much of the discussion has centered on the character of our personhood and the dynamic normativity of the process of human knowing. It is now time to put that account into context and to develop a bit further the implications it holds for Etzioni's crucial project. Accordingly, we next will turn to a fuller consideration of the notions of community, values, the common good, and the unavoidability of the question of religion.

COMMUNITY, ITS LEVELS, AND ITS GROUNDS

Community of any sort represents the achievement of shared sentiments and common meanings.[16] Thus, I largely agree with Etzioni's characterization of community as "a web of affect-laden relationships" that rest on "a measure of commitment to a set of shared values, norms, and meanings."[17] Nevertheless, consistent with the discussion of personhood advanced previously, I would like to flesh out the account of community a bit further than does Etzioni. If successful, this will produce a fuller heuristic scheme of the common good than the one Etzioni provides and will suggest how its authentic commonality transcends the categories of sheer convention or simple majoritarian assent.

As the Canadian philosopher Bernard Lonergan points out, because meanings and our commitments to them exist at various levels and stages, so do communities. These levels, in turn, directly correspond to the four levels of human consciousness previously discussed. [18] At the first level, a body of shared experiences offers the potential for the attainment of a body of common meanings. To retreat from this common realm, or to refuse to attend to these shared experiences, dissipates this opportunity, leaving it stillborn. When such inattentiveness becomes a trend, both community and the prospects for effective self-rule wither.

However, we do not merely experience. We seek to interpret and explain what we have sensed, and we do not do this alone. The formation of common understandings constitutes the second level of community, one in which what was potential becomes formal. At this level, common experiences become mediated through shared understandings of their meaning and significance. Only infants live in a world of immediacy, and then only very briefly. Coming to adulthood involves being brought into a world constituted and mediated by meanings, and bringing us into this world as attentive, intelligent, and responsible participants is the goal of all our formational and educational undertakings. Try as we might at times to suppress or ignore them, questions about what events and experiences actually mean always surround us. In the stream of our lives, they constitute the steady undertow. These questions insistently invite us to go past the narrow world of our immediate, personal experience to consider what really is and what our answers might imply. These questions constitute the primordial, erotic drive that never can be entirely ignored and, when authentically pursued, leads to the formation and maintenance of community in its fullest sense.

This demand for meaning highlights one of the critical aspects of community. As Etzioni observes, our values and mores have a pedigree. Our "starting point," he properly notes, "is shared values, not individual choices or formulations of the good."[19] He realizes, as Edmund Burke put it, that individuals cannot "live and trade each on his own private stock of reason," but instead must "avail themselves of the general bank and capital of nations and ages."[20] Etzioni is correct: meanings and the communities that form around them do have a history. The implications of this fact, however, are more profound than Etzioni implies, or may wish to recognize.

Because we are humans, we only exist in communities, which give us our orientations and identities. They tell us who we are and what our lives are for and indicate the ends toward which we should strive. Likewise, these communities exist not only within specific geographical areas and temporal eras but across space and time as well. None of us generates ideas out of whole cloth. We live and work only in traditions, even when we consciously act against them or seek their undoing. The very languages we speak shape and condition our self-understandings, as they organize and mediate our experiences and the meanings we give them. Thus, just as we never can fully escape the worlds of our forebears, our descendants never will be entirely free of us. Human consciousness has an inherently timeless quality about it, and the reality in which we participate transcends us, to bind us with everyone who has ever or will ever live. As a result, even as we benefit from the good our predecessors did, so do we participate in the structures of their wrongs. Václav Havel has observed that everyone in a totalitarian state ends up as a collaborator with evil. That observation can be extended to all of us, regardless of our situation, and suggests some of what is implied by the theological idea of original sin.

Mere meaning, however, is not enough. We will not mindlessly accept just any set of understandings or beliefs. We not only seek meaning in our lives, but we spontaneously demand that the meanings by which we live be justifiable, both to ourselves and to others. We would not consistently collaborate on the basis of anything less. Hence, common understandings are one thing, but common judgments about those understandings are something else. It is through the latter that community ascends from a formal to an actual level. This third level, constituted by judging, also marks the point at which community becomes in the truest sense personal. As previously described, when we judge, we unavoidably make a commitment. With a question of fact, we evaluate the evidence and work through our own questions about its weight and significance, but we still must settle the question, "Is it so?" With a question of value, we go through the same process, but with the aim of answering the question, "Is it desirable?" A question of fact inquires into what is. Questions of value go further and ask whether it would be good to bring some situation, relationship, or state of affairs into existence. Our answers to these questions of worth make up part of the moral reality in which we live. It is through them, to paraphrase the rabbis, that we cooperate in the completion of creation.

In either case, we constitute ourselves through our judgments and commit ourselves through them to certain sorts of meanings. Reasonable judgments, in turn, do not represent some sort of exclusive preserve open only to an elect few. What is authentically reasonable stands independently of us and our purely private imaginings, desires, and wishes. As Joseph Flanagan observes, "in every correct judgment, you are not asserting what you think is so; you are actually affirming a fact that is true or probably true independently of your saying so. Such independent judgments commit you to a realm of factual realities that other knowers may in turn verify for themselves."[21] To the extent that anything is true, it is radically public and constitutes something in which everyone potentially may share. We might well make mistakes or allow our judgment to be clouded by our own biases and inauthenticities. Our common and spontaneous drive for meaning, however, points past ourselves as well as past particular times, places, and people. Not only does it set the conditions for community, it ensures the eventual collapse of social, legal, economic, and political orders that do not make sense. The self-correcting tendency of the human mind suggests that there may be far more to the notions of tradition and community than most realize.

Consequently, the fact that we are born into communities and a body of meanings is not the end of the story. We may be conditioned by history, but we are not wholly determined by it. Etzioni's discussion is on the right path, even if the account he offers ultimately falls short of the goals he has set for it. There is a normative basis for community that transcends any form of convention and that allows us to distinguish authentically desirable forms of community from deformed or deficient ones. Likewise, Etzioni's emphasis on the "moral voice" moves toward the recognition of a crucial fact. Our capacity for speech grounds the specifically human characteristics of our natural sociality. Unlike other animals, whose utterances are limited to expressing pleasure or pain, the human voice manifests an apprehension of the desirable and the harmful, the just and the wrongful. Communities constitute themselves through a consensus over just these issues. However obscurely, people appeal to ideas of fairness and equity whenever they seek to achieve agreement by explaining and justifying their conclusions to one another. Since speech is the vehicle by which we reveal and test our understandings and judgments, speech is a normative activity, a good in itself. Our involvement in what the ancients referred to as the "civil conversation" literally actuates our capacity for self-rule, at both an individual and a social level. Etzioni's term *the moral voice* represents more than a metaphor. There is a normativity to the human voice; nothing engages our personhood more fully than our involvement in a serious conversation about how we should conduct our lives.

As noted, communities exist through and define themselves along the lines of shared judgments. They become most fully realized, however, through concrete undertakings and commitments that reflect those shared understandings and meanings. It is at this fourth stage that we are challenged to put our money where our mouths are and to live out what we profess to be true. Unfortunately, knowing what ought to be done is not the same thing as doing it; all of us have had firsthand experience with the fault that Aristotle called "moral impotence." Failing to act in accordance with our moral judgments is not a problem of cognition, but of motivation. As Etzioni points out, we are not disembodied spirits, perfect reasoners who somehow mysteriously have become trapped in clay vessels.[22] Although much modern thinking overlooks this fact, human beings consist of both a mind and a body. Our consciousness and our corporeality fully suffuse and condition one another, and are coprinciples in the constitution of the person.

One of the consequences of this fact, to use Martin Heidegger's characterization, is that we are "mooded beings." Our feelings align and move us; they give a "bottom" and a direction to our conscious activities of experiencing, understanding, and judging. In a significant and powerful way, our feelings guide and influence our knowings and actions. What we find worthwhile and contemptible, and that for which we will willingly work and sacrifice, reflects the values that give us our motives and identify our objectives in life. These values also constitute the core about which communities form and condition the meanings and the sentiments on which communities rest. It is appropriate here to briefly discuss them.

VALUES, THEIR RELATION, AND ORDER

"Values," Etzioni observes in the final chapter of *The New Golden Rule*, "combine the kind of affect that true emotions evoke (without such cathartic involvement, values tend to become little more than icons for lip service) with an intellectual account."[23] As previously discussed, Etzioni's intellectual account of values rests on the notion of "self-evident" moral propositions. Having identified "moral order and autonomy" as the basic social virtues, Etzioni proceeds briefly to discuss their relation to what he refers to as the "social and personal virtues" and "corollary and secondary values."[24] Once again, there is something to Etzioni's portrayal. The understanding of the character of our personhood that was previously set forth, however, permits the development of a more comprehensive heuristic framework than the one Etzioni provides.

Etzioni rightly notes the tie between affect and values: values represent a response to feelings. This statement, however, does not imply some version of what Etzioni refers to as "emotivism," which finds values "favored or rejected because ego feels so."[25] Rather, it must be understood in view of the foregoing anthropological sketch. Feelings are immediate and spontaneous to us; in the first instance, at least, we do not decide whether we will "have" or experience them. In contrast, we do determine how we will react to the feelings that we experience. Thus, it falls to us to come to an understanding about the possible meanings of the feelings and desires we encounter in ourselves and to decide whether they should be regarded as pleasant or perverse. Likewise, we must judge whether those feelings should move us to act, which reinforces them and invites their reoccurrence, or whether we should redirect the impulses they incite. In a real sense, we "suffer" emotions; desires of all sorts inflict themselves on us, but we ultimately determine how we respond to them and how we should regard the feelings they arouse in us. Our answers represent the judgments of value previously mentioned, and because they become part of the moral reality we inhabit, each of them contributes to the advance or to the decline of human history. In sum, our values mark out the horizon by which we take our bearings and map out our understanding of the human good. For our purposes, we can classify five sets of values in an ascending order.[26]

At the first level stand vital values. These values represent our concerns with health, physical safety, and bodily well-being and our willingness to work to secure ourselves against the consequences that flow from their absence. Social values constitute the next level of goods. These include the concrete social, economic, legal, and political institutional orders through which the demands for the vital values are met. Because the intelligent and responsible arrangement of these ordering schemes set the conditions for meeting the aggregate needs of the members of a community, social values stand at a higher level of significance than the vital values. If the social order breaks down, the well-being of every individual is threatened.

Cultural values represent the third level of human goods. These values suggest our purpose and our identity. They recount the community's story and help us to locate our place within it, within history, and within the greater world. Because cultural values mediate the meanings that explain and justify the social order, and its goals and purposes, cultural values stand at a higher level of significance than either the social or vital values. Cultural values supply the shared motives and sentiments that promote social cohesion and ongoing cooperation, which in turn anchor the schemes of the social order. Thus, when the cultural order disintegrates, the social order loses its coherence. A new and stable social order emerges only after a new set of cultural meanings has been accepted.

The culture's tasks are to identify what is authentically worthwhile and to criticize what is not. To the extent that it successfully carries out these tasks, a culture is normative; to the degree that it falls short, it is deficient, and it threatens the flourishing of those who live within its body of meanings. As noted previously, our spontaneous demand for meaning ensures that nonsensical cultural values, and the communities that form about them, eventually will deteriorate. Like humans, communities and cultures are contingent "beings" who do not sustain themselves from their own, self-generated resources. Their continued existence and development rest upon their authentic intelligibility.

Community of any sort exists for the individual; it grounds and conditions the possibilities for the achievement of one's true individuality. Hence, personal values constitute the fourth level of the human good, and when rightly ordered, the other values underpin and serve them. Authentic personal values find their expression in the individual's ability to engage in the most distinctly human of activities: experiencing, deliberating, choosing, and loving in an intelligent, reasonable, and responsible fashion. They are informed by, and represent the expression of, a rightly ordered self-love, which properly values that which is best in a human being. Personal values thus embody an appropriation of the intentional operations of one's own consciousness. For the reasons outlined previously, personal values find their full expression in authentic self-transcendence. As mentioned, this self-transcendence is a function of our innate demand for meaning. It is represented in the movement from purely personal imaginings, desirings, and feelings to some apprehension of, and participation in, what actually is. Our pursuit of meaning and the facts of good and evil in our concrete experiences in life raise questions about the character of the universe and the sufficient conditions for truth and seek some identification of that for which we can hope.

These and related questions turn us to the question of God and religion. This question not only lies within the human horizon; it is one by which our consciousness is drawn and to which our consciousness directs us. For that reason, religious values constitute the final level of the scale of values. These represent the core of our meanings and constitute that for the sake of which we do everything else. They orient our other values and shape and direct the course of our inquiries, our doings, and the identity of that which we love. In this context, it is important that our ideas of religion not be cabined by some crabbed notions of sectarianism. Everyone has a religion; no one gets away without one. In the final analysis, the question is not whether we are religious, but what we are religious about, and thus who or what we find ourselves worshipping. It is appropriate briefly to address this matter here.

RELIGION, VALUING, AND THE COMMON GOOD

Etzioni ends his argument in *The New Golden Rule* by asking, "Must one be religious to be communitarian?"[27] A few paragraphs into his response, he apparently reframes the question by asking, "Must a person be religious to be virtuous?" Etzioni's answer is clear: "being religious does not guarantee virtue." Etzioni also assures us that being religious is optional to one's being a communitarian. We can prescind from addressing the question of whether one must be a communitarian to be virtuous, but from Etzioni's perspective, at least, the answer to this query seems self-evident. Perhaps it is not going too far to suggest that in the final analysis, communitarianism constitutes a variation on the theme of civic religion. In any event, communitarianism constitutes Etzioni's faith, and he is unquestionably the movement's foremost theologian.

Because it embodies questions about reality and the nature of meaning, religion is a vast and complex topic, and there is room here only to reiterate and to expand slightly upon a few of the points previously mentioned. The first is that the question of God and religion is the natural product of our unrestricted desire to know. Etzioni's own work exemplifies this fact: Etzioni seeks a basis for community and values that transcends mere convention. This pushes him to ask what the basis for values might be and whether our values can have any ultimate meaning. These are questions about God, and such is Etzioni's honesty that he forthrightly asks whether the world and our moral enterprise can have intelligibility for us apart from our participation in a being that transcends us and in an intelligible order that goes beyond the level of sensible presentations.

Nevertheless, Etzioni's discomfort with the topic of religion is palpable. The call to know fills us all with a certain sort of dread, and as Etzioni nears the burning question, he flinches. Indeed, he responds to the issue of the relation between virtue and religion by pointing out the not very remarkable fact that the "devout" not infrequently "have conducted themselves in ways few would consider moral."[28] That observation is certainly true enough, but the fact of human failure (i.e., sin, which "religious" people do not deny, and which in any event is a condition not restricted to them) does not make the question of ultimate meaning go away. Explicitly and implicitly, in a constant and incremental fashion, all of us must answer it, because each of us must work out a solution to the question of how we will be a human being. That is the essence of human freedom. Hence, for all of us, the identity of what we worship is an unavoidable question.

The scale of values discussed previously allows a quick illustration of this point. As mentioned, Etzioni's chief concern is to find some middle way between the sort of romantic or expressive individualism that threatens to undermine any form of community and some form of group bias, which by reifying the community, dissolves our unique and distinct personalities into the mass. Etzioni's anxieties about the seeming exclusivity of these alternatives are well founded. While these positions typify much of contemporary life and thinking, both truncate the character of our true personhood, and both represent distortions of valuing. Hence, both put the conditions for authentic human flourishing at risk.

The problem with the first perspective is that it short-circuits the hierarchy of goods at the level of personal values, which results in their distortion. This attempt to value the individual grows out of a problematic account of the limits on human knowing and reveals the influence of a disordered form of self-love. Because of its canted understanding of the person as a sovereign self, this framework emphasizes the vital values but tends to slight the social and cultural good, and it sputters out entirely at the fourth level of valuing into some version of romantic selfhood. If questioning moves us to meanings that go beyond ourselves, a key difficulty with the various versions of expressive individualism is that they suggest that as persons we are autoteleological beings, and as such, constitute the source of our own meanings. Among many other things, this viewpoint reduces community and ideas of the good to matters of contract and largely limits their intelligibility to being nothing more than an expression of one's ultimately inscrutable tastes. [29] From this perspective, human liberty principally implies the freedom of each self-made individual to worship his or her own creator.

The second of these frameworks, which results in the reification of the group, presents not dissimilar errors in valuing and in understandings of our personhood. Here, the scale of values terminates at the third level, in a particular group or culture, which makes it the standard of the good. This approach displaces personal values and telescopes religious values into the level of cultural values, thereby making the community or the group its own end, a "religion" unto itself. In the more perverse appearances of this bias, the group and its meanings become the sole reality; individuals disappear, and those without the group become unrecognizable as humans. Etzioni is right to be anxious about the implications that flow from both of these frameworks. Getting beyond them, however, pushes him—and the rest of us—into questions that we all would like to ignore, if only we could.

This observation leads to a final point. In the course of his argument, Etzioni raises the notion of the common good, which he defines as "a core of shared values."[30] Perhaps enough now has been said to indicate something about both the shortcomings of this formulation and the articulated and ordered whole that the term intends.

For the reasons outlined previously, this good transcends particular individuals and groups and constitutes something in which we all, by the very operation of our consciousness, are invited to share, and which constitutes the satisfaction of all of our most human longings. In short, Etzioni is right when he states at the close of his book that, "community provides one with a normative foundation."[31] True community, however, is a far broader and more significant good than he allows himself to realize.

NOTES

1. Amitai Etzioni, *The New Golden Rule* (New York, N.Y.: Basic Books, 1996).

2. Etzioni, *New Golden Rule*, xvii–xix.

3. Etzioni, *New Golden Rule*, 247.

4. Etzioni, *New Golden Rule*, 241–2.

5. On this point, and on the account of knowing presented in this chapter, see Bernard J. F. Lonergan, *Insight: A Study of Human Understanding* (San Francisco: Harper & Row, 1978), especially chs. 6–7 and 9–11. Also see, Bernard J. F. Lonergan, "Cognitional Structure" and "Dimensions of Meaning," in *Collection: Papers by Bernard Lonergan,* ed. Frederick E. Crowe and Robert M. Doran (Toronto: University of Toronto Press, 1988), 205–21; 232–45.

6. See Aristotle, *Nichomachean Ethics*, Books II–III.

7. See Lonergan, *Insight,* especially chs. 11–12; also see the discussion in Bernard J. F. Lonergan, *Method in Theology,* (Toronto: University of Toronto Press, 1990), 3–124.

8. Etzioni, *New Golden Rule*, 244–5.

9. Etzioni, *New Golden Rule*, 249–50.

10. Etzioni, *New Golden Rule*, 71.

11. Etzioni, *New Golden Rule*, 85.

12. Etzioni, *New Golden Rule*, 249.

13. Subsidiarity is an organizational norm that recommends that social institutions of all descriptions be ordered so that decision making can occur at the lowest capable level. Thus, communities and institutions should not take up what individuals can do, and larger groups should not assume what smaller groups can accomplish. Conversely, the state and other large institutions have the responsibility to undertake those tasks that neither smaller groups nor individuals can accomplish. On subsidiarity, see Thomas C. Kohler, "Lessons from the Social Charter: State, Corporation, and the Meaning of Subsidiarity," *University of Toronto Law Journal* 43(3) (Summer 1993): 607–28.

14. Etzioni, *New Golden Rule,* 160.

15. Etzioni, *New Golden Rule,* 165.

16. Lonergan, *Method,* 79.

17. Etzioni, *New Golden Rule,* 127.

18. See Lonergan, *Method,* 6–20, 73–85.

19. Etzioni, *New Golden Rule,* 93.

20. Edmund Burke, *Reflections on the Revolution in France* (Indianapolis: Bobbs-Merrill Educational Publishing, 1983), 99.

21. Joseph Flanagan, *Quest for Self-Knowledge: An Essay in Lonergan's Philosophy* (Toronto: University of Toronto Press, 1997), 232.

22. Etzioni, *New Golden Rule,* 97–101, 241–4.

23. Etzioni, *New Golden Rule,* 218.

24. Etzioni, *New Golden Rule,* 244–52.

25. Etzioni, *New Golden Rule,* 244.

26. On this scale of values and its relation to meaning, see Lonergan, *Method,* 30–4, 76–90.

27. Etzioni, *New Golden Rule,* 252–6.

28. Etzioni, *New Golden Rule,* 253.

29. The problem is an ancient one, cf. Plato, *The Republic,* Book II; also see Eric Voegelin, "The Concrete Consciousness," in *Anamnesis,* ed. and trans. Gerhart Niemeyer (Columbia: University of Missouri Press, 1990), 200–5.

30. Etzioni, *New Golden Rule,* 90.

31. Etzioni, *New Golden Rule,* 257.

5

What Can the Study of Communities Teach Us about Community?

Benjamin D. Zablocki

Community seems to be one of these things that we humans can't live with and can't live without. When we have it in abundance, we find it stifling and we run off to find a place where we can "be more ourselves." When we lack it, we feel lost and alienated and we go around searching for that "cheerful" bar where "everybody knows your name and you can see that troubles are all the same." Currently, we Americans seem to be at a time when we don't feel we have enough of it. But it is reasonable to ask whether we'd be better off were it somehow made available to us in greater abundance.

Amitai Etzioni has sparked an interesting debate within sociology on the subject of community, with his writings on the subject of the sociopolitical movement known as "communitarianism." There is a double thrust to communitarian writings. The first is concerned with the kind of society that will emerge from increasing the salience of community in our lives as a mediating institution between the state and the individual. The second is concerned directly with that mediating institution itself—that is, the formation and maintenance of the communities that form the presumed basis of a communitarian society. My contribution will be aimed only at the second of these two concerns of the communitarian movement.

I will focus in this chapter on a limited portion of the communitarian debate.[1] I will limit my discussion, first of all, to its sociological dimensions, ignoring, for the most part, its political and philosophical dimensions, although the latter are at least as important. Secondly, I will limit my discussion to just two of the three major sociological issues that emerge from communitarian writing. Etzioni's work confronts sociologists with a challenge to find answers to the following three questions: (1) *Definition.* What do we mean by community and how may we define it in terms of its essential features? (2) *Feasibility.* Is it feasible at this time in history to strengthen the role of community (or communities) in contemporary U.S. life? (3) *Desirability.*

71

Are there unanticipated consequences of strengthening the role of community in contemporary life and might many people find some of these consequences undesirable?

Although all of these questions are important, I am going to ignore the first in order to concentrate on the second and third. In ignoring the issue of definition, I do so by provisionally accepting Etzioni's own definition of community: "Community is defined by two characteristics: first a web of affect laden relationships among a group of individuals, relationships that often crisscross and reinforce one another (rather than merely one-on-one or chainlike individual relationships), and second, a measure of commitment to a set of shared values, norms, and meanings, and a shared history and identity—in short, to a particular culture" (p. 127).

In insisting that community include both the dimension of believing and the dimension of belonging, Etzioni is on solid ground. He differentiates himself thus from those who define community solely in terms of relational networks. I will say that I am somewhat troubled by the blithe assumption made in this definition that ties of belief and ties of belonging can always be counted on to reinforce each other (or at least to not work against each other). This assumption is the essence of the so-called Homans' Law.[2] But the empirical association between believing and belonging does not entirely bear George Homans out in this matter. There is reason to believe that this association is far more complex and problematic than one of simple mutual reinforcement. Especially at the less individualistic end of the believing and belonging scales, where Etzioni places his communities, there is reason to believe that the very strength of interpersonal ties, so necessary for group survival, can actually undermine group solidarity. Andreas Flache and Michael W. Macy, taking the obverse of Mark Granovetter's famous principle of the strength of weak ties, refer to this capacity to undermine as "the weakness of strong ties." They show how tightly bonded social networks can actually, under some circumstances, diminish rather than strengthen the collective capacity to act in support of shared beliefs and values.[3] As network ties grow stronger, effort that could have gone into the support of collective objectives is diverted instead into network management.[4] Ironically, Etzioni himself was one of the first sociological theorists to point this out, in his earlier precommunitarian work on cohesiveness in complex organizations.[5]

But an attempt to untangle the reciprocal causal effects linking believing with belonging in communities would require an entire additional chapter at least the length of this one. So let us grant, for the sake of the argument, that the two dimensions of believing and belonging, which Etzioni correctly identifies as indispensable for real community, can coexist in an unproblematic, if not always a mutually supportive, association. Making this assumption will allow us to devote our attention more fully to the problems of feasibility and desirability.

Communitarian feasibility and desirability would not provoke such a fascinating debate if there were not much to be said both for and against. Let me start on the positive side of the ledger. It seems to me that three arguments can be made to support the contention that an increased role for community participation in twenty-first-century U.S. society may be difficult to achieve but is, nevertheless, both a feasible and desirable goal.

The first of these arguments stems from the pragmatist philosophical approach to sociology. Traditionally, American sociological theory has been marked by something of a pragmatic flavor, and this flavor is clearly present in communitarian writings. Two basic premises of pragmatism applied to sociology are that solutions to social problems can sometimes be engineered and, despite what theory may tell you, you never know until you try whether something will work. The economic, political, and social restructuring of U.S. society that came to be called the New Deal was an achievement of pragmatists who refused to be guided by a priori theory and who made many interim mistakes while developing their program. They kept on trying different solutions until they found some that worked well enough. This is very much the mode of operation of the contemporary communitarians, and there is no reason to assume that it cannot in time turn out to be equally successful.

A second point that supports communitarianism is that community's perceived utility for most people is directly proportional to its scarcity. This is reflected on even such a fundamental level as real estate value. In the wake of massive suburbanization of the outlying regions of expanding metropolitan areas, those enclaves that, for whatever reason, have been able to retain something of a distinctive and well-bounded community character have found that this translates into a premium in the market price for commercial and residential property. And, judging from advertising campaigns, even the illusion of community then becomes an important selling point in real estate transactions.

Max Weber discussed a similar point in his essay on Protestant sects.[6] His point, which I will return to later in discussing the relative success of contemporary "strict" religions, is that visible membership (in good standing) in a moral community has tangible economic value, particularly in business. Especially to the extent that trust becomes a scarce commodity in the society at large, the ability of the community to stamp a trustworthiness seal of approval on the brows of its participants is useful and treasured. Such communities have the teeth not only to espouse but to require individual compliance with consensually agreed-upon moral standards.

A third point, closely related to the second, is that we *want* more community in our lives. Maybe more to the point, public opinion surveys show that baby boomers want more community in their lives, especially as they grow older. And we know from experience that baby boomers are good at finding ways to get what they want out of society. Abraham Maslow has argued that community is one of the basic needs of human self-actualization and that, as society becomes better at providing for fundamental survival needs, issues of community become a more important part of the civic agenda.[7] Whether or not you buy into this somewhat metaphysical argument, it is impossible to ignore the fact that human beings have been remarkably inventive in their attempts to find or carve out islands of community in an increasingly acommunal world.

Against these three arguments, however, can be posed three counterarguments, out of classical sociological theory, that appear to me, on the whole, to be somewhat more compelling. These are arguments against the feasibility or desirability of increasing the importance of community in our lives. The first of these is the Weberian argument that there is a long-term trend toward ever-greater rationality and ever-greater individualism in our society that nothing can reverse. The second is the Simmelian argument that communities are defined primarily by their boundaries and that on the other side of the boundary are strangers to be distrusted and enemies to be hated and feared. The third is an argument based on the free rider problem, that moral community for you might be exploitative opportunity for me. Let us discuss each of these three in turn.

Max Weber marshaled considerable evidence in support of his proposition that there has been an ever-increasing rationality in human relationships in Western societies in recent centuries and an increased importance of the individual as a social actor.[8] An implication of this proposition is the increasing importance of the economic institution as opposed to other institutions in our society, and a corollary that is relevant for our current discussion is that communities over time will come to be more and more organized around economic needs. It is true that U.S. communities, which tend to be considerably newer than their counterparts in Europe and Asia, tend also to be much more exclusively organized around economic functions.

Now there is nothing about being organized around economic functions that necessarily precludes increasing the importance of such communities in social and political life. However, the problem is that another well-supported proposition of Weberian sociology is that vertical integration always undercuts and weakens horizontal integration. Most communities as we know them are horizontally integrated and Max Weber's writings suggest that they are relatively helpless to resist the vertical restructuring of our contemporary economy, particularly the global aspects of that restructuring. Whether a particular community benefits or loses in this restructuring, its role is still one of a relatively passive recipient of vertical pushes and pulls that it cannot influence and that its citizens often don't even understand.[9]

Georg Simmel argued for the importance of boundaries in the definition of community.[10] A point too often ignored in communitarian literature is that communities are often defined as much by who is on the outside as by who is included. This again is not so much intrinsically a problem as something that becomes a problem when set against the racism, ethnic conflict, and economic segregation that have been part of the U.S. cultural heritage. Indeed, much of the history of the past half-century of progressive social reform has involved the deliberate weakening of the exclusionary powers of community. In this regard, see, for example, first the campaigns against restrictive neighborhood covenants against Irish, Italians, and Jews, later compulsory racial integration of community schools, and still later legal decisions like the Mount Laurel decision in New Jersey, which limited the right of communities to zone out the poor.[11] It is reasonable to ask whether, if communities become strong again, they will take back their traditional powers to choose who gets to belong and who must remain an outsider.

The third and, to my mind, the most serious problem is the free rider problem.[12] Community is an example of a public good par excellence. The free rider argument is that it is not rational for me to contribute to the production of a public good if I cannot be penalized for not doing so and if I cannot be deprived of the right to enjoy the good after others have produced it. I may indeed very much want to live in a moral community. I will feel safe and relaxed if all my neighbors are committed to upholding high moral standards. But there is no reason why I should impose those same irksome standards on myself. Of course, the community is only minimally weakened as long as I am the only one following this selfish path. Problems arise, however, when the rest of you are tempted to free ride in a similar way.

Historically, communities have protected themselves against free riders through the mechanism of civic reputation. Traditionally, communities have controlled their own internal markets for prestige/disdain. Where the costs of leaving a community are high, reputational sanctions can be a powerful disincentive to free ride. The problem is, however, that community exit costs[13] in the United States have historically been quite low, owing in large part to our frontier tradition. I am aware of no evidence that it is becoming less costly to exit one community and enter another with any previous bad reputation wiped out in the process. This might not be quite as true for professionals and public figures, but it remains very much the case for the average citizen. Under such circumstances, the temptation to foul one's own nest periodically and move on to a new clean nest can be high. Are there ways to engineer greater costs to nest fouling and moving on? In some other cultures, wrongdoers have been branded or mutilated to prevent just this form of escape. Our own society has, of course, been reluctant to impose such sanctions on wrongdoers, with the notable exception of child molesters (e.g., Megan's Law).[14] If U.S. society moves in the direction of requiring uniform mandatory identification cards, this may provide a way to make nest fouling more difficult. But it is not clear that public opinion is or should be ready to accept the trade-offs in terms of loss of privacy.

Etzioni is, of course, aware of these counterarguments and prepared to rebut them. His rebuttal, however, rests heavily on the claim that modern communities are quite different from traditional communities and are thus immune from the weaknesses and dangers that I have enumerated. Etzioni states his rebuttal as follows:

> Behind many of these criticisms lies an image of old or total communities, which are neither typical to modern society nor necessary for, or even compatible with, a communitarian society. Old communities (traditional villages) were geographically bounded and the only communities of which people were members. In effect, other than escaping into no-man's-land, often bandit territories, individuals had few opportunities for choosing their social attachments. In short, old communities had monopolistic power over their members. (p. 128)

There is a great deal of slippage in the exposition of Etzioni's argument at precisely this point. His desirability arguments tend to be framed in terms of these modern nonpropinquitous nonexclusive alternatives to traditional community. But his feasibility arguments all fall back on the old standby of the traditional geographically based community. For example, in trying to show that community need not be oppressive of individual liberty, Etzioni makes much of the fact that the average person is simultaneously a member of multiple new communities: "New communities are often limited in scope and reach. Members of one residential community are often also members of other communities—for example, work, ethnic, or religious ones. As a result community members have multiple sources of attachments, and if one threatens to become overwhelming, individuals will tend to draw more on another community for their attachments" (p.128). He argues further that these new communities, because people spend considerable amounts of their time in them, can "fulfill many of the social and moral functions of traditional communities."[15]

But we have to question whether such weakly bonded communities can really serve to create the kind of moral regeneration that Etzioni is looking for. An indication that Etzioni himself is dubious about this prospect can be seen in the fact that all of the specific examples that he gives of community regeneration (pp. 87, 149, 152) involve activities organized within geographical (old style) communities. The same is true for all the examples of state policies to strengthen the community institution. Indeed it is hard to imagine how fair and evenhanded national policies could be framed to strengthen the institution of community on any but geographical criteria, especially if such policies involved (as surely they must) significant amounts of public revenue redistribution.

Despite Etzioni's confusing differentiation between what he calls "old" and "new" communities, there is reason to believe that both sorts of communities have existed in many different historical periods and that both continue to thrive today. The real difference is that most people today have the opportunity to participate in both types of community, whereas this privilege was usually reserved for the elite (and perhaps some parts of the professional middle class) in the past. It follows that communitarian transformation of society is not some newly emergent opportunity associated with late modernity or postmodernity, but that it was an option in the past as well. Let us then turn to the historical record to see how issues like this were met in earlier times.

HISTORICAL EVIDENCE

Communal regeneration movements such as Etzioni's are not new. Similar movements have arisen at other times in history. Of course, every historical epoch is unique in terms of the social opportunities and challenges that it poses for social reform. Nevertheless, it is possible that we can learn something about the pitfalls facing the current communitarian movement by looking at what happened to other similar movements in the past.

Although American communitarianism is a fairly new social movement, pleas for a greater role for community in our social life are part of an ancient tradition in Western civilization. In the Bible, Jonah, one of the first communitarian activists, albeit a reluctant one, played to mixed reviews in Nineveh. But the biblical prophet Amos (who was in some ways the Etzioni of his era), with his fervent call for increased community morality, apparently was talking about a problem that, even way back then, was recognized as real within ancient Hebrew society. There is no biblical evidence that Amos's plea was heeded, except perhaps by various small separatist cults of religious extremists like the Essenes.[16]

During the Middle Ages, the Confraternities of the Holy Spirit, which were to be found in most reasonably large towns and cities throughout Western Christendom, represented a communitarian recognition on the part of the Catholic Church of the need for a middle community layer between the hierarchical church and the individual Christian.[17] The fact that these confraternities, after the first few centuries, never remained a particularly important part of civic life, except at times in Ireland and in parts of France, can serve as a historical warning of the difficulties of maintaining sustainability even of well-organized communal institutions in a strictly hierarchical society.

I want to mention briefly the Paris Communes of 1848 and 1968 as more recent examples of a recurring historical tendency to overestimate the amount of community that people want, particularly during times of social crisis and alienation. A problem with community movements is that they tend to awaken in people romantic longings for a utopian way of life. To the extent that these serve as a goad to actively seek Utopia and, in the process, find a better way of life, there is nothing wrong with the misty perspective of romanticism. However, sometimes, a romantic longing for community can lead people to overcommit resources to a communal venture that turns out to involve greater surrender of autonomy than they had bargained for. Historically, such enterprises, rather than readjusting their demand for self-investment to the available supply, tend rather to disintegrate or to turn morbidly inward as in Calvin's Geneva.[18] A more recent example of this phenomenon can be seen in the proto-communitarian social movement, Moral Rearmament, with its intermittently fascistic and sadistic outcomes.[19]

Probably the most direct historical evidence relevant to communitarianism can be found by examining the Kehillah experiment among New York's Jews in the early part of the twentieth century.[20] The Kehillah experiment was a very deliberate attempt at social engineering on the part of U.S. Jewish leaders during the first two decades of the twentieth century to cope both with the adjustment problems of the large waves of recent Jewish immigrants from Eastern Europe and to prevent these problems from eroding the careful accommodation that earlier generations of Jews had made to the U.S. gentile majority with whom they lived.

The Kehillah experiment attempted to build upon a well-established cultural tradition of authoritarian community that the immigrants brought with them from Eastern Europe and that was still very much alive both in their memories and in their expectations. Moreover, it was a response to a very real crisis that had emerged at the time, as the institutions of the established informal Jewish community of New York were increasingly overwhelmed by the demands of the new immigrant groups. The plan, which was backed by the considerable resources of leading Jewish financiers and businessmen and led by the Jewish visionary Judah L. Magnes, was to transform the Kehillah model of Eastern Europe but give it a democratic basis more fitting for U.S. society.

The ultimate (although far from total) failure of the Kehillah movement provides an object lesson for contemporary communitarianism, whose task it is to mobilize support for new and revived community institutions during a period of less evident crisis and with less of an immediate cultural tradition to build upon. As Arthur A. Goren concludes:

> One had to agitate for community, then, by persuading individuals to affiliate with the organized communal body; joining entailed an act of personal self-identification. In the early days of the Kehillah movement, the emphasis had been different. Magnes had assumed the existence of an ethnic solidarity which, grounded in the group's minority experience and the national-religious quality of Judaism, led to collective responses to outside threats. He had proposed channeling these group sentiments in to the creation of an integrated community—the Kehillah. Its utility and reasonability, he believed, would bring the institution stability and recognition. This process fitted his understanding of the thrust of American society, which he saw as evolving into a "republic of nationalities." But in the declining period of the Kehillah, Magnes came to understand that under the free conditions of American life, ethnicity was but one of the many attachments shared by group and individual. (p. 252)

Although communitarianism does not propose the development of community institutions along ethnic lines, it must nevertheless contend with the multidimensionality of most people's involvement with U.S. society. Historically, community has generally fared best when the relations of the individual to society are closer to the unidimensional.

It seems to me that the failure of the Kehillah movement offers strong historical evidence against the feasibility of communitarianism. If ever there was a time when all the conditions were right, the desire was there, and the necessary resources were available, it was among the New York Jews in the early decades of the twentieth century. Moreover, history does not offer us any obvious communitarian success stories to juxtapose to the Kehillah saga. We are forced, I think, to conclude that the historical evidence is not very promising for the communitarian agenda.

It may be, however, that, as Etzioni suggests, emergent characteristics of late twentieth-century society (widespread prosperity, the Internet, widespread involvement in multiple affiliative networks) are necessary to make communitarianism possible.

Let us turn now from the historical record to contemporary evidence to see if we can find data more encouraging for communitarian plans.

CONTEMPORARY EVIDENCE

Contemporary U.S. society provides overwhelming evidence of the creativity of its citizens in seeking a greater degree of community in their lives both by creating new social institutions and modifying those already in existence. We can take this as evidence that communitarianism is on fertile soil on the demand side. On the supply side, the evidence is less encouraging. We confront a deep-seated ambivalence in widely shared positive attitudes toward the potential core of communities and widely shared negative attitudes regarding community boundaries. In particular, the new community institutions that have been created exemplify, on the one hand, salutary collective desires for the decentralization of civic life and the desire to be held to more robust moral standards of conduct. However, on the other hand, many of them exemplify an exclusionary spirit—a desire to attain moral purity by shunning the impure and a desire to relieve the strains on traditional cultural legacies by fragmenting U.S. society into separate but interdependent culturally homogeneous enclaves. A useful litmus test to use on community experiments in this regard is to ask how they treat the traditional shunned seven of U.S. society: Jews, Blacks, Hispanics, Asians, Native Americans, homosexuals, and the poor.

Let us now look briefly at five particularly vigorous areas of community experimentation, all of which could be found in some abundance in the United States at the close of the twentieth century: (1) tightly networked, high-demand communes or intentional communities; (2) strict churches; (3) planned communities of various sorts; (4) ethnic and racial communities; and (5) communities without propinquity, especially social networks and virtual communities on the Internet.

Communes are an extreme but interesting site to investigate with regard to the desire for community and the willingness of people to adapt to it. Communes typically demand a great deal of surrender of personal autonomy from their members but offer in return the promise of a radically improved lifestyle. Recent enthusiasm for starting communes peaked during the 1960s and 1970s but has remained high ever since. Moreover, most communes, in their early stages, do well by the litmus test offered above. They are typically open to all who appear to sincerely embrace their vision.

The problem with communes is that they are extraordinarily unstable, typically lasting no longer than two or three years.[21] Very few survive even to a second generation. Data that I collected on a national sample of 120 rural and urban communes followed for twenty-five years (between 1974 and 1999) bear this out. At the twenty-five-year mark, only 8 percent of these 120 groups were still in existence. What is perhaps worse news from the communitarian point of view is that the ten communes that did survive for a quarter of a century were all either strict religious communes with charismatic leaders or live-and-let-live anarchist or semi-anarchist communes with no shared moral or ideological core. Of the thirty-eight communes in the initial sample that met Etzioni's standard of sharing a moral core without being authoritarian, none was still in existence at the twenty-five-year mark. Few of them had survived even as long as ten years.

As Rosabeth M. Kanter and others have argued, among communes that demand more than minimal Hobbesian courtesy from their members, those that tend to survive are the ones that institute very serious commitment mechanisms, requiring a great deal of investment of individual autonomy.[22] Evidence from the kibbutzim in Israel suggests that even in a society, unlike our own, that provides a legitimate and honored place for such communal experiments, they are likely over time to become overwhelmed by socioeconomic changes to which they are unable to adapt.[23] With a few notable exceptions like the Bruderhof and the Shakers,[24] U.S. communes have proven on the whole too fragile to be satisfactory models of community building. Another problem has been that, while communes generally start out with an inclusive outlook toward the "shunned seven," in particular the poor and minorities, those that survive and prosper develop an increased tendency over time to look at the world from a somewhat apocalyptic "us" versus "them" perspective.

Somewhat more encouraging than communes from a communitarian perspective has been the relative success of strict churches in the religious marketplace. One of the most interesting (although still hotly debated) findings to come out of recent research in the sociology of religion is that churches that make heavy demands on their members tend to retain member loyalty to a greater degree than the more permissive liberal churches.[25] To the extent that we can assume that these findings are robust, they offer suggestive evidence that many people are willing to pay a personal price for moral community.

This phenomenon needs to be closely studied by communitarians to see if it has applicability outside of the religious domain. I suspect it does not and that the unique ability of religion to bind congregations into moral communities suggests that religion must have an increased role in any communitarian society. Etzioni is, I think, a little defensive on this topic. He frames the question: "Must a person be religious to be virtuous?" (p. 253). His answer to this question is that religious and the secular communitarians need to cooperate to make the movement succeed. "The communitarian endeavor requires a broad coalition rather than a situation in which those on the side of regeneration condemn one another, because some do not recognize the importance and role of religion, and others deny the possibility of secular recommitment to virtues. At best, if both religious and secular advocates of the return to virtue will join their endeavors, their commitments may suffice to carry the day" (pp. 255–6). But I think that Etzioni is specifying the question using the wrong unit of analysis. It is not whether nonreligious people can be communitarians that is at issue. The real issue is whether strong moral communities without a religious foundation can survive over time with any degree of regularity. Comparisons of religious with secular communes in the United States and of religious with secular kibbutzim in Israel suggest that perhaps they cannot. Evidence from religious communes, Orthodox kibbutzim, and strict U.S. churches suggests that religion is near to being an essential ingredient of the stable moral community.

But maybe we are just not looking for secular communitarian success stories in the right places. After all, both religious communes and strict churches demand a great deal more from their participants than the minimum envisioned by Etzioni and his colleagues. Perhaps planned communities provide a better model. Planned communities differ from communes (or intentional communities) in that they are less demanding, do not offer a utopian agenda, require less of a modification of lifestyle, and are generally secular in worldview or at least liberally ecumenical. Planned communities have been an important part of the U.S. cultural landscape for more than two hundred years. We do not have space here to do more than touch on a couple of manifestations of this very complex and important phenomenon, however, I do want to mention two examples, one that is encouraging to the communitarian agenda and one that is discouraging.

The cohousing movement[26] is an example of one of the more encouraging trends in contemporary U.S. society for the communitarian movement. Cohousing is a form of residential design that is inspired not only by the longing for greater community but also by an important phenomenon that we have not yet addressed: the super-stressing of the contemporary nuclear family. Cohousing retains the mainstream concept of individual family-based economically autonomous households but makes the boundaries between home and neighborhood less rigid. Particularly, for two-career families raising children and for one-parent household units, cohousing offers a way to shift some of the functions of the overburdened family onto the cooperative community. Although cohousing has been slow to catch on in U.S. society, it has shown slow growth for more than twenty-five years. It is a development worth watching.

Also worth watching, but with a gloomier message for communitarian idealists, is the phenomenon of the gated community. In a recent article, Andrew Stark quotes *Time* magazine editor, Richard Stengel, as arguing, "neither gated suburbs nor business improvement districts could be considered salutary for the republic. Both represent the secession of a smaller more privileged community from the larger one. Each is, in some respects, driven by fear."[27]

Starting with a trickle of such enclaves after World War II, gated communities have rapidly proliferated in the United States. Edward J. Blakely and Mary Gail Snyder estimate that new ones are being developed at a rate of more than one thousand per year and that, in 1997, there were twenty thousand such communities in the United States, cumulatively containing more than three million housing units.[28] On the whole, the shunned seven, spoken of earlier, do not do well in such environments unless they have enough money to build gated communities of their own.

It is sad to note that, while the cohousing movement has enjoyed very slow but steady growth in the last quarter of a century, the gated community movement has enjoyed such a rapid and steady growth. The urge to define an "us" and then to separate "us" from "them" has been a significant part of the U.S. conglomerate culture since precolonial times, and the gated community is only the latest manifestation of this urge. Research on this phenomenon sums up the sentiments driving it as follows:

> In gated communities across the nation, we heard people say they want to take their neighborhoods back. They want safety, they want quiet, and they want to feel secure. Though they do not often say so explicitly, they want community as well; they are pleased and proud when they feel they are part of a residential area that has a sense of community. Given these desires, the movement toward gates, guards, fences, walls, and concrete barricades is understandable. These physical security measures seem to offer protection and peace of mind. If they also divide neighborhood from neighborhood, encourage privatization, and send signals of exclusion, that may seem a small price to pay. Some residents of gated communities told us that their first obligation must be to look after their families, their blocks, and their neighborhoods before worrying about the rest of the world.[29]

To keep the communitarian movement from being captured by the proponents of the gated vision seems to me the greatest single challenge facing this movement.

The whole area of ethnic and racial communities is one deserving of a far more complete treatment than I can give it here. The desire for ethnic and racial solidarity seems to me on the whole to be a good thing and, whether good or bad, a persistent feature of U.S. political and cultural life. There is, however, the legitimate concern that this solidarity, if bolstered by communal separation, will eventually contribute more to the fracturing than the healing of U.S. society. It is important to emphasize that we are not talking here about imposed patterns of segregation through formal exclusion. Studies of suburbanization have shown that, even where choice is relatively free, both Blacks and Whites quite often choose patterns of voluntary racial segregation.[30] Similar patterns are shown for voluntary age segregation.[31] The Simmelian argument suggests that an unanticipated outcome of success in developing the communitarian agenda may be increased voluntary ghettoization of significant portions of U.S. society.

Homogeneous ethnic communities are not always a bad thing. The Amish are perhaps the best example of an ethnic community that has been able to hold itself and its members to a higher moral standard than that generally found within U.S. society without walling itself off from that larger society. The secrets to its success are, I think, first its deeply shared religious faith and second a kind of pragmatism that has allowed the Amish to adapt to the changing economic and social conditions of the surrounding society. Although the Amish have tended to be romanticized by contemporary U.S. culture, close study of this ethnic enclave shows that there have been many mistakes made and false steps taken in its accommodation with its host society and that its success has really been a series of compromises, sometimes painfully arrived at, with the outside world.[32]

Finally, I want to say a few things about another aspect of community about which little is yet known or understood. I speak of communities without propinquity.[33] These comprise a bewildering array of new social forms, including support networks of dyadic relationships, virtual cybercommunities, and communally inspired social movements such as Promise Keepers, Million Man Marches, Honesty Markets, Posses Comitatus, and Ten Commandment Societies. All of these represent eloquent testimonies both to the longing for community and the inventiveness of human beings in finding outlets for this longing. All of them also exemplify the ambivalence between core and boundary that I mentioned previously, the desire to reach out with closer ties to some while all the more effectively shunning others.

The rapid explosion of cybercommunities in the last few years bears eloquent testimony to the high degree of unmet demand for community that there is in the United States. It is now beyond dispute that significant numbers of sane individuals can and do enter into networks of meaningful relationship with people whom they have never met and may never meet. These communities offer advice, comfort, and companionship and have been known to provide effective contexts for the rituals of courtship, the celebration of birth, and the shared mourning of death. At the same time, there have been many instances (some of them well publicized) of betrayal and misrepresentation within these cybercommunities. Because communications are entirely electronic, the opportunities for fraud are nearly unlimited. Those that seem to work best are those that supplement a large amount of cyber communication with at least an annual occasion for face-to-face contact. Even in such situations, online communities have proven to be paradise for free riders and con artists.

The controversies surrounding the Promise Keepers provide a good example of the effects of ambivalence. The primary overt function of the Promise Keepers is to provide an institutionalized mechanism whereby men of diverse ethnic and religious backgrounds can voluntarily hold themselves and one another to a higher moral standard than the one to which they had become accustomed. However, an important latent function of this social movement is to provide its members with a male bonding association, examples of which have been rare in recent U.S. history. Since many of the particular moral issues with which members of Promise Keepers grapple have to do with their members' relationships with women, it is perhaps understandable that some women's groups have been uncomfortable with this male bonding latent function. Because of this functional ambivalence, the Promise Keepers serves simultaneously as a source of integration and a source of segregation in U.S. society.

Honesty Markets are examples of experimentation with moral community in the economic sphere. An outgrowth of the consumer co-op movement of the 1960s, these are buying clubs to which membership is open by invitation only and for which perceived honesty is the major criterion of membership. The idea is to offer a wide range of Price Club-type consumer goods to members at prices even cheaper than Price Clubs can offer, by putting the act of purchasing on the honor system, thereby being able to dispense with most store personnel. Member volunteers provide (supposedly) just enough spot checks of customers exiting the store (with any member not able to show a receipt for all purchased items immediately drummed out of the club in disgrace) to give some teeth to the club's ability to enforce its code of honest consumer behavior. Members are also limited to one visit to the store per week and are limited in the bulk of items they can carry out at any given visit, which presumably reduces the temptation to engage in a single act of nest fouling before moving away. This type of store is still too new for us to be able to draw any conclusions as to its efficacy. Its success will obviously rest heavily on its ability to confer a measurable degree of prestige on its members. Those participants I have talked to have indicated that the price savings, although welcome, are hardly large enough to be worth the various inconveniences of membership. For them, the real payoff comes from being recognized by their peers as being persons honest enough to belong to such a club.

Ten Commandment societies are based on a similar principle, although without the clear economic motivation. Individuals enter into an agreement to voluntarily follow the Ten Commandments and to hold one another to these standards. Here again, the major payoff seems to be the prestige of being accepted as a member of such a society. Understandably, TC societies have been more reluctant to expel members than Honesty Markets because violations of the Ten Commandments are often less visible and less clear-cut than walking out of a store with a quart of milk that hasn't been paid for. A representative of one of these groups acknowledged frankly that compliance among members is far from universal. "The club will have served its purpose," he said, "if it just makes members think twice before violating a commandment."

I think it is clear from this rapid survey of a wide variety of contemporary forms of communal expression that there is no lack of demand for community and no lack of ingenuity in attempts to meet this demand. It is less clear that the communities we know how to develop can be stable over time. Least clear of all is that innovative contemporary communities will serve to knit U.S. society together rather than providing fracture points for its division.

CONCLUSIONS

The empirical data that I have discussed in this chapter suggest a number of hesitations that we should have about communitarianism as a social movement and some areas for further research. But they provide us with no final conclusions to tell us with certainty whether communitarianism as a social movement is viable or whether its goals are desirable. To the extent that communitarians seek merely toothless communities of discourse within which moral issues can be discussed and within which members can mutually exhort one another to maintain high standards of social behavior, I think it is probably safe to say that its goals are benignly attainable but its social effects will be minimal. To the extent, however, that the movement seeks the creation of new communal forms with teeth, its task will be more difficult and its potential impact greater. By "teeth" I mean the ability to enforce consensually agreed-upon normative standards among its members or at least impose costs for violation of these standards. Even if such communities with teeth prove to be viable there is a very real risk that their impact on society will be more negative than positive.

Communitarian writing thus far has paid more attention to political and philosophical theory than it has to sociological data. To progress further, it needs to pay more attention to historical and contemporary evidence of the sort I have discussed in this chapter. In connecting itself to empirical findings, communitarianism will need to stop playing fast and loose with the vital distinction between communities of shared geographical space and nonpropinquitous communities of shared activity or interest. Although communities of both sorts can be found in abundance in contemporary society, a lack of precision in specifying which of these two types is envisioned creates too much confusion when we try to evaluate some of the claims of the communitarian movement empirically. Slipping too casually back and forth between these two forms allows communitarians to claim moral persuasiveness for their envisioned communities without having to fully face up to the attendant problems of oppressiveness and authoritarianism.

A more empirically grounded communitarianism will need to acknowledge that the kind of society it envisions will have costs as well as benefits. Historical and contemporary evidence suggests that it is likely to be a society that is more religious, more ghettoized, and less forgiving than our own.

When I speak of a more religious society, I don't mean to imply that anything in the communitarian agenda threatens our constitutional freedom of religious affiliation. Although people will still remain free to chose from a diverse menu of religions, the evidence suggests that they may well be less free, in a communitarian society, to check "none of the above" without negative consequences. Although from a philosophical perspective, there is no reason to assume that secular moral communities cannot thrive alongside religious moral communities, empirically, the latter are so much more stable that they will eventually crowd out the former.

When I speak of a more ghettoized society, I don't mean to imply that communitarianism will lead us back to the days of enforced residential segregation by race. The designer ghettos or semighettos in which we will increasingly live will be ones chosen by ourselves rather than imposed upon us. And the U.S. population will not be ghettoized solely on the basis of racial or ethnic differences. These criteria will persist but self-segregation on the basis of economic status, lifestyle, and age will be at least as important.

When I speak of a less forgiving society, I don't mean to suggest the likelihood of a return to the harsh colonial morality of the Puritan Commonwealth. The less forgiving nature of this society will not necessarily be as strict as the kind of scarlet letter-imposing communities written about by Nathaniel Hawthorne. But it will be harder in such a society to live down past mistakes and make fresh starts or obtain new deals. Community without accountability breeds free riders, as we have seen. But accountability requires a long collective memory that is slow to erase records of its citizens' past mistakes. In order to give communities moral teeth, we probably will need more extensive individual records that follow you around as you move from one place to another.

If this is the sort of society we think we want, communitarianism provides as plausible a road map as any contemporary social movement instructing us how to achieve it. It doesn't very much appeal to me. But, even if this is not the sort of society we think we want, it would be wise to pay serious attention to the warnings of Etzioni and his fellow communitarians. The alternative—a society bled dry of significant moral community—may turn out, in the long run, to be an even less attractive and less sustainable option.

NOTES

1. Etzioni's writings on this topic have been extensive. In this chapter, I respond mainly to his arguments as presented in two of his books: Amitai Etzioni, *The Spirit of Community: The Reinvention of American Society* (New York: Simon & Schuster, 1993) and Amitai Etzioni, *The New Golden Rule: Community and Morality in a Democratic Society* (New York: Basic Books, 1996). Since most of my specific citations of his work refer to the latter book, I do not annotate these citations in the text of the chapter but simply include page numbers in parentheses within the text. Any such page references should be assumed, therefore, to refer to pages in *The New Golden Rule*.

2. George Homans, *Social Behavior: Its Elementary Forms* (New York: Harcourt Brace Jovanovich, 1974).

3. Andreas Flache and Michael W. Macy, "The Weakness of Strong Ties: Collective Action Failure in a Highly Cohesive Group," in *Evolution of Social Networks*, eds. Patrick Doreian and Frans N. Stokman (Amsterdam: Gordon and Breach, 1997), 19–44. Mark Granovetter, "The Strength of Weak Ties," *American Journal of Sociology* 78 (1973): 1360–80.

4. Jeff Goodwin, "The Libidinal Constitution of a High-Risk Social Movement: Affectual Ties and Solidarity in the Huk Rebellion," *American Sociological Review* 62 (1997): 53–69. James Coleman has also noted this phenomenon as a form of second-order free rider problem in closely bonded collectivities: James S. Coleman, *Foundations of Social Theory* (Cambridge, Mass.: Harvard University Press, 1990). Similar phenomena have also been noted elsewhere in sociological literature: Herman Schmalenbach, "The Sociological Category of Communion," in Talcott Parsons, Edward Shils, Kaspar D. Naegele, and Jesse R. Pitts, *Theories of Society*, vol. 1 (New York: Free Press, 1961), 331–47; Edward Banfield, *The Moral Basis of a Backward Society* (New York: Free Press, 1967).

5. Amitai Etzioni, *A Comparative Analysis of Complex Organizations* (New York: Free Press, 1975).

6. Max Weber, *The Sociology of Religion* (New York: Beacon Press, 1963).

7. Abraham H. Maslow, *Toward a Psychology of Being* (Princeton, N.J.: Van Nostrand, 1968).

8. Hans Gerth and C. Wright Mills, *From Max Weber: Essays in Sociology* (New York: Oxford University Press, 1946).

9. For an example of this, see Arthur Vidich and J. Bensman, *Small Town in Mass Society* (Princeton, N.J.: Princeton University Press, 1958).

10. Georg Simmel, *Conflict and the Web of Group Affiliation* (Glencoe, Ill.: Free Press, 1965).

11. James S. Coleman and Thomas Hoffer, *Public and Private Schools: The Impact of Communities* (New York: Basic Books, 1987).

12. Mancur Olson, *The Logic of Collective Action* (Cambridge, Mass.: Harvard University Press, 1965).

13. Benjamin D. Zablocki, "Exit Cost Analysis: A New Approach to the Scientific Study of Brainwashing," *Nova Religio* 1 (1998): 216–49.

14. But, even with respect to the public stigmatization of former child molesters, the fifty states have been far from uniform in their willingness to require registration and public identification. The belief that one is entitled to a new start after paying for one's mistakes is deeply cherished within U.S. culture. This belief is likely to make it difficult for communities to exercise the long arm of disrepute to prevent people from wiping their slates clean by moving to a new geographical place.

15. Etzioni, *The Spirit of Community*.

16. A. Powell Davies, *The Meaning of the Dead Sea Scrolls* (New York: The New American Library, 1956).

17. Pierre Duparc, "Confraternities of the Holy Spirit and Village Communities in the Middle Ages," in *Lordship and Community in Medieval Europe*, ed. Fredric Cheyette (New York: Holt Rinehart & Winston, 1968), 150–61.

18. William H. Swatos Jr., "Charismatic Calvinism: Forging a Missing Link," in *Charisma, History, and Social Structure*, eds. Ronald M. Glassman and William H. Swatos Jr. (New York: Greenwood, 1986), 73–81.

19. See, for example, Geoffrey Best, *The Oxford Movement: Twelve Years, 1833–1845* (Chicago: University of Chicago Press, 1970), for a discussion of the historical precursor to Moral Rearmament.

20. Arthur A. Goren, *New York Jews and the Quest for Community: The Kehillah Experiment, 1908–1922* (New York: Columbia University Press, 1970).

21. Benjamin D. Zablocki, *Alienation and Charisma: A Study of Contemporary American Communes* (New York: Free Press, 1980).

22. Rosabeth M. Kanter, *Commitment and Community: Communes and Utopias in Sociological Perspective* (Cambridge, Mass.: Harvard University Press, 1972). Benjamin D. Zablocki, *The Joyful Community* (Chicago: University of Chicago Press, 1980).

23. Eliezer Ben-Rafael, *Crisis and Transformation: The Kibbutz at Century's End* (Albany: State University of New York Press, 1997).

24. For a discussion of how the Shakers avoided this problem, see Diane Sasson, "The Shakers: The Adaptation of Prophecy," in *When Prophets Die: The Postcharismatic Fate of New Religious Movements*, ed. Timothy Miller (Albany: State University of New York Press, 1991), 13–28. For a discussion of how the Bruderhof avoided this problem, see Yaacov Oved,

The Witness of the Brothers: A History of the Bruderhof (New Brunswick, N.J.: Transaction, 1996) and Benjamin D. Zablocki, *The Joyful Community* (Chicago: University of Chicago Press, 1980).

25. Lawrence R. Iannaccone, "Why Strict Churches are Strong," *American Journal of Sociology* 99(5) (1994): 1180–211.

26. Haya El Nasser, "Residents Share Values, Sense of Community," *USA Today* (July 15, 1997): 1–2.

27. Andrew Stark, "America, The Gated?" *Wilson Quarterly* 22(1) (1998): 58–79.

28. Edward J. Blakely and Mary Gail Snyder, *Fortress America: Gated Communities in the United States* (Washington, D.C.: Brookings Institution Press, 1997).

29. Blakely and Snyder, *Fortress America*, 161.

30. Avery M. Guest, "The Changing Racial Composition of Suburbs: 1950–1970," *Urban Affairs Quarterly* 14 (1978): 195–206.

31. M. Powell Lawton, "Environments for Older Persons," *The Humanist* (September/October 1977): 20–4.

32. Albert N. Keim, *Compulsory Education and the Amish: The Right Not to Be Modern* (Boston: Beacon, 1975).

33. Melvin Webber, "Order in Diversity: Community without Propinquity," in *Cities and Space: The Future Use of Urban Land*, ed. Loudon Wingo Jr. (Baltimore, Md.: The Johns Hopkins University Press, 1963), 211–38.

6

Defining Community:
A Psychological Perspective

Tom R. Tyler and Robert Boeckmann

In his recent book *The New Golden Rule* Amitai Etzioni[1] addresses a fundamental question that has long preoccupied social scientists, philosophers, and political theorists: "What makes a good society?" Etzioni links this question to an understanding of the desirable features of the political and social communities within a society. He suggests that one way to evaluate a community is to look at the behavior of its citizens: that is, to examine whether those citizens follow social rules and engage in community-oriented behaviors that help the society. A good society should be composed of citizens who both follow social rules and engage in community-oriented behaviors. Our goal in this chapter is to discuss the motivations that lead people to engage in both of these types of behavior. In addition, we will present empirical results of a study that examined the motivations that lead to engagement in community-oriented behavior.

Desirable social behaviors of the type just mentioned can be motivated in many ways. One basic distinction psychologists make is between behavior that is shaped by instrumental judgments about the incentives or punishments associated with engaging in the behavior and behavior that is value-driven. Instrumentally motivated behavior is shaped through the promise of rewards (incentive approaches); through threatened or actual punishments (deterrence approaches); or by both approaches. Value-driven behavior is shaped by people's attitudes and values. These attitudes and values reflect people's internal sense of what they think is appropriate or right for them to do. Value-driven behavior is voluntary in that people are motivated to engage in such behavior by their own internal values, without the promise of reward or the threat of punishment.

One common approach to social regulation within groups, communities, organizations, and societies is to shape citizen behavior instrumentally via incentives or punishments. Such strategies have been described as "command and control,"

"rational choice," or "deterrence" strategies. They seek to encourage socially beneficial behavior through some combination of promising rewards for some behaviors
and/or threatening to or actually punishing undesired behaviors.

In his discussion of the meaning of community Etzioni argues that the degree to
which a society is a "good" society is a reflection of the type of behavior engaged in
by its citizens, and is shaped by the motivations that lead to those behaviors.

Etzioni suggests that "good societies" of the type advocated by communitarians
rely upon having some form of internal values among their citizens that shape people's
social behavior. That is, they are not societies that rely upon incentives or threats of
punishment to secure desired behavior from their citizens. In a "good society" people
engage in socially desirable behaviors because they follow the internal "values in
which they believe, rather than because they fear public authorities or are driven by
economic incentives."[2] In such a "good" society the social order is maintained by
the moral and social values that exist among the population, rather than by "inspectors, auditors, the police, courts, and prisons." People want to engage in socially
desirable behavior because it accords with their own social values about the right
and proper way to behave.

A central issue that Etzioni raises in *The New Golden Rule* is the need to identify
the type of social or community conditions that encourage the development and
maintenance of moral and social values among citizens, and through them the occurrence of cooperative behaviors. To address this issue, we need to follow Etzioni's
lead and focus on understanding the social conditions that facilitate voluntary citizen behavior.

While Etzioni raises this issue as a general philosophical proposition, we will address it empirically through an examination of research exploring the influence of
social values on citizen behaviors. Our analysis considers how citizen judgments about
the community influence whether people engage in socially desirable voluntary behaviors within their community.

We will focus upon voluntary participation within the community. In examining this behavior, we are exploring the degree to which citizens engage in proactive
behaviors designed to help their communities—that is, talk about community issues with neighbors, read about community issues, or attend community meetings.
We will compare such participation to the more formal act of voting, a discretionary prosocial action of a more structured character. We are not concerned with a
second type of behavior, following social rules, since the antecedents of rule following have already been studied and discussed.[3]

We could imagine a wide variety of community conditions that might promote
voluntary cooperation of the type we have outlined. Our goal in this chapter is to
examine the importance of two antecedents of voluntary cooperation that are articulated in Etzioni's writing. In his analysis Etzioni suggests two social conditions
that he thinks might facilitate voluntary citizen behavior. One is the perceived existence of a moral consensus within a community. Another is the belief that the

community consists of people who have shared social bonds or a common ethnic/ social background. We will examine the influence of both of these factors.

While we explore the issues raised by Etzioni, our goal is to present a different view about moral consensus than that advocated by Etzioni. We will argue that people are not especially concerned about whether they think there is a broad moral consensus or common agreement about a set of core moral values. Instead, we will argue that people are concerned that at least some other members of their community agree with and share their personal moral values.

If people are more strongly focused on whether others share their own values than on whether there is a consensus on values, this suggests the possibility that people are more open to moral pluralism than is often suggested—and is suggested by Etzioni. This openness would be possible because people would not be focusing on whether everyone in the community shares a common set of values. Their focus would be on whether at least some others in the community share their views.

In addition, to better understand people's views about morality, our analysis will expand the model proposed by Etzioni. To enlarge the possible antecedents of co-operative behavior explored, we will consider the influence of people's psychological connection to the community, a factor that we have elsewhere argued is important in shaping voluntary behavior toward groups, organizations, and societies.[4]

This psychological connection reflects three aspects of people's feelings about their social connection to their community: the degree to which they draw an important aspect of their sense of themselves from their membership in the community (identification); the degree to which they feel proud to be a member of the community (pride); and the degree to which they feel respected by others in their community (respect).

Our goal is to empirically test Etzioni's argument that judgments about the community encourage desirable citizen behavior. Since prior research has examined the antecedents of rule-following behavior, we will focus on voluntary helping behavior.

THEORETICAL BACKGROUND: THE IMPORTANCE OF A SOCIETY IN WHICH CITIZENS HAVE INTERNAL VALUES

The beginning point of Etzioni's analysis is the argument that a "good society" is one in which people's behavior is largely shaped by people's attention to their own personal moral values, rather than to their concerns about external incentives, such as possible rewards and punishments for their behavior. This aspect of Etzioni's argument is similar to the argument that has recently emerged within the literature on compliance with the law.[5] That argument is that authorities benefit from the existence of internal values that encourage desired behavior among citizens.

Punishment-based systems are primarily used with social regulation, with an emphasis on threatening punishment to produce deterrence. Such systems have the difficulty of requiring surveillance of people's behavior, when people are motivated to hide undesirable behavior. Research suggests that such actual or threatened punishments are seldom sufficient for the control of citizen behavior in democratic societies. This is the case because authorities are not in the position to monitor citizen behavior sufficiently closely to make the risks of rule breaking high enough to engage the fear of being caught and punished for wrongdoing.[6] As a consequence, when legal authorities can only rely on the threat of sanctions to gain compliance with the law, their ability to effectively function is very limited.

An illustration of the difficulties of enforcing laws using only the threat of punishment is provided by recent efforts to control the problem of drug use. Although there have been massive expenditures for police officers and penalties for drug use have been made very high, drug use continues. Why? A recent review of deterrence research on drug use suggests that, at best, 5 percent of the variance in law-related behavior can be explained by variations in the perceived certainty and severity of punishment.[7] This finding is consistent with the results of recent panel studies of deterrence, which suggest that deterrence has only a minor influence on rule-breaking behavior.[8]

Social authorities can function much more effectively when those within society are willing to act voluntarily based on their internal values. In a direct comparison of the influence of the threat of punishment and of internal values on compliance with the law, Tom R. Tyler found that internal values had more influence on people's behavior than did the threat of punishment.[9] Two types of internal values were found to be important: judgments about the morality of lawbreaking and judgments about the legitimacy of the law. Each of these internal values is more important in shaping people's law-related behavior than is the threat of punishment.

These findings from the area of social regulation strongly support Etzioni's argument that the effective functioning of society is facilitated when the people within society have supportive internal values, since people then voluntarily engage in the behaviors society desires. They do not have to be compelled to behave in socially beneficial ways, since desired behavior reflects their own judgment about the behavior that is appropriate or desirable in a given situation. As Etzioni suggests, "Voluntary compliance reflects society members' convictions that rules of behavior which they are expected to follow in their private pursuits, and in directly serving the common good, are values in which they believe."[10] Because people believe in the value of the behaviors they are enacting, they take the personal responsibility for monitoring their behavior. Consequently, society does not need to use as many social resources to monitor and enforce social rules. This frees these collective resources for use in other pursuits.

Etzioni emphasizes that the "spirit" of a society in which people are actively choosing to follow rules because they feel it is right and proper to do so is quite different from that in a society where people must be compelled to behave in particular ways by police officers, judges, inspectors, and other social authorities. In societies with extensive systems of surveillance and control it is possible to maintain social order, although inefficiently and at considerable cost to society and social authorities, but it is difficult to feel that a "good society" is being attained.

This discussion focuses on deterrence, which shapes behavior through the use of threats of punishment. Another model that is similarly instrumental in character involves incentive systems, which focus on rewards instead of punishments. Such systems are widely used by work organizations and by governments seeking to shape people's behavior. Such systems have the benefit of encouraging people to bring their behavior to the attention of authorities. However, such systems do not encourage people to act in innovative, creative, or nonrequired ways. Hence, they have been found to be most effective in situations in which the behaviors required are clearly specifiable and routinized. Incentive systems do not work well when people need to exercise initiative or engage in creative tasks.

Legitimacy versus Morality as a Basis for Society

Research on social regulation indicates that both judgments that rules are moral and judgments that authorities are legitimate support voluntary compliance with the law.[11] However, the role of these two types of judgment points to very different approaches to constructing a "good" society of the type outlined by Etzioni. The literature on the legitimacy of authority focuses on understanding why people defer to government. The literature on morality focuses on why people defer to their judgment about what is right or wrong.

This distinction between deference to government and deference to personal moral values is by no means an abstract one. It speaks directly to the viability of pluralistic societies. If a core of common moral values is required for a society to be effective, then pluralistic societies are at risk. Consider the case of the United States. Our society is founded on the belief that a common society could be composed of people who had different religious and moral values. It is believed that those people could be held together through a common commitment to a governmental system and their obligations to that system. If people have to believe that a law is morally right to obey it, a pluralistic society has problems. The success of such a society requires a consensus on core moral values. The need for such a consensus on moral values is contrary to the idea of value pluralism.

The Procedural Basis of Government Legitimacy

Because of the problems of trying to manage a pluralistic society based on moral consensus, the U.S. government bases the legitimacy of government authorities on procedural grounds. That is, we encourage people to defer to societal authorities because of the way those authorities make decisions. By focusing on the procedures of government, the problem of agreement about the moral correctness of government decisions and policies is minimized.

Studies of the psychology of legitimacy suggest that the legitimacy of authorities can be maintained by the belief that those authorities exercise their authority through decision-making procedures that are judged to be fair. This procedural justice effect has been replicated in studies of legal, political, and managerial authorities. The procedural justice effect is quite robust and occurs when outcomes are important and important issues are at stake.

In his discussion of "procedural commitments" Etzioni suggests that commitments to procedures that occur without developing a consensus about the right or appropriate answer to underlying value conflicts are unstable. However, research on the influence of procedural justice judgments on people's willingness to defer to authorities suggests the contrary conclusion that procedural commitments are often quite robust. At least within U.S. society, people seem to focus primarily on issues of procedure when judging the legitimacy of government institutions and authorities.

Consider the specific issue of abortion policy. Tom R. Tyler and Gregory Mitchell studied the willingness of a random sample of adults in the Bay Area of northern California to defer to the abortion decisions made by the United States Supreme Court.[12] They found that people's moral views about abortion had little influence on whether they were willing to defer to the Court's abortion decisions. Deference was primarily shaped by evaluations of the fairness of Court decision-making procedures. If citizens judged that the Supreme Court made its decisions in fair ways, they felt obligated to defer to those decisions, irrespective of their own views about what was morally right or wrong.

A more extreme example that illustrates the same point is Stanley Milgram's study on obedience to authority.[13] In that study, participants were ordered to shock another person in the guise of a teacher-learner situation. Many did so, even delivering what they believed to be high and potentially lethal levels of shock. However, those delivering the shock did not want to do so and manifested many signs of stress. Their behavior did not occur because being told to engage in the behavior led them to believe that the behavior was the correct or appropriate thing to do. Instead, participants felt that their role in the study required them to engage in the behavior in response to "legitimate" orders from the experimenter. Such behavior is fundamentally different in character from that which might result for the development of a consensus about appropriate or desirable behavior.

Hence, if our concern is about the legitimacy of authorities, a focus on procedural issues is quite reasonable. Proceduralism underlies legitimacy, and does so quite robustly. To a striking degree, people defer their own moral judgments and personal and group interests to follow the directives of legitimate authorities. And they judge legitimacy in procedural terms.

Because of the power of proceduralism, pluralistic societies such as the United States can function in the absence of a set of shared core moral values. They can do so because citizens defer to government based on the procedures through which government exercises its authority. Without such a procedural underpinning of government legitimacy, it would be difficult, if not impossible, for government to be effective in the United States. In the case of abortion, for example, those who viewed abortion as "murder" would simply disregard the government and seek a society in which their moral views were enacted as public policy. Conversely, those who believe that abortion is morally acceptable would expect their moral views to be enacted as public policy. Such an approach to government quickly leads to discontent, conflict, and civil war. Instead, both sides of this emotional controversy have generally deferred to the framework of government established in our society.

This discussion in the empirical literature ignores Etzioni's normative arguments, which suggest that proceduralism is a value "in and of itself." Drawing on the work of Jurgen Habermas, Etzioni suggests that we can evaluate the normative "rightness" of procedures that involve dialogues among citizens to construct shared moral values. From the perspective of moral philosophy, it seems clear that we can make normative judgments about what constitute fair and unfair procedures for conducting dialogues about moral right and wrong. These judgments can be distinct from the consensus or lack of consensus about moral values that results from those values. However, these normative arguments are quite separate from an empirical examination of the consequences of procedural variations.

The empirical literature makes clear that people are very much influenced by their evaluations of the fairness of decision-making procedures. Hence, subjective normative evaluations have important behavioral implications for the viability of society.

Morality and Moral Consensus

There are clearly additional potential benefits to developing a moral consensus about the desired course of action within a given society beyond the benefits of engaging in normatively appropriate procedures for dialogue about moral consensus. One benefit is that judgments of moral right and wrong are found to have an impact on behavior that is beyond the impact of evaluations of legitimacy. Hence, if people genuinely believe that a social policy is morally correct and feel that it is being articulated by a legitimate social authority, their levels of compliance with that policy should be very high. In addition, as we have noted, their motivations for compliance will be internal and compliance will be voluntary.

Past discussions of social authority have focused on government legitimacy because personal morality can be a double-edged sword in terms of the impact of individual behavior on society. While morality facilitates acceptance of social decisions when people think the decisions are moral, to those whose moral views are violated by a law, the motivation to *not* comply is equally strong. This illustrates the problem of basing social authority on morality. In such a situation, those whose moral values are violated will be less inclined to obey the law.

EMPIRICAL ANALYSIS

The empirical aspect of this chapter will focus on issues of perceived moral consensus, rather than on citizens' perceived obligations to follow laws or social rules. The same logic that underlies the importance of legitimacy to the effectiveness of government authorities underlies the value of moral consensus. If people believe that the ethical or moral climate of society is appropriate and reasonable they will be more likely to voluntarily engage themselves in society. Such engagement is an important underpinning of Etzioni's vision of a "good society." As a consequence, society should benefit from the belief that there is a moral consensus within the group. We will test empirically this suggestion that perceived moral consensus enhances voluntary behavior.

Etzioni argues for the benefits of having a developed consensus about core social values. How might such a consensus be developed? In his view, through "moral dialogues." These dialogues are fair procedures for discussing moral values. Etzioni suggests that having fair ways to develop a moral consensus about policy issues is an important part of a "good society." Etzioni advocates such dialogues and presents rules of engagement that he argues will enhance the likelihood of their success. These rules "basically reflect the tenet that one should act on the recognition that the conflicting parties are members of one and the same community."[14]

The focus on rules of engagement links the idea of moral dialogues to the issues of procedure that have already been shown to underlie the legitimacy of governments. To some degree, in other words, the ability to develop a consensus about the right policy for handling a particular societal issue is linked to discussing that policy, using procedures that all of the parties involved in the discussion will regard as dignified, respectful, and fair. These procedures will facilitate the development of consensus by encouraging commitment to the procedure.

Other aspects of procedures are also important to the development of consensus in Etzioni's analysis, because they facilitate the process of decision making. One example of a key procedural element important in decision making is participation. All parties to a fair procedure want to feel that they have a chance to present their arguments. This is also a key to a rule of engagement for developing consensus, since people need to exchange information as a beginning basis for establishing consensus. Hence, fair procedures facilitate the development of moral consensus both by encouraging commitment to the process and by facilitating the effective making of consensus decisions.

Interestingly, studies of what people mean by a fair procedure for decision making indicate that citizens typically consider treatment with dignity and respect by societal authorities to be the key component of a fair procedure. Hence, the issues that Etzioni mentions in his discussion of moral consensus accord well with the findings of the procedural justice literature that examines the psychological underpinnings of the legitimacy of social authorities.

To build support for accepting a policy as a solution to a social issue, people need to feel that their "needs, wants, and interests" are being respected and taken seriously in the decision-making process. Similarly, people need to feel that others are sincerely trying to consider and take account of their arguments during the dialogue that leads to a common policy.

However, despite these similarities between the procedural basis of political authority and the procedural basis of moral consensus, it is important to clearly state the difference between deference to legitimate authorities, whose legitimacy is based upon procedural grounds, and the development of a moral consensus about the appropriate solution to a social problem.

In the previously mentioned study of abortion,[15] for example, people deferred to the Supreme Court and empowered it to make abortion policy if they felt that the Court made policy using fair procedures. However, people's views about the morality of abortion were not changed by the *Roe v. Wade* decision. The Court's decision, in other words, did not stimulate a moral consensus about values among Americans. And we would not necessarily expect that it would, since it had none of the properties of a consensus-creating procedure of the type outlined by Etzioni. Instead, a Supreme Court decision is, by its very nature, an authoritative pronouncement to be accepted or rejected based on loyalty to the institutions, authorities, and rules of government.

The Tyler and Mitchell study found that people's assessments of the Court's views were unrelated to their own personal sense of the moral right and wrong of abortion. Hence, while it has been argued that the Supreme Court can sometimes sway public views about what is the appropriate moral stance to take over some issue, that was not true in the case of abortion. In this case, people deferred to government, but did not change their moral values. Hence, abortion policy illustrates how a procedural approach proceeds without necessarily developing a moral consensus about the substance of a particular policy. People defer to a policy because of their feelings of obligation to the authority that makes the policy. The authority "authorizes" the policy, substituting its institutional legitimacy for the legitimacy that flows from people's judgment that the policy is morally appropriate.[16]

A dialogue to develop moral consensus of the type advocated by Etzioni has higher ambitions than simply gaining deference. It seeks "true" consensus about moral values. Etzioni wants people to actually agree on a set of core values. This involves agreeing about what areas will be covered by core values and which are open to different individual values. Within the core areas, people must then agree on what the correct core values will be. For example, if abortion falls within core values, will society be against abortion or in favor of it?

This higher aspiration for a "good society" suggests the need to go beyond pluralism. It raises the interesting and important question of whether a good society must reach agreement about core moral values. If it must, then the traditional openness of U.S. society to diverse values may pose problems for the good society. Consider the example of American attitudes toward homosexuality. Many Americans take the position that, while they personally disapprove of homosexuality, everyone's personal life is their own concern. Such a view is supported by the U.S. Constitution, which defines spheres within which people have the "right" to act as they personally choose. In other words, the Constitution defines our society in a pluralistic way. Hence, what citizens view as moral deviance by others is seen as outside of their universe of societal concerns. People do not, in other words, view developing a common attitude about the morality of homosexuality as necessary to living in U.S. society. However, a consensus model requires decisions about other people's values and lifestyles.

We will empirically test the argument that a core set of moral values matters. However, we need to distinguish this question from the societal equivalent of the procedural argument about government decision making. The equivalent question involves studying people's views about the fairness of the cooperative decision-making procedures through which a community creates a moral consensus. In other words, there is an important question that involves judgments about the procedures through which a moral consensus is arrived at that is distinct from what that moral consensus is. We might imagine that people would defer to procedural justice in the process of consensus building, as they do in the case of government.

Perceived Moral Consensus

We are not addressing the impact of the procedure through which a moral consensus is developed in this empirical analysis. Instead, we are looking at whether people feel that there is a moral consensus—however arrived at. We are looking at people's views about the content of public morality, not about how that common morality is developed.

Does having a consensus about core values facilitate having a "good society?" We can test this argument here on a psychological level by asking whether perceived moral consensus influences citizen's voluntary behavior in ways that facilitate a "good society." To do so, we need to have criteria that identify behaviors that represent a "good society." We will focus on one such criterion: whether people voluntarily participate in society. Voluntary participation was assessed in two ways. First, whether people informally participate in their neighborhood. Second, whether they vote.

Our exploration of the influence of perceived moral consensus is based on interviews with a group of 166 citizens living in the East Bay area of northern California. These citizens were a random sample of adults living in the East Bay, and they were selected using a two-stage random sampling process—random selection of homes and random selection of people within those homes. Of those residents identified as potential respondents, 71 percent were successfully interviewed over the telephone.

The mean age of the sample was forty-three. The respondents were 43 percent male. Sixty-six percent were European-American; 20 percent African American; 7 percent Hispanic/Latino; and 6 percent Asian American. Sixty-one percent of respondents had a bachelor's degree or higher, and 39 percent made more than $50 thousand per year. Finally, 49 percent described themselves as liberals, 34 percent as moderates, and 17 percent as conservatives.

Respondents were interviewed about their views concerning the nature of society. Two frames of reference were used. Some questions asked respondents to consider conditions in their community. The scope of community was not defined. Other questions asked respondents about conditions in California. The items framed in these two ways were found to generally fall together empirically, suggesting that both frames evoked similar feelings about respondent's "communities." For this reason, these two types of items will be used interchangeably.

Voluntary informal participation in the community was established by asking respondents how frequently they: "attended public meetings on community or school issues (33 percent very or somewhat frequently)"; "met with neighbors for a social evening (39 percent very or somewhat frequently)"; "communicated their views about local issues to community leaders (32 percent very or somewhat frequently)"; and "discussed their views about local issues with their neighbors (27 percent very or somewhat frequently)." Voting was established by first asking respondents if they were eligible to vote. Those eligible to vote were asked whether they had voted in the last major election (98 percent were eligible to vote; of those 82 percent had voted).

Moral Consensus and Participation

The first issue we address is the degree to which people's judgments about whether there is a value consensus within their community shape whether they voluntarily participate in that community. The underlying assumption is that the degree of voluntary participation indicates, to at least some degree, whether that community is a "good society." Hence, our concern is with the influence of perceived moral consensus on the existence of "good" societies.

This relationship between perceived moral consensus and voluntary participation was tested by asking people whether they believed that a moral consensus existed within their own community, that is whether they felt that people agreed with each other about what is right and wrong. Respondents were asked to agree or disagree that "There is a lot of agreement about what is right and wrong nowadays"; "There are so many different points of view in California today, it is hard to know what is right and wrong behavior (reverse scored)"; and "You have similar values to most Californians."

Moral consensus was distinguished from the degree to which people felt that others shared their moral values. To establish this latter aspect of moral values, respondents were asked to agree or disagree that "Others in your community have similar values to your own."

Respondents were also asked if they felt that moral values shaped society and the social behavior of citizens. This issue was addressed in two ways. First, people were asked whether they felt that people in their community had moral values. Second, they were asked whether those social values could be appealed to in efforts to change other people's behaviors. Without the ability to make moral appeals that could change people, seeking to make or enforce a moral consensus would be of little effectiveness.

The degree to which the respondent felt that moral values are strong was assessed by asking, "Do you agree that social bonds between family members are not as strong as they used to be (reverse scored)?"; "Do you agree that many teenagers lack a sense of moral direction (reverse scored)?"; "Do you agree that the breakdown of the family has led many children to grow up without knowing what is right and wrong? (reverse scored)"; "Do you agree that society has become more violent and dangerous as traditional moral values have decayed? (reverse scored)"; "Do you agree that families do not do enough to discipline their children? (reverse scored)"; and "Do you agree that teenagers in gangs will assault a person like you without feeling any guilt or remorse? (reverse scored)."

Respondents were also asked whether citizens had moral values that could be effectively appealed to in seeking to change other people's behavior. The questions used to operationalize this idea asked about social mechanisms that might be used to deal with deviants in the community. Respondents were asked to indicate their assessment of the likely behavioral change effectiveness of "publishing the names of deviants in their communities so that their friends and neighbors are aware of their crimes," of "requiring that offenders make public apologies," and of "using schools to encourage values of mutual respect and discipline."

The impact of these judgments about moral consensus on voluntary participation in the community is shown in table 6.1. The table shows regression analyses in which indices of voluntary participation are the dependent variables. Judgments of moral consensus are included as independent variables and used to predict voluntary participation.

The regression equations that are shown in table 6.1 indicate that the degree of perceived moral consensus within the community influences both indices of voluntary participation. In the case of participation in voluntary activities within the community, people are more likely to participate when they believe that other people have moral values that can be appealed to in change efforts (beta = .16, p < .05). In addition, people are influenced by whether they think that others share their own moral values (beta = .22, p < .01). There is no direct influence of whether or not people think there is a moral consensus (beta = .06, n.s.).

Voting behavior was shaped by people's views about whether or not a consensus about moral values exists within their community (beta = .16, p < .05) and by whether or not people believe that others share their moral values (beta = .36, p <.001).

These findings suggest a very different image of the importance of moral consensus than that which is outlined by Etzioni. Consider the case of voluntary informal community participation. Whether there is a perceived moral consensus had no impact on whether people participate in their communities. Instead, people were influenced by whether or not they think that there are other people in the community who share their values.

Interestingly, people are influenced by two factors. The first is whether they believe that moral values have an impact on society, in that moral appeals can change

Table 6.1   Moral Consensus and Participation in the Community

	Voluntarily Participate?	Vote?
Do people generally agree with each other about what is right and wrong?	.06	.16*
Do other people agree with you about what is right and wrong?	.22**	.36***
Are moral values strong?	.08	.11
Do appeals to values work to change people?	.16*	.13
adj. R-squared	7%**	15%***

Entries are beta weights in an equation in which all terms are entered at the same time. Each reflects the relative importance of the independent contribution of the variable it represents. The adjusted R-squared terms reflect the percentage of the variance in the dependent variable explained by all of the variables considered at the same time.

High scores indicate participating; believing that people agree with each other about right/wrong; believing that others agree with you; believing that moral values are strong; and believing that appeals to values work.

*p < .05; **p < .01; ***p < .001.

others. The second factor is whether people think that at least some others in the community share their values. That is, people do not focus on whether all members in the community share common values. Instead, they are influenced by whether they think that there are others in the community who agree with them about moral values. This suggests that people are influenced by whether they think they are part of a subgroup of the community that has a particular perspective. While this study does not directly address the issue, people might define such a group as a religious or ethnic subgroup. Further, people participate more when they believe that others can be changed via appeals to their values.

Moral consensus does have an impact. It influences whether or not people vote. So, more formal participation of the type represented by voting in elections is responsive to whether or not people think that there is a consensus about core moral values among the members of their community. This finding supports Etzioni's view about core moral values.

These findings suggest that people are open to a morally pluralistic society. Their participation does not depend on feeling that people within society agree about core moral values. If it did, then a society such as the United States would potentially be difficult or impossible to maintain. Our society is based on the belief that agreement about core moral values is not a prerequisite to effective social functioning. These findings support the argument that such a pluralistic society is possible by suggesting that people are reacting to whether or not they think that at least some others in society share their values, not to whether there is general agreement about commonly held core moral values.

Inclusion within the Community

Up to this point our focus has been on the respondent's view of society—the perspective emphasized by Etzioni in *The New Golden Rule*. That is, we have been examining how people's views about the nature of their community—that is, the degree of perceived value consensus in that community—influences their willingness to participate in their own community.

There is a second potentially important issue that flows from psychological research on people's relationships to their communities. That issue is how people view their own relationship to the community. Here the focus is on people's views about the nature of their connection to the community, not upon the nature of the community itself. Of course, we would expect that people's views about the nature of the community would be related to their feelings concerning their connection to the community. Nonetheless, we can explore these issues separately.

Three indices of status are important as possible elements in evaluating one's personal connection to the community.[17] First is people's views about the status of their community—how people evaluate the things they feel their community stands for and represents (pride in the community). This judgment reflects the degree to which people agree with and view as personally important the principles and values of their community. The second index is people's views about whether they are valued and respected members of their community (respect from the community). This judgment reflects people's assessment of what the community thinks of them. Does the community include them within its boundaries, as citizens entitled to citizen rights and decent and respectful treatment from others? The final index is the degree that people use the community to define themselves (identification with the community). To some citizens membership in the community is central to their definitions of themselves, while to others it is peripheral.

Pride

The issue of community status reflects the extent to which people think that the values, norms, and principles that their community represents are positive and favorable. Studies suggest that people's pride in the groups, organizations, and communities to which they belong shapes their voluntary acceptance of group rules and norms. Hence, people voluntarily follow the expectations of the community when they regard the community as an important and valuable one of which to be a member.

Pride in the community was established by asking people to agree or disagree that: "You are proud to tell others about the community you live in" and "Your community is a great place to live."

Respect

The issue of status in a community is also an important one for people. Communities are not simply collections of people who live within a particular set of geographical boundaries. Communities are socially created entities within which some people are included and others are excluded. This definition of the social boundaries of the community is important, since societies are more willing to deny material benefits, procedural protections, and entitlement to treatment with dignity and respect to people they define as outside of their community.

Historically, persecution of minorities and other "deviants" has typically occurred after there have been efforts to define potential victims as outside of the scope of the community and, hence, outside of the boundaries to which the rules of justice apply. Further, those who engage in hurting others, typically engage in a variety of types of psychological activity to justify their behavior. One of the major forms of justification is "dehumanization," the development of beliefs that the victim is not a member of one's community. Hence, people who live in geographical proximity are very concerned to have evidence that they are included within the social community and entitled to its rights and protections.

Recent psychological research supports the argument that people are influenced by their assessments of their own status within the community. Those who feel respected by the community are found to voluntarily engage in prosocial behaviors that benefit the group. Such actions are often called "extra-role" behaviors, since they are discretionary behaviors that are individually motivated and unique. Each person engages in the unique pattern of actions that they feel will help their community.

Respect from others was assessed by asking people whether the other people within their community: "respect their values," "respect what they have accomplished in their lives," and "approve of how they live their lives."

Identification

Identification with a community reflects the degree to which people draw their sense of themselves from a community. Highly identified people make greater use of the community to define themselves and are, as a result, more invested in the well-being of the community. Those who are more strongly identified with a group, organization, community, or society should do more to help it do well as a community. Highly identified individuals are more invested in the group and are more motivated to undertake voluntary action designed to help it.

Identification with the community was established by asking respondents how important being a member of the community was to "the way they think of themselves as a person." Do people's feelings about their status shape their behavior toward the community? To test this argument the influence of the three aspects of status was examined. The results, shown in table 6.2, suggest that status judgments do influence voluntary behavior on behalf of the community. In the case of participation, people are more likely to participate in a community when they feel respected by others in that community and when they identify more strongly with that community. With voting behavior, people are more likely to vote when they feel proud of the community and when they identify more strongly with it.

Table 6.2 Inclusion within the Community and Participation in the Community

	Voluntarily Participate?	Vote?
Are you proud to be a community member?	−.01	.19*
Are you respected by others in the community?	.21**	.04
Do you identify with the community?	.24**	.19*
adj. R-squared	11%***	7%**

Entries are beta weights in an equation in which all terms are entered at the same time. Each reflects the relative importance of the independent contribution of the variable it represents. The adjusted R-squared terms reflect the percentage of the variance in the dependent variable explained by all of the variables considered at the same time.

High scores indicate participating, voting, feeling proud, feeling respected by others, and identifying with the community.

*p < .05; **p < .01; ***p < .001.

The pattern of influence found mirrors that could be predicted based on prior status-based studies.[18] While voting is a voluntary behavior, it is part of the norms of society that one ought to vote (i.e., voting is a duty and people who fail to vote feel that they have neglected an important civic duty). Hence, we would expect that those who feel pride in their community would be more likely to follow this community norm and vote.

On the other hand, informal participation in one's community is not a clear normative requirement. Such participation is more open to discretion, and people who do not take to their neighbors do not typically feel guilty or uncivic as a consequence. Such discretionary behaviors are typically strongly shaped by the respect one feels from others. That is also the case here, with participation linked to the respect people feel they are receiving from others in the community.

Finally, those who identify more strongly with the community engage in both types of voluntary behavior—voting and informal participation—to a greater degree. Since they are more invested in the community, they would be expected to voluntarily act to develop and maintain it. And the findings of this study suggest that they do so.

These findings about the antecedents of voluntary participation in the community support the prior argument that people are primarily concerned about whether there are others in the community who share their views rather than with whether there is a moral consensus within the community. In this case, people are influenced by whether they think that others in the community respect their values and lifestyle. People want to believe that their views are respected by the community, but not necessarily that they are shared.

These findings suggest considerable support for moral pluralism among those studied. We do not find that people react negatively to believing that there is no moral consensus within their society. Instead, they react negatively to believing (1) that they are alone in their community in endorsing the values that they hold and (2) that their views are not respected by others in the community. This set of beliefs supports the arguments for a pluralistic society composed of a variety of subgroups that respect each other's views and lifestyles. Such a community requires that each group be willing to think about and be persuaded by the arguments of others, and that factor is also found to be important in this study.

The findings about respect that we have outlined should not be confused with the ideas of political or social tolerance for others. People are expressing the desire to have their views respected by others, not merely tolerated. Hence, the findings about respect should not be confused with the belief that others should be allowed to engage in their own desired lifestyle, even though others see it as being disgusting or intrinsically undesirable. People are looking for respect and acceptance from others, not mere tolerance. On the other hand, they are not concerned about whether everyone shares their beliefs.

Social Bonds

While social bonds are less strongly emphasized by Etzioni in his discussion of the "good society," his analysis of communities does recognize the potential importance of social bonds in promoting a "good society." People may participate in communities not because of a perceived consensus about moral values but because of interpersonal connections and loyalties. In other words, it may not be moral dialogue that is needed, but interpersonal efforts to build a net of social friendships and perceived interpersonal loyalties among the members of a community. This argument is consistent with Robert Putnam's argument that associations whose purpose is not political form a framework within which democracy works. For example, people who bowl with others are better citizens.[19]

Is it important that people feel that they have social bonds with others in their community? We test this argument by examining the importance of three types of social bonds in shaping voluntary participation within communities. Those three types of social bonds are trust in other people, the belief that the people in one's community share a common social background, and the belief that people have interpersonal ties.

Trust in people was established by asking respondents whether "most people are basically good and kind," "most people are basically honest," "if a person does not look out for themselves, no one else will" (reverse scored), "given the opportunity, most people will take advantage of you (reverse scored)," and "life is basically a struggle for survival (reverse scored)."

Whether people think that others in their community share a common social background was established by asking whether people agree or disagree that "there are so many different types of people in California" that (1) people have very little in common, (2) there are many places where it is hard to feel safe, (3) it is dangerous to rely upon others, and (4) it is hard to know if others would help you if you were in trouble (all reverse scored).

Whether people are regarded as having shared social bonds was established by asking respondents to agree or disagree that "many of the people in your community are good friends with each other," "people in your community help each other in times of need," "if you fell on hard times, you could count on members of your community to help you," and "the people in your community are working together on the problems they face."

The influence of beliefs about social bonds on voluntary behavior is shown in table 6.3. The findings indicate that social bonds have an important influence on whether or not people engage in voluntary behavior in their communities. Those respondents who feel that social bonds do not exist are less likely to voluntarily participate in society. Neighborhood participation declines when respondents feel that others do not share their social background (beta = .23, p < .01) and do not have ties with one another (beta = .39, p < .001). Further, people are less likely to vote if they do not trust others in their community (beta = .20, p < .01) and do not feel that people have ties with one another (beta = .17, p < .05).

These findings suggest that thinking that others in society share a common social background encourages voluntary participation in society. When people think others share their own background, they are more likely to indicate that there is agreement about morality within the community (r = .32, p < .001), and that moral values are strong (r = .36, p < .001). This social force is not supportive of pluralism in society, since it suggests that societies are most effective when they are homogenous in terms of people's backgrounds.

However, the findings suggest a distinct influence of social bonds upon voluntary participation in society. This finding is encouraging, since social bonds can be created and built across group boundaries. As we might expect, people are more likely to say that they have social bonds with others when they say that others share their social background (r = .16, p < .05). However, there is a stronger influence of whether

Table 6.3   Social Bonds and Participation in the Community

	Voluntarily Participate?	Vote?
Is there a shared social background?	.23**	.04
Do you trust others in the community?	.06	.20**
Do people have social bonds?	.39***	.17*
adj. R-squared	20%***	9%***

Entries are beta weights in an equation in which all terms are entered at the same time. Each reflects the relative importance of the independent contribution of the variable it represents. The adjusted R-squared terms reflect the percentage of the variance in the dependent variable explained by all of the variables considered at the same time.

High scores indicate participating in activities, voting, believing that there is a shared social background, trusting others, and feeling that there are social bonds between people.

*p < .05; **p < .01; ***p < .001.

people feel that some others in their community share their moral values (r = .52, p < .001), and of whether they think others in the community respect their values (r = .53, p < .001). As this finding suggests, thinking that others share one's moral values and feeling respected by others in the community are closely related (r = .51, p < .001).

These two patterns suggest two distinct effects on behavior. Voluntary cooperation with the community is enhanced by believing that the community shares a common social background (r = .27, p < .001) and by thinking that one has social bonds with others in the community (r = .41, p < .001). However, the perception of shared social bonds has a stronger psychological impact. It encourages identification with the community (r = .36), pride in the community (r = .59), and feelings of respect from the community (r = .53). In contrast, thinking that one shares a social background with others in the community has little impact on identification (r = .10), pride (r = .25), or respect (r = .09). In terms of the quality of a "good society," a society based upon social bonds seems much more robust than a community based upon shared background.

Similarly, thinking that at least some others in the community have your moral values has a strong psychological impact. It leads to identification with the community (r = .35), pride in the community (r = .48), and feeling respected by the community (r = .51). Judgments about whether the community shares common moral values have less impact on identification (r = .28), pride (r = .11), and respect (r = .13). Thinking that moral values exist in the community has little impact on psychological connection to the community (average r = .04). Finally, believing that appeals to moral values can shape behavior influences identification (r = .32), but has little impact on pride (r = .08) or respect (r = .01).

These findings suggest that engagement in one's community is linked to feeling that one's values are respected by the community and that others in the community have similar values. These feelings reflect the desire to be a respected member of the community, rather than a desire to have a community of common values.

SUMMARY

In his book *The New Golden Rule* Etzioni tries to identify the components of a "good society." He then discusses how those components might be developed or maintained. One important component is that most citizens engage in voluntary behavior that helps their community.

This analysis suggests that three aspects of people's views about communities encourage them to voluntarily participate in those communities. These three aspects are views about morality in society, status judgments that define people's relationships with the community, and views about social bonds in the community.

Etzioni emphasizes the value of the belief that society shares core moral values. This argument suggests the need to define core values within civil society. Doing so would make civil society different from the traditional form of U.S. government, which emphasizes moral pluralism held together by a state authority that governs based upon procedurally created institutional legitimacy. The finding of this study suggest that people are less concerned about moral consensus that is suggested in Etzioni's analysis. Instead, people are concerned about having their views respected by others in the community and having some others in the community that share their values, that is, being part of a subgroup with shared values.

These findings suggest one possible model for civil society—a set of distinct groups that respect one another. Such a model of civil society puts an emphasis upon a mutual respect among social groups for each other's lifestyle and values. Instead of seeking a method to achieve a value consensus, in other words, we might better be seeking methods for developing mutual respect among the members of different groups within society.

NOTES

I would like to thank several anonymous reviewers for their comments on this chapter. I also received valuable feedback during a presentation of this paper at the Communitarian Summit, February 27, 1999, Washington, D.C.

1. Amitai Etzioni, *The New Golden Rule: Community and Morality in a Democratic Society* (New York: Basic Books, 1996).

2. Etzioni, *The New Golden Rule,* 86.

3. Tom R. Tyler, *Why People Obey the Law* (New Haven, Conn.: Yale University Press, 1990).

4. Robert J. Boeckmann and Tom R. Tyler, "The Antecedents and Consequences of Civic Engagement," Unpublished manuscript, Flinders University; and Tom R. Tyler, "Why People Cooperate with Organizations," in *Research in Organizational Behavior,* ed. Barry Staw and Robert Sutton (Greenwich, Conn.: JAI Press, 1999), 201–46.

5. Tyler, *Why People Obey the Law;* Tom R. Tyler, "Procedural Fairness and Compliance with the Law," *Swiss Journal of Economics and Statistics* 133 (1997): 219–40; Tom R. Tyler, "Citizen Discontent with Legal Procedures," *American Journal of Comparative Law* 45 (1997): 869–902; Tom R. Tyler, "Compliance with Intellectual Property Laws, *Journal of International Law and Politics* 28 (1997): 101–15; Tom R. Tyler, "Public Mistrust of the Law: A Political Perspective," *University of Cincinnati Law Review* 66 (1998): 847–75.

6. H. Laurence Ross, *Deterring the Drinking Driver: Legal Policy and Social Control* (Lexington, Mass.: Heath, 1982).

7. Robert J. MacCoun, "Drugs and the Law: A Psychological Analysis of Drug Prohibition," *Psychological Bulletin* 113 (1993): 497–512.

8. Raymond Paternoster, Linda Saltzman, Gordon Waldo, and Theodore Chiricos, "Perceived Risk and Social Control: Do Sanctions Really Deter?" *Law and Society Review* 17 (1984): 457–79.

9. Tyler, *Why People Obey the Law.*

10. Etzioni, *The New Golden Rule,* 121.

11. Tyler, *Why People Obey the Law.*

12. Tom R. Tyler and Gregory Mitchell, "Legitimacy and the Empowerment of Discretionary Legal Authority," *Duke Law Journal* 43 (1994): 703–814.

13. Stanley Milgram, *Obedience to Authority* (New York: Free Press, 1965).

14. Etzioni, *The New Golden Rule*, 104.

15. Tyler and Mitchell, "Legitimacy and the Empowerment," 703–814.

16. Herbert C. Kelman and V. Lee Hamilton, *Crimes of Obedience* (New Haven, Conn.: Yale University Press, 1989).

17. Tyler, "Why People Cooperate with Organizations.

18. Tyler, "Why People Cooperate with Organizations."

19. Robert Putnam, "Bowling Alone: America's Declining Social Capital," *Journal of Democracy* 6 (1995): 65–78.

7

Community and Its Discontents: Politics and Etzioni's *The New Golden Rule*

Wilson Carey McWilliams

The founder of a significant movement and an important presence in U.S. public life, Amitai Etzioni exemplifies political engagement, but he looks beyond the barricades, seeking first principles and things that endure. It is no surprise, consequently, that his argument for a "community of communities," while thoroughly contemporary, also stands in a grand U.S. tradition, linked to Randolph Bourne's hope for a "trans-national" America and Josiah Royce's precept, "be loyal to loyalty," as well as to that founding mystery, *e pluribus unum*.[1] And as a critic, Etzioni is admirable in recognizing and confronting the shortcomings of intellectual fashion, even among his sometime allies.

The recent political vogue accents America's plurality, with calls for "multiculturalism" echoed, in a somewhat distorted way, by postmodernist suspicions of the universal. But while Aristotle warned against trying to reduce the sounds of political society to a mere unison, he knew that harmony requires an even more complicated discipline.[2] In itself, diversity is often only the occasion for domination, following the old maxim, *divide et impera*, or for civil strife—witness Yugoslavia, where the collapse of Communist hegemony has led to competing ethnic cleansings. It is pretty generally recognized that in any political society, some institutions must reliably prevail in cases of conflict, "or else," John Locke noted, "it is impossible it should act or continue one body, *one community*."[3] Yet Locke appealed to the natural rule of majorities—or, more precisely, to their "greater force"—and majorities can repress or tyrannize, just as a political society can include a variety of peoples while maintaining that some are naturally superior to others, or at least entitled to rule.[4] Etzioni goes a step further in realizing that a "community of communities," like a mosaic, must be *framed* and *glued*, that is to say that it requires both institutions and attachments, norms as well as procedures. His good society is not morally neutral; it depends on a fairly substantial creed.

111

An inclusive democracy—especially one that, like America in G. K. Chesterton's describing, seeks to make a nation "literally out of any old nation that comes along"—is accepting, paradoxically, because it is judgmental.[5] Democratic inclusiveness, as Abraham Lincoln taught us, is dedicated to equality as a ruling norm, a principle that, while it embraces all communities, denies that any of them is entitled to public rank. Equality, as Etzioni understands, welcomes diversity because, more or less gently, it deprecates all cultures and particularities. In the mirror of equality, all differences are mere varieties and accidents, frequently delightful and ordinarily valuable, but subordinate to what is humanly natural and common. In Etzioni's vision, as in Royce's, the customs and creeds of the communities must, in the last analysis, yield precedence to the hope of the Great Community.[6] Etzioni's prescription is attractive, and he makes his case with force and erudition. Still, I will be arguing that Etzioni understates the elements in American life that work against a "community of communities" and the extent to which, in the United States, politics both contributes to the problem of community and is indispensable to any possible solution. It is hardly a secret, after all, that our political culture, the cornerstone of our commonality, is pervaded by a devotion to individual liberty that views community with suspicion, if not hostility. And to overcome that bias, so deeply planted in our institutions and habits, we will need not only public deliberation—Etzioni's "megalogues"—but also authoritative policy: in Etzioni's metaphor, because the frame of our political mosaic is loose, we need stronger glue.[7] As Alexis de Tocqueville suggested, democratic politics offers the best antidote to the disorders of democratic culture.[8]

To be sure, the U.S. tradition includes a deeply rooted communitarian strain best articulated in biblical religion. In the high versions of that teaching, communities exist to nurture the human capacity for love, coaxing the human soul out of "timid and suspicious privacy" toward a truer understanding of human nature.[9] Human individuals are not independent or separate, but parts of wholes—families, polities, and nature or creation—on whom common goods have rightful claims. In the same spirit, those teachings speak easily of equality, since our commonalities make us all one and all accountable to the same standard; in this version of equality, however, it is much easier to enunciate duties than rights.[10] Those cadences still reverberate in the United States, but the echoes are growing fainter, and for most Americans, the language of strong communitarianism is articulated with difficulty, if at all.[11] In fact, a large part of Etzioni's work, and that of the communitarian movement in general, consists in the effort to bring that old idiom back into civic speech.

At the moment, however, the terms of public debate are defined, with very little challenge, by an individualism premised on our bodily separateness and spiritual uniqueness, and hence on our title to liberty. In this account, we are equal, as Locke taught, chiefly in being free from obligations to others, or from any claim on them beyond the recognition of our own individual rights.[12] Long familiarity, together with new teachers and new times, has exaggerated or amplified the original bases of this persuasion, and great numbers of Americans would agree with Ralph Waldo

Emerson's then-startling saying, "Nothing is at last sacred but the integrity of our own mind. . . . Expect me not to shew cause why I seek or why I exclude company. Then again, do not tell me, as a good man did today, of my obligation to put all poor men in good situations. Are they *my* poor? I tell thee, thou foolish philanthropist, that I grudge the dollar, the dime, the cent I give to such men as do not belong to me, and to whom I do not belong."[13]

Political society, in this view, is created as a matter of utility for the better fulfillment of private purposes, chiefly material well-being—"a joint-stock company," Emerson said, "in which the members agree, for the better securing of his bread to each shareholder, to surrender the liberty and culture of the eater."[14] Hence political institutions aim at more bread, more securely guaranteed, at economic growth and the dominion over nature; government is the creation of human beings who themselves seek mastery. The liberty human beings cherish, in this understanding, is the freedom to pursue private ends, unencumbered by limits and duties, liberty *from* community.

Of course, Americans have always thought and felt other, more generous, ideas and impulses, but at least as early as Tocqueville's time, individualist doctrine was regnant in public speech. "Americans . . . are fond of explaining almost all their lives by the principle of self-interest rightly understood. . . . In this respect, I think they frequently fail to do themselves justice; for in the United States as well as elsewhere, people are sometimes seen to give way to those disinterested and spontaneous impulses that are natural to man; but the Americans seldom admit that they yield to emotions of this kind; they are more anxious to do honor to their philosophy than to themselves."[15] As Tocqueville knew, what begins as a somewhat disingenuous habit of rhetoric becomes, across the generations, a basis for self-understanding.

This is especially true because the Constitution—the frame of Etzioni's mosaic—has at best an ambivalent relation to community. It was designed, James Madison tells us, on the principle that government exists, not to produce virtue or public spirit, but to protect "the diversity in the faculties of men."[16] Traditionally, democracy had been associated with an open politics in a relatively closed and small society, as in Tocqueville's description of America's roots in Puritan New England: "in the moral world everything is classified, systematized, foreseen and decided beforehand; in the political world everything is agitated, disputed and uncertain. In the one is a passive though a voluntary obedience; in the other, an independence scornful of experience and jealous of all authority. These two tendencies, apparently so discrepant, are far from conflicting; they advance together and support each other."[17] Diverse peoples in large states had been thought to require monarchy, with the unity of the state substituting for moral coherence or love for the community as a whole.[18] By contrast, the U.S. Founders linked popular government to a radically *open* society within a relatively *closed* politics, multiplying diverse communities in order to subordinate them and to undermine their authority in the interest of republican laws and personal liberty. Hence Madison's celebrated argument, making a desideratum out of the greatest variety of groups and factions possible within the Constitution's forms.[20] That plurality allows for the uniting of government's goal, liberty, with the just basis of its power, majority rule: making rule by any one faction or community difficult or impossible, it also weakens the hold of such groups on the allegiances and affections of individuals.

The Framers expected national allegiance to be a relatively "diffuse" sentiment, lacking the strong positive attachments characteristic of more intimate and coherent communities and less able, under ordinary circumstances, to subordinate individual interests to common endeavors.[21] Most of them reckoned this limitation as a virtue: champions of a rather prosaic liberty, they were wary of heroic politics. But they did think that the national regime would be effective *negatively*, by offering rights and opportunities that would detach individuals from state and local loyalties, especially by limiting—potentially, in very severe ways—local power to regulate the commercial economy. The Pennsylvania Anti-Federalist John Smilie had it right when he declared that if the people "find their governments . . . divested of the means to promote their welfare and interests, they will not . . . vainly idolize a shadow."[22] And the existence of federal rights, courts, and authorities, of course, was bound to encourage an appeal by discontented individuals or subgroups from the local community to the national government: as all communitarians know, one cannot speak in favor of community to a contemporary audience without evoking specters of local repression—particularly racial—and reminders of the federal government's role as a defender of individual and civil rights.

In fact, the Constitution today is in crucial ways less favorable to diversity than it was at the time of the founding. Originally, after all, the Constitution accommodated the culture of slavery and it allowed the states to establish churches, while the Bill of Rights did not apply to, or limit the varieties of, state government and politics.

As Etzioni notes, by establishing a national citizenship, the Fourteenth Amendment made states and local communities subject to new restraints, in the spirit of Lincoln's redefinition of the republic as "dedicated" to equality, that high communitarian norm. Of course, for the better part of a century, the Reconstruction amendments were largely ignored or distorted, treated as compatible with Jim Crow and a politics for Whites only. But the amendments are also a striking instance of the power of constitutional forms, which—by requiring a deference to principles—affirm standards. If a form "cannot guarantee the result it wants," Harvey Mansfield writes, "it can indicate the direction toward which it wants to go, and thus become the cause of going if not getting there."[23] Gradually, if too slowly, the national norms proclaimed by the amendments have come to govern states and localities and, via civil rights legislation, wide areas of civil society.

Etzioni, in fact, testifies to the success of the Framers' design of effacing local authority. His discussion of the ongoing "megalogue" regarding the Bill of Rights is cast in terms of a tension between our "national normative stance" and the rituals and values of "particular communities," in which "the community" refers to religio/ethnic collectivities (the Native American Church, followers of Santería, and hypothetical advocates of female circumcision) but *not* to the local regimes that are attempting to regulate them.[24] Etzioni's analysis seems to presume that states and localities have authority only when they reflect national norms (and not even then, when as in the case of Santería, the national value—the protection of animals—seems weak when set against the right to practice one's religion). In every other case, Etzioni implicitly discounts state and local claims. Ironically, Etzioni's definition of "constituting communities" within the "community of communities" appears to exclude the only subgroups—the states—that are actually recognized in the Constitution. That stance, John Smilie would surely have argued, is quite consistent with the Framers' long-term intent.

Moreover, the Constitution's distrust of subcommunities does not stop with the states. While Etzioni describes the Supreme Court as assessing the place of *community values* within the nation as a whole, the Court itself speaks of *individual rights*, in terms of the claims of persons rather than those of congregations and communities. So it must, since the Constitution acknowledges such rights, but—states aside—speaks of communities not at all, and is virtually silent on the question of any duties beyond the "obligation of contracts."[25] Implicitly, Etzioni attempts to minimize this by contending that the Court's arguments, while "couched in legal terms," are in practice dealing with conflicts between communities, and in a sense he is right. Tocqueville reminds us, however, that the laws—our most authoritative public speech—tend, over the long term, to shape the way we talk about public things and personal duties, just as they exert a powerful influence on the habits of the heart.

The founding generation knew that republics depend on an element of virtue—self-preservation will not move citizens to risk their lives in the country's defense, and self-interest will not lead them to see contracts as sacred and liberties as beyond price—and they expected families and churches to provide the fundamentals of moral education. Consequently, the Constitution leaves considerable room for communities in private life, and even values them, up to a point.[26] But it does so silently and interstitially: in its dominant teaching, the Constitution speaks emphatically in the language of individual rights and liberties.[27]

To borrow Albert Hirschman's terms, in any contest between individuals and a community, if the persons involved are not content simply to be loyal, it is almost always difficult to find a voice—to make a case for change in the community—that has a realistic chance of being effective.[28] Political organization takes time and requires resources; imposing costs and risks, it offers no guarantee of success. Having a personal voice on any but the most local or intimate matters is likely to be impossible: in any reasonably large association or public, only a few of us can speak and most of us will have to content ourselves with being spoken for.[29] That principle surely applies to Etzioni's megalogues and promises to weaken any sense of moral obligation that might grow out of them.

By contrast, U.S. institutions proliferate opportunities to exit—to leave or resign from community, moving oneself or one's resources—with little need to consult others and in ways that get relatively quick results, although not always the results we want. That encouragement to exit, almost inevitably, thins all communities, including the nation as a whole, in the name of liberty. As Lewis Lapham writes, "a man can feel shame before an audience of his peers, within the narrow precincts of a neighborhood, profession, army unit, social set, city room, congregation or football team. The scale and dynamism of American democracy grants the ceaselessly renewable option of moving one's conscience into a more congenial street."[30]

Alarm at the rise of the "unencumbered self," combined with the prevailing distrust of the state, defines the enthusiasm for "civil society" that is one of Etzioni's starting points.[31] The strongest voices among U.S. public intellectuals, for all their variety, tend to unite in appreciating the alternative, more communitarian modes and orders preserved in families, churches, localities, and associations.[32] That disposition, too, has found confirmation and encouragement in resistance to Marxist-Leninist totalitarianism in Eastern Europe. But while civil society has its subsidiary autonomy, it remains decisively *civil*, affected by the subtle disciplines of political society. In fact, the subtext of the eulogy for civil society is lament.

In 1927, John Dewey was already writing that, while community had once been relatively autonomous, relying primarily on economic and social sanctions—so that the state was "hardly more than a shadow" on the life of society—its affairs were now "conditioned by remote and invisible organizations."[33] In our times, communities are defending their last bastions: their cultures, relationships, and ways of life are being reshaped, if not shattered, by markets and technologies, mobility and the media.[34]

Everyday experience testifies that communities are pervaded and reformed by an increasingly global economy. Jobs move or disappear; local banks and retailers give way to corporate giants; the homey practice of the family physician is impinged on by the cost-cutting imperatives of the HMO. Businesses, less and less tied to locality, use threats to relocate or downsize as economic blackmail, and local governments, even with the best intentions, seem reduced to hat-in-hand or beggar-my-neighbor politics.[35]

Culturally, communities find outsiders even in their sanctuaries. Socialization in families and neighborhoods once preceded any influence from the media: reading required schooling, even radio largely presumed speech, and for children, access to movies—shown in public settings—was controlled by adults. By contrast, television enters the home as a presence in socialization before reading and even before speech, challenging if not displacing the curricula of communities.[36]

Our local relationships matter less, and our ties to distant others, more. These remote connections, however, are too abstract, specialized, and impersonal to constitute anything but the thinnest sort of community. They are more effective than affective, separating us from what is close without binding us to what is far.[37] In our rhetoric and experience, community is increasingly associated with the trapped. The successful "secede," as Robert Reich observes, but they do not reconfederate: their symbol is the modish suburban house without sidewalks, drawn back from the streets, cherishing private spaces, and visibly minimizing any tie to a common life.[38]

Etzioni's insistence on inclusiveness—its philosophic force aside—reflects the extent to which other peoples, institutions, and nations have become part of our *immediate* world, so that parochialism is disabling and supremely impractical. Yet while it make sense to ask Americans to learn more about other cultures, it has to be recognized that doing so leaves less time to devote to the dominant culture, or to any culture we think of as our own. Human time is limited, and, all things being equal, extending breadth implies a loss of depth. In fact, the ordinary course in "comparative world cultures," when it avoids the excesses of identity politics, is very likely to be a superficial, celebratory travelogue, its language shaped by relativism.[39] In practice, in other words, the danger is that Etzioni's "principle of respect" for the cultures of others—which presumes a knowledge of the things that *deserve* to be respected—will take second place to an exit from any serious engagement with our own.

Community, after all, draws strength from habit and memory, from the expected continuity of past and future.[40] For us, by contrast, virtually exponential transformations have become almost routine, making the past less relevant, the present less comprehensible, and the future less predictable. Aware of the risks, we are apt to be more guarded in our commitments to places, persons, or beliefs.[41]

The great majority of us know that our communities do not have the political resources to govern economic and social life effectively. In the first place, communities suffer from a constitutional disability: the regulation of the commercial economy, like the conduct of foreign affairs, belongs to the federal sphere. Any serious attempt to deal with those shaping forces requires a turn to *national* authority (and these days, more and more Americans fear or are convinced that even federal power, in practice, may prove to be inadequate). Localities depend on grants of power and money from state or federal governments; even "devolution," that conservative nostrum, is tied to federal block grants. And with very few exceptions, communities across the board make pilgrimages to state capitals and to Washington, seeking subsidies or vouchers or laws to enforce moral norms and duties. In crucial areas of policy, local leadership is less engaged in governing than in representing and lobbying for the community at higher levels.[42]

The communities, in other words, need the community. Politics cannot do everything for communities, but it can be a deadly enemy or an invaluable ally. For all their variety, communities are being led, by the logic of U.S. life, to ask government, and particularly the national government, to give their distinctive goods—home, family, culture, and stable relationships generally—status as public goals and interests.

At the moment, public policy leans to the other side. As it should, government accepts a duty to protect outsiders, especially racial minorities, who buy into ethnic neighborhoods. By intervening, however, government does more than protect the rights of individuals: it sides with the market and with change, emphasizing the mutability of relationships and values. Confirming fears that loyalty is futile and that voice is ineffective, it reinforces the impulse to exit, a dynamic evident across the urban United States. Government could balance the scales, giving some support to community stability—for example, by offering property tax reductions to long-term residents. Policies of this sort involve economic costs, of course, but a willingness to pay that piper is a ground of Etzioni's *New Golden Rule*: our first principle ought to be democratic self-government, not economic gain, and to that end, civil order and community are worth a high price.

Of course, some communities are not worth supporting—the Jim Crow South is the inevitable example—and even admirable ones may have indefensible practices. All communities, moreover, constrain individuals, although they regard their discipline as protecting members against temptation and self-betrayal, while pointing them toward the good life.[43] The "French-only" regulations in Quebec, about which Etzioni comments, are efforts to protect that language—and the culture associated with it—against the greater material rewards of speaking English. For similar reasons, communities may raise the walls of exclusivity, separating insiders from outsiders, as in taboos on intermarriage. But while there is sometimes a good case for such restrictions—and more often, reason for sympathy—it is also true that communities can exaggerate both the extent of their unity and its value. Etzioni is right to observe that the partisans of "identity politics" tend to treat groups as monolithic, underrating their internal differences and the ways in which individual members are linked to people and things outside. It is a major virtue of Etzioni's argument that he recognizes the need for, and does a creditable job of discovering, moral standards by which the claims of community can be judged and limited.[44]

In the contemporary United States, however, repression is a much smaller danger to democratic liberty than fragmentation, privatization, and the conviction that collective action is hopeless. Linked by law—especially given the virtual incorporation of the Bill of Rights into the Fourteenth Amendment—and by the market forces associated with it, local communities are relatively open societies, often to the regret of their members. Meanwhile, the diversity of the nation as a whole is increasing in startling ways: even Madison might be taken aback by the incoherence of present-day majorities. The scale of life and the pace of change, moreover, leave increasing numbers of Americans baffled and feeling powerless, in a situation that is broadly paranoid. The opinion that economics and technology are fundamentally ungovernable is paralleled, among a substantial fraction of the public, by the conviction that our lives are being scripted by hidden powers and conspiracies. And there is something like a common denominator in the wish—reflected in movies like *Independence Day*—for someone to "take charge," even at great cost. Too many Americans "hate politics" because they have lost faith in democratic institutions and forms.[45]

Etzioni is right to urge policies designed to strengthen our sense of national community. As he argues, we need to teach a history that includes all of America's voices, with all their continuing discords, but also develops an ear for commonalities, especially that American leitmotiv, the doctrine of equality.

Similarly, there is a strong case to be made for an extended—ideally, universal—form of national service that, more utilitarian benefits aside, would affirm the proposition that every citizen has the duty and the right to contribute to the common life.

Ultimately, however, any hopes for a "community of communities" depend on organized public support and hence on a revitalized democratic politics, particularly the kind of "megalogues" in which all communities can press their claims through civil speech and majority votes—and which, at the highest level, presume that we know how to be spoken *for*.[46]

In practice, however, Americans are becoming less likely to learn civil speech and the "arts of association."[47] Technological change, particularly, poses a problem for democratic community. It may challenge the position of old elites, but it also creates new ones, drawing a sharp distinction between those who have mastered the latest innovation and those who have not. And by the time the laggards learn the new skills, those skills are likely to have become relatively obsolete.[48] Adding to the difficulty, the local forums that served Tocqueville's America as the common schools of citizenship have been attenuating in favor of national media that speak in sound bites to a passive audience that resists chiefly by inattention.[49] Moreover, as Etzioni notes, despite the hopes of various enthusiasts, the prospects for electronic community are severely limited. John Dewey came very close to the political truth of the matter when he wrote that "the local is the ultimate universal, and as near to an absolute as exists."[50] The body remains stubbornly physical, and the bonds people form in "virtual reality" lack the erotic dimension and the qualities of special place and occasion that Tocqueville associated with the "power of meeting."[51] These shortcomings are most evident in electronic politics, which can enable us to *vote* easily enough, but cannot overcome the time constraints that make it impossible for any more than a tiny fraction of the citizenry to *speak* to any significant part of the electorate. The new media do allow minorities to overcome pluralistic ignorance and find like-minded others. Yet while this heartens some bands of angels, it emboldens at least as many demons, without fundamentally assuaging their feelings of indignity and resentment.[52] In fact, more and more associations dealing with public affairs are centralized, largely self-directed bureaucracies that relate to their supporters almost solely through fund-raising, so that "membership" is reduced to the choice of whether to donate and how much. Needing the arts of politics more, communities are less likely to have mastered them.

Education can help: public policy should be urging schools to teach civil speech, particularly the techniques and implicit ethics of deliberation to be found in *Robert's Rules of Order* and the arts of rhetoric and hearing that allowed leaders, at one time, to speak to the larger public and for their own communities. In the end, however, the prospects for a community of communities depend on a rebuilding of local political institutions, where participation can have an effect on the immediate lives of citizens, linking voice to power.

Limiting the weight of money in campaigns, of course, is also an imperative in any attempt to restore confidence in the democratic process. Ordinary citizens, particularly those at the lower end of the income scale, are right to suspect that monumental spending and the corresponding fixation on fund-raising, come close to rigging the game against them.[53] Ideally, the Court would reverse its opinion, in *Buckley v. Valeo*, which held that donations of money are the equivalent of speech, entitled to the protection of the First Amendment.[54] Yet even within those terms, it may be possible to restrict campaign expenditures on electronic media—by banning paid political advertising on television, for example—and redirecting spending into "retail" campaigns that are more local and face-to-face.

Similarly, among the institutions of democratic civil society, political party organizations have a compelling claim to support. Historically, party organizations, rooted in precincts and wards, linked communities—by a chain of personal relationships, memories, and affections—to higher levels of government.[55] If their concerns, like those of human beings, were often petty or sordid, they developed allegiance and reciprocity, crucial "social capital" for a community of communities.[56] In this century, of course, party organizations have been damaged by a series of "reforms," like the direct primary and the evisceration of patronage, which have had the ironic effect of strengthening the hand of money and organized interests relative to ordinary citizens and communities.[57] And while national party committees have been growing stronger in recent decades, they epitomize the fund-raising bureaucracies of centralized, media-dominated politics. When Congress exempted money used for "party-building activities" from federal contribution and spending limits, it left parties free to use the bulk of such "soft money" in media advertising, and rather ingeniously, the parties have done just that.[58] The scandals associated with the scramble for such funds have inspired a contradictory set of proposals for reform that, promising little, have so far come to nothing. From a communitarian viewpoint, it would make good sense to limit the amount or percentage of such funds that can be spent on the electronic media, pointing such monies toward the rebuilding of party organizations, especially at the local level.

Etzioni is right, however, to recognize that the possibilities for reform or reconstruction rest, finally, on moral foundations. In critical ways, civil society and democratic politics are "inefficient": relying on deliberation, they are ordinarily slower to decide and more amateurish than technicians and elites; they are likely to begin with perspectives that are shortsighted and parochial; most important, they may incline to make stability a rival of productivity in the scales of value. But to the extent that they respect the dignities of their members, such communities are more apt to *be* respected.[59] Formal authority has a stronger basis in personal commitments, so that collective judgments, when arrived at, speak with moral force.[60] Citizenship, a mutuality in governance, is an example of the golden rule, not the least admirable, and an excellence essential to Etzioni's high vision.

NOTES

1. Randolph Bourne, "Trans-National America," *Atlantic Monthly* (July 1916): 86–97; Josiah Royce, *The Philosophy of Loyalty* (New York: Macmillan, 1908).

2. Aristotle, *Politics*, 1261a18–b17; on the contemporary modes, see Sheldon S. Wolin, "Democracy, Difference and Re-cognition," *Political Theory* 21 (1993): 466, 481.

3. John Locke, *Second Treatise on Civil Government*, § 96.

4. The Old South is the obvious U.S. case. For a forceful statement of the problem, see Genesis 26: 12–16.

5. G. K. Chesterton, *What I Saw in America* (New York: Dodd Mead, 1922), 14.

6. Josiah Royce, *The Hope of the Great Community* (New York: Macmillan, 1916); see also John Dewey, "The Search for the Great Community," in John Dewey, *The Public and Its Problems* (New York: Holt, 1927), 143–84. Terry Ball argues that identity politics offers a place to "begin or stand," but not a place to "stay." *Reappraising Political Theory* (New York: Oxford University Press, 1995), 296.

7. On the limits of deliberation, see Amitai Etzioni, *The New Golden Rule: Community and Morality in a Democratic Society* (New York: Basic Books, 1996), 97–101.

8. Alexis de Tocqueville, *Democracy in America* (New York: Knopf, 1980), II: 105, 115.

9. Mark Twain, *A Connecticut Yankee in King Arthur's Court* (Berkeley: University of California Press, 1979), 300.

10. For example, see Galatians 3: 28–9.

11. Robert Bellah, et al., *Habits of the Heart* (Berkeley: University of California Press, 1985).

12. Locke, *Second Treatise*, § 54.

13. Ralph Waldo Emerson, "Self-Reliance," in *Emerson's Essays*, ed. Sherman Paul (New York: Dutton, 1976), 33–4.

14. Emerson, *Emerson's Essays*, 32.

15. Tocqueville, *Democracy in America*, II: 122.

16. James Madison, *The Federalist* #10.

17. Tocqueville, *Democracy in America*, I: 43–4.

18. Montesquieu, *The Spirit of the Laws*, book III, chs. 5 and 6.

19. See my "Democratic Multiculturalism," in *Multiculturalism and American Democracy*, ed. Arthur Melzer, et al., (Lawrence: University Press of Kansas, 1998), 120–9.

20. Madison wrote that "notwithstanding the contrary opinions which have been entertained, the larger the society, provided it be within a practicable sphere, the more duly capable it will be of self-government." *The Federalist* #51.

21. James Madison, *The Federalist* #17.

22. John Bach McMaster and Frederick Stone, eds., *Pennsylvania and the Federal Constitution 1787–1788* (Philadelphia: Pennsylvania Historical Society, 1888), 270–1. As David Pearson writes, communities "are necessarily, indeed by definition, coercive as well as moral, threatening their members with the stick of sanctions if they stray, offering them the carrot of certainty and stability if they don't." "Community and Sociology," *Society* (July/August 1995): 47.

23. Harvey C. Mansfield, *America's Constitutional Soul* (Baltimore: Johns Hopkins University Press, 1991), 12.

24. Etzioni, *The New Golden Rule*, 200–202.

25. Article I, section 10.

26. In *Wisconsin v. Yoder*, 406 U.S. 205 (1972), the Court appreciated the private virtues of the Old Order Amish. On the limitations of this principle, however, see *U.S. v. Lee*, 455 U.S. 252 (1982).

27. See my comments in the introduction to *The Constitution of the People*, ed. Robert E. Calvert (Lawrence: University Press of Kansas, 1991), 7–8. This is true even where the Framers pretty clearly intended otherwise. The Second Amendment, for example, is concerned with the common defense, asserting that a free state must be defended, primarily, by a popular military. It thus implicitly enunciates an *obligation* to serve in a militia whose *arming* and *discipline* are subject to congressional regulation (Article I, section 8). But in public debate, this tends to be reduced to a putative personal "right to keep and bear arms."

28. Here and in what follows, I borrow terms from Albert Hirschman, *Exit, Voice and Loyalty* (Cambridge, Mass.: Harvard University Press, 1970).

29. Bertrand de Jouvenel, "The Chairman's Problem," *American Political Science Review* 55 (1961): 368–72.

30. Lewis Lapham, "Supply-Side Ethics," *Harper's* (May 1985): 11.

31. Michael Sandel, "The Procedural Republic and the Unencumbered Self," in *The Self and The Political Order*, ed. Tracy B. Strong (New York: New York University Press, 1992), 79–94.

32. For example, Robert D. Putnam, *Making Democracy Work: Civic Traditions in Modern Italy* (Princeton: Princeton University Press, 1993) or Jean Bethke Elshtain, "In Common Together: Unity, Diversity and Civic Virtue," in Calvert, *The Constitution of the People*, 64–82.

33. Dewey, *The Public and Its Problems*, 41, 98.

34. Robert D. Putnam, "Bowling Alone, Revisited," *Responsive Community* 5 (Spring 1995): 18–33.

35. For an anticipation of the contemporary problem, see Charles Beard, *The Open Door at Home* (New York: Macmillan, 1934), 78–9.

36. Robert D. Putnam, "Tuning In, Tuning Out: The Strange Disappearance of Social Capital in America," *PS* 28 (1995): 664–83.

37. See Dewey, *The Public and Its Problems*, 126–7.

38. Robert Reich, "The Secession of the Successful," *New York Times Magazine* (January 20, 1991): 16ff; see also Richard Thomas, "From Porch to Patio," *Palimpsest* (August 1975): 120–7. This is true even of those forms that attempt to pass as communities. Evan McKenzie, *Privatopia* (New Haven, Conn.: Yale University Press, 1994).

39. Arthur Melzer, "Tolerance 101," *New Republic* (July 1, 1991): 11.

40. Sheldon S. Wolin, *The Presence of the Past* (Baltimore: Johns Hopkins University Press, 1989); Dewey, *The Public and Its Problems*, 140–1.

41. Norval Glenn, "Social Trends in the United States," *Public Opinion Quarterly* 51 (1987): S109–S126.

42. Wolin, *Presence of the Past*, 191.

43. Pearson, "Community and Sociology," n. 22.

44. Ronald Beiner, *What's the Matter with Liberalism?* (Berkeley: University of California Press, 1992), 28–9.

45. E. J. Dionne Jr., *Why Americans Hate Politics* (New York: Simon and Schuster, 1991).

46. Brutus, essay in the *New York Journal* (October 18, 1787), in *The Complete Anti-Federalist*, ed. Herbert Storing (Chicago: University of Chicago Press, 1981), I: 370–1;

Stanley Cavell writes that "The alternative to speaking for yourself politically is not: speaking for yourself privately. . . . The alternative is having nothing to say. . . . (I)f I am to have my own voice . . . I must be speaking for others and allow others to speak for me." *The Claim of Reason* (Oxford: Oxford University Press, 1979), 28.

47. Tocqueville, *Democracy in America*, II: 110.

48. Jacques Ellul, *The Technological Society* (New York: Vintage, 1964), 208–18.

49. Samuel Popkin, *The Reasoning Voter* (Chicago: University of Chicago Press, 1991), 226–31.

50. Dewey, *The Public and Its Problems*, 215.

51. Tocqueville, *Democracy in America*, I: 192, II: 102–03, 116.

52. Darrell M. West and Richard Francis, "Electronic Advocacy: Interest Groups and Public Policy Making," *PS* 29 (1996): 25–9; see also W. Russell Neuman, *The Future of the Mass Audience* (New York: Cambridge University Press, 1991).

53. Thomas Byrne Edsall, *The New Politics of Inequality* (New York: Norton, 1984).

54. *Buckley v. Valeo* 424 U.S. 1 (1976). See Scott Turow, "The High Court's 20-Year-Old Mistake," *New York Times* (October 12, 1997): WK 15.

55. Woodrow Wilson, *Constitutional Government in the United States* (New York: Columbia University Press, 1908), 208–10; see my essays, "Parties as Civic Associations," in *Party Renewal in America*, ed. Gerald M. Pomper (New York: Praeger, 1980), 51–68 and "Tocqueville and Responsible Parties," in *Challenges to Party Government*, ed. Jerome Mileur and John K. White (Carbondale: Southern Illinois University Press, 1992), 190–211.

56. It should be noted that the term *social capital* involves a misleading metaphor: see Nancy Tatum Ackerman, *Congregation and Community* (New Brunswick: Rutgers University Press, 1997), 4.

57. Michael McGerr, *The Decline of Popular Politics* (New York: Oxford University Press, 1986).

58. Anthony Corrado, "Financing the 1996 Election," in Gerald M. Pomper, et al., *The Election of 1996* (Chatham: Chatham House, 1997), 135–6, 165–6.

59. Donald Wittman, *The Myth of Democratic Failure* (Chicago: University of Chicago Press, 1995).

60. The proposition is illustrated, in a somewhat ironic context, by John McKay, *Foundations of Corporate Success* (New York: Oxford University Press, 1993), 70–2.

8

Integrating Diversity: Boundaries, Bonds, and the Greater Community in *The New Golden Rule*

Paul Lichterman

PLURALISM IN A "THICK" SOCIAL ORDER: A WORTHY CHALLENGE

The New Golden Rule is a courageous work. Amitai Etzioni pursues a communitarian agenda that faces up to the toughest issues in community life, refusing to indulge in fuzzy talk about community or moralistic condemnations. On the issue of diversity in America, Etzioni faces the communitarian agenda with an absolutely crucial challenge: He asks "how the bonds of a more encompassing community can be maintained without suppressing the member communities."[1] The answer is a "community of communities," a greater community that coheres with a "thick" (*NGR,* 192) framework of shared values while member communities maintain their own integrity. Albeit a very challenging answer, the community of communities is the best of the alternatives for integrating diversity that Etzioni discusses.

Not surprisingly, a thin proceduralism of individual rights will not do for Etzioni, who along with other communitarians is skeptical of negative freedoms that lack counterbalancing commitments to shared visions of the good (*NGR,* 198). The liberal individualism with which Etzioni takes issue tends to assume that diverse individuals, or groups, exist prior to the social whole and have a moral primacy too. Etzioni is right to advocate a thick social order rather than a thin agreement over procedure— a few figurative traffic signals monitoring the routes to insular communities and private lives. It is not enough to hope that in a democratic, greater community, more people of color will know their right to file suit for discrimination or more local communities will know their right to petition against dump sites, important as these rights are.

Etzioni also takes care to mark off his arguments from authoritarian or assimilationist versions of social conservatism. While some have tarred communitarians as authoritarians who value order above all,[2] Etzioni's argument values individual

125

and subcultural autonomy too much to settle for easy formulae of social conformity. Characterizing melting-pot assimilationism as "a case of strong oversteering," Etzioni shares with celebrants of cultural diversity a distaste for bland, if not coercive, monocultural answers to the challenge of diversity within unity (*NGR*, 196). Cultural variety results as a substantive good for Etzioni. This is worth underscoring: After *The New Golden Rule*, it is more difficult for critics to argue that communitarians ignore the joys and richness of a diverse society and concentrate only on its challenges to moral order. In Etzioni's argument, the greater community not only functions more effectively when diverse groups secure respect and autonomy, but it becomes the setting for a multicultural kind of public happiness.

Etzioni's communitarian pluralism is all the more challenging, then, for rejecting the popular "rainbow" image of racial and ethnic diversity. The problem with the rainbow metaphor is that, for many of its proponents, it pictures groups that coexist side by side but actively engage one another mainly to compete for power or complain about injustices inflicted on one's own group (*NGR*, 192, 197, 207). A communitarian insists that diverse groups share something besides social space. Rainbow multiculturalism ends up replaying a kind of liberal individualism writ large. Etzioni makes the point effectively with a telling quote from an education professional who holds that democracy is "about establishing the processes whereby these conflicts [resulting from diversity] can be played out" (*NGR*, 198). For communitarians, and anyone who treasures the public happiness a diverse society offers, the central trouble with this version of liberalism is that it locates the shared life mostly within subcultural enclaves; the greater community exists largely to safeguard more particular, communal quests.

Communitarian pluralism means more than a set of procedures for resolving grievances and marking off space. Etzioni implies we need to understand communitarian pluralism as a way of life, a way of practicing membership in society (*NGR*, 142, 205), not adherence to abstract principles or an expanded set of rights alone. The greater community, in other words, must cohere through the ways we practice communal membership in our daily rounds, and not only when we adjudicate explicit conflicts across communities.

It follows from this very agreeable insight that we ought to look closely at how communities create and maintain themselves. And that is no simple task: Americans tend not to talk about the communal bonds that we take for granted a lot of the time as we go about pursuing communal goals. When Americans, from grassroots volunteers to the president, do talk about "community-building, " we often talk as if there is one way to do it and as if we all agree on that one way. Further, many of our communities are "imagined communities" that we call into being through print and electronic media rather than through face-to-face contact.[3] To assess the possibilities for communitarian pluralism in practice, we need language that can help us locate different textures and depths of relationships that we do not always experience directly.[4] We need good metaphors.

Chapter seven of *The New Golden Rule* makes several troublesome assumptions about the ways communities relate to one another. Etzioni's discussion highlights the unarguably real problems of crossing group boundaries, and it makes a case for shared values that few proponents of a public-spirited society could oppose. But the terms of discussion are too abstract, the metaphors too limiting. The discussion needs to pay more attention to concrete relationships that create social *bonds* as well as boundaries, relationships that hold communities and the greater community together. The community of communities that Etzioni envisions, it turns out, is not communitarian enough.

While this chapter will be challenging the conceptions of boundaries and bonds most prominent in Etzioni's discussion of the greater community, my goal is also to tease out and augment a second, less prominent vision in the discussion that a focus on concrete relations helps us to see. In this picture, communities are mutually constitutive and interpenetrating, with permeable boundaries. And the community of communities holds together by means of many, specific, greater communities. In the same spirit of specificity, I will show that Americans create different kinds of social bonds even when they share the same, binding values. In all, this is the vision that best embodies the communitarian tradition with its focus on particularity and concrete relationships. This vision of communities, grounded in specific traditions, yet mutually engaged too, also complements recent efforts in democratic theory to imagine public-spirited citizenship in a diverse society.[5] In all, a close look at relationships in the community of communities can enhance communitarian pluralism in conceptual terms and improve its prospects in state policy arenas as well as in the civic sphere that this chapter will emphasize most.

A SECOND LOOK AT BOUNDARIES

Discussions of diversity often emphasize group boundaries, weighing the possibilities for transcending them. Older discussions picture a diverse United States in terms of interest groups that vie for influence over national or local policy. In this liberal pluralist view, diverse groups work together because they commit themselves to democratic procedures—and to the shared goal of cutting a good deal—and because group members' and leaders' multiple affiliations result in cross-cutting cleavages.[6] A steelworker from a Slavic neighborhood votes for an Irish Catholic candidate because the candidate advances workers' concerns; a representative from an agricultural state votes to end farm subsidies because a congressional colleague from an industrial northeastern district has convinced her that the two can help pass a big defense spending bill benefiting both. More recent explorations of diversity tend to emphasize ethnic, racial, or religious differences that may defy negotiation. Critical diagnoses of contemporary U.S. culture often find identity groups refusing to recognize cross-cutting ties that might unite them; critics of cultural fragmentation search for some common commitment that can transcend identity groups' celebrations, or denunciations, of cultural differences.[7] The liberal pluralist view is often normative as much as descriptive, while in its starkest, "culture wars" terms, the prospect of cultural fragmentation is almost dystopic to those who have written about it—and certainly it appeals little to Etzioni, for good reason. But despite these differences in evaluative stance as well as substance, there is still a striking similarity in the two views of the United States: Each pictures groups who imagine their own interests to be stakes in a zero-sum game. Communities build boundaries around separate interests, albeit shifting and negotiable interests under liberal pluralism. In either view, one group's (or coalition's) win is another group's loss, even if only temporary.

Etzioni's terms of discussion borrow much from a zero-sum view of community boundaries that, I will argue, unnecessarily narrows the prospects for communitarian pluralism. The discussion takes for granted that people want, and will continue pursuing, lives defined by a succession of autonomous if not greedy community interests. Etzioni advocates an "equilibrium" between greater community and member communities that will endure if people can adopt a "split loyalty, divided between commitment to one's immediate community and to the more encompassing community" (*NGR*, 203). Elsewhere, Etzioni counsels that the politics of the greater community will be communitarian when constituent groups "realize that they must fight for their causes with one hand tied behind their back" (*NGR*, 207). Etzioni's guiding metaphor of diversity, the mosaic, pictures the community of communities in more positive, enabling terms: The mosaic's "elements of different shapes and colors"—the separate communities—add up to a beautiful whole that is more than the sum of the parts (*NGR*, 192). The separate communities connect to one another, and to a larger community, because they submit to the binding force of a "frame and glue" of shared, democratic values (*NGR*, 192, 199–200). I will have more to say about the "glue" of social bonds, but will point out for now that the mosaic metaphor suggests that the greater community results from an external imposition on its members. Greater and smaller communities still meet one another as competitors, if not in a strictly zero-sum game.

Some critics of liberal pluralism might go on to ask why Etzioni's discussion does not remark more on the consequences of boundary drawing for social inequality. Groups draw boundaries on hierarchical grids of class, gender, race, or sexuality; the boundary drawing itself is an important means of reproducing inequality.[8] In leaving this theme largely unexamined Etzioni comes that much closer, the critic might say, to a liberal pluralist stance on the greater community. But that in itself is not the trouble with this view of boundaries. Etzioni's main goal is to understand the consequences of boundaries for identity and for morality in Émile Durkheim's sense of the term: social bondedness. Certainly groups draw boundaries that often privilege their higher-status, more powerful members. But at the same time, questions about social solidarity should not simply be reduced to questions about power; Etzioni's focus is fully defensible and valuable in analytic terms.

One may argue, alternatively, that if Etzioni's metaphors highlight the divisions within the greater community just as liberal pluralists, rainbow advocates, and critics of cultural fragmentation have before him, it is because that is simply what realism dictates: Americans, as Alexis de Tocqueville observed, dwell mostly inside parochial circles of group interest unless goaded outward by more public-spirited intuitions, and these intuitions serve self-interest too—if rightly understood. But by assuming parochial, communal interests within its terms of discussion, chapter seven weakens its grasp of communitarian potentials.

A proactive communitarian project, in contrast, ought to develop new metaphors of community attachment that can apprehend the more expansive as well as more defensive sentiments alive in real communities. Realistically speaking, many communities do define themselves as competing interest groups, so the images of boundaries and zero-sum competitions do reflect the way many people experience their own communities at least some of the time. But it is also realistic to note as Etzioni does that individuals always carry multiple community affiliations; the experience of community boundaries must be more complicated in real life than the picture of zero-sum community relations suggests. Going from communitarian theory to community practice ought to mean questioning the commonsense metaphors of community that frustrate real communities' goals as well as scholars' normative visions. An example of a gay community interest group illustrates the point that zero-sum thinking about community boundaries may not always be so realistic after all.[9]

At the start of 1995, lesbian and gay activists in an East Coast city felt threatened as a new cohort of conservative Republican congresspeople were arriving in Washington, and local pastors were decrying a curricular initiative in the public schools that would teach kids about lesbian- and gay-headed households. The activists initiated a network that would promote the interests of "the gay community." The network mounted a campaign urging gay voters to support a gay-friendly city council candidate. And it sought to build a long-term coalition of groups, gay and straight, to fight the political right. These community activists kept assuming that ordinary lesbians and gays would support a seemingly unambiguous gay interest. Yet, other participants in gay community life, and these activists themselves, kept expressing other interests too—even in the heat of an election campaign that the network had outlined in starkly pro-gay/anti-gay terms.

During the city council campaign, for instance, one lesbian community leader said that while it was important to guarantee insurance for same-sex partners of city employees, other issues concerned her more. She went on to explain that she opposed an initiative to fund schools with revenue from gambling because she did not want her daughter attending a school "financed by boozers." And the network's coalition-building attempts found network activists themselves struggling to conceive a unitary, and superordinate, gay community interest. At a meeting dedicated to the problems of gay youth, members named a broad range of issues that concerned them, including child abuse and the declining fortunes of public education, and they rated many issues higher on their list of priorities than specifically lesbian and gay issues.

Yet, at succeeding meetings, members assumed that their network needed to be strategizing around a specifically gay community interest. For the same reason, the network assumed that lesbians and gay men would care about welfare reform only if they could be convinced that welfare reform was a properly gay issue, even though these network members themselves sounded concerned about welfare policy quite apart from its impact on sexual minorities.

Active members of the lesbian and gay communities, in other words, worked at hardening the boundaries between their community and others. They thought politically savvy citizens were supposed to mark off gay community boundaries that way in order to be "realistic," not because gay community members necessarily had such single-minded attachments. The trouble was that these firm boundaries were not realistic for all the participants in that community. A Black, gay leader chafed at the network's presumption of a unitary gay community. He argued at a public forum that straight people are not all the same, and so "the gay community" ought not be stereotyped as being uniform either.

Etzioni's metaphors of community relations tend to normalize the kind of "realism" that the gay interest group tried to enact. The image of mosaic pieces, suspended in glue, conjures up solid, self-contained communities and identities that coexist without intermixing. The metaphors of layered loyalty and hands tied behind the back connote individuals who each carry segments of community affiliation, compartmentalized roles. Yet, the example of the gay network illustrates how people maintain multiple commitments simultaneously that inform one another; people may have to work hard at making themselves proponents of one, undifferentiated, rigidly bound group identity. Assumptions about firm boundaries may be a sign that it is difficult to imagine a community of communities, from the smaller community's standpoint, in positive terms. That is all the more reason for communitarian pluralists to work at challenging the commonsense realism that supposes communities by definition pursue relatively narrow interests and guard their boundaries jealously.

Etzioni's discussion offers important insights toward a more nuanced understanding of community membership, even if these do not always get communicated in the metaphors. Counter to the arguments made about some communitarian thinking, for instance, Etzioni's is not an essentialist view of communities.[10] Etzioni is careful to note that groups such as Puerto Ricans, African Americans, or Mexican Americans hardly share views uniformly; neither do all members of one racial or ethnic group value their cultural particularity to the same degree (*NGR*, 193, 207). Any exclusive form of identity politics oversimplifies people's communal attachments by "defining people as if they had only one social status, as if they were members of only one community" (*NGR*, 205). Implicit in Etzioni's discussion, in other words, is the view that communities are often overlapping rather than discrete entities and that people enact multiple community memberships simultaneously rather than in succession.

PERMEABLE BOUNDARIES, EVOLVING IDENTITIES:
SPECIFIC GREATER COMMUNITIES

Once we look closely at communal boundaries with Etzioni's more complex notions of community in mind, we see not one greater community reining in the smaller, but multiple circles of community—some overlapping, some concentric, some barely touching. Etzioni points toward these multiple levels of community life when he pictures an "immediate" community encircled by "more encompassing wholes" rather than by a single, national community of communities (*NGR*, 203). This passage suggests that we should expand the picture of the greater community. In addition to the national community that gets defined in legislative chambers, summoned through the Pledge of Allegiance, ritualized in national holidays, or addressed in the nightly news, the greater community works through a vast congeries of alliances, coalitions, networks, associations, and fellowships, which in themselves engage many more particular communities. If the greater community is a way of life, a way of creating unity in diversity, then much of the community building it requires must happen in this vast "middle" level of community between the most particularly de-fined groupings and the national, greater community that we experience largely in mass-mediated forms.

This vast, middle level is teeming with what I will call "specific greater commu-nities." The lesbian and gay interest group, to give one example, created a specific greater community as it built alliances with schoolteacher groups and Black com-munity advocates who may not have been lesbian or gay. Creating a regional net-work around lesbian and gay issues, it imagined itself, too, as participating in the national debate about whether tolerance for sexual diversity ought to become a broadly shared value. Specific greater communities may include many textures of community relationship, then: the face-to-face relationships of a local advocacy group, the parliamentary relationships of representative associations, the electroni-cally mediated relationships of E-mail users, or the imagined relationships that any of these groups may construct to a mass-mediated, ongoing national debate. De-spite the discomforting evidence that civic groups have been on the decline over the past thirty years,[11] U.S. civil society still hosts myriad specific greater communities as well as local community advocacy groups. If U.S. society is going to achieve plu-ralism within unity mostly through voluntary moral commitment, as Etzioni rec-ommends, then specific, issue-oriented civic groups, alliances, networks, and imag-ined arenas of debate become key places to put the community of communities into practice. As communitarian Harry Boyte has observed,[12] many if not most civic groups exist to take action on specific issues, to solve problems, and not solely to deliberate about a greater, national community. If we look for the integuments of the greater community only in groups that claim to address the broadest, national good, we excuse the great bulk of civic life from responsibility for the greater community's well-being.

Specific greater communities live up to the promise of communitarian pluralism when their members act as if their particular community boundaries are permeable to other communities' interests. Ideally, members of the particular, or in Etzioni's term *immediate,* communities invoke the good of other particular as well as greater communities *as they go about pursuing their own goals.* Communitarian pluralism depends, in other words, on people like the woman mentioned earlier who can talk about her parental concerns for public schools and her citizenly concerns about gambling *as* she is practicing gay community leadership. A communitarian pluralist's greatest hope, then, ought to be that Americans see ourselves as empowering different communities and images of community simultaneously, not that we resign ourselves to fighting for causes "with one hand tied behind the back." Interpenetrating loyalties, not layered loyalties, would inform Americans' sense of boundaries in a community of communities.

Permeable boundaries also open up the possibility that communal identities evolve in relation to one another. In fact, smaller and greater communities are often more mutually constitutive than the terms of Etzioni's discussion imply. Sometimes, the smaller communities and specific greater communities cocreate themselves as relatively self-contained entities that complement the simpler view of boundaries I discussed before. In the gay-initiated network pictured previously, for instance, people who identified themselves as spokespersons for a unitary gay interest imagined a greater specific community made up of other, unitary interest groups. They talked of how "the gay community" should ally with "the Black community" and enlarge "the progressive community." And this image of a progressive community, in turn, ratified the notion of a unitary interest groups with single identities to match. Further civic interchange between the smaller communities and the spokespersons for the specific greater community of progressives would only reinforce the notion of firm communal boundaries and unitary interests.

In some instances, though, smaller communities and specific greater communities cocreate new or more flexible identities that are not simply the sum of the parts. In these instances, civic interchange between smaller and greater communities evolves a new sense of "we," a more cosmopolitan definition of community interest among local participants, and a greater respect for local traditions among spokespersons for the greater community. The particular communities themselves begin to *change.* The following brief example of a faith-based urban ecumenical association will illustrate[13]:

Congregational leaders and lay people gave themselves a challenge rather like that which Etzioni defines for communitarian pluralism: They wanted to create a greater community out of their liberal Protestant, evangelical, and Catholic church communities, dedicated to pursuing the greater good of their locale. They wanted not to suppress particular faith traditions or to meld themselves into bland advocates of generic goodness. At difficult monthly meetings representatives tried, haltingly at first, to talk their way toward a collective stance on racism in their locale. After a half year, members were condemning what they had learned to call "structural racism," in specifically Christian terms. They learned that Black families had difficulties renting apartments all over town, that local police stopped Black motorists more frequently than others. They developed strategies for dealing with structural racism on several levels: by drawing out the antiracist content of their own theologies, creating ties with ethnic community centers, summoning their denominational head offices to become proactive on race issues, and sponsoring religiously inflected, cultural diversity celebrations for the city at large.

In other words, the ecumenical association created a specific greater community of faith communities with permeable boundaries and a slowly evolving sense of members' identities. Member congregations did not layer their loyalties between their own congregation and the alliance; rather, membership in the alliance began to influence the way individual congregations defined their own mission. Active members became agents of the alliance's values *as* they carried on life in their own congregations. Given the broad range of Christian faiths represented in the alliance, it is all the more interesting from a communitarian perspective that evangelical congregations could see their way to identify with an alliance strongly influenced by liberal Protestantism. The point is not that individual congregations were trying to transform their core priorities, much less their theologies. Rather, the congregations started creating a new community face. They brought a slowly evolving, flexible, collective identity into being, an identity they could announce together in unison—at a press conference to counter a Ku Klux Klan rally, for instance—or one they could inflect with their own denominational traditions in church.

Attending closely to concrete relationships, we realize that communities create greater wholes in a variety of mass-mediated and face-to-face settings. Etzioni's discussion opens the way for this more complex and constructionist view of the greater community, without thereby taking community as a purely strategic "deployment," as some postmodern writers have it. A communitarian imagination reminds us that social relationships, even if mediated ones, and lived traditions lie behind the settings and the constructions of identity.[14] In the same vein, that imagination reminds us that communities depend on social bonds as well as boundaries. Earlier in his book, Etzioni defines community itself partly in terms of integrative social bonds (*NGR*, 127). So with the same communitarian concern for concrete relationships in mind, we can seek out the integrative social bonds that make a community of communities compelling to members. But to identify those bonds, we will need to rethink the conceptualization of civil society.

VALUES AND SOCIAL BONDS IN CIVIL SOCIETY

For Etzioni, civil society is a necessary though not sufficient condition for a good community of communities. On the one hand, Etzioni values a sphere of social membership, the sphere of neighborhoods, voluntary associations, and communities apart from the state. Civil society—or in Etzioni's preferred expression, civic society—is the "third leg" of society, apart from the market and the state, "on which the communitarian society particularly leans" (*NGR*, 142). In a succinct riposte to some liberal criticisms of communitarianism, Etzioni holds that "the communitarian society is not first and foremost one of law-and-order, but one based on shared moral values . . . the main social body is not the state . . . but the body is the society (as a community of communities) and the actors are members in it" (*NGR*, 140–1).

On the other hand, Etzioni insists early on that the existence of a vibrant civil society is not enough to ensure a good moral order. Criticizing civic order as "far too thin a concept" (*NGR*, 14), Etzioni tends to define civic order and civil society in terms of procedure, because that is how some proponents of civil society define it: Civic order obtains when people uphold the sense of propriety necessary for discussing public issues civilly (*NGR*, 95). But "a virtuous society requires a core of shared values" (*NGR*, 95–6) that anchors civic life with a vision of the good. Chapter seven devotes considerable effort to identifying core values or elements integrating the community of communities: respect for democracy, adherence to the Constitution, "layered loyalties" as discussed already, and a rejection of identity politics are the most salient for my discussion (*NGR*, 199–208). These core elements make up the glue that bonds the social mosaic.

The potential benefits of civil society certainly do depend on the public morality that sustains civic spaces. If, for instance, civic clubs favor local boosterism over uncomfortable self-examination and ignore complaints that local businesses discriminate by race, few would argue those civic clubs are advancing the good society simply by their existence. But I also argue that the chapter interprets the currently popular discourse about civil society in unnecessarily thin, abstract terms. The problem is more than purely theoretical. The discussion underestimates the distinctive, substantive importance of civil society, while giving general values too exclusive a role in bonding the community of communities.

First, the discussion sometimes mishandles the distinctions between civic relationships and legal mandates, even as Etzioni perceptively points out the difference between *membership* in civil society and *citizenship* in the state (*NGR*, 141–2).[15] The difference should matter for communitarians who appreciate civic alternatives to legislated social change. This claim hardly contravenes the spirit of Etzioni's book; the book effectively illustrates the differences between a social order that leans heavily on legal codes and legal remedies and a society that sustains order largely through the voluntarily shared moral understandings of civil society. Civic relationships are more egalitarian, and people enter them more freely, than those between the state and its citizens. And the diverse, specific customs and traditions of a region or a people can play a bigger part in civic relationships than they can in the state with its stronger accent on administrative rationality and its claim to generality.[16]

For those reasons, then, it is somewhat jarring to include the Constitution and Bill of Rights, along with much less formalized normative orientations, as "elements" of the shared framework that glues the greater community together (*NGR*, 200–02). The problem is not that constitutional law is an unworthy guide, or that a communitarian society can rely only on the force of community opinion to keep itself whole. The Constitution provides an indispensable baseline for relations between minority and majority individuals and between localities and the nation. But it is the less formalized mores of civil society that determine whether the Constitution serves as a focal point for unity or instead becomes a weapon in culture warriors' battles over the meaning of free speech or a free press. In the same vein, it is generalizing too much to treat local political jurisdictions and cultural identity groups as commensurate examples of smaller "communities" within the community of communities. For it would be hard to argue that most Americans' municipal jurisdictions or states of residence make them feel the same sense of bondedness with which many Americans experience religious, racial, or ethnic identities. The blur here between formal citizenship and social membership obscures the concrete bonds on which a successful community of communities depends. Advocates of the greater community can appreciate the formally binding force of national law, while also inquiring into the civic bonds through which people enact the law.

Focusing in on the treatment of civil society we find a second, deeper problem: the discussion dichotomizes civil society and binding values as formal procedure and moral substance. Civic order, however, is not simply an abstract, procedural framework awaiting substantive, moral values. And as many sociologists now argue,[17] the same general values—such as the core values Etzioni promotes for a community of communities—can affect action differently through different everyday customs. People enact civic order and core values through particular community-building customs that have important consequences for the greater community. These community-building customs in themselves produce different kinds of social bonds. A communitarian imagination can sensitize us to these particular relationships through which abstract values achieve their integrative power.

Different community-building customs produce different kinds of social bonds, different ways of carrying group responsibilities, different ways of enacting core values.[18] The gay network pictured previously, for instance, was creating a community of interest. To many groups in U.S. public life, it is customary, a matter of common sense, to build community on the basis of a unitary group interest. A good member of such a community identifies unambivalently with the strategic interest and depends on other members to do the same, even if that means bracketing off their other communal identities. Groups follow this custom of community building even when their members envision wider horizons of concern outside the group and even when it does not serve strategic interests to define community in such a unitary way—as the Black gay leader's dissent suggested. Communities of interest are not simply rational or logical reflections of group interest; they are cultural and custom bound.

The community of interest is pervasive in U.S. civic life, but it does not exhaust the community-building customs available to Americans. Some groups in civil society, for example, construct themselves as very localized, narrowly communitarian kinds of community—to be distinguished from the more pluralistic communities Etzioni upholds. Such a group defines its community in terms of a unitary will, somewhat as communities of interest do. But it is a will that the group articulates in terms of long-standing moral traditions and shared history, and not simply strategic interests, even if defining its will this way is not immediately valuable in strategic terms.

Different kinds of community-building customs would make the proposed framework of core values mean different things in different communities. To understand the potentials for a community of communities, then, it is not enough to stipulate a general framework of binding values—important as those values are. We must focus, too, on the customs that determine the ways those values exert their binding force.

An African American environmental group offers a good example of how particular social bonds inflect the meaning of general, core values.[19] We could find a number of the core values operating in the group's relations with county agencies, local corporations, and local neighborhoods. First, the group embraced democracy as a core value (*NGR*, 199), not simply a tool of expediency that could be discarded for strategic reasons: The group rejected an allied group's proposal to shout down a state-sponsored public hearing on local pollution, instead of participating with other local interests and state regulators. Second, the group's leaders expressed "layered loyalties," another core value (*NGR*, 202–03), by accepting that their locale was obligated to host some of the more "encompassing" community's toxic waste sites, rather than simply saying all waste sites should be removed from their neighborhoods. Third, the group in effect affirmed the value of "limiting identity politics" (*NGR*, 205); its mostly Black constituency presented itself as local residents with reasonable stakes in the larger community, not solely as Blacks with race-specific grievances against a White power structure.

And yet, neither the group's dedication to democracy, nor its sense of place in a larger society, nor its lack of any overt identity politics, kept it from a parochial outlook on its own community. Though group members insisted the group was an environmental alliance open to any local residents, the group assumed that *being a member* meant having an unquestioning stance toward a single, morally grounded communal will. Residents who favored different strategies than the group's for dealing with their pollution-damaged homes and chronic illnesses got written off as merely "self-interested" and not really part of "the community." When one local resident spoke out in favor of a local company that provided jobs to young people, after the environmental group had castigated the way the company managed its toxic waste, group members were stunned and found nothing more to say than that the woman was "bought off." But didn't those young people need jobs after all? It would be unfair to say the group contradicted its own core value of democracy by discounting this woman. Rather, the group enacted the values of democracy and loyalty through community-building customs that sustained a tight-knit, almost organic "we." This kind of bond gave the group some admirable strengths, but also made it difficult for members to validate competing priorities in the community without sounding like they were breaking ranks.

Communitarian values by themselves cannot guarantee that people will enact them in a way that always strengthens the greater community. Communitarian pluralists need to examine social bonds as well as guiding values. We need to talk explicitly about the patterns of community building that people often take for granted.

POLICY AND CIVIL SOCIETY WITHIN THE GREATER COMMUNITY

Chapter seven's policy recommendations invite the same tensions between general framework and concrete relationships that strain the thinking about boundaries and values in Etzioni's otherwise promising argument. I read the policy proposals in light of Etzioni's dictum "there should (not) be a law" (*NGR*, 138). There is much to appreciate in this call to seek community goals through moral suasion in civil society when possible, rather than turning automatically to legislatures or courts in pursuit of new rights. Still, I want to affirm Etzioni's commitment to give the state a meaningful role in his project for a greater community. The dilemmas of housing policy constitute a brave test for communitarian ideas about the state's role in a community of communities.

Housing, as Etzioni notes, is one of the most important if difficult issues on the agenda to strengthen community life. That is all the more reason to acknowledge the concrete boundaries and bonds Americans create through our housing preferences, for better or worse, even as we affirm core values of diversity and equal opportunity. The faith-based association introduced previously evolved in a city in which at least some White, majority-culture parents affirmed the communitarian value of intercultural respect, attended Martin Luther King Day celebrations with their children, and lauded schoolteachers' efforts to promote cultural diversity in their kids' classrooms, all the while living in suburban enclaves whose residents had few relationships with people culturally different from themselves. These local residents wanted to experience the public happiness that a community of communities makes possible. Surely these residents experienced, or avoided, or tripped over, social priorities that would make an integrated, greater community a highly conflicted goal for many Americans. Here, the economic dimensions of communal boundaries become especially salient. But even if free of anxieties over maintaining their own class standing, these residents still needed more than good values in the abstract to make their own neighborhood life reflect more of America's diversity. They needed to make boundary crossing a part of their working definition of "community" itself. They

needed to know *how* to create a community of communities. A high-powered housing commission as briefly advocated (*NGR*, 215) is not likely to model new kinds
of community-building practices—though official proclamations about neighborhoods and diversity may carry ritual value we should not underestimate in a time
when more Americans are choosing to shut out the greater community beyond their
guarded neighborhood gates.

Most Americans are likely to define housing in terms of a fundamental, passion-
ately defended free choice.[20] A national commission could not hope to speak legitimately on the issue without first engaging broad, popular, local debates about what
constitutes a good neighborhood and a good community. At stake here is the larger
question of how communitarian ideas relate to state power. Policy recommendations
within a communitarian pluralist agenda need to evolve in tandem with public discussion. The society-wide moral dialogues that Etzioni advocates elsewhere in *The
New Golden Rule* ought to influence state policy making, as well as the moral voice
of civil society. The high stakes in these debates, their potential to create cultural
and economic barriers anew as well as moral deadlocks, would sorely test the limits
of moral deliberation.

That said, I will venture that the best community-promoting policies from a
communitarian standpoint will be ones that are general enough to allow communities the autonomy to select from a large range of strategies as long as these stay within
the parameters set by core values. Clearly, a locality that refuses to address school
segregation, for instance, with anything other than vague recommendations for "further study" would soon fail the core value of equal rights contained in the Constitution. But to argue that a specific strategy, such as busing for racial integration,
"breaks communal bonds and undermines communal institutions" (*NGR*, 216) is
to assume that *all* communities define themselves in parochial terms. Communitarian
policy initiatives ought not assume that communities are always rigidly bound by
definition or always defined by geography. Any number of housing and neighborhood policies may complement the community of communities model, depending
on the kinds of social bonds and civic customs community members share.

While cognizant of real boundaries and real parochialism in U.S. communities,
communitarian policymakers ought to uphold the vision of the greater community's
potential I have introduced here. A communitarian and pluralistic community of
communities sustains interpenetrating loyalties, not layered ones; permeable boundaries, not rigid ones; self-reflective identities, not narrowly partisan ones. And it reflects on the strengths and weaknesses of its customary social bonds as well as its
explicit values. In policy-making arenas as well as the arenas of civil society I have
discussed already, citizens need to cultivate the sense that their individual choices
often contribute to immediate communities and specific greater communities simultaneously. More than a product of legislation, the greater community must become
a way of life.

NOTES

1. Amitai Etzioni, *The New Golden Rule: Community and Morality in a Democratic Society* (New York: Basic Books, 1996), 191. Subsequent references to this work will be noted parenthetically in the text by *NGR* and page number.

2. See, for instance, Derek Phillips, *Looking Backward: A Critical Appraisal of Communitarian Thought* (Princeton, N.J.: Princeton University Press, 1993).

3. See Benedict Anderson's oft-cited argument in *Imagined Communities: Reflections on the Origins and Spread of Nationalisin* (London: Verso, 1991).

4. For a discussion of indirect community relationships and social cohesion, see Craig Calhoun, "Populist Politics, Communications Media, and Large Scale Social Integration," *Sociological Theory* 6(2) (1988): 219–41.

5. Theorists of democracy have been exploring the kinds of communities and institutional relationships that would make lively, public-spirited citizenship possible in a society of diverse identities and inequalities. See, for instance, Nancy Fraser, "Rethinking the Public Sphere: A Contribution to the Critique of Actually Existing Democracy," in *Habermas and the Public Sphere,* ed. Craig Calhoun (Cambridge, Mass.: MIT Press, 1992), 109–42; Seyla Benhabib, ed., *Democracy and Difference: Contesting the Boundaries of the Political* (Princeton, N.J.: Princeton University Press, 1996); Seyla Benhabib and Drucilla Cornell, eds., *Feminism as Critique* (Minneapolis: University of Minnesota Press, 1987); Steven Seidman and Linda Nicholson, *Social Postmodernism* (Cambridge: Cambridge University Press, 1995). These diverse inquiries share a critical engagement with Jurgen Habermas's writings on the public sphere; see *Theory of Communicative Action,* 2 vols. (Boston: Beacon Press, 1987, 1984); "The Public Sphere: An Encyclopedia Article," *New German Critique* 3 (1974): 49–55.

6. A classic statement and illustration of the position is Robert Dahl, *Who Governs? Democracy and Power in an American City* (New Haven, Conn.: Yale University Press, 1961).

7. See James Hunter, *Culture Wars* (New York: Basic Books, 1991); Todd Gitlin, *The Twilight of Common Dreams* (New York: Henry Holt, 1995); Robert Hughes, *Culture of Complaint* (New York: Oxford University Press, 1993).

8. This is an argument that Michele Lamont makes convincingly in *Money, Morals and Manners* (Chicago: University of Chicago Press, 1992). Sociologists of culture and inequality increasingly make this argument. For examples, see Michele Lamont and Marcel Fournier, eds., *Cultivating Differences* (Chicago: University of Chicago Press, 1992). In a related vein, see Pierre Bourdieu's work, especially *Distinction: A Social Critique of the Judgment of Taste* (Cambridge, Mass.: Harvard University Press, 1984).

9. I have adapted this example from Paul Lichterman, "Talking Identity in the Public Sphere: Broad Visions and Small Spaces in Sexual Identity Politics," *Theory and Society* 28(1) (February 1999): 101–41.

10. In an otherwise perceptive treatment of communitarian thinking, Chantal Mouffe implies that communitarians treat communities as premodem, essential wholes. See her argument in "Democratic Citizenship and the Political Community," in *Dimensions of Radical Democracy,* ed. C. Mouffe (London: Verso, 1992), 225–40.

11. Arguments about the state of civic life in the United States often refer to Robert Putnam's findings that memberships have dropped sharply in a wide variety of civic groups—from PTAs and fraternal organizations to bowling leagues—since the 1960s. See "Bowling Alone: America's Declining Social Capital," *Journal of Democracy* 6(1) (January 1995): 65–78.

12. See Harry Boyte, "The Pragmatic Ends of Popular Politics," in *Habermas and the Public Sphere,* ed. Craig Calhoun (Cambridge, Mass.: MIT Press, 1992): 340–55.

13. This example comes from my ongoing research project, tentatively titled "Love Thy Neighbor: Religion and Civic Renewal in America," unpublished manuscript, Department of Sociology, University of Wisconsin.

14. On this point, communitarian thinking offers a corrective to other lines of political thought that focus too narrowly on community as a discursive construction. My discussion is influenced by radical democratic theorists who share the communitarians' concern with shared public goods, but highlight the ways identity and community continually get redefined in deliberation and conflict. See, for instance, Chantal Mouffe, *Dimensions of Radical Democracy;* William Connolly, *The Ethos of Pluralization* (Minneapolis: University of Minnesota Press, 1995). Yet, these treatments of community tend to neglect the grounded, ongoing social relationships that one cannot see from analyzing community as a discourse alone.

15. Here I follow the more restricted usage of "citizen" as a subject of the state, because Etzioni's well-taken point is to contrast a state-centered understanding of membership with more autonomously defined forms of belonging in society at large. Radical democratic political theorists, in contrast, tend to define "citizenship" in terms similar to those of social membership, signifying that the state is but one locus of power in society. See, for instance, the essays in Steven Seidman and Linda Nicholson, *Social Postmodernism.*

16. I am counterposing civil society to a simply drawn, coolly administrative state, rather than elaborating on the state's own integrative pull and its own rituals and customs, only to bring the less remarked-upon customs of civic life into high relief in this short chapter. A large body of research explores the state's integrative rituals; for a recent study, see Lyn Spillman, *Nation and Commemoration* (Cambridge: Cambridge University Press, 1997). The terms of my discussion are influenced by an authoritative theoretical account in Jean Cohen and Andrew Arato, *Civil Society and Political Theory* (Cambridge, Mass.: MIT Press, 1992). But state and civil society are not as neatly divisible as my discussion suggests; for a good example of the difficulties in making these distinctions cleanly on the ground, see Michael Brown's study of state-supported AIDS service workers and volunteers, *Replacing Citizenship* (New York: Guilford Press, 1997).

17. Sociologists increasingly point out the empirical and logical difficulties in relating values to action. They reject the conventional, Weberian understanding of values as end-goals for action. See, for instance, the forceful critique in Ann Swidler, "Culture in Action: Symbols and Strategies, *American Sociological Review* 51 (April 1986): 273–86.

18. The community-building customs concept is adapted from separate and coauthored projects by the author and Nina Eliasoph. See the "culture of commitment" and "practice" concepts in Paul Lichterman, *The Search for Political Community: American Activists Reinventing Commitment* (New York: Cambridge University Press, 1996); see "civic practices" in Nina Eliasoph, *Avoiding Politics: How Americans Produce Apathy in Everyday Life* (New York: Cambridge University Press, 1998), and Nina Eliasoph and Paul Lichterman, "Cultural Style in Civic Life" (revised version of paper presented at the annual meetings of the American Sociological Association, New York, 1996).

19. This example is adopted from Lichterman, *Search for Political Community.*

20. The relatively affluent, weekend multiculturalists portrayed in my brief sketch here could be very much like the interviewees in Robert Bellah et al., *Habits of the Heart* (Berkeley: University of California Press, 1985), who used individualistic moral language even when

they sustained communitarian attachments. This could be even more true of working-class or lower-middle class Americans. As Herbert Gans writes, "middle Americans" weigh public issues in terms of their own chances for winning and protecting a piece of the economic pie. See Herbert Gans, *Middle American Individualism* (New York: Free Press, 1988).

9

Communitarianism: The Issue of Relativism

Nicos Mouzelis

There are two standard critiques against communitarian theories: (1) that these theories always entail authoritarian connotations, with their emphasis on the importance of communal values and order undermining individual freedoms; and (2) that their focus on the context-bound nature of communal values results in the relativistic idea that, since every community has its own values, there is no supracommunal or extracommunal way of assessing conflicting views of the good life.

THE GOLDEN-RULE PERSPECTIVE

Communitarianism, as expounded by Amitai Etzioni, attempts to overcome both the authoritarian and the relativistic critiques. He responds to both with his notion of the "golden rule"—with the idea that when advocating or promoting "community" in the modern world, one should strive to achieve a balance between order and individual autonomy. It is the imbalance between these two cardinal virtues that creates difficulties: overemphasis on order at the expense of autonomy leads to authoritarianism, overemphasis on autonomy at the expense of order leads to anarchy.

If the golden rule is applied, there can be no authoritarianism because of communal order taking repressive forms, undermining autonomy, and therefore breaking the order–autonomy balance. More specifically, Etzioni is in favor of a voluntary social and moral order that, without being contractarian, is based on an ongoing dialogue leading to communal consensus. If *intra*communal dialogue avoids authoritarianism, relativism for Etzioni can be dealt with by the notion of *inter*communal dialogue: respect for the values and ways of life of other communities and the promotion of open-ended dialogue between them will undermine communal isolation and so encourage procedural and even substantive mechanisms of intercommunal integration. Such integrative mechanisms combat the postmodern relativistic idea that there is no common framework, no common moral vocabulary by means of which one can compare and assess the ways of life of different communities or civilizations.

In addition, Etzioni argues that the values of specific communities should be compatible with the values or moral order of the "community of communities," of the superordinate social entity (e.g., the nation-state, global system) within which communities are embedded. However, as he points out, this does not solve the problem of relativism but simply shifts it upward from the community level to that of the "community of communities." Concerning this difficulty, he argues that the values of the community of communities should, in the last analysis, be compatible with the golden rule, with the twin cardinal virtues of moral order and bounded autonomy: "As I see it, moral order and autonomy crown the communitarian normative account. They provide the final, substantive normative criterion this account requires."[1]

According to Etzioni, this compatibility is the result of the values of moral order and bounded autonomy being "morally compelling" and therefore self-evident. No utilitarian, consequentialist reasoning is required for the legitimation. They are accepted by people of good will as a matter of course—in as unmediated a manner as religious revelation is accepted by believers. In other words, the balance between the basic virtues of moral order and bounded autonomy is as manifest and morally compelling as is the value of health for the medical sciences.[2] Moreover, the golden rule is universal and applies to all communities—while at the same time, provided they do not offend against it, it allows for the myriad particularistic judgments of specific communities.

I think that Etzioni's attempt to avoid the absolutism of any single value by stressing that the crucially important balance between moral order and individual autonomy will lead to a mutual reinforcement of social virtues and individual rights, as well as his dialogic approach to intracommunal communication, does indeed provide an adequate normative framework for refuting those critics who stress the authoritarian character of all communitarian theories. Where he seems to me to be rather less successful is in tackling the critique of relativism.

ON THE SELF-EVIDENCE OF THE GOLDEN RULE

My difficulty with Etzioni's solution to the matter of relativism is that the virtue of a balance between order and autonomy is not as utterly self-evident and morally compelling as he implies. To take an extreme example: in highly segmental, non-differentiated communities with low or nonexistent individuation, the idea of bounded autonomy (entailing negative and positive liberties as well as the notion of self-expression) is neither self-evident nor morally compelling. The idea of the right to self-expression, or the idea of the individual having rights of his/her own, develop only in conditions of what U. Beck has termed individualization.[3]

Even if we ignore such extreme examples and restrict ourselves to traditional village communities as they exist today in various parts of the so-called third world—the contention that a moral social order as it may be developed and defined by a specific community should *prevail* over individual autonomy cannot be simply dismissed as ideological brainwashing, or as a "misunderstanding" that can be cleared up by open dialogue, as advocated by Etzioni.

To take an example used by the author of *The New Golden Rule* himself: the father who finds a much older husband for his daughter, one rich enough to afford the dowry price, may seem to us as "selling" his daughter to the highest bidder.[4] But the situation can be interpreted very differently from the point of view of a culture where kinship solidarity or economic survival of the family unit take clear precedence over the expressive needs, preferences, or individual rights of family members. To put it bluntly, sacrificing the individual rights of a kin-member on the altar of family solidarity or survival may be self-evidently immoral to a U.S. university professor, but not at all to an impoverished Egyptian or Bolivian peasant. In other words, for a huge part of humankind still living in quasi-traditional settings, the *imbalance* between moral order and individual autonomy (in favor of the former) might be more morally compelling or more self-evident than the balance between these two cardinal virtues. To dismiss such orientations as the result of confusion or "distorted communication" simply won't do. It is as unconvincing as the Marxist argument of false consciousness that is supposed to explain why the proletariat does not revolt.

BASIC ASSUMPTIONS AND DIFFICULTIES OF THE RELATIVIST POSITION

These difficulties with the golden-rule concept do not necessarily result in total relativism. But I do think that, in order to overcome the relativistic position, the focus should shift from moral and political philosophy to sociology and adopt a more historically oriented macrocomparative, evolutionist perspective. It would then be quite feasible to show that the golden rule, without being *universally* self-evident, does become morally compelling for a growing number of people living in *post-traditional* contexts all over the globe.

I shall begin by looking more closely at how postmodern, relativistic arguments are deployed. According to most postmodernist discourses, if we take into account the social and cultural pluralism that characterizes the contemporary world—as well as the fact that what is ethical/unethical, good/bad, valuable/nonvaluable is strictly related to specific sociohistoric contexts—then we are bound to conclude that there is no way of assessing or hierarchizing cultural values and modes of life based on them. There is no foundation, no Archimedian principle, no universal norm that would help us stand above multiple and often contradictory cultural codes or para-digms in order to judge which of them is more or less good, just, or true.

On a more practical level this relativistic attitude means that, in our postmodern condition, even practices that are inhuman or repulsive from the Western point of view (such as female circumcision, infanticide, etc.) cannot be condemned on the basis of some universal standard—whatever it might be. On the other hand, in con-trast to relativism, there is the view that values like moral order, individual freedom, respect for basic human rights, or a combination of them, are of transhistorical, universal character, and as such can be used in the assessment or evaluation of so-cial practices in specific contexts.

In what follows I shall develop a position that avoids the postmodern type of rela-tivism without subscribing to Etzioni's idea that certain values (like the balance be-tween social virtues and individual rights) are morally compelling or self-evident in a universal, transhistorical manner. It is true of course that Etzioni does not explic-itly emphasize the universal, transhistorical character of his golden rule. His whole argument, however—insofar as it does not distinguish between people still living in traditional and others living in posttraditional contexts today—implies that the bal-ance between moral order and individual autonomy appeals to all people of good-will. This is definitely not so.

Let us consider first total relativism. It generates severe difficulties in two particular areas. *First*, notwithstanding the fact that values like those entailed by the golden rule are not universal, there is a very small number of human values that, because they are based on what evolutionists call biological or sociological universals,[5] are indeed universal or quasi-universal. Example: because all known human societies have a kinship system and because Homo sapiens need a long period of primary social-ization, a certain altruism of the mother toward her biological child is to be found, as a norm,[6] in all sociocultural formations from the least to the most differentiated. This statement does not necessarily lead to teleological functionalism,[7] because one can argue that cultures/societies without such altruistic values simply could not and did not survive.[8]

Second, and more important, as Ernest Gellner pointed out long ago, the notion of total relativism assumes the existence of societies or communities that are entirely self-contained, that have no linkages whatsoever with other societies or communi-ties. It is based on a hypothetical, nonexistent world where values do not spread from one sociocultural whole to another via trade, war, migration, and so on.[9] Such a totally compartmentalized world not only has never existed but is the extreme op-posite of what we are witnessing today: that is, the growing interpenetration and interdependence (via globalization) of cultures, civilizations, societies, and so on. The more advanced this interdependence and interpenetration, the less ground there is for postmodern relativism to stand on. It loses its footing because it is precisely the growing overlap between various cultural traditions that provides a basis both for comparison and for serious assessment and evaluation of conflicting ways of life.

STEPPING STONES TOWARD GROWING SOCIOCULTURAL INTERPENETRATION

This becomes clearer if we view processes of growing interdependence or interpenetration from a perspective not of *specific* but of *general* evolution[10]—pointing out in an illustrative, nonsystematic manner, some of the key turning points or institutional breakthroughs that have led to the present extraordinary, unprecedented fusion and interpenetration of cultural traditions.

1. Starting from the city-states of antiquity, not only in Mediterranean Europe but also in Mesopotamia and Asia Minor, these miniscule sociocultural formations were embedded in larger cultural-civilizational wholes. These wholes extended far beyond a specific city-state's walls and its military-administrative organization.[11]

2. The tendency of cultural values and norms to transcend specific juridico-administrative entities was dramatically reinforced by the shift from local, primitive to the so-called historic, or world, religions, which developed quasi-universal discourses—discourses whose abstractions made them "detachable" from local, particularistic conditions, thus increasing their appeal to millions of people across a variety of societies, polities, and civilizations.[12]

3. According to I. Wallerstein, it was in the sixteenth and seventeenth centuries that the first "world system" came into existence: a system of various states competing with one another in the international economic, political, and cultural arenas. What was unique about the system was that no one state was strong enough to destroy interstate economic and politico-military competition by establishing an imperial order.[13] This "primitive" world system was, of course, very much strengthened in the eighteenth century by the emergence of the nation-state and the shift from the inter*state* to an inter*nation-state* world system.

4. Another crucial breakthrough during the process of growing sociocultural interpenetration was the dominance of the capitalist mode of production in eighteenth-century Western Europe. If by capitalist mode of production we do not simply mean commercialization in the sphere of trade/distribution; if (following Karl Marx) we use the narrow definition of capitalism as the entrance of capital into the sphere of agricultural and industrial production and the consequent creation of wage labor[14] on a massive scale—then the dominance of the capitalist mode of production not only peripheralizes noncapitalsit modes, but it also, together with the nation-state, systematically destroys the economic, political, and cultural segmental localisms of the precapitalist era.

   Furthermore, it dramatically advances the internationalization or globalization of the economy. If in the nineteenth century international capital was mainly oriented toward infrastructural investments (e.g., ports, railways), and in the twentieth, toward the global production of consumer goods (e.g., cars), on the eve of the twenty-first century the globalization of the economy is being completed by its massive entrance into the service sphere (banking, insurance, management, accounting, etc.).[15]

5. The global process of democratization after the collapse of the Soviet Union[16] —although often superficial and extremely uneven—is another fundamental mechanism that is bringing late-modern societies closer together on the level of political, social, and cultural values.

Summing up: world religions in the cultural sphere, the system of nation-states and the more recent trend of global democratization in the political sphere, the massive entrance of capital into the sphere of national and international production in the economic sphere—all these, as well as the extraordinary technologies with which they are inextricably linked, have brought us to a situation that is the exact opposite of total societal self-containment and cultural isolation.

Today's situation creates conditions that encourage the gradual spread and acceptance of the core values of late modernity—values such as productivity in the economic sphere, democracy in the political, solidarity in the social, and individual autonomy/self-realization in the cultural sphere. These values, as I have argued already, are certainly not transhistorical or universal, but they do appeal to the growing number of people who live in *posttraditional* settings, whether in Blairite Britain, social-democratic Sweden, authoritarian Korea, or quasi-totalitarian China. It is precisely because the previously mentioned values are gradually becoming global among "late-modern" individuals that it is possible to transcend relativism and condemn the violation of human rights, whether this occurs in Israel, Turkey, Northern Ireland, or China.

EUROCENTRISM

Of course, the "politically correct" relativist may argue that the previously described way of founding transcultural values is clearly Eurocentric, since values relating to parliamentary democracy and entailing individual freedoms are specifically Western cultural products that have been imposed on the rest of the world via imperialism or the less violent Western-dominated mechanisms of the world market. The Eurocentrism debate is a highly complex one, and I do not intend to tackle it at all systematically.[17] What I do want to point out here is that the values of democracy and of human liberties and rights—without being universal or "eternal" in the Platonic, idealistic sense of the term—transcend the narrow limits of Western European culture or civilization. This is so because:

- Despite the fact that parliamentary democracy and the civil, political, and social rights associated with it took their most developed form in the "West," important elements of such institutions are to be found in various non-European civilizations, past as well as present.

- As the historian William McNeill has persuasively argued,[18] the types of revolution (scientific, technological, economic, and political) that have "modernized" Western Europe could equally well have happened in other "civilized" parts of the preindustrial world. The fact that they occurred in the West has more to do with conjunctural factors than with the uniqueness or superiority of Western culture. Another way of putting this is to say that the reason why the breakthrough happened in Western Europe was due less to "unique" elements (such as the Protestant work ethic) than to the combination and timing of elements that were not unique but could be found in several other complex civilizations during the breakthrough period.[19]

- The modernization of the non-Western world took various forms. Some of these proved less "effective" (e.g., Soviet collectivist modernization) than the Western one, whereas others might, in the long run, prove more so (i.e., the Japanese or Chinese type of modernization). This is particularly so if one takes into account that democracy is not always compatible with development. In fact, contrary to Etzioni (see *The New Golden Rule*, 234–42), I am not at all sure that "late-late"-comers, whatever the stage of their development, can overcome the usual bottlenecks created by underdevelopment without—*at least at some initial state*—a strong dose of authoritarianism. Etzioni gives India as an example of development without authoritarianism, but I do not think he is convincing. India is still a country where a large part of the population lives in conditions of utter poverty and degradation.

Considering certain features of Japanese modernity that sharply distinguish it from the Anglo-Saxon variant—such as concern for long-term growth and development rather than immediate profit maximization, horizontal cooperation between branches of industry, selective and flexible state support for growth industries, more emphasis on training and developing human resources and less on "downsizing," reluctance to let the market set the level of unemployment, and so on, and so on—it is highly possible that in the next century quasi-authoritarian Asian capitalism could prevail over its more liberal Anglo-Saxon competitor.[20]

This prognosis becomes particularly plausible in view of the at present rather spectacular development of Chinese modernization—a modernization combining foreign-capital led economic development with rigid capital controls. As has frequently been argued, it is highly likely that, as Chinese capitalism develops further, there will be both internal and external pressures for the democratic opening-up of the political system. (This has happened in Korea.) Such an opening-up might lead to a Japanese style of authoritarian modernity, with weak liberal-democratic political institutions providing some degree of political pluralism and democratic representation. On the other hand, the possibility cannot be excluded that, in the long term,

Chinese modernity might combine effective capitalist development with political forms that continue to remain strongly authoritarian-totalitarian.

However, regardless of which modernizing route China follows, perhaps with lower rates of economic growth than now, there is no doubt that in the decades to come a more developed China will, with its demographic weight, drastically change the global capitalist landscape.

It is true, of course, that at present the Asian economies are experiencing serious difficulties. But however serious the crisis, there is no doubt that in terms of both production and distribution of wealth, Asian capitalism is greatly superior to Indian or Latin-American capitalism, for instance.

If we take this into consideration it becomes clear that values related to political rights, for example (regardless of where they became fully institutionalized for the first time), constitute what Talcott Parsons has called *evolutionary universals*: at a certain stage in the evolution of human societies they become basic preconditions if a society is to move up to higher levels of differentiation and "adaptive capacity."[21] As such they have a very broad, transcultural appeal, which, as I have already argued, addresses itself to posttraditional individuals all over the world. This does not mean, of course, that the previously mentioned values are totally accepted, always respected, or followed in practice. It does mean, however, that they have become a basic reference point for assessing and legitimizing or condemning political practices on a global, transcultural level.

What, therefore, distinguishes today's major living cultural traditions or civilizations is not their focus on radically conflicting values, but rather the way in which a small number of commonly accepted core values articulate with each other. For example, in the Anglo-Saxon world, at least at the level of the elites, political pluralism (as a core dimension of liberal democracy) has much more weight than social solidarity. In Japan, on the other hand, the priorities are reversed. And if for Europeans and North Americans the political repression in China is totally unacceptable, for many Asians this negative feature of the Chinese regime must be seen in the light of Russia's disastrous "democratic" revolution and of China's spectacular economic growth—a growth that, for the first time in the country's history, has freed millions of peasants from the specter of starvation or chronic undernourishment.[22]

SUMMARY AND CONCLUSIONS

Etzioni deals with relativism by saying that his "golden rule," that is, balance between individual autonomy and the moral, social order, constitutes a self-evident, morally compelling truth. I have argued that this is not the case and that a more effective way of overcoming postmodern relativism is adopting an evolutionist, macrohistorical perspective. If this is done certain values, or combinations of values (like the combination of individual autonomy and order), without being universally valid, tend to have a transcultural, global appeal today for those individuals who live in posttraditional settings. I have tried to support this claim by saying that:

a. Relativism takes into account neither certain common biological and socio-logical features of all human societies nor the fact that societies and civiliza-tions are not isolated, totally self-contained wholes.

b. From an evolutionist point of view, the interrelatedness/interdependence of societies is dramatically increased by the emergence of world religions, the de-velopment of a system of nation-states, the penetration of capital not only into the sphere of distribution but also of production, present-day globalizing trends, and so on.

c. Despite the fact that some of the above values were first institutionalized (on a large scale) in the West, they are not just Western but constitute *evolution-ary* universals. As such, in different combinations, they appeal to all "modern" people, whether in Europe, Asia, or Africa.

d. What, in late modernity, distinguishes various sociocultural wholes is not so much the absolute "uniqueness" of their values, but rather the unique way in which a small number of common, transcultural values are related to each other.

NOTES

1. Amitai Etzioni, *The New Golden Rule* (New York: Basic Books, 1996), 246.

2. Etzioni, *The New Golden Rule*, 244–7.

3. According to Beck, individualization entails three fundamental dimensions: (1) *disembedding*, or removal from "historically prescribed social forms and commitments"; (2) *the loss of traditional security* with respect to practical knowledge, faith, and guiding norms; and (3) *re-embedding*, or reintegration into a new context, requiring a posttraditional type of social commitment. U. Beck, *Risk Society: Towards a New Modernity* (London: Sage, 1992), 128. See also U. Beck and E. Beck-Gernsheim, "Individualization and 'Precarious Freedoms': Perspectives and Controversies of a Subject-Object Oriented Sociology," in *Decentralization*, ed. P. Heelas et al. (Cambridge: Blackwell, 1996). Also U. Beck, A. Giddens, and S. Lash, eds., *Reflexive Modernization: Politics, Tradition and Aesthetics in the Modern Social Order* (Cambridge: Polity Press, 1994).

4. Etzioni, *The New Golden Rule*, 245–7.

5. On the concept of biological and sociological universals, see T. Parsons, "Evolutionary Universals in Society," *American Sociological Review* 29 (1964): 339–57; and his *Societies: Evolutionary and Comparative Perspectives* (Englewood Cliffs, N.J.: Prentice Hall, 1968).

6. I emphasize *norm* because, obviously, there are always discrepancies between normative expectations (as these are embedded in specific rules and institutions) and actual performance.

7. Teleological functionalism in a methodologically illegitimate manner transforms social needs into causes, i.e., it explains the emergence, persistence, or transformation of social wholes in terms of society's functional requirements for stability, adaptation, cohesion, and so on.

8. For the theoretical elaboration of such an argument, see R. Dore, "Function and Cause," *American Sociological Review* 26 (1961): 843–53.

9. Of course, value overlap or similarities between different societies is due not only to diffusion. Given similar structural conditions or systemic requirements, the same values may emerge in disconnected parts of the world. On this point, see T. Parsons, "Evolutionary Universals."

10. Specific evolution refers to a process of cumulative growth that is historically and geographically specific, in the sense that it takes place within a specific social whole evolving through time (e.g., the process of bureaucratization in postrevolutionary France). General evolution, on the other hand, refers to a process of cumulative growth that, historically and geographically, cuts across specific evolutionary lines. It is a process that can be understood by looking at the evolutionary patterns of all or of several societies or cultures. A good example is Auguste Comte's three-stage evolutionary theory, which argues that one can identify a general pattern of growing rationalization as humanity moves from theological to metaphysical and, finally, positivistic modes of social explanation. Comte's mistake was to consider this pattern of rationalization not in terms of general but of specific evolution. He wrongly thought that all societies go through these three stages. For the concepts of general and specific evolution, see M. D. Sahlins and E. R. Service, eds., *Evolution and Culture* (Ann Arbor: University of Michigan Press, 1960). In what follows, I consider the growing interdependence of societies/cultures as a process of general evolution.

11. See M. Mann, *The Sources of Social Power*, vol. 1 (New York: Academic Press, 1974).

12. Comte, in discussing the theological stage of his evolutionist theory, is one of the first classical social theorists who focused on the connection between the growing "abstraction" of religious belief (as one moves from animism to polytheism and monotheism) and the decline of cultural localism. The link between growing differentiation and the emergence of "free-floating," "disembedded" religious ideas and values constitutes a central theme in the work of Parsons and some of his disciples (Eisenstadt, Bellah, etc.).

13. See I. Wallerstein, *The Modern World System*, vol. 1 (New York: Academic Press, 1974).

14. For a systematic discussion of Marx's definition of capitalism, see M. Dobbs, *Studies in the Development of Capitalism* (New York: International Publishers, 1968), 1–32. For a debate on the meaning of capitalism and the relevance of diverging definitions in explaining the transition from feudalism to capitalism in Western Europe, cf. R. Hilton, ed., *The Transition from Feudalism to Capitalism* (London: New Left Books, 1976).

15. See C. Chase-Dunn, *Global Formation: Structures of the World Economy* (Oxford: Basil Blackwell, 1989).

16. See L. Diamond and M. Plattner, eds. *The Global Resurgence of Democracy* (Baltimore, Md.: Johns Hopkins University Press, 1996).

17. For a more detailed treatment of the Eurocentrism issue, see my "Modernity: A Non-Eurocentric Conceptualization," *British Journal of Sociology*, forthcoming.

18. See W. H. McNeill, *The Rise of the West* (Chicago: Chicago University Press, 1963).

19. See W. H. McNeill, "A Swan-Song of British Liberalism?" in *The Social Philosophy of Ernest Gellner*, ed. J. Hall and I. Jarvie (Amsterdam: Poznan Studies in the Philosophy of Sciences and Humanities Series, 1995).

20. For the difference between Anglo-Saxon and Japanese capitalism, see S. Berger and A. Dore, *National Diversity and Global Capitalism* (Ithaca, N.Y.: Cornell University Press, 1996).

21. See T. Parsons, "Evolutionary Universals."

22. On this point, see N. Mouzelis, *Rethinking the Left: Social Democratic Tasks and Prospects* (Department of Sociology, London School of Economics Series, 1998).

10

Moral Dialogue across Cultures: An Empirical Perspective

Shalom H. Schwartz and Anat Bardi

In the culminating chapter of *The New Golden Rule*, Amitai Etzioni extends his analysis of social morality to apply it to the global community.[1] He asserts that one limited set of core values can serve, in varying balances, as the basis for good societies around the world. In presenting this view, Etzioni confronts the fundamental relativist challenge. In a world of diverse communities, societies, and cultures, is there really a set of shared values? If not, how can one community make moral claims on others? How can one cultural group use its values to challenge those of another cultural group? The key to Etzioni's argument for the viability of a worldwide moral dialogue is the presumed existence of a set of core values that is shared around the world.

Etzioni acknowledges that it is necessary to justify the choice of these core values and of the other values in whose name groups may legitimately make moral claims. He therefore sets out a sequential series of normative criteria for evaluating the moral acceptability of values. Values gain greater legitimacy to the extent that they (1) are based on community consensus building, (2) comport with values embodied in the laws or other frames of the wider society, (3) are endorsed as an outcome of cross-societal moral dialogues, and (4) are endorsed as an outcome of cross-cultural, global moral dialogues (currently rare). Even if these criteria are met, however, the values endorsed may be morally unacceptable. Etzioni's final criterion is that the values should speak to all people as self-evident: people should experience them as having compelling moral force. This is a novel position for a communitarian, making the subjective response of individuals the final arbiter of the community's values.

Etzioni proposes two core values as underlying all others—autonomy and social order. In his view, these two values are self-evident and endowed with compelling moral force. He asserts that maintaining a proper balance between this pair of social virtues is the key to promoting the joint welfare of individuals and communities.

155

A sociological analysis persuasively argues that autonomy and social order are attractive and necessary social virtues. Yet, to support the claim that they are self-evident core values requires evidence for their endorsement not only by social analysts like Etzioni but by a broad spectrum of humanity across cultures.

In building his argument, Etzioni remarks that empirical evidence regarding the possible universality of certain basic values is of limited importance as a criterion for legitimacy. Global endorsement, as in the case of the low status of women until very recently, does not ensure moral acceptability. Nonetheless, the absence of widespread endorsement may be a sign that a value is not self-evident and that it lacks compelling moral force. Etzioni notes that historical and cultural factors may obscure the compelling nature of the core values unless it is brought to light through moral dialogue. Nevertheless, if core values are indeed self-evident, traces of their importance should be found in the responses of individuals across cultures.

If the balance of autonomy and social order is essential for societal and individual health, moral dialogues within communities should have engaged these values in the past and made them salient. If Etzioni's choice of these two as shared core values is not merely idiosyncratic, evidence to support their widespread endorsement should therefore emerge. In search of such evidence we will examine data from our own cross-cultural research. We will discuss the priority that people from around the world assign to values related to autonomy and social order. Cross-cultural variations in the importance of autonomy and social order are likely. These variations may point to the kinds of historical and social structural circumstances that influence the acceptance of these values or obscure their presumed compellingness.

Etzioni points to a second probable deficiency of empirical research as an instrument for identifying core values. He claims that any list of universal values is likely to be quite thin. Perhaps so. But only empirical research on a broad array of values across many cultures can determine how scant or elaborate is the list that emerges. The research we will describe used a set of values that aspires to be comprehensive of the different major content categories of values recognized across cultures. It is therefore capable of revealing a substantial subset of values that enjoy widespread support, if such values exist. It might reveal instead, of course, that very few values indeed are universally endorsed.

If particular values do in fact emerge as widely endorsed, we may ask whether they are shared core values. Perhaps Etzioni has overlooked other candidates for the grounding of global moral dialogues. By analyzing the particular values that are or are not widely endorsed, we can learn about the origins of cross-cultural agreement. Knowledge of the extent to which members of different cultural groups agree or disagree about a relatively comprehensive set of basic values allows us to address additional questions relevant to Etzioni's concerns: Do value priorities exhibit enough in common to provide a general context for global moral dialogues? What are the values on which we can anticipate conflict as efforts are made to establish such dialogues? In sum, this chapter examines empirically whether a limited number of core values speaks to people worldwide. We seek to understand sources both of value consensus and of value difference. And we consider the implications of our findings for the possibilities and pitfalls of global moral dialogues.

In what follows, we briefly describe a comprehensive set of ten types of values that were recognized in almost every one of sixty-two nations we studied (e.g., security, hedonism, achievement.)[2] We then present the average importance ratings given to these values across these nations from around the world. We also report the average order of importance of the ten types of values across nations. These data establish a pancultural baseline of value endorsement. Cultures vary substantially around this baseline in the importance attributed to values. At the same time, there is considerable consensus regarding the relative importance and unimportance of certain values. This consensus suggests that there are core values that are universally shared. Moreover, it enables us to identify these values. We then address the question of why these particular values enjoy such widespread endorsement and why other values are assigned lesser importance.

THE NATURE OF BASIC VALUES

We define values as desirable, transsituational goals, varying in importance, that serve as guiding principles in people's lives.[3] The crucial content aspect that distinguishes among values is the type of motivational goal they express. We derived ten motivationally distinct types of values, intended to be comprehensive of the core values recognized in cultures around the world, from three universal requirements of the human condition: needs of individuals as biological organisms, requisites of coordinated social interaction, and survival and welfare needs of groups.

In order to coordinate with others in the pursuit of the goals that are important to them, groups and individuals represent these requirements cognitively as specific values about which they communicate. A *conformity* value type was derived, for example, from the prerequisites of interaction and of group survival. For interaction to proceed smoothly and for groups to maintain themselves, individuals must restrain impulses and inhibit actions that might hurt others. And a *self-direction* value type was derived from organismic needs for mastery and from the interaction and group requirements of independence and creative problem solving.

The ten motivationally distinct types of values cover the content categories we found in earlier value theories, in value questionnaires from different cultures, and in religious and philosophical discussions of values. Each type of values can be characterized by describing its central motivational goal. Table 10.1 lists the value types, each defined in terms of its central goal. A set of specific single values that primarily represent each value type appears in parentheses, following that value type. A specific value represents a type when actions that express the value or lead to its attainment promote the central goal of the type.

Table 10.1   Definitions of Motivational Types of Values in Terms of Their Goals and the Single Values That Represent Them[a]

ACHIEVEMENT: Personal success through demonstrating competence according to social standards. (successful, capable, ambitious, influential)

BENEVOLENCE: Preservation and enhancement of the welfare of people with whom one is in frequent personal contact. (helpful, honest, forgiving, loyal, responsible)

CONFORMITY: Restraint of actions, inclinations, and impulses likely to upset or harm others and violate social expectations or norms. (politeness, obedience, self-discipline, honoring parents and elders)

HEDONISM: Pleasure and sensuous gratification for oneself. (pleasure, enjoying life)

POWER: Social status and prestige, control or dominance over people and resources. (social power, authority, wealth, preserving my public image)[b]

SECURITY: Safety, harmony, and stability of society, of relationships, and of self. (family security, national security, social order, clean, reciprocation of favors)

SELF-DIRECTION: Independent thought and action—choosing, creating, exploring. (creativity, freedom, independence, curiosity, choosing own goals)

STIMULATION: Excitement, novelty, and challenge in life. (a daring life, a varied life, an exciting life)

TRADITION: Respect, commitment, and acceptance of the customs and ideas that traditional culture or religion provide the self. (humble, accepting my lot in life, devout, respect for tradition, moderate)

UNIVERSALISM: Understanding, appreciation, tolerance, and protection for the welfare of all people and for nature. (broad-minded, wisdom, social justice, equality, a world at peace, a world of beauty, unity with nature, protecting the environment)

---

[a]The following values that were included in the inventory are not used in forming indexes of the importance of each value type, because they do not exhibit equivalence of meaning across cultures: social recognition, intelligent, self-respect, inner harmony, true friendship, a spiritual life, mature love, meaning in life, detachment, sense of belonging, health.

[b]The inventory contains two lists of values, one phrasing values as nouns, the other as adjectives. For a discussion of the rationale for the dual approach see Shalom H. Schwartz, "Universals in the Content and Structure of Values: Theoretical Advances and Empirical Tests in 20 Countries," in *Advances in Experimental Social Psychology*, vol. 25, ed. Mark P. Zanna (New York: Academic Press, 1992), 1–65.

Earlier multidimensional analyses of the relationships among the single values within each of forty-seven societies provided replications that supported the discrimination of the postulated ten value types.[4] These analyses within each society also established that the forty-five single values listed in table 10.1 have nearly equivalent meanings across cultures. These forty-five values formed consistent and internally reliable subsets, and serve to index the ten value types.[5]

In order to assess the comprehensiveness of the ten value types in covering the full range of motivational goals, we invited local researchers to add values of significance in their culture that were missing from the survey. Researchers in eighteen countries added up to six values each. We assigned these values a priori to the existing value types whose motivational goals we believed them to express. Analyses including the added values revealed that these values did not identify any missing motivational content. Rather, they correlated as expected with the core values from the motivational value types to which we had assigned them. This supported the view that the set of ten types probably does not exclude any significant types of basic values.[6] The assumption of near comprehensive coverage of the basic values recognized across cultures is important when interpreting the findings we present later.

Individuals and groups may differ substantially in the importance they attribute to the values that make up the ten value types. However, our research has established the existence of a near-universal structure of relations among these value types. That is, people's values are apparently organized by the same structure of motivational oppositions and compatibilities across cultures.[7] For example, in all cultural groups, people who value obedience highly tend to attribute little importance to creativity, and vice versa. Another example, reflecting value compatibility, is that people who value creativity highly tend to value an exciting life, and vice versa.

More generally, values that emphasize one's own independent thought and action and favoring change (self-direction and stimulation types) are compatible in virtually all cultures, whereas these values are opposed to values that emphasize submissive self-restriction, preservation of traditional practices, and protection of stability (security, conformity, and tradition). Equally widespread is the opposition between values that emphasize acceptance of others as equals and concern for their welfare (universalism and benevolence) and those that emphasize the pursuit of one's own relative success and dominance over others (achievement and power).

The values studies we have cited and that we will use to assess the existence of globally accepted core values are based on individuals' self-reports of the importance they attribute to various values. Such self-reports might reflect lip service to values rather than true endorsement. It is therefore critical to establish that the self-reports of value priorities relate meaningfully to actual behavior. For this purpose, we briefly mention some of the work from around the world that addresses this issue.

The structure of relations among value types has been used to generate and test hypotheses that relate individual differences in value priorities to a large variety of attitudes, behaviors, and background variables. We list a sample of the behaviors and behavioral intentions to which values, measured with the same instruments we employ, are related in the hypothesized manner: choice of medical specialty, choice of university major, consumer purchases, cooperation and competition, counselee behavioral style, delinquent behavior, environmental behavior, intergroup social contact, occupational choice, religiosity and religious observance, and voting.[8]

This evidence for the systematic relation of value priorities to behavior comes from an impressive range of countries around the world (Brazil, China, Czech Republic, Denmark, Finland, France, Germany, Greece, Hong Kong, Hungary, Israel, Italy, Mexico, the Netherlands, Poland, Portugal, Spain, the United States, and Venezuela). There is evidence, moreover, that self-reported values are not confounded by socially desirable responding.[9] That is, the tendency to report that values are important is not related to the general tendency to present oneself as graced by socially approved qualities. The confirmation of various hypotheses relating values to attitudes, behavior, and sociodemographic characteristics supports the assumption that the self-reported values in the current study reflect real priorities rather than mere verbalizations.

Many studies have used individual differences in values to predict and explain individual differences in behavior and attitudes. Researchers have also sought to identify and explain differences between the value priorities of groups and societies.[10] Few if any have attempted, however, to determine whether there are any similarities in value priorities across cultures. Such similarities would imply that there are basic, knowable principles that account for the order of values in human societies. We next present empirical research whose aim is to identify cross-cultural similarities in value priorities. We will then develop explanations for the similarities we identify.

We are particularly interested in the importance across cultures of values that might represent the presumed core values Etzioni proposes—autonomy and social order. Is there near universal consensus on their importance, or is there variation in their importance that can be linked to particular characteristics of societies? Eztioni defines autonomy as a value expressed as a societal attribute "that provides structured opportunities and legitimation for individual and subgroup expression of their particular values, needs, and preferences."[11] The value type we label self-direction closely parallels Etzioni's autonomy. It refers to the desirability and legitimacy of individuals' independent pursuit of their own ideas and goals. In a society whose members strongly endorse self-direction values, these values will find expression in the institutions of the society (e.g., the legal, political, market, and educational systems) and in daily interactions among individuals and groups.[12]

The match between Etzioni's social order value and our value types is less obvious. His definition of social order refers to the absence of hostility and violence among members of society and to voluntary commitment to promote ordered social relations out of a sense of moral responsibility.[13] The value type ostensibly closest to Etzioni's social order is security—safety, harmony, and stability of society, of relationships, and of self. Indeed, one of the specific values that serves as an indicator of security is "social order." Conformity values, in their focus on avoiding disturbance or harm to others, also capture an element of social order. But the voluntary, moral responsibility element is missing in the conformity value type.[14] In order to assess the importance of social order across cultures, we will need to examine the importance of both security and conformity values.

IDENTIFYING THE IMPORTANCE OF VALUE TYPES ACROSS NATIONS

The value survey we employed included fifty-six single values sampled to represent the ten types of values in our theory,[15] plus values added by local researchers. Each value was followed by a short explanatory phrase in parentheses. For example: SOCIAL ORDER (stability of society), AN EXCITING LIFE (stimulating experiences).

In keeping with the definition of values, respondents rated the importance of each value as a guiding principle in their own lives. They used a nine-point scale from -1 (opposed to my principles) to 0 (not important) to 7 (of supreme importance). Because values are typically seen as desirable, they generally range from somewhat to very important. The asymmetry of the response scale reflects this natural distribution of distinctions that individuals make when thinking about the importance of values to them. We computed indexes of the importance of each of the ten value types by averaging the importance ratings of the single values representative of that type. Table 10.1 lists the specific values used to measure each type following the definition of the type.

We will base our arguments on consistencies across three different sets of samples. First we discuss findings in a set of representative or near representative samples of twelve nations or of regions within them (N = 7,639). These samples cover the variety of ages, occupations, educational levels, and so on, found in the world fairly well. Moreover, the set of nations (Australia, China, East Germany, Finland, France, Israel, Italy, Japan, the Netherlands, Russia, South Africa [Whites], West Germany) is quite variegated. It includes nations from Asia, Africa, the Middle East, East Europe, West Europe, and Oceania. Of course, a larger set of nations is needed to draw firm conclusions about any worldwide pattern.

As a second step, we ask whether the findings for the representative samples replicate in a much larger set of nations. For this purpose, we investigate the value priorities of an occupationally matched set of schoolteacher samples (grades 3–12) from fifty-five nations (N = approximately 13,000). Finally, we examine whether the pattern of value priorities observed among representative and teacher samples replicates data from yet another type of matched sample—college students from fifty-three nations (N = approximately 19,000). The nations in the three sets of samples only partly overlap. Consequently, our conclusions are based on data from sixty-two different nations or cultural groups.

Let us make explicit an important assumption about the use of findings from teacher and student samples. The mean ratings for teacher and student samples in a nation are not likely to be the same as those for representative samples in that nation. And teacher and student samples from the same nation are not likely to yield exactly the same mean value ratings. The assumption we make is that the *order* of nations on the value means, using the matched samples, resembles the *order* one would obtain with representative samples from the same set of nations. We will provide empirical support for this assumption. If the assumption is correct, there will be consistencies across the representative, teacher, and student sample sets that will enable us to draw inferences about a broad pancultural normative order of value ratings.

Table 10.2 lists the nations, locations within them where the data were gathered, type of sample, and year in which data were gathered. All samples included at least one hundred respondents. Most samples were in the 180–300-respondent range; several included more than a thousand. Where there were multiple samples from

Table 10.2   Nations, Locations, Samples, and Year Data Were Gathered

Nation/Location	Samples/Year
Argentina-Buenos Aires	T-1995; S-1995
Australia-Adelaide and Queensland	T-1992; S-1988, R-1992
Austria-Graz	T-1997
Belgium-Flemish	S-1991
Bolivia-La Paz	T-1993
Brazil-Brasilia	T-1993, 95; S-1989, 95
Bulgaria-Sophia	T-1992, 95; S-1992, 95
Canada-Toronto	T-1993; S-1993
Chile-Santiago, Temuco, National	T-1995, 97; S-1994
China-Guangzhou, Hebei, Shanghai	T-1988, 89; S-1988, 95; R-1990
Cyprus-Limassol (Greek)	T-1992; S-1992
Czech Republic-Prague	T-1993; S-1993
Denmark-Copenhagen	T-1991, 95
England-Surrey, London	T-1995; S-1990
Estonia-Tallinn and Rural	T-1990; S-1990
Fiji-Suva	S-1991
Finland-Helsinki and National	T-1989; S-1989; R-1991, 94
France-Paris, Lyon, and National	T-1991; S-1996; R-1994
Georgia-Tbilisi	T-1992; S-1992
Germany(E)-Berlin, Chemnitz	T-1991; S-1991, 94; R-1996
Germany(W)-Trier, Berlin, National	T-1990; S-1989, 94; R-1996
Ghana-Accra	T-1995; S-1995
Greece-Athens	T-1989; S-1989
Hong Kong-Hong Kong	T-1988, 96; S-1988, 96
Hungary-Budapest	T-1990, 95; S-1990, 95
India-Allahabad and Patna (Hindu)	T-1991; S-1992
Indonesia-Jakarta, Yogyakarta	T-1994, 96; S-1994
Ireland-Dublin	T-1996
Israel Jewish-Jerusalem and National	T-1990; S-1990, 95; R-1996
Israel Arab-Galilee, Jerusalem	T-1990
Italy-Rome and National	T-1989; S-1989, 91; R-1997
Japan-Hyogo, Osaka, Tokyo, Hokaido	T-1989; 96; S-1989, 90, 96; R-1991
Macedonia-Skopje	T-1995; S-1995
Malaysia-Penang	T-1989; S-1989
Mexico-Mexico City	T-1990, 1995
Nepal-Katmandu	T-1993; S-1992, 93
Netherlands-Amsterdam and Nationwide	T-1988, 96; S-1988; 96; R-1989
New Zealand-South Island	T-1998; S-1988
Nigeria-Ile-Ife	T-1995; S-1995
Norway-Olso	T-1994; S-1994
Peru-Lima	S-1996
Philippines-Metropolitan Manila	T-1996; S-1996

(*continued*)

Table 10.2   Continued

Nation/Location	Samples/Year
Poland-Warsaw	T-1998; S-1990, 96
Portugal-Porto	T-1989; S-1989
Romania-Bucharest	S-1996
Russia-Moscow, Leningrad	T-1995; R-1995
Singapore-Singapore	T-1991; S-1991
Slovakia-Bratislava	T-1991; 96; S-1991
Slovenia-Ljubljana	T-1991; S-1991-92
South Korea-Nationwide	S-1993
South Africa-Pochefstroom, Midrand	S-1994, 96; R-1992
Spain-Madrid	T-1988, 96; S-1988
Sweden-Stockholm	T-1993; S-1993
Switzerland-Lausanne (French)	T-1988; S-1988, 96
Taiwan-Taipei	T-1993, 95
Thailand-Bangkok	T-1991
Turkey-Istanbul and Ankara	T-1990; S-1994, 95
Uganda-Kampala	T-1995; S-1995
USA-Illinois, Seattle, California, Mississippi, Washington, D.C.	T-1990, 95, 96; S-1989, 90, 93, 94, 96
Venezuela-Caracas	T-1993; S-1989
Zimbabwe-Harare	T-1989; S-1989

Note: T signifies teacher samples, S signifies student samples, R signifies representative or near representative samples.

one nation or location, we averaged their ratings to obtain a single, more reliable rating. Each nation was given equal weight in the analysis.

Table 10.3 summarizes the key findings regarding value importance. The left side of the table presents the mean importance ratings of the ten value types averaged across the twelve representative or near representative samples. As can be seen, benevolence was the value type rated most important. Self-direction was rated second most important, universalism third, security fourth, and conformity fifth. The five less-important value types were, in order, achievement, hedonism, stimulation, tradition, and power. The range of importance of the value types was substantial, covering more than two full scale points (4.73 to 2.34).[16] Self-direction, security, and universalism did not differ significantly from one another in importance, nor did achievement differ much from hedonism. Differences among all other value types were significant (p < .05 two-tailed), however. Most differences were a full standard deviation unit or more, indicating strong differentiation in the value hierarchy.

The order of value priorities observed across the twelve nations may or may not represent a wider pancultural value pattern. To ascertain whether it does, we examine the findings for schoolteachers from fifty-five nations and students from fifty-three nations. We ask: Does the same order of priorities among the types of values

Table 10.3 Cross-National Importance of Individual Value Types

Value Type	Representative (12 Nations)		Teachers (55 Nations)		Students (53 Nations)		Difference
	Mean Rating (sd)	Mean Rank (sd)	Mean Rating (sd)	Mean Rank	Mean Rating	Mean Rank	Teacher-Student
Benevolence	4.73 (.29)	1	4.68 (.28)	1	4.60 (.25)	1	.08
Self-Direction	4.45 (.26)	2	4.45 (.31)	2	4.58 (.31)	2	−.13*
Universalism	4.44 (.18)	3	4.42 (.31)	3	4.25 (.29)	3	.17*
Security	4.40 (.44)	4	4.25 (.39)	4	3.99 (.36)	5	.26**
Conformity	4.16 (.48)	5	4.16 (.47)	5	3.96 (.49)	6	.20*
Achievement	3.87 (.40)	6	3.85 (.34)	6	4.02 (.30)	4	−.17*
Hedonism	3.80 (.46)	7	3.42 (.59)	7	3.84 (.65)	7	−.42**
Stimulation	3.12 (.38)	8	2.91 (.41)	9	3.44 (.34)	8	−.53**
Tradition	2.77 (.50)	9	3.01 (.45)	8	2.73 (.48)	9	.28**
Power	2.34 (.43)	10	2.38 (.55)	10	2.39 (.43)	10	.01

**p < .001, *p < .05, 2-tailed

replicate with data from much larger and more diversified sets of nations and from different types of samples? Teachers are of special interest because they constitute the largest occupational group in most societies. Moreover teachers presumably serve as value carriers in their society.

The middle section of table 10.3 presents the mean importance ratings of the ten value types averaged across seventy-six teacher samples from fifty-five nations. Benevolence was again the value type rated most important, self-direction was second, universalism third, security fourth, and conformity fifth. The five less-important value types were, in order, achievement, hedonism, tradition, stimulation, and power. This order was identical to that for the representative national samples, except for the reversal of tradition and stimulation. The range of importance of the value types covered more than two full scale points (4.68 to 2.38) here too, and the differences of importance among the values were once again substantial. Every value type differed significantly (p < .01) from every other type, except for tradition/stimulation.

Oversampling nations from some regions of the world and undersampling nations from other regions might distort the observed order of the value types. With only twelve representative samples, this could not be assessed. With the teacher samples, we checked this possibility. We recalculated the mean importance of each value type, giving equal weight to samples from eight different regions (Western Europe [fifteen nations], Eastern Europe [eleven], North America [two], South and Central America [six], East Asia [eleven], Africa [four], Oceania [two], and the Middle East [four]).[17] The order of importance of the ten value types obtained by equally weighting the world regions was identical to the order based on weighting the fifty-five nations equally.

The similarity of the order of value priorities between the representative and the teacher samples is striking. Forty-six of the nations that contributed to the teacher priorities were not included in the representative sample set, and the priorities were based on samples with different characteristics.

As a further assessment of whether the relative value priorities identified thus far constitute a pancultural value pattern, we examined the ratings by matched samples of college students. The proportion of the population that attends college varies considerably across nations. Hence students may not be well matched on background and other characteristics across countries. Nonetheless, if they too order values in ways similar to the national samples, they can add to our confidence that the value ratings we observed reflect a "true" pancultural pattern.

Results for seventy-nine student samples from the fifty-three nations are shown on the right side of table 10.3. Benevolence and self-direction values were most important on average, and did not differ in importance. Universalism values were third, followed by achievement, security, conformity, hedonism, stimulation, tradition, and power. This order is similar to that for the representative national samples, except for the reordering of achievement, security, and conformity in the middle of the value hierarchy. The Pearson Correlation between the value ratings by the student and representative samples is 0.97. The range of importance of the value types

(4.60 to 2.39) was similar to the ranges in the representative and teacher samples. With the exceptions of benevolence/self-direction and security/conformity/achievement, every value type differed significantly in importance (p < . 01) from every other type.

For the student samples, we also recomputed the means in order to give equal weight to samples from the eight different regions: West Europe (thirteen nations), East Europe (twelve), North America (two), South and Central America (five), East Asia (ten), Africa (five), Oceania (three), and the Middle East (three). This yielded an identical order of importance among value types for student samples.

The consistent findings across these three sets of samples lead us to conclude that the pancultural value hierarchy we have identified may reflect a "true" order of pancultural norms fairly well. Benevolence, self-direction, and universalism consistently emerge at the top of the value hierarchy, in that order. Security, conformity, and achievement are located in the middle of the hierarchy. Hedonism, stimulation, tradition, and power are consistently at the bottom of the hierarchy.

These findings may surprise those who are convinced that there is great cultural diversity around the world. It is important to recognize, however, that even when groups order values quite similarly overall, small differences between specific value priorities can be meaningful and foster disagreement. This is critical, because it suggests that broad similarity of value priorities may not be sufficient to ensure easy moral dialogue. We illustrate the phenomenon of difference within similarity by comparing the values of the teacher with the values of the student samples. The average value priorities of the teacher and student samples are quite similar. The Pearson Correlation between these ratings is 0.93, and the Spearman Correlation between ranks is 0.95. Nonetheless, there are significant and meaningful differences between teachers and students on eight of the ten value types (see table 10.3, last column).

The differences are what one would expect considering differences between these two occupational groups. Teachers are older than students, more embedded in established social institutions and roles, and more caught up in networks of mutual obligation. Thus they are more tied to the status quo and less open to change. This can account for why teachers attribute more importance than students to security, tradition, and conformity values and less importance to hedonism, stimulation, and self-direction values. The advanced academic studies that students are currently pursuing encourage openness to and tolerance of new and different ideas; yet they demand that students meet socially defined standards of achievement.[18] This can account for why students attribute more importance than teachers to self-direction, universalism, and achievement values. The student-teacher comparison shows how groups that exhibit high overall similarity in their ratings of values may nonetheless differ substantially and meaningfully in their specific value priorities.

In sum, the pancultural averages in three sets of samples from sixty-two different nations or groups reveal that, on average, people around the world attribute high importance to self-direction and benevolence values. This provides initial support for Etzioni's claim that autonomy (parallel to self-direction) is a shared, core value. It also identifies another potential core value, benevolence. The component of social order measured most closely by security values received relatively high average ratings, especially in the representative samples. The average ratings of the conformity values component of social order were somewhat weaker.

CONSENSUS ON VALUE PRIORITIES

The average orderings of the importance of the ten value types based on many nations may or may not reflect the ordering of value priorities in particular nations. We must therefore ask whether these are merely averages or whether they also represent a high degree of agreement regarding value priorities across nations. Only if there is a consensus on the importance of values can we identify specific basic values such as benevolence and self-direction as core values with near universal endorsement.

In order to address this issue, we assessed the degree of agreement on value priorities across nations by comparing the ratings of the ten value types and their order of priority in each sample with the average (= pancultural) ratings and order. This was done separately for the sets of near-representative samples, teacher samples, and student samples. Specifically, we computed Pearson Correlations between the average rating of the value types across each set of samples (representative, teacher, student) and their rating within each national sample from that set. We also computed the Spearman rank correlations between the average ranking of the value types across each set of samples and their ranking within each national sample. Table 10.4 presents results of these analyses.

For the twelve near-representative national samples, the mean Pearson Correlation across nations was 0.92, and the median correlation was 0.95 (median Spearman rank correlation was 0.91). Even the weakest correlation, for the sample from China, was still 0.82, indicating that two-thirds of the variance in its value ratings was shared with the pancultural ratings. Moreover, this relatively lower correlation may reflect the fact that the Chinese sample represented factory workers rather than the general public. These correlations indicate a substantial degree of agreement regarding which value types are relatively important and which are relatively unimportant. Might this consensus hold when we study a much larger set of nations? Results for the teacher and student samples shed light on this question.

For teachers, the mean Pearson Correlation between the national hierarchy and the average teacher sample hierarchy across the fifty-five nations was 0.89, and the median correlation was 0.90. Only 7 percent of the correlations were less than 0.75. Thus the teacher samples also point to substantial agreement regarding the hierarchy of value types around the world. Of course, samples from different nations

Table 10.4   Cross-National Consensus Regarding Value Importance: Correlations between the Average Priority Ratings of Value Types across Samples from around the World and the Ratings in Each Nation

Samples	Number of Nations	Average Pearson Correlation	Median Pearson Correlation	Range of Pearson Correlations	Median Spearman Rank Correlation
Representative	12	.92	.95	.82–.97	.91
Teacher	55	.89	.90	.71–.98	.88
Student	53	.89	.92	.56–.98	.82

showed varying degrees of agreement. But even for the samples with the least simi-larity to the average teacher sample (Uganda and Nigeria), more than 50 percent of the variance in value ratings was shared.

This high degree of consensus is striking. Equally significant is the fact that, with one exception, the degree of consensus varied little across the regions of the world from which the samples came. The mean Pearson Correlation was similar for four Middle Eastern nations (0.93), eleven East European nations (0.91), fifteen West European nations (0.89), six Latin American nations (0.92), two North American nations (0.94), two nations from Oceania (0.95), and eleven East Asian nations (0.86). The four African nations (0.76) had priorities relatively less similar to the pancultural average, however. Four nations are a small sample for drawing conclu-sions, so we postpone comment until we examine the student data that included five African nations.

For students (table 10.4, third row), the mean Pearson Correlation across the fifty-three nations was 0.89, and the median correlation was 0.92. Only 11 percent of the correlations were less than 0.75. These findings too reflect a substantial degree of agreement regarding the relative importance of the different value types. Once again, the African samples were the exception. Otherwise, consensus was high re-gardless of the region of the world from which the samples came. Mean Pearson Correlations were similar for three Middle Eastern nations (0.93), twelve East Eu-ropean nations (0.94), thirteen West European nations (0.93), five Latin American nations (0.95), two North American nations (0.92), three nations from Oceania (0.89), and—somewhat lower—ten East Asian nations (0.84). The five African na-tions had a mean Pearson Correlation of only 0.70. For samples from four nations (Ghana, Fiji, Nigeria, and Uganda), less than 50 percent of the variance in value ratings was shared with the pancultural baseline.

All five African student and four African teacher samples were unusual in that the average persons in these samples attributed more importance to conformity than to any other type of values. They also attributed unusually little importance to self-direction and universalism values. The Fiji student sample, the one non-African sample whose value ratings shared less than 50 percent of their variance with the pancultural baseline, also rated conformity most important and self-direction was unusually unimportant. Apparently, this is an alternative ordering of value priori-ties. We will discuss the conditions under which this order prevails.

The high degree of overall consensus on value priorities across nations does not yet tell us whether any of the ten value types are core values that are highly endorsed around the globe. For this purpose, consider the ranks across the many samples of the most highly endorsed values—benevolence, self-direction, and universalism. Benevolence values ranked first or second in importance among the ten value types in at least three-quarters of all three sets of samples—representative, teacher, and student. Benevolence ranked as one of the five most important value types in 119 of the 120 samples. Recall that a rating of 3.0 on the rating scale signifies that a value is important as a guiding principle in life. In every sample, benevolence values received an average rating of at least 4.1. Thus, these values are considered quite important everywhere. Benevolence, it appears, qualifies as a core type of values across cultures.

Self-direction values were second in importance overall. They ranked first or second most important in 57 percent of the samples. They ranked as one of the five most important value types in 97 percent of the samples. Self-direction values also received average ratings above 4.0 in 113 of the 120 samples. Thus, except for the African and Fiji samples, self-direction values also receive high endorsement around the globe. This gives considerable support to Etzioni's claim that autonomy is a shared core value.

Universalism values were also widely endorsed. They received average ratings above 4.0 in 110 of 120 samples. Nonetheless, the data suggest that they are not so widely shared across cultures. They ranked first or second in importance in only 20 percent of the samples and were in the bottom half of the ranking in 16 percent of the samples.

There was even less agreement that security values are particularly important. They received average ratings above 4.0 in only 78 of 120 samples. They ranked first or second in only 18 percent of the samples and were in the bottom half of the ranking in 25 percent of the samples. Hence their status as core values shared across nations is questionable.

Conformity values, the remaining value type that measures a component of social order, received average ratings above 4.0 in only 69 of 120 samples. Reflecting the special pattern of African samples, conformity values ranked in the top two ranks in 22 percent of the samples; but they were in the bottom half of the ranking in 42 percent of the samples. There is thus little global consensus regarding the importance of conformity values.

Interestingly, there was widespread agreement about the relative lack of importance of one type of values. Power values ranked ninth or tenth in 92 percent of all samples. Endorsement of the remaining types of values varied more across nations. Variation was especially great for hedonism values.

In sum, examination of this large body of data supports the idea that there is a substantial consensus worldwide (except for Africa) regarding the relative importance of most of the ten value types. The existence of cross-cultural consensus regarding the importance of the comprehensive set of ten value types raises three intriguing questions: First, why does the pancultural baseline of value priorities show the pattern that it does? That is, why is benevolence most important, power least important, and the other value types ordered in the ways observed? Second, what might lead to the relative consensus on this order? Third, why do the African samples diverge from the pancultural order? There can be no definitive empirical answers to the first two questions. Nonetheless, we can propose plausible, theory-based answers to all three, answers we will then relate to Etzioni's claims.

PANCULTURAL NORMS: WHY?

As noted earlier, the typology of ten types of values that differ in their motivational content was derived by reasoning that values represent, in the form of conscious goals, three universal requirements of human existence: biological needs, requisites of co-ordinated social interaction, and demands of group survival and functioning.[19] One or more of these requirements underlies each value type.[20] Groups and individuals represent these requirements cognitively as specific values about which they communicate in order to explain, coordinate, and rationalize behavior.

Individual differences in the importance attributed to values reflect individuals' unique needs, temperaments, and social experiences. But the pancultural similarities in value importance are likely to reflect the shared bases of values in human nature and the adaptive functions of each type of value in maintaining societies.[21] Most individuals are likely to oppose the pursuit of value priorities that clash with human nature. Socializers and social control agents are likely to discourage the pursuit of value priorities that clash with the smooth functioning of important groups or the larger society.

The basic social function of values is to motivate and control the behavior of group members.[22] Two mechanisms are critical. First, social actors (e.g., leaders, interaction partners) invoke values to define particular behaviors as socially appropriate, to justify what they demand of others, and to elicit the desired behaviors. Second, and equally important, values serve as internalized guides for individuals, relieving the group of the necessity for constant social control. Value transmission, acquisition, and internalization occur as individuals adapt to the everyday customs, practices, norms, and scripts to which they are exposed. Through reinforcement, modeling, and explicit verbal teaching, socializers consciously and unconsciously seek to instill values that promote group survival and prosperity.

From the viewpoint of human nature and societal functioning, we propose that the following three requirements, ordered according to their importance, are especially relevant for explaining the observed pancultural value hierarchy.

1. Most important is the promotion and preservation of cooperative and supportive relations among members of primary groups. For without such relations, daily life in the group would be filled with conflict and group survival would be at risk. Developing commitment to positive relations, identification with the group, and loyalty to its members is therefore the most critical focus of value transmission.

2. Positive relations are insufficient to ensure the survival and prosperity of societies, groups, and their individual members, however. Individuals must also be motivated to invest the time and the physical and intellectual effort needed to perform productive work, to solve problems that arise during task performance, and to generate new ideas and technical solutions.

3. Some gratification for the self-oriented needs and desires of group members is also critical. Rejecting all expression of self-oriented desires would produce individual frustration, withdrawal of investment in the group, and refusal to contribute to group goal attainment. Hence, it is socially functional to legitimize self-oriented behavior to the extent that it does not undermine group goals.

We now use these principles to develop our tentative explanation of the observed pancultural value hierarchy.

Positive, cooperative social relations, the basic requirement for smooth group functioning, are especially important in the context of the family, with its high interdependence and intense interaction.[23] Value acquisition occurs first in this context and later in other primary and secondary groups.[24] Benevolence values (helpfulness, honesty, forgiveness, loyalty, responsibility) provide the internalized motivational base for cooperative and supportive social relations. These values are reinforced and modeled early and repeatedly, because they are critical to ensure required behaviors even in the absence of real or threatened sanctions. Benevolence values are therefore of utmost importance panculturally (first).

Universalism values (e.g., social justice, equality, broad-mindedness) also contribute to positive social relations. But universalism values differ from benevolence values in their focus on *all* others, most significantly, on those outside the in-group. Universalism values are functionally important primarily when group members must relate to those with whom they do not readily identify. Commitment to the welfare of others with whom one is not close is critical in schools, workplaces, and other extrafamilial settings. Universalism values are less crucial when most interaction is limited to the primary group. Indeed, universalism values might even threaten in-group solidarity during times of intergroup conflict. Therefore, although universalism values are high in the pancultural hierarchy (third), they are less important than benevolence values.

Security (fourth, fifth) and conformity (fifth, sixth) values are also fairly important panculturally, probably because harmonious relations among group members also depend upon avoiding conflict and violations of group norms. Security and conformity values are likely to be acquired in response to demands for self-restriction, avoiding risks, and controlling forbidden impulses. Hence these values may interfere with gratifying self-oriented needs and desires, the third basis for value importance mentioned previously. As a result, some negative affect is likely to accompany socialization for these values. Moreover, security and conformity values emphasize maintaining the status quo.[25] They may therefore interfere with the motivation to innovate in finding solutions to group tasks, the second basis for value importance we proposed. Thus, despite their contribution to harmonious social relations, security and conformity values are rated lower in the pancultural importance hierarchy than benevolence and universalism values.

Accepting and acting on tradition values can also contribute to group solidarity and thus to smooth group functioning and survival. However, tradition values are largely concerned with individuals' commitment to the abstract beliefs and symbols that represent groups.[26] They find little expression in the everyday social behavior that interaction partners have a vital interest in controlling. As such, tradition values are attributed relatively low importance as guiding principles (ninth, eighth) in the lives of people in most countries.

Power values are located at the bottom of the pancultural hierarchy (tenth), with very high consensus regarding their relatively low importance as guides. This is also attributable to the requirement of positive relations among group members. By definition, power values emphasize dominance over people and resources. Pursuing them often entails harming or exploiting others, thereby disrupting and damaging social relations. On the other hand, power values are congruent with the gratification of self-oriented desires, the third basis of importance noted previously. It is probably necessary to grant some legitimacy to power strivings in order to motivate individual efforts to work for group interests and in order to justify the hierarchical social arrangements in all societies.

Self-direction values have strong implications for meeting the functional requirement of motivating individuals to work productively. By promoting exploration, creativity, and independence of thought and action, self-direction values foster group members' innovativeness and their intrinsically motivated investment in finding the best ways to get the group's tasks done. Action based on self-direction values contributes to group prosperity in normal times; it is crucial to meet the challenges posed by change in times of crisis. Moreover, intrinsically motivated actions satisfy self-oriented needs and desires by definition. Because self-direction values constitute an intrinsic source of motivation, their pursuit need not come at the expense of others who compete for social rewards. Hence, they rarely pose a threat to positive relations in the group. Thus self-direction values substantially advance the second and third basic social functions of values without undermining the first. As a result, they receive high importance (second) in the pancultural hierarchy.

Achievement values are attributed moderate importance panculturally (sixth, fourth). This level of importance may reflect a compromise among the three bases of value importance. Achievement values, as defined and operationalized here, emphasize demonstrating competence according to social standards of success. On the positive side, achievement values motivate individuals to invest their time and energy in performing tasks that serve group interests. They also legitimize self-enhancing behavior, so long as it contributes to group welfare. On the negative side, achievement values may motivate individuals to devote so much effort to demonstrating their own worth that they thwart optimal attainment of group goals. Moreover, such self-interested behavior is also likely to disrupt harmonious, positive social relations. By assigning moderate importance to achievement values, a balance is found between motivating people to work for the group, gratifying self-oriented desires, and avoiding disruption of social relations among group members.

The location of hedonism (seventh) and stimulation (eighth, ninth) values in the pancultural hierarchy reflects their irrelevance for the first two requirements that underlie value importance. These values acquire some importance, nonetheless, because they are relevant to the third requirement. Hedonism and stimulation values are social transformations of the needs of the individual, as a biological organism, for physical gratification and optimal arousal.[27] Societies must be organized to allow and legitimize some gratification of self-oriented desires, but socializers are unlikely to invest in inculcating such values because they serve mainly the interests of the individual. Hedonism and stimulation values are attributed greater importance than power values probably because, in contrast to power values, their pursuit does not necessarily threaten positive social relations.

Self-determination theorists[28] provide a more psychological basis for the high importance attributed to benevolence and self-direction values across all human cultures. They argue that relatedness, community, autonomy, and personal growth are the major psychological needs whose fulfillment is intrinsically satisfying. Consequently, the goals to which these needs direct us are salient and central to most individuals. Benevolence and self-direction values, respectively, express the goals based on relatedness and community and on autonomy and personal growth. These theorists also designate a set of needs that underlie extrinsic goals—money, fame, power, and image. They argue that the pursuit of these goals does not bring direct satisfaction, so they are inherently less salient and central. Note that these are the goals of power values, the least important value type across cultures.

Our analysis of the bases of the pancultural value hierarchy does not account for the different pattern observed in the Black African samples and in Fiji. The average respondents in these samples differed from the pancultural norms primarily in the very high importance they attributed to conformity values and the low importance they attributed to self-direction values. If the preceding analysis is correct, then we should look to aspects of the social structural context to which these samples are exposed to explain their unusual pattern of value priorities. A full explication is beyond the scope of this chapter, but we will provide some suggestions.[29]

Most obviously, these samples all come from nations that are neither industrialized nor Westernized. Perhaps even more important is the large size of the households in which respondents in these samples grew up (average above ten persons) and the diversity of the members (e.g., multigenerational, with children of different mothers). Most primary groups in these nations consist of large numbers of persons, organized in a hierarchical family, living in close proximity and high interdependence, with little room for privacy. Under such circumstances, successful coordination of behavior requires the operation of norms in almost all domains of life, obedience to these norms and to the demands of authority, and restraint of individual impulses or inclinations that might violate normative arrangements. By definition, conformity values are therefore crucial to group survival and positive relations. The large number of people and the diversity of relationships in the household may weaken the identification with close others that underlies benevolence values. Hence, conformity values may even be more important than benevolence values.

In contrast, self-direction values are likely to disrupt group relations in these circumstances, because they encourage individuals to develop their unique modes of action and thought. They are therefore less likely to be reinforced and cultivated. A key mechanism for the development of a sense of an autonomous, self-directed self, according to Richard Shweder and Edmund Bourne,[30] is the granting of privacy to children. This is not possible in large but poor households, and its absence may inhibit the growth of self-direction values. Equally important, most groups in these societies have lived in relatively stable environments in which the daily challenges are fairly routine.[31] Consequently, fostering innovativeness in times of change and crisis, a critical social function of self-direction values discussed previously, is less relevant. This brief analysis of the divergent African findings implies that the widespread pancultural normative value hierarchy depends upon social structural features shared by most contemporary nations.

The convergence theory of modernization suggests that the emergence of a pancultural value hierarchy may reflect adaptations to the common structural characteristics of industrialized societies. This theory argues that, as societies industrialize, they develop similar institutional structures.[32] We do not think, however, that industrialization accounts for the relative consensus on value priorities we have found. Even excluding Africa, our sample of nations varies considerably in level of industrialization. But the degree of agreement between the value hierarchies in particular nations and the pancultural normative order is related at most weakly to level of industrialization. Some nations high in industrialization are among those whose value hierarchies correlate strongly with the pancultural value hierarchy (e.g., Norway, 0.97) but also among those whose hierarchies correlate relatively weakly (e.g., Switzerland, 0.80). This is the case for nations that are relatively less industrialized (e.g., Turkey, 0.95; China, 0.78) as well. Thus, the pancultural hierarchy is apparently based in shared requirements of human existence that are present in all societies that are at least minimally industrialized.

IMPLICATIONS FOR ETZIONI'S ARGUMENTS

Etzioni dismissed the idea that the empirical search for values that are globally endorsed is useful for establishing their moral force. He noted that morally unacceptable values might enjoy global endorsement (e.g., prejudice against minorities) while historical and cultural factors might hide the compelling nature of morally acceptable values. He also argued that any list of universally endorsed values is likely to be quite thin. In contrast, we believe that the current empirical findings considerably increase the power of Etzioni's postrelativist assertion that certain global values can be used legitimately to make moral claims across societal borders. Moreover, these findings provide at least as "thick" a list of values as he has proposed. The empirical research also raises questions regarding the nature and components of Etzioni's social order value. Although it justifies the notion that certain values can be drawn upon to lay a claim on all humanity, it suggests likely areas of contention if people make such claims across certain borders.

We touch first on the question of a "thick" versus "thin" set of core values. The crucial issue is the level at which one conceptualizes the notion of a value. Etzioni's stance in presenting his own position is highly abstract. Consequently, he arrives at two core values, autonomy and social order, which he defines broadly. He argues persuasively that the balance of commitments to these two values is central to many of the most important decisions that individuals, groups, and nations must make. Variation in the weight given to each value leads to different policies regarding education, government, trade, human rights, and so on. Thus these core values are deeply involved in determining social policy; they provide a thick, substantive base for decisions and action. When critiquing empirical approaches, however, Etzioni attributes to them a much less abstract position. We read, for example, that the empirical criterion of core values is thin "because it embraces only a few values such as condemning murder, theft, and rape."[33] And even the violation of these values may be legitimated in some situations (e.g., war).

True, some empirical researchers do conceptualize values at this more specific level; but it is not necessary to do so. We conceptualized the ten motivationally distinct values we study as transsituational. The value types are abstract, but they come into play as guiding principles that influence decisions in all situations that have relevance to goal attainment (the vast majority of decisions). We too emphasize that decisions are made by balancing or making trade-offs between competing values.[34] Social actors draw upon such broad, abstract values as benevolence, self-direction, and so on to generate and justify a wide range of specific social policies and actions. Thus, this empirical approach can point to core values that serve as the substantive grounds on which people may base compelling moral claims in most life domains.

Consider next the overlap between the empirical evidence for globally endorsed values and Etzioni's designation of autonomy and social order as shared core values. Etzioni notes that the elements of his conception of autonomy referring to freedom of expression for subgroups and social boundedness are unusual. Self-direction values (e.g., independence, creativity, choice of own goals) signify that it is desirable for all social actors—subgroups as well as individuals—to be free to pursue their own chosen paths. That autonomy is socially bounded is not inherent in its essence. Rather, it is a product of Eztioni's assertion that autonomy should be balanced with social order. Consequently, we interpret the nearly worldwide agreement that self-direction values are an important guiding principle in life as evidence that people in the large majority of world societies perceive autonomy as having moral force. This lends substantial support to Eztioni's view that autonomy is a shared core value.

Recall, however, that the African and Fiji samples attributed relatively little importance to self-direction values. One might argue that this does not undermine the self-evident moral force of autonomy values. According to our analysis, social structural factors—large household size, poverty, and relatively stable environments, in particular—may account for the low importance of self-direction and the high importance of conformity values in these societies. If so, members of these societies may come to recognize the importance of autonomy if and when the societies shift toward smaller families, confront more change in their social and technological environments, and become wealthier. But is it legitimate to make moral claims on these societies in the name of autonomy so long as the priority they give to conformity over self-direction is anchored in the functional appropriateness of their value hierarchy? Perhaps so, but we can hardly expect these claims to be accepted.

Etzioni's concept of social order includes the commonly understood notion of preventing hostilities among individuals and groups and imposing laws and institutions that regulate social interchange. It is expressed in the value types we call security and conformity. When Etzioni notes that social order is inherently opposed to autonomy, it is these values that are critical. Indeed, conformity and security oppose self-direction values in our theory of the structure of values and in our empirical findings across cultures. If our interpretation of social order is correct, the cross-national ratings of security and conformity values do not suggest that it is a shared, core value. The importance of these values varies across cultures. Although both receive very high ratings in some cultures, both are rated among the less-important values in a substantial minority of cultures. Hence one may question whether their moral force is self-evident.

The global importance of self-direction and benevolence values provides empirical support to Etzioni's assertion that it is legitimate and practical for cultures to call one another to account in the name of shared values. These two value types have implications both for social welfare and freedom, for the distribution of resources and of rights. Societies may therefore draw upon these values as moral anchors to buttress their stance on a vast range of issues, when they challenge others or defend themselves. Moral dialogues across societies with different cultures are likely to be more fruitful to the extent that they probe the implications of the policies or practices at issue for autonomy and for benevolence.

Recognizing an inherent conflict between autonomy and social order, Etzioni emphasizes the need for balance between them. In a "virtuous society . . . there is continuous tension between two forces," which are "kept in a carefully crafted, continuously challenged, but ultimately restored balance."[35] In this view, a range of relative weightings of autonomy and social order is acceptable. But Etzioni offers no firm guidance concerning how to determine the optimal balance. When the cultures of societies move too far in either direction, he says, those who are morally active throw their weight in the opposite direction. The continuous pressures and counterpressures needed to maintain an acceptable balance within societies can be justified by appeals to a presumably shared value culture. In cross-cultural moral dialogues, the search for balance is liable to be much more treacherous, especially because cultures differ widely in the priority they give to the components of social order opposed to autonomy—conformity and security.

Consider four of the distinct cultural regions identified in our value studies— Africa, Southeast Asia, Western Europe, and North America.[36] The findings suggest that in Africa, as noted, conformity values are substantially more important than benevolence and security values, and self-direction values have relatively little importance. The pattern is similar, but less extreme in Southeast Asia. The opposite pattern, high importance of self-direction and low importance of conformity and security values, appears in Western Europe. In North America, benevolence is most highly endorsed, self-direction is next, and both conformity and security values are also fairly important. Thus a different balance of autonomy and social order characterizes each cultural region.

In moral dialogues across the boundaries of these cultural regions, differences in the balance of values are critical. West Europeans attack female genital mutilation in Africa arguing that it violates core values of self-direction and benevolence. Africans defend female circumcision on the grounds of conformity to tradition and stable, secure social relations, social order values that are self-evidently more important in their view. Southeast Asians attack massive social decay in the United States in the name of the social order values of security and conformity. They reject a U.S. defense of individual freedom based in a value hierarchy that gives precedence to self-direction values. Note that self-direction values, even in Africa, and conformity values, even in Western Europe, averaged above 3.0 ("important") on the rating scale. This suggests that both are recognized as having *some* legitimacy around the world. But even extended moral dialogues are unlikely to lead to consensus regarding how they should be balanced. Communitarians would do well to address the problems of balance more explicitly.

Moral dialogues, within or across cultures, rarely take the form of debates over the relative importance of abstract, core values. Interlocutors typically debate the merits of concrete practices or policies—child labor, abortion, free trade, overconsumption of resources, arbitrary arrest. Each practice or policy may be denounced or defended in the name of a variety of values, even if positions on them have little actual basis in values.

A body of social psychological theorizing and research[37] points to an aspect of moral dialogues that deserves more attention. Groups or individuals with different positions on issues (e.g., arming the nation with nuclear weapons) tend to differ in their value priorities, as expected. Less obviously, they often agree on some of the values they see as relevant to deciding these issues. However, they differentially cite those values that can justify or rationalize their own positions. Thus proponents and opponents of nuclear weapons both regard world peace as a value relevant to their position. Proponents view national security as a more relevant value than do opponents, however, and opponents view social justice (a universalism value) as more relevant. This analysis suggests that the value dialogue on concrete issues is as likely to be over which values are relevant as over the importance of those values themselves. This further complicates moral dialogues. Even when both sides can reach agreement regarding the importance of core values, they may argue for the moral superiority of their own position by claiming that it expresses one or another of these values better.

In sum, Etzioni's call for the moral voice to be raised across cultural borders has empirical support in our finding of core values that speak to all people around the world. These values provide a rich, substantive value base for groups to make claims on one another. A cross-cultural moral dialogue can be built on shared commitments to benevolence and self-direction values. Incorporation of claims based on social order values, such as conformity and security, is more problematic. There are substantial differences among cultural regions in the extent to which these values are experienced as having moral force. Hence the balance between opposing values varies greatly across cultures. Even where agreement on value priorities exists, dialogue over concrete issues will not be easy. In our highly interdependent world, dialogue will take place, nonetheless. Abstaining from making moral judgments will not advance such dialogue, grounding it in a few shared values might.

NOTES

This research was supported by grant No. 94-00063 from the United States–Israel Binational Science Foundation (BSF) to the first author and facilitated by the Leon and Clara Sznajderman Chair Professorship in Psychology. We thank the following persons, who gathered the data on which this chapter is based: Charity Akotia, Hassan Bacanli, Krassimira Baytchinska, Suzanne Beckmann (Grunert), Gabriel Bianchi, Klaus Boehnke, Edna Bonang, Michael Bond, Glynis Breakwell, Steven Burgess, Bram Buunk, Bartolo Campos, Maria Casullo, Agnes C. Chang, Weining Chang, Patrick Chiroro, Gisela Dahme, Ake Daun, Rolando Diaz-Loving, Ken Dion, Karen Dion, Igor Dubov, J. P. Dupont, Andrew Ellerman, Norman Feather, Johnny Fontaine, Maggye Foster, Kathryn Frost, Adrian Furnham, F. Gendre, James Georgas, Hector Grad, Andreas Gronningsaeter, Aydan Gulerce, Gyuseog Han, Judith Howard, Sipke Huismans, Sumiko Iwao, Saburo Iwawaki, Maria Jarymowicz, Neil Johnston, David Karp, Uichol Kim, Dan Landis, Kwok Leung, Alexey Levinson, Mei-chi Li, Eva Mautner, Michael McCarrey, Isabel Menezes, Paolo Mercado, Kyrre Moen, Leo Montada, John Munene, Regmi Murari, Kathleen Myambo, George Nidharadze, Toomas Niit, Solo Olowu, Henri Paicheler, Michaelis Papadopoulos, Wu Peiguan, Darja Piciga, Penkhae Prachonpachanuk, Deepa Punetha, Martti Puohiniemi, Mark Radford, Sharon Reimel de Carrasquel, Bert Richmond, Sonia Roccas, Maria Ros, Viera Rozova, Jose Saiz, Jose Miguel Salazar, Manfred Schmitt, Loraine Scholtz, Renuka Sethi, Leonid Smirnov, Dario Spini, Jan Srnec, James Starr, Anna Szuster, Osamu Takagi, Alvaro Tamayo, Giancarlo

Tanucci, Ilina Todorova, Harry Triandis, Shripati Upadhyaya, Antti Uutela, Zsuzsa Vajda, Erika van der Watern, Markku Verkasalo, Jyoti Verma, Genevieve Vinsonneau, Monique Wach, Colleen Ward, Marie Wissing, Louis Young, Vladimir Zahkarov, Wei Zhi-gang.

1. Amitai Etzioni, *The New Golden Rule: Community and Morality in a Democratic Society* (New York: Basic Books, 1996).

2. Shalom H. Schwartz, "Universals in the Content and Structure of Values: Theoretical Advances and Empirical Tests in 20 Countries," in *Advances in Experimental Social Psychology*, vol. 25, ed. Mark P. Zanna (New York: Academic Press, 1992), 1–65; Shalom H. Schwartz, "Are There Universal Aspects in the Content and Structure of Values?" *Journal of Social Issues* 50(2) (1994): 19–45.

3. For a fuller elaboration, see Schwartz, "Universals in the Content"; cf. Milton Rokeach, *The Nature of Human Values* (New York: Free Press, 1973); see also Clyde Kluckhohn, "Values and Value-Orientations in the Theory of Action: An Exploration in Definition and Classification," in *Toward a General Theory of Action,* ed. Talcott Parsons and Edward A. Shils (Cambridge, Mass.: Harvard University Press, 1951), 388–433.

4. Schwartz, "Universals in the Content" ; Schwartz, "Are There Universal Aspects"; Shalom H. Schwartz and Lilach Sagiv, "Identifying Culture Specifics in the Content and Structure of Values," *Journal of Cross-Cultural Psychology* 26(1) (January 1995): 92–116.

5. For details on reliability of the value type indexes, see Manfred J. Schmitt, Shalom H. Schwartz, Rolf Steyer, and Thomas Schmitt, "Measurement Models for the Schwartz Values Inventory," *European Journal of Psychological Assessment* 9(2) (1993): 107–21. Note that the achievement value type refers to meeting social standards and attaining social approval, not to meeting personal standards. This differs from McClelland's "need for achievement," which resembles self-direction values. See David C. McClelland, John W. Atkinson, Russell A. Clark, and Edgar L. Lowell, *The Achievement Motive* (New York: Appleton, 1953).

6. The fact that there were no extensive empty regions in the spatial representation of relations among the single values in the multidimensional space analyses also supported the argument for comprehensiveness.

7. Schwartz, "Universals in the Content"; Schwartz, "Are There Universal Aspects"; Schwartz and Sagiv, "Identifying Culture Specifics."

8. Marina Barnea and Shalom H. Schwartz, "Values and Voting," *Political Psychology* 19(1) (1998): 17–40; Gabriel Bianchi and Vera Rosova, "Environment as a Value: Intraindividual, Interindividual and Intercultural Differences," in *Culture, Nature, Landscape,* ed. Hana Svodoba (Zdar n/Sazavou: International Association of Landscape Ecology, 1992), 37–45; Michael H. Bond and Vinnie M-Y Chi, "Values and Moral Behavior in Mainland China," *Psychologia* 40(4) (1997): 251–64; Suzanne C. Grunert and Hans J. Juhl, "Values, Environmental Attitudes, and Buying Organic Foods," *Journal of Economic Psychology* 16(1) (March 1995): 39–62; David G. Karp, "Values and Their Effect on Pro-Environmental Behavior," *Environment and Behavior* 28(1) (January 1996): 111–33; Martti Puohiniemi, "Values, Consumer Attitudes and Behaviour: An Application of Schwartz's Value Theory to the Analysis of Consumer Behaviour and Attitudes in Two National Samples," (Ph.D. diss., The University of Helsinki, 1995); Sonia Roccas and Shalom H. Schwartz, "Church-State Relations and the Association of Religiosity with Values: A Study of Catholics in Six Countries," *Cross-Cultural Research* 31(4) (November 1997): 356–75; Maria Ros, Hector Grad, and Jose L. Alvaro, "The Meaning and Hierarchy of Values and Political Orientation"

(paper presented at the 23rd International Congress of Applied Psychology, Madrid, Spain, July 1994); Lilach Sagiv, "Process and Outcomes of Vocational Counseling: The role of Clients' Values." (Ph.D. diss., The Hebrew University of Jerusalem, 1997); Lilach Sagiv and Shalom H. Schwartz, "Value Priorities and Readiness for Out-Group Social Contact," *Journal of Personality and Social Psychology* 69(3) (September 1995): 437–48; David B. Schubot, William Cayler Jr., and B. Clair Eliason, "Personal Values Related to Primary Care Specialty Aspirations," *Family Medicine* 28(10) (November-December 1996): 726–31; Shalom H. Schwartz, "Value Priorities and Behavior: Applying of Theory of Integrated Value Systems," in *The Psychology of Values: The Ontario Symposium,* vol. 8, ed. Clive Seligman, James M. Olson, and Mark P. Zanna (Hillsdale, N.J.: Erlbaum, 1996), 1–24; Shalom H. Schwartz and Marina Barnea, "Los Valores en Orientaciones Politicas: Aplicaciones en Espana, Venezuela y Mejico" (Value Bases of Political Orientations: Applications in Spain, Venezuela, and Mexico), *Psychologia Politica* 11 (November 1995): 15–40; Shalom H. Schwartz and Sipke Huismans, "Value Priorities and Religiosity in Four Western Religions," *Social Psychology Quarterly* 58(2) (June 1995): 88–107; Jan Srnec, "Attitudes to Ethical Dilemmas and Value Orientation," *Praticky Lekar* 75(1) (1995): 35–8.

9. Shalom H. Schwartz, Markku Verkasalo, Avishai Antonovsky, and Lilach Sagiv, "Value Priorities and Social Desirability: Much Substance, Some Style," *British Journal of Social Psychology* 36(1) (March 1997): 3–18.

10. Geert Hofstede, *Culture's Consequences: International Differences in Work-Related Values* (Beverly Hills, Calif.: Sage, 1982); Milton Rokeach, *The Nature of Human Values* (New York: Free Press, 1973); Shalom H. Schwartz and Maria Ros, "Values in the West: A Theoretical and Empirical Challenge to the Individualism-Collectivism Cultural Dimension," *World Psychology* 1(2) (April 1995): 91–122.

11. Etzioni, *The New Golden Rule*, 23.

12. Shalom H. Schwartz, "Values and Culture," in *Motivation and Culture,* ed. Donald Munro, John E. Schumaker, and Stuart C. Car (New York: Rout, 1997), 69–84; Shalom H. Schwartz, "Cultural Value Differences: Some Implications for Work," *Applied Psychology: An International Review* 48(1) (1999): 23–47.

13. Etzioni, *The New Golden Rule*, 10–13.

14. Voluntary commitment to the welfare of others is the essence of benevolence values—values that express a proactive goal of fostering the welfare of close others (e.g., helpfulness, responsibility, honesty, loyalty). However, benevolence values are not a key component of Etzioni's concept of social order. The voluntary commitment to which he refers is to maintain order in society. This goal is not necessarily related to fostering the welfare of close others, though it rarely conflicts.

15. Schwartz, "Universals in the Content."

16. We adjusted all reported means to eliminate national differences in use of the response scale by centering the means for each sample around 4.00, the approximate pancultural mean.

17. These regions are from the classification in George P. Murdock, *Outline of World Cultures,* 5th ed., (New Haven, Conn.: Human Relations Area Files, 1975), substituting Eastern Europe for Russia. Theoretical and empirical studies of world cultures suggest that the eight regions specified by Murdock probably capture the major distinctive, broad cultures of the world. See Hofstede, *Culture's Consequences*; Samuel P. Huntington, "The Clash of Civilizations," *Foreign Affairs* 72 (Summer 1993): 22–49; Schwartz, "Cultural Value Differences"; Schwartz and Ros, "Values in the West." Giving equal weight to world regions is

one of many potential weighting schemes for estimating pancultural norms. One could weight regions by the number of nations they include, for example, and nations and regions by their populations.

18. Samuel Bowles and Herbert Gintis, *Schooling in Capitalist America* (New York: Basic Books, 1976); Melvin L. Kohn and Carmi Schooler, *Work and Personality: An Inquiry into the Impact of Social Stratification* (Norwood, N.J.: Ablex, 1983).

19. Shalom H. Schwartz, and Wolfgang Bilsky, "Toward a Universal Psychological Structure of Human Values," *Journal of Personality and Social Psychology* 53(3) (1987): 550–62; Schwartz, "Universals in the Content."

20. Schwartz, "Universals in the Content"; Schwartz, "Are There Universal Aspects."

21. Donald T. Campbell, "On the Conflicts between Biological and Social Evolution and between Psychology and Moral Tradition," *American Psychologist* 30(12) (December 1975) 1103–26; Talcott Parsons, *The Social System* (New York: Free Press, 1951); Shalom H. Schwartz and Anat Bardi, "Influences of Adaptation to Communist Rule on Value Priorities in Eastern Europe," *Political Psychology* 18(2) (1997): 385–410; Robin M. Williams Jr., *American Society: A Sociological Interpretation,* 3rd ed. (New York: Knopf, 1970).

22. Parsons, *The Social System.*

23. Cigdem Kagitcibasi, *Family and Human Development across Cultures: A View from the Other Side* (Hillsdale, N.J.: Erlbaum, 1996).

24. Orville G. Brim Jr., "Socialization through the Life-Cycle," in *Socialization after Childhood,* ed. Orville G., Brim Jr. and Stanton Wheeler (New York: Wiley, 1966), 3–49; Kohn and Schooler, *Work and Personality."*

25. Schwartz, "Universals in the Content."

26. Schwartz, "Universals in the Content."

27. Schwartz, "Universals in the Content."

28. Edward L. Deci and Richard M. Ryan, *Intrinsic Motivation and Self-Determination in Human Behavior* (New York: Plenum, 1985); Richard M. Ryan, "Psychological Needs and the Facilitation of Integrative Processes," *Journal of Personality* 63(3) (September 1995): 397–427.

29. Discussions of social structural, political, demographic, technological, religious, and ideological factors that influence national or cultural differences in values are provided in Hofstede, *Culture's Consequences*; Shalom Schwartz, "Toward Explanations of National Differences in Value Priorities," presented at the XXIV Congress of the Inter-American Society of Psychology, Santiago, Chile (July 1993); Schwartz and Bardi, "Influences of Adaptation"; and Schwartz and Ros, "Values in the West." Here, we comment only on differences in the structured experience of individuals that may affect the importance of their personal values.

30. Richard A. Shweder and Edmund J. Bourne, "Does the Concept of the Person Vary Cross-Culturally?" in *Cultural Conceptions of Mental Health and Therapy,* ed. Anthony J. Marsella and Geoffrey M. White (New York: Reidel, 1982), 97–137.

31. Daniel Lerner, *The Passing of Traditional Society* (Glencoe, Ill.: Free Press, 1964); Andrew Webster, *Introduction to the Sociology of Development* (London: McMillan, 1984).

32. Shmuel N. Eisenstadt, *Tradition, Change and Modernity* (New York: Wiley, 1973); Alex Inkeles and David H. Smith, *Becoming Modern* (Cambridge, Mass.: Harvard, 1974); Joseph A. Kahl, *The Measurement of Modernism: A Study of Values in Brazil and Mexico* (Austin: University of Texas Press, 1968).

33. Etzioni, *The New Golden Rule.*

34. Schwartz, "Value Priorities and Behavior"; cf. Philip E. Tetlock, Randall S. Peterson, and Jennifer R. Lerner, "Revising the Value Pluralism Model: Incorporating Social Content and Context Postulates," in *The Psychology of Values: The Ontario Symposium,* vol. 8, ed. Clive Seligman, James M. Olson, Mark P. Zanna (Hillsdale, N.J.: Erlbaum, 1996), 25–54.

35. Etzioni, *The New Golden Rule,* 248.

36. Schwartz, "Cultural Value Differences"; Schwartz and Ros, "Values in the West."

37. Milton Rokeach, *The Nature of Human Values* (New York: Free Press, 1973); John R. Eiser, *The Expression of Attitude* (New York: Springer Verlag, 1987); Connie M. Kristiansen and Mark P. Zanna, "The Rhetorical Use of Values to Justify Social and Inter-group Attitudes," *Journal of Social Issues* 50(4) (Winter 1994): 47–65.

11

The Cycles of Moral Dialogue

Joel H. Rosenthal

POSTRELATIVISM

The portrayal of society as a bicycle is one of the most compelling images in *The New Golden Rule*. The image is only enhanced by the prospect that the rider depicted might be Amitai Etzioni himself, skillfully navigating between the perils of excessive autonomy on one side of the path and excessive order on the other. Keeping the bicycle upright is the momentum generated by constantly evolving moral dialogues—dialogues that raise consciousness, clarify, and educate. Etzioni, the virtuous leader and teacher, introduces us to a virtuous social tool, the moral dialogue. With each dialogue, the bicycle rolls gently forward down the wide, flat path to the ultimate goal, the good society.

There is likely to be little argument that the use of moral dialogue as a vehicle to achieve the good society is desirable. Dialogue properly structured is fair, balanced, and reasonable. Participants air their views in a rational and civilized manner. Sometimes new understandings are reached; other times the participants agree to disagree.

Yet Etzioni's approach to moral dialogue in *The New Golden Rule* could benefit from attention to another key consideration: the unremitting realities of power. Power is to moral dialogue as gravity is to the bicycle. Power, like gravity, is an omnipresent and inescapable force of nature. You defy power or gravity at your own risk, with predictable consequences.

Etzioni's current account of moral dialogue is curiously one-dimensional; that is, it lacks an accounting mechanism for the irresistible forces of power and politics. Etzioni speaks as a reasonable man to reasonable people, and this is another virtue, to be sure. But his lack of attention to power is perhaps limiting in the harsh world of practical politics and the competitive arena of local community life. Etzioni clearly means to move beyond his previous work emphasizing social structures and coer-

185

cive power and alienation in favor of normative power and the power of moral suasion. As Edward W. Lehman points out in his analysis of Etzioni's intellectual trajectory of the past thirty years, "The communitarian Etzioni is unequivocal in touting the superiority of the moral voice over more alienating forms of compliance."[1]

Many passages in *The New Golden Rule* assure us that Etzioni has not forgotten the insights of his past work and that he is acutely aware that the world is often governed by passions and interests. He makes numerous references to the twin perils of intolerance and greed. These perils often lead to the eclipse of dialogue in favor of a descent into oppression and violence. Yet despite these gestures toward the uncomfortable facts of life, somehow Etzioni's idea of moral dialogue remains a world apart. It is my contention that in searching for a vision of the good society, Etzioni might do better to account for the stubborn realities of power and politics right from the start.

In reading *The New Golden Rule* one might come to the conclusion that the primary challenge for the moralist is to choose between conflicting pathways to the good life. As the image suggests, this would mean that the cyclist's most difficult challenge would be to select the proper path among a number of reasonable inviting alternatives. The choice is seen as a trade-off rather than a confrontation. Pain such as it exists is manageable as society inevitably glides on.

Reliance on moral suasion alone underestimates the moralist's challenge. Can moral suasion really eclipse the tragedy inherent in moral choice? History tells us that the biggest obstacle for the moralist is not navigating between relatively benign choices but rather confronting powerful, malignant, and often irreconcilable interests. Our most influential and respected moralists have always acknowledged this tougher side of the job. They have known that in pursuing the good society they are not invoking moral principles in isolation, but are in effect questioning the most basic facts regarding the distribution of society's political power, wealth, and social status.

The moralists we most admire have seen it as their obligation to "speak truth to power." These moralists have understood that standing in their way are not only competing conceptions of the good life and the inevitability of making compromises, but powerful coalitions of political and economic force who are formidable if not insurmountable adversaries. An effective moralist knows that he or she must often combat the status quo and the power structures that support it. An effective moralist also knows that it is precisely his or her deeply held moral principles that gave him or her the ability and authority to act.

What ideas emboldened the great moralists of our time—moralists such as Mohandas Gandhi and Martin Luther King Jr.—to challenge the social structures of their respective societies? First, they were emboldened by the fact that their claims for justice had universal appeal and validity. Their claims resonated beyond the local community to others outside of it. Second, they were emboldened by the insight that their claims for justice would lead them to a direct confrontation with the established power structure. They reasoned that by invoking the power of principle they might be able to meet political power with another kind of power, thereby effecting real social change. For Gandhi, the enemy was imperialism and colonialism—an entire way of life for generations of people who had lived under its influence. For King, the enemy was racism and its devastating effects on African Americans and all who shared his vision of the American Dream. Just as Gandhi knew that his trek would be all uphill, King knew that not every American shared his dream, particularly many powerful local leaders in the South.

Prototypical moralists like Gandhi and King begin with the understanding that the advancement of morality is, by definition, a struggle. Half of the struggle is intellectual and conceptual; the other half is political. As the American theologian Reinhold Niebuhr pointed out in his work of the 1930s and 1940s, it is folly to think that the intellectual and conceptual side of the equation is all that matters. In his famous critiques of John Dewey and other early twentieth-century liberal pragmatists, Niebuhr cautioned against the simple conclusion that ignorance is the principal cause of injustice. History tells us that better educated men and women are not necessarily less predatory, selfish, cruel, or unjust. Self-interest—and as Niebuhr would add, man's sinful nature—is the principal cause of injustice.[2]

In his "Letter from Birmingham City Jail (1963)," Martin Luther King Jr. wrote, "History is the long and tragic story of the fact that privileged groups seldom give up their privileges voluntarily. Individuals may see the moral light and voluntarily give up their unjust posture, but as Reinhold Niebuhr has reminded us, groups are more immoral." The mere fact that King wrote his famous treatise while incarcerated is testament to the fact that power and justice are not easily divided. Power depends on justice for its legitimacy; justice depends on power for its implementation. With both sorrow and anger detectable in his prose, King reminded his readers that "we have not made a single gain in civil rights without determined legal and non-violent pressure."

Pressure was the key to King's approach. "This may sound shocking," he wrote, "but I must confess that I am not afraid of the word tension. I have earnestly worked and preached against non-violence, but there is a type of constructive nonviolent tension that is necessary for growth." For King, tension is creative—it creates possibilities for reform by putting unjust policies under the direct and relentless stress of the power of principle. Tension forces dialogue and negotiation in situations where the other side does not want to speak or deal. It is important to remember the crude facts of King's predicament. From his jail cell he explained that "only yesterday in Birmingham, Alabama our children, crying out for brotherhood, were answered with firehoses, snarling dogs, and even death." Confronting these harsh circumstances, King concluded, "for too long our beloved Southland has been bogged down in the tragic attempt to live in monologue rather than dialogue."[3]

Gandhi too realized that creating moral dialogues did not come without cost. Gandhi considered his life to be an ongoing series of manufactured tensions and tests. He arranged his life in ways that would put his theories to practical tests. The subtitle of Gandhi's autobiography is telling, "The Story of My Experiments with

Truth." Whether he was addressing personal, national, or world problems—ranging from dietary principles to racism to geopolitics—Gandhi's approach was always the same: every theory was tested in the crucible of lived experience. Working first in South Africa and later in India against the evils of imperialism and the remnants of colonialism, Gandhi coined the term *Satyagraha*—the Force that is born of Truth and Love.

Gandhi was careful to explain that his concept of *Satyagraha* was more proactive than "passive resistance" or "civil disobedience." *Satyagraha* built upon the previous concept of *Sadagraha,* which meant "firmness in a good cause." Gandhi's intention was to give every citizen the means, or the "weapon," he or she needed to embark on a campaign for nonviolent social change. As one commentator has observed, Gandhi's concept was "meant for the common people, not the saints," and it was a "weapon of the brave, not the weak." Change would come at a cost, and *Satyagraha* would demand discipline, self-sacrifice, suffering, fasting, imprisonment, and perhaps even death.[4] The sources of the enemy's strength were the very social institutions that defined public life. It was precisely these institutions that would become the target of Gandhi's activism.

As a sociologist, Etzioni knows better than most that "we live through institutions."[5] He also knows that institutions—particularly local community institutions—are bastions of power and therefore are by definition difficult to change. Institutions can be thought of as either patterns of behavior (ritualized customs such as shaking hands) or concrete organizational structures (such as families, schools, churches, or corporations). But whatever definition one decides upon, one thing is certain: institutions embody and symbolize the values and moral commitments of those whom they serve. When change comes to an institution, it is because certain values and objective circumstances have changed. New patterns of power are then mobilized behind the new vision of what the institution should be. Successful change comes for the moralist who understands that his or her appeal to principle must be anchored in considerations of institutional and social structures.

The genius of Gandhi and King can be summarized in four points. First, they recognized this intrinsic connection between power and justice. Second, they understood that their own moral authority stemmed from the universal appeal of their moral principles, as opposed to narrow, local, or parochial appeal only. Third, they adopted strategies that combined moral suasion with nonviolent confrontation, giving reason a chance to prevail. And finally, they demonstrated that any good society needs moralists of conscience who are articulate and courageous and who can appeal to the best aspects of human nature.

Amitai Etzioni is clearly a moralist of the first rank and should be recognized as such. His work in transforming communitarian theory into a communitarian "movement" is laudable to be sure, and his political prowess in bringing this transformation about proves that he is not naive when it comes to politics, power, and the difficult task of reforming society's institutions. He has shown us how moral dialogue can be most helpful in providing a vehicle for communities to check their own commitments against those of others. The power of principle, as his work attests, lies in its ability to transcend the local, the particular, the individual community. Only principles that resonate outward across communities and across cultures are likely to create lasting social change on a wide scale. In this way, moral dialogue is necessary for both legitimacy and social action. Moral dialogue might help us to achieve incremental and marginal moral change if not comprehensive reform.

But in searching for a "postrelativist" answer to the problem of regenerating moral values, we would do well to remember the *limitations* of dialogue in addition to its possibilities. For example, can all societies be expected to value the very concept of dialogue in the same way we do in the Anglo-American, Western political tradition? Is it reasonable to expect the hierarchical Confucian societies of the East to give the same weight to the idea of dialogue as we do in the West? Moral voices can and should be raised across boundaries, but we must be realistic about how those voices will be received.

Also, it may be a mistake to consider moral dialogue exclusively in the context of the autonomy/social harmony debate symbolized by the East–West debate. Perhaps our perspective is skewed. Would it make sense to highlight a second axis of the debate to feature universalism on one end and particularism on the other? Etzioni alludes to this theme (pp. 247–9) but never engages it fully. A more forceful and systematic treatment of the problem of universalism versus particularism would enable us to view Etzioni's bicycle as one that must always account for the push and pull of the local versus the cosmopolitan. On this second axis we would ask, are local moralists able to transcend their particular circumstances to connect with larger cosmopolitan values? Do their arguments resonate beyond their local communities? If the answer is yes, are they then able to marshal the appropriate political power and political will to create change?

Successful moralists must connect with the historic moral traditions that provide them with their moral compass, with the universal human values to which they aspire, and with the power centers of society. Successful moralists must analyze their predicament and gauge it against something larger than themselves and the current moment. In this regard, our current fixation on the East–West debate over excessive individualism and excessive order may be too circumspect. Perhaps we would do better not only to enlarge but also to redirect our focus.

Such a redirection might lead to a series of debates over fairness, justice, and equity in the new postindustrial, post–Cold War, consumer-oriented society. This new society must be measured against the best of our moral traditions. In this new age, we may not need a single vision of the good society brought about by some version of the moral dialogue. To paraphrase Gandhi, what we might need is for Hindus to become better Hindus, Muslims to become better Muslims, Christians to become better Christians, and humanists to become better humanists. Particular communities will likely be judged according to their ability to deliver on their self-professed ideals. Future conflicts are unlikely to be confined to East/West differences and are unlikely to be judged in these terms. In fact, it appears that the new paradigm pits modernity against tradition. Dangerous fault lines are appearing between religious and secular worldviews, orthodox (fundamentalist) and liberal religions. The much-debated "clash of civilizations" may or may not materialize as a war of "the West against the rest." But we already know for certain that there are serious cleavages within several civilizations that have already deteriorated into internal culture wars.

Let us remember that the animating idea behind Etzioni's *New Golden Rule* is the need to regenerate moral values and commitments that have waned in the face of modern social change. The word *regenerate* is important, for it reveals Etzioni's own commitment to tradition. In order to regenerate, one must first go back to the original power source. The sources for moral regeneration are varied: Hebraic, Hellenistic, Confucian, and so on, but in a very real sense, the precise location and condition of each source is not the most important factor. Jaroslav Pelikan puts it best in *The Vindication of Tradition* (1984) when he writes that tradition can show us "the way that we who are heirs must follow to go beyond it . . . to a universal truth that is available only in a particular embodiment." In engaging our own moral traditions, we enter into a dialogue with the authoritative presence of a continuously transmitted past.[6] This understanding of tradition calls for yet a third axis by which to consider moral dialogue, this time a vertical axis that would feature moral traditions at the bottom, current social issues in the mid-range area, and desirable societal outcomes at the top.

Unlike horizontal dialogue, which takes place *between* communities with different backgrounds and commitments, vertical dialogue takes place *within* communities of similar belief and tradition. The history of the Christian church and all of its schisms is one such extended vertical dialogue, with all of the survivors of Jesus debating among themselves the proper interpretation of his message. Today, vertical dialogues dominate life within the Jewish and Islamic communities. As is painfully evident, the regeneration of moral values is almost never self-executing despite the so-called authoritative tradition that exists to govern the internal affairs of each of these communities. Vertical dialogue is necessary. Without it, each of these communities is without a consensus as to where it has been, and it is unlikely to find a moral compass to give it a fix on where it is, and where it is going.

As with any other moral dialogue, vertical dialogue within communities will also be closely connected to issues of power and control. In fact, vertical dialogue is certain to mirror the interests of the powerful individual and institutional forces that are the pillars of the community. These dialogues can be expected to be every bit as contentious as dialogues between communities if not more so, just as family feuds and conflicts among those with minor differences can be especially destructive.

The tension between individual freedom and social harmony will not disappear, but it will need to be considered within new and different contexts. Horizontal connections involving East–West conceptions of autonomy and order will remain, but their immediate relevance may wane. It seems appropriate for moral dialogue to be considered in accordance with a second, more expansive, horizontal axis: one that seeks equilibrium between coordinates labeled "universalism" and "particularism."

This would make the concept less time-bound and circumstantial. The concept of moral dialogue also needs the capacity to shift at least ninety degrees to include the vertical challenge of connecting past and present to the future. Finally, as history makes clear, we must remember that it makes little sense to consider morality outside of its relationship to the dominant social forces of power and interest. Etzioni's remarkable insights aside, it would be a mistake to think that moral dialogue alone will relieve us from the steep hills that all moralists, by their very nature, seek to climb.

NOTES

1. Edward W. Lehman, "From Compliance to Community in the Works of Amitai Etzioni, *The Responsive Community* 9(1) (Winter 1998/1999): 38–47.

2. For this interpretation of Niebuhr and Dewey I rely on Robert B. Westbrook, *John Dewey and American Democracy* (Ithaca, N.Y.: Cornell University Press, 1991) 523–32.

3. Martin Luther King Jr., *Testament of Hope: The Essential Writings and Speeches of Martin Luther King, Jr.,* edited by James M. Washington (New York: HarperCollins, 1986) 289–302, 340–77.

4. Homer A. Jack, *The Gandhi Reader* (New York: Grove Press, 1956), v–ix, 59–84.

5. The phrase is taken from Robert N. Bellah, et al., *The Good Society* (New York: Vintage Books, 1992).

6. Terry Nardin and David R. Mapel, eds., *Traditions of International Ethics* (New York: Cambridge University Press, 1992) 6–9.

12

Accounting for Order

J. Russell Muirhead

> In all governments, there is a perpetual and intestine struggle, open or secret,
> between AUTHORITY and LIBERTY; and neither of them can absolutely pre-
> vail in the contest.
>   —David Hume, "Of the Origin of Government"[1]

"Values are not broccoli," insists Amitai Etzioni. One might take or leave broccoli—
its healthful effects notwithstanding—simply on whim or preference. But values,
Amitai Etzioni hopes, should be firmeer than this.[2] Etzioni comes to defend the need
for an account of values in the conclusion of his attempt to advance a communitarian
public philosophy.[3] Defending communitarianism is tricky if only because of the
persistent difficulty in locating precise and important differences between communitarianism and the philosophy it aims to amend, liberalism.[4] The distinction
of interest to Etzioni concerns the status of society's core values. Where some liberals (especially foundational liberals such as John Locke or Immanuel Kant) root values
in something universal, like the law of nature or the preconditions of rational agency,
communitarianism is often allied with the claim that core values can only reflect the
shared understandings of a particular community,[5] Etzioni's defense of a "communitarian agenda" insists that values be subjected to a higher test than the community. After surveying a variety of procedures by which a community's values might
be judged and finding them inadequate, Etzioni in the end lands on the moral sense
as the final arbiter of community values. "In searching for the final touchstone . . . ,"
Etzioni says of his attempt to find a source of value, "I draw on the observation that
certain concepts present themselves to us as morally compelling in and of themselves."[6]

Two values that "speak compellingly for themselves" are autonomy and order, the
two core values of any good society.[7] The "communitarian paradigm" is distinguished

from common liberalism and conservatism, in Etzioni's view, by its aim to secure a balance between autonomy and order, instead of exaggerating one at the cost of the other.[8] Each is necessary, yet as David Hume says, "neither of them can absolutely prevail."[9] The central focus of *The New Golden Rule* is on core values as they apply to societies as wholes. Societies need some kind of moral order if they are to survive Etzioni points out. At the same time, autonomy is also socially functional, for it equips society to adapt to changing circumstances. Throughout his analysis, Etzioni brings a judicious sociological sensibility both to soften the philosophic differences among competing political theories and to point to the important social and political implications that follow.[10] Yet in the closing chapter, Etzioni turns to a different, more philosophic question. There, he considers the need for a final arbiter or ultimate test by which to gauge society's core values. This notion, that we need a test by which to assess social values, goes beyond what is necessary for society to function well. Why, we might ask, do we need an account or higher framework of value? And if we do, can we rely in the end on what might be called a "moral sense," or the conviction that certain primary moral concepts are "self-evident," or "compelling in and of themselves?"[11]

The first section of this chapter will address Etzioni's central claim that we need an account that locates a higher framework for value than social conventions can provide. Although I agree with Etzioni about this need, I will argue that in the end we should not rely on the moral sense understood as the conviction that elemental values present themselves to us as morally compelling in and of themselves. Values that seem compelling in and of themselves are often commonsense moral intuitions that redescribe conventional values and sidestep the burden of their justification. These conventional judgments and commonsense intuitions are indispensable starting points in moral analysis. But they are only starting points; to understand their implications and inadequacies, it is necessary to examine what they presuppose. They need to be complemented by a deeper and more extensive account.

To clarify the inadequacies of the moral sense and at the same time defend the need for an account of value, the second section of the chapter will examine the value of moral order, which along with autonomy is one of the two core social values Etzioni identifies. Common sense tells us that moral order is necessary for societies if they are to survive, prosper, and ensure the safety of individuals within them. But moral order involves more than this commonsense concern with stability and safety. Moral order involves an account of those inequalities that, in different degrees, are inevitable in any society. In any actual social order, some have more and others less of what is generally desired. An effective account of order needs to address this unequal distribution. In order to do this, an account of moral order needs to show why social and economic inequality cannot be reduced to a matter of the strong dominating the weak, and why moral order does not simply serve the private interests of a few. It needs, in other words, to provide an account of the common good that links individual interest with the social order. The general endorsement of moral order, while sensible and judicious, is too abbreviated to provide such an account.

To consider a more complete account of order, I turn to two particular accounts of moral order. One comes from John Winthrop's *Arabella* sermon, where Winthrop invokes the famous image of a "city on a hill." The second more familiar account comes from John Locke. Winthrop's organic account justifies—but also tempers—inequality by reference to a shared ideal, while Locke's liberal account reconciles inequality with the equal moral claim of each human being to life and liberty. Winthrop's account reminds us, I argue, that the liberal account of order needs to be supplemented by a shared purposive ideal if it is to enlarge individual interests in a way that is necessary both to the liberal defense of rights and to effectively address inequality.

There is an important methodological point involved in considering two accounts of order. No matter how much we may need an account of value, it is a mistake to reach for a single source that can serve as a "final arbiter" of all value. To grasp directly for such a final arbiter is likely to result in either unearned skepticism or an account of value that bypasses the complexity of the moral world. Rather than reach directly for a final account of value, it is better to begin with the values that are evident to us, for we do inescapably inhabit a moral world. What we are likely to find when we take seriously the values that give life meaning, purpose, and justification is not one final account but several accounts. One may appear most insightful or seem to offer the best articulation of the moral meanings we know, but even this is likely to be surrounded by rivals, perhaps within the same moral tradition. The enterprise of understanding a value like moral order, for instance, is essentially comparative: we need to consult more than one account, and compare them to each other in order to forge a "best available account." Only by this method can we deepen and extend our understanding of a value like moral order.[12]

DO WE NEED AN ACCOUNT OF VALUES?

The very claim that we need an account of core values is itself controversial, for many hold that contemporary politics can do without such an account. For instance, to understand political justice it is sufficient to begin with the conventional agreement on central values such as religious toleration and the rejection of slavery, according to John Rawls.[13] The values that give rise to an understanding of justice do not need, in this view, to look to a source of authority that lends them universal truth. In a pragmatic mode others claim that politics can get along just fine without an account of moral truth by focusing instead on what works: what matters for politics is how effective we are at eradicating cruelty, not how proficient we are at explaining why it's wrong.[14] There is much to be said for this sort of pragmatism. We may not need to know why human beings have a right to live or why they should be treated as moral equals to develop a coherent and workable account of morality. "The study of judgments and justifications in the real world moves us closer, perhaps, to the most profound questions of moral philosophy, but it does not require a direct engagement with those questions," Michael Walzer argues. "Indeed," he continues, "philosophers who seek such an engagement often miss the immediacies of political and moral controversy and provide little help to men and women faced with hard choices."[15] Since the judgments many of us agree about (for example, that "intentional killing of those who constitute no threat to others is wrong") are sufficient to support further reasoning about applications and implications, practical moral reasoning does not need to venture all the way down and attempt to build up moral theory from the beginning.[16] That bolder venture might tempt those whose wonder drives them to see why the morality of ordinary life might "mesh with the world."[17] Laudable though this wonder is, it points to a long and difficult path that can distract us from the practical tasks of morality.

Etzioni, on the contrary, insists that politics needs more than clear and careful efforts to trace the implications of our moral agreements. We must, he argues, not only take points of moral agreement as given moral facts but also seek a higher framework of value that serves to decide and justify political decisions. In search of such a framework, Etzioni first looks to four main possibilities: democratic, or majoritarian, decision procedures; foundational, or constitutional, frameworks; cross-cultural moral dialogues; and global declarations of rights. Each of these provides a crucial and useful guide by which to test our moral judgments. As citizens, legislators, or judges consult the authority of majorities or the constitution, so societies more generally may find guidance in the outcome of cross-cultural dialogue or global declarations of rights. But none of these tests gives a sufficient account of core moral values, Etzioni rightly claims.[18] Although majorities, constitutions, cultural dialogues, and global declarations represent a wide agreement that has its own moral and practical force, agreement is not the same as truth. Another way of putting this view is that we are never so free as to be the original source of moral value. We do not—as individuals, as members of a political majority, or as participants in a cross-cultural dialogue—simply *make up* morality. This conviction (or worry) that moral truths are not of our own making stands behind the need for a higher framework of value.

The Force of Convention

Neither the worry nor the conviction is obvious. Many values plainly exist or are true only insofar as they are believed. The value of a dollar, to take a ready case, depends entirely on convention. Should enough persons cease valuing dollars, dollars will be worthless. No higher framework or final arbiter can defend the value of a dollar against all dissent. Moral values may be of the same sort. The value of a human being, even what we sometimes take to be the infinite value of each human being, may be like this: it may exist only insofar as we agree to the value, or enough of us agree so as to effectively institutionalize this value in the form of legal protections equally extended to each. Around here, we might say, we take each human being, no matter how lonely or weak or lacking in what is conventionally admired, to be worthy beyond measure, such that her or his life and liberty is inviolable. If asked why we take this to be the case, we might reply, "It's true simply because we believe it, and should your actions reveal that you dissent from our belief, we'll punish you." On this view, moral value, like the value of a currency, is a convention. And its binding force suffers little for its conventional status. Just as one would court hazard by treating white pebbles as currency when the larger society places currency in dollars, so it would be imprudent or perilous to live by moral values radically different from those embraced by social conventions.

Why not, then, rest content with convention, and simply forego the quest for a "final arbiter" of values? A number of considerations show convention alone, no matter how powerful, to be insufficient. First, conventional agreements are often very general, and agreement loosens at the level of concrete application. The general notion that governmental establishment of a religion violates human freedom, for instance, does not itself decide whether the proper way of respecting freedom involves funding only nonreligious schools or funding all religious schools on an equal basis, and it does not answer how the state should regulate the employment practices of religious associations.[19] Answering such practical questions requires not only a careful assessment of policies but also some examination of the underlying principles that bear on the question. Second, conventions are not themselves consistent, nor are what they conventionally entail. The core values Etzioni distills—autonomy and order—are in tension, and in their practical application often point in different directions. Negotiating this tension requires not only a compromising and generous spirit but also, again, careful reasoning about how to best understand the underlying principles. It requires, in short, that we get beyond what we passively take from conventions. Third, confidence in our conventions may waver given the judgments we make about the conventions that prevailed in our past, or that continue in other cultures. If we were wrong before—about the status of women and Blacks or the treatment of prisoners—perhaps we are also wrong now. If we are to criticize across cultures, certainly we need to think values are not wholly ours. This last sort of consideration points to Etzioni's worry with convention. In his view, conventions alone are inadequate because, in short, they could be wrong. The fact that conventional agreements are so powerful is no cause for moral complacency but rather makes the business of assessing convention the more pressing.

Morally Compelling Concepts

To find a basis for morality more firm than convention, Etzioni looks to a simple and universal natural capacity in order to ground values: the moral sense. This capacity issues, he says, in primary regulative concepts of morality that do not require reasoning or analysis or investigation. The moral notions we know through our moral sense "present themselves as morally compelling in and of themselves," Etzioni claims.[20] This view, which is akin to the claim that the primary concepts of morality are given by a universal moral sense, has a heritage that goes back to the seventeenth-century Scottish resistance to Hobbesianism. And as long as the moral sense theory has been around it has motivated intense criticism.[21]

The ineradicable problem with the claim that elemental moral concepts are compelling in and of themselves is that it offers nothing to arbitrate disagreement. And it often cannot make sense of disagreement, at least where basic moral propositions are at stake. The moral sense alone cannot determine when and how privacy should be defended and protected, for instance, and for that matter it cannot explain why privacy itself, which is a concern of relatively recent vintage, should count as a core moral value. More problematic than the difficulties the moral sense thesis has with arbitrating moral disagreement is the problem it incurs in deciding the scope of the moral. Questions about the distribution of benefits and burdens—especially where benefits are diffused and burdens are concentrated, as arise in deciding the location of airports, waste dumps, power plants, and prisons—involve both interests and principles. Yet the moral sense cannot bring the moral aspects of such questions into focus or orient the deliberation about such questions.

The moral sense, as Jeremy Bentham charged, is more a "principle in name than in reality: it is not a positive principle of itself, so much as a term employed to signify the negation of all principle."[22] Kant too thought that the moral sense and allied notions left morality a motley patchwork of conflicting notions, which in part is what motivated his effort to found morality on a ground wholly stripped of all contingency.[23] For both Bentham and Kant, the problem with the moral sense is that it is too indeterminate, too subjective, and too arbitrary. It renders moral value a matter of individual taste and thus makes the status of moral value like broccoli—exactly what Etzioni hopes to avoid.

To be sure, Etzioni does not suppose that self-evident moral concepts will settle every moral conflict. On the contrary, he expects that at best we will find as self-evident only general values that occupy a special elemental status, such as the concepts of moral order and autonomy. Even when it does not settle everything, the notion that some basic values are self-evident and beyond disagreement is comforting: it asserts something that many of us *want* to be true. That everyone has access to primary moral precepts is a comfort to democrats, for instance, by virtue of the faith it supports in the moral capacities of everyday men and women. When moral knowledge is not the special possession of experts, philosophers, or the holy, but instead is available to all human beings, then democracy rests not only the strength of numbers but also on the moral quality of the people. Democracy is right not only because the people can rule, but because they deserve to. The conviction that some values are compelling in and of themselves comforts also in a different way, by the strength it lends to the understanding that morality is, underneath all our doubts and examinations, something solid and real. Faith in something like a moral sense sets to the side nettlesome doubts about the status of morality. As it does this, so it also gives confidence to those who cherish something about the current order of things yet worry that some form of moral skepticism will corrode the present order and yet fail to replace it with anything better.

Confidence in a basic moral sense speaks to two strong, if competing, tendencies: it strengthens the convictions of a democratic age in itself and assuages the doubts about the status of morality. It could not do this if it did not describe something about ordinary experience that many both find true and want to be true. Professions of "relativism" notwithstanding, many experience themselves and most other people as moral and yet find morality either tedious or difficult to explain. The conviction that some values are self-evident calls to mind a student who, when asked to explain why Kant thought lying is wrong, replied, "I don't know what Kant would say; it just IS!" He was not the finest student of Kant but was utterly trustworthy as a matter of character. His example reminds us that the moral life, at least from the perspective of the moral, usually needs little explanation, only occasional exhortation. [24] What needs to be explained is what is out of the ordinary, and in ordinary life it is not fair-mindedness or decency that is unusual, but rather prejudice, hatred, violence, and criminality. Moral sense theory tells us what much in everyday life seems to show: that the moral life, the life of loyalty, truth telling, decency, fairness, and respect, is the norm. This is the baseline against which deviations are measured.

But attributing basic moral concepts to the moral sense obscures the fact that the order and autonomy that characterize our social life, as well as the decency, honesty, and respect that normally characterize our common life result from an historical achievement that should not be taken for granted. And the struggle against snobbery, intolerance, aggression, duplicity, and hatred is not complete. The comforts of the moral sense support an unjustified complacency that ends up displacing what Etzioni says we need: an account of moral values. The moral sense actually neglects the need for an account of values by falsely showing that it is really not a need; we do not need to account for what we can readily enough perceive. What goes by the name of moral sense is something real. It reflects assumptions that—although reliable—are unexamined and unreflective. These assumptions or moral intuitions constitute what is at best a first step, and not the final point, of moral analysis. To rest moral analysis on the moral sense is to escape from the project of evaluating and justifying values. Taken as a resting place (rather than a first step), the moral sense is more of a wish than a theory; it does not justify anything. It fulfils the wish that we could escape the burdens and doubts of engaging the moral world. Such an escape is certainly possible, and possibly even relaxing. But the cost of resisting the need of accounting for values is remaining deaf and blind to the disagreements, the conflicts, and the dilemmas contained in our moral world. The respite the moral sense offers denies the reality of moral conflict as it resists the possibility for moral improvement.

Accounting for Values

If the moral sense cannot provide a final account of value, Etzioni is right about the deeper matter at stake here: we do need an account of value, even if the account only covers *our* values or fails to provide the sort of final accounting that puts all moral controversy to rest. But the need for an account of value cannot rest entirely on the promise that such an account might offer a way of deciding every vexing moral question. To be sure, an account of value that could serve as a steady and true guide by which to navigate through our most difficult ethical dilemmas, here and now, would be of much assistance. But no general account of value will be able to decide every practical question in all its detail. It would betray the tragic complexity of competing values, for instance, to suppose that an account of value could simply settle every particular involved in deciding whether the terminally ill should be able to control the time and manner of their deaths. An account of value should bring some clarity to what is at stake in such dilemmas, but the need for an account of value cannot depend on the promise of it carrying a single right answer. Any general account of value will likely be too abstract and incomplete and its application to the "real world" too hazardous to cover every detail.

The need is instead rooted in the inescapable fact that we inhabit a moral world. We live in and among values that are points of orientation, commitment, and contestation. Values are woven into the social and political practices of everyday life, and regardless of whether we know it or much like it, when we participate in everyday life we live out and live by an array of values. For instance, the two central and generally unavoidable arenas of everyday life—work and family—implicate each of us in an intricate weave of values. At critical moments (in deciding about careers, the education of children, or marriage or negotiating the balance of work and family) we engage choices that make some threads of this fabric explicit. Political life too necessarily engages a range of values. Often these values are an unnoticeable backdrop to the daily give and take of politics. But they come up with special prominence when navigating more occasional questions like those that bear directly on a fundamental clash of values (such as abortion), or when deciding questions that involve great risks, such as matters of war and peace. Even for those who do not share the Socratic temperament that seeks a whole understanding for its own sake, the need to reflect on the values that give shape and direction to life arises from the inevitable crises of individual and political life. And this is not to be regretted, for if the project of accounting for values is difficult and hazardous, it also issues in the promise that we might act through a deeper and truer self-understanding to effectively give shape to our social and political life.

THE VALUE OF MORAL ORDER

The need for an account of value arises especially with a value like moral order, which along with autonomy is one of the two core social values Etzioni identifies. It is fair to suppose that these are the core social values our moral senses, or unreflective moral intuitions, would identify. As individuals whose aspirations and pride are nourished in a liberal democracy, we want to rule ourselves; we want autonomy—and even when we do not, we want to retain the power of deciding when and how to forgo it, which amounts to the same thing. Common sense also suggests that all societies need some measure of order as a precondition to other social goods; the protection of individual autonomy, for instance, itself requires order. Social order and individual autonomy are not antithetical, Etzioni points out, though they are in tension. The "good society," Etzioni prudently argues, negotiates the tension between them, preserving and augmenting each for the sake of the other.[25] Thus order and autonomy are what we find through our moral sense. This is a judicious and accurate description of what common sense, or at any rate, *our* common sense identifies.

But this commonsense account masks the fact that neither order nor autonomy is ever a simple matter. The basis of moral order—to take only one of the two core values—is one of the most elemental and contested questions of political life, and the way we account for it carries immense implications. The commonsense account, which tells us that some order is necessary, is only a beginning. Certainly there are some extremes that show order in general to be crucial. The value of order generally comes into focus, for instance, against the background of chaos and unpredictable violence, in places where there is no safety to be had. Order in general is desirable because it makes possible calculations about safety; violence and anarchy make any stable order look choiceworthy.

Yet, as Etzioni points out, the choice citizens often face is not between any order and the lack of all order.[26] When anarchy is not at the gates, one kind of order is usually confronted with another, which is thought to be better, fairer, and more just. In more peaceful moments, one must ask, "What *kind* of order is it to be?"[27] Questions about the *kind* of order we should endorse arise with special force because of the connection between moral order and inequality. Some inequality is inevitable in society: some have, and others lack, what is generally desired: money, honor, authority. Some are eminent, others obscure, some command, others obey. These differences might be fixed or fluid, but in either case an account of moral order serves to diminish contestation over inequality by explaining how the inequalities are fair or just.

An account of moral order attempts to show why a given order is more than an arrangement where some dominate over others for their private benefit. Because some seem to get more from any given order than others, it is often possible to unmask an order and to show that all it amounts to is the self-interested rule of some over others. The need for an account of order is an expression of resistance—both to the temptation to interpret particular orders as essentially matters of domination and also to the real possibility that this is all order can ever amount to. Striving to account for moral order expresses the real desire to understand and to inhabit an order that is just. And every particular order must sooner or later give an account that explains its justice. To be stable, order needs not only physical force but also the persuasive force of words. Even tyrannies are full of enemies, and when the effectiveness of fear runs short even tyrannical rulers need to depend on something more than fear to sustain order—they need some story, or argument, that serves to persuade people that those in power deserve their power.[28] Order of any sort occasionally needs words made in its defense that show why order, with all its attendant inequalities, is just. Assessing what counts as a just order moves us far beyond the general endorsement of order. Here, where matters become more complicated, the notion that some moral values are compelling in and of themselves is of little help. The conviction that some values are self-evident cannot itself supply words of the sort that might justify an order.

The need for such words is most explicit in moments of political founding, when habitual assent or what Hume called "the sanction of antiquity"[29] is absent. To see how we might more fully answer the need for an account of order, consider two accounts of order, both of which are indirectly connected to the establishment of the American order. One comes from John Winthrop, the other John Locke. The two accounts do not stand on par. Where Locke's account abides by the liberal premise we share—that human beings are free and equal—Winthrop's is stranger, as it relies on the ideal of a Christian nation. But the contrast suggests a weakness in the Lockean, or liberal, account of order that can be partly remedied by Winthrop's organic account of order.

For the sake of this argument, I will not attend to the full accounts each offers in all their richness and depth but will isolate a strain in each that bears on the justification of inequality. Winthrop and Locke each explain and justify inequality, especially material inequality. Yet Winthrop, unlike Locke, argues that inequality should be tempered by charity, which for Winthrop is a duty that places great demands on the advantaged. The difference here issues from the way each reconciles order with interest. Locke shows how an order can appeal to the basic interests of each person in self-preservation, comfort, and liberty. Winthrop, on the other hand, connects individual interest to the social order by appealing to a comprehensive ideal that can be better realized collectively than individually. Where Winthrop attempts to expand and extend the sense of self to include others in service to a shared ideal, Locke seems to ask less of individuals, invoking plain interests each person can be presumed to possess. The comparison to Winthrop suggests that while the strategic element of the Lockean order gives it great strength, it is also both limiting and misleading. Even a strategic order needs to complement the bonds of interest with ties of social affection.

The Organic Account of Order: John Winthrop

To begin with the less familiar, the organic argument for order depends on showing how different individuals together form an admirable whole. Such an account is what John Winthrop offered aboard the ship *Arabella* in 1630, just prior to its arrival in what would become Massachusetts.[30] The problem motivating Winthrop's sermon was not set only by scripture, but by politics. As a founder, Winthrop needed to offer a reason for the new political community that would strengthen its coherence and justify individuals in sacrificing something of their own good for the whole.

Winthrop grasped the way inequality breeds indifference, spite, and envy, in the process undermining confidence that the moral order serves the common good. Yet he also thought some inequality inevitable. Societies necessarily create a variety of tasks, and not all are equal in the authority, status, or remuneration they entail. The human condition is such, he says, that "in all times some must be rich, some poor, some high and eminent in power and dignity; others mean and in subjection."[31]

Winthrop needed to offer an account of moral order that could square inequality with the common good. His account locates a powerful source of affective unity in inequality. Individuals in unequal roles are drawn together by society in relations of mutual need, and together form a functional whole. Societies have rich and poor, high and low, Winthrop notes, so that each "might have need" of every other. But in order for mutual need to generate affection rather than envy and spite, the community must be more than a functional whole. The satisfaction of mutual need is not itself sufficient for individuals to be all knit more nearly together in the bonds of brotherly affection."[32] Social affection requires that the community stand for not only the satisfaction of individual needs but also for a shared moral purpose. Winthrop locates this purpose in the way that a community as a whole can imitate Christian virtue, especially Christian love.

This ideal demands an expanded sense of self that can identify with one's fellow members of society, who make possible a society that approximates that ideal. By invoking the ideal of Christ's love, Winthrop asks his listeners to get beyond themselves: "We must," Winthrop urges, "delight in each other, make other's conditions our own, rejoice together, mourn together, labor and suffer together, always having before our own eyes our commission and community in the work, our community as members of the same body." Connecting the individual to others through a shared moral purpose allows Winthrop not only to justify an inegalitarian order but also to temper it. Because social relations are not oriented only to the satisfaction of private wants but also to the collective approximation of a shared ideal, Winthrop can insist on very demanding duties of charity. The point of society after all, is not private opulence of a few, and especially not the sort that depends on the privations of others. By placing inequality (however inevitable it might be) in service to a shared moral ideal, he can ask that those on top "be willing to abridge ourselves of our superfluities, for the supply of others' necessities."[33] The shared moral ideal offers a powerful source of social unity. By appealing to a conception of the ideal that the community as a whole serves, order connects to each individual and is not simply for the sake of those on top. This is also why Winthrop can claim that those on top use what they have to the advantage of the rest.

If Winthrop's account of order answers the political need of sustaining social unity amid inequality, it cannot serve as an account for us. With neither the united faith that we are "fellow members of Christ," nor some agreement about the implications of this fellowship, Winthrop's invocation of organic order is relegated to the irrecoverable past. And we do not view this as an important loss, since the kind of agreement the organic account requires could only be secured if individuals were deprived of the liberty to form and act from their own moral ideals. Our account of order needs to start from a different premise, the natural equality and freedom of human beings. It looks, at least initially, not to the individual's part in a whole but to an interest that attaches to each person.

Locke, who justifies order in terms of a universal interest in self-preservation and comfort, does not appeal to any ideal that the community as a whole might imitate, and he does not explicitly ask that individuals expand their sense of self or develop an expanded conception of self-interest. On its face, Locke's account of order is more strategic and less idealistic than Winthrop's. Looking only to its strategic dimension, the Lockean order elicits less affection than Winthrop's and because of this also has less to say about the importance of remediating inequality. Attending to this strategic side of Locke's account of order serves as a reminder that an account of order needs to do more than appeal to interest. It needs also to connect allegiance and affection to the values that form the moral core of any order.

The Strategic Account of Order: John Locke

Like Winthrop's, Locke's account of order justifies inequality. As social and economic inequality looked unavoidable to Winthrop, so it looks choiceworthy to Locke: "men have agreed," Locke says, "to disproportionate and unequal possession of the Earth."[34] Yet Locke begins with the fact of natural equality and rejects the possibility that natural difference can justify the fact that some have and others lack or that some command and others obey. Nature makes "nothing more evident," he says, than that human beings should "be equal among one another without subordination or subjection."[35] Why would moral equals choose material inequality? Locke's answer centers on the shared benefits that inequality makes possible.

By stimulating industriousness, inequality makes everyone better off. The promise of appropriation gives people a reason to labor, and it is only by labor that the earth's latent value becomes actual. "For whatever *bread* is more worth than acorns, wine than water, and cloth or silk than leaves, skins, or moss, that is wholly owing to labor and industry,"[36] Locke says. The use of money amplifies the incentive to labor by facilitating even greater accumulation. Without something like money, there would be no point to appropriating more than one could use. This, Locke points out, would be "dishonest," since it wastes what could benefit others, and "foolish," since it wastes effort. Only money—or the agreement to place a value on "something both lasting and scarce" like gold or silver, allows accumulation without limit.[37] Although they introduce material inequalities, it makes sense to agree to both private appropriation and the use of money since in the end these give a point to human effort and augment what gives security and comfort to human life. The sum of this added effort is that everybody is better off. Comparing the paltry production of the United States' uncultivated lands with Britain, Locke observes, "And a king of a large and fruitful territory there feeds, lodges, and is clad worse than a day laborer in England."[38]

To be sure, the Lockean order offers something more profound than material gain. It grants everyone the more elemental protection of their lives and security from the "inconstant, uncertain, unknown, arbitrary will of another man."[39] The power of command does not accompany the comforts of money. Locke limits the power of rule to defined roles or offices and in turn restricts the reach of official authority by limiting the purposes of the state to the protection of rights. By restricting the reach of government and by making ruling a job—or rather a series of functionally related but separate jobs—Locke denudes inequality of the domination that threatens to accompany it.

The Lockean order can seem a wholly strategic affair. The weak have a profound interest in the protection of the state, while the strong have an interest in the accumulation it facilitates. And both share, though to different degrees, in the promise of prosperity. So long as the protection of rights is secure and prosperity is shared, even the lowliest has something to gain. The affinity of this strategic order to our order should be clear. Like Locke's, our order takes rights seriously, especially the elemental right to the protection of our lives and bodies. It too offers security or freedom from fear for one's physical safety or domineering will of others and gives something to the capable and ambitious by protecting property and stewarding accumulation. Something much like Locke's account may offer the best account of our moral order. For this reason it is important to see why a single emphasis on the strategic dimension of order, even for a regime that focuses on shared prosperity and the equal protection of basic rights, misses something critical.

The Moral Core of Strategic Order

Connecting order to the elemental interests of each is a source of great strength, both with Locke's order and with ours, yet it tends to exaggerate the place of interest. Even a liberal order concerned with securing equal respect and general prosperity needs to appeal to something more than individual interest. Indeed the strategic appeal can obscure the moral core of liberal order. The vulnerabilities of an order that looks more strategic than it can afford to be reveal themselves especially in moments of crisis, when the preservation of an order particularly requires individuals to sacrifice something of their own to carry off critical common tasks. This occurs of course in the occasional need to go to war but also in the more frequent need to observe the demands of equal respect. A strategic appeal alone cannot induce individuals to follow the law or respect the rights of others when it is not in their interest to do so. This depends not only on a strategic commitment to one's own rights but on a moral commitment to the protection of rights more generally. In this respect, the Lockean order does not ask for less than Winthrop's, for it demands that we identify not solely with the claims of our neighbors but with human beings generally as "sentient creatures." Its thrust is even cosmopolitan, for it insists that "an insult to the life and liberty of any race or group in any part of the world" should at the least elicit empathy, and in certain cases action.[40] Focusing only on the strategic dimension of order obscures the fact that liberal order too depends on an expanded sense of self.

In times of peace, few things threaten to constrict this expanded sense of self more effectively than a widening distribution of wealth, where the winners appear to "take all," and where all strive to ensure they don't fall on the shallow side of the divide that separates the top tenth from the rest. Widening inequality, entrenched through the practice of inheritance, divides the society into isolated communities of consumption. The best-off opt out of the wider public by privately purchasing those goods that for the rest come from common provision: education, recreation, safety, even water. All this tends to sap the common identification and expanded sense of self on which the protection of rights occasionally depends.[41] Even when inequality carries common benefits, its widening degree has social consequences that shroud the shared moral commitment at the core of liberal order.

There is reason to think that the moral commitment at the heart of Locke's account of order is insufficient on its own to support the expanded sense of self that it in practice requires. This moral commitment—in short, the principle that each stands to every other as a moral equal—on the one hand demands we identify with the interests of every human being, while on the other hand restricts this identification to the most basic human interests. The universal duty of equal respect in practice limits the burden of that duty. At the same time, the pursuit of prosperity encourages an instrumental relation to others—precisely the kind of relation that needs to be partially overcome if we are to identify with the moral claims of others. The limits of equal respect are particularly evident when considering material distribution. Something more limited in scope than the moral equality of human beings, but more powerful in its demands, is necessary to support a distributional principle that tends toward greater equality.

The principle of moral equality needs to be complemented by a measure of affection or a sense of fraternity to prod individuals to go beyond the requirements of respect and take into account the general material condition of others. From a sense of fraternal affection, people may not *want* to be part of an order that benefits some to the exclusion of others. To a system that gives each what they can get while securing the elemental requirements of equal respect, they might prefer a distributional principle that better expresses affective bonds. John Rawls's difference principle, which asks people to "view the greater abilities of some as a social asset to be used for the common advantage,"[42] is an example. Affection, limited though it must be in its civic form, goes beyond the demands of equal respect by singling out some for special concern. Such special concern must be grounded in something more particular than the principle of equal respect. Winthrop's example of calling forth "brotherly affection" suggests that it needs to be rooted in an ideal that finds its particularity not because it is parochial but because it can best be expressed by the complementary energies of those who make up a particular community. Of course, the ideal Winthrop looked to, a community of faith, is unavailable to the liberal order because it too pointedly contradicts the demands of equal respect. This in turn raises an important question: can a shared ideal—one that supports fraternal affection and is necessarily expressed by a particular community—be consistent with the claims of moral equality?

This is a serious issue for our order, founded as it is on moral equality. For without something like an element of fraternal affection, the liberal order is limited not only in remediating inequality for the sake of the least advantaged but also in supporting the kind of bonds that are occasionally necessary to the defense of rights and freedom. The liberal order needs a source of that affection that allows individuals to expand their conception of interest and identify (in a partial and restricted way) with others. It is possible to meet this challenge, although doing so requires some judicious balancing. Meeting it does not require denying respect for the equality and freedom of human beings but attending to the promise implicit in the moral commitment to equal respect. A shared ideal that supports civic affection can be founded in an appreciation not only of the harms individuals may suffer but also of the possibilities they may achieve.

This ideal looks to the achievement of individuality that is expressed when a person through sustained and vigorous engagement with the world unites talent with passion, discipline with enthusiasm, and sensitivity with commitment in a distinctive and definitive self. Although focused on the individual, individuality is not a private achievement. It requires a social and political commitment that is not only protective but also enabling. Individuality is nourished by the political protection of freedom but also relies on the communal provision of those resources that allow individuals to develop and display their talents. In addition to the political and social support it requires, the achievement of individuality is public in another sense. It depends on a kind of exchange between individuals that occurs when each gives something of himself or herself through their own example. Although the inspiring example of heroic effort in the face of great impediments is rare, both the working life and family life offer a more everyday location for such examples. Individuality requires a community where persons exchange not just goods and services, but also "humane gifts," the gifts that come when people put something of themselves in what they attempt and accomplish. [43] This is why the ideal of individuality is necessarily rooted and why it is the kind of ideal that extends individual affections. This ideal is not at odds with the liberal concern for free choice. On the contrary, the generalized achievement of individuality requires an order that respects human freedom and equality. Yet at the same time it offers a powerful resource on which society can draw not only to prevent the worst harms but also to enable individuals to develop their capacities and direct their energies such that their own life inspires by the way it reflects human possibility.

To be sure, there is a tension between the romantic ideal of individuality and the liberal ethic of moral equality—for some definitive individual traits may threaten or violate the rights of others. At times the ethic of individuality will need to be constrained by the obligations of equal respect. But this tension does not make it impossible to supplement the liberal account of order with an ideal of individuality.

The ideal of individuality recognizes that in practice order is cemented not only by force, or only by interest and reason, but also by affection. Such affectionate concern is not absent from our common life, and its source need not be omitted from a full account of our order. This is only to gesture toward the sort of ideal that can augment and complement the liberal account of order. An account of order akin to Winthrop's cannot be *our* account—it too much neglects our moral commitment to equal respect. But consulting it offers a reminder that built into our order is a tendency to view it as more strategic than it can afford to be and that liberal principles especially need the auxiliary support of affection for their support.

This account of order does not, alas, ascend to the level that "final arbiters" of a community's values might occupy. It starts where we are, in the moral order we inhabit. If it does not break free of every conventional value, still it submits convention to careful scrutiny by consulting a familiar account of our order, as articulated by Locke, and examining this in light of the rival account found in Winthrop. Even Winthrop's account is not utterly strange; it too is located within our tradition. But it bears on our order only indirectly and is sufficiently distinct from the more familiar account Locke offers to illuminate some of its strengths and weaknesses and to direct us in remedying those weaknesses. This method does not promise a final account of value, only the prospect of a better account. If it does not fully satisfy Etzioni's quest for a final arbiter of values, still it reflects the spirit of his larger argument: in practice, a "good society" needs to balance and combine values that do not easily fit together, and the task not only of moral theory but also of politics is to negotiate what must always contain some tension.[44]

NOTES

1. David Hume, "Of the Origin of Government," in *Essays, Moral, Political, and Literary,* ed. Eugene F. Miller (Indianapolis, Ind.: Liberty Fund, 1985), 40.

2. Amitai Etzioni, *The New Golden Rule: Community and Morality in a Democratic Society* (New York: HarperCollins Basic Books, 1996), 217. Perhaps the analogy is misplaced, for it would be no small achievement to show that many conventional values like broccoli are beneficial, even if they don't always go down well.

3. Etzioni, "The Final Arbiters of Community's Values," *The New Golden Rule,* 217–57.

4. One of the most careful and instructive accounts of the distinctions between communitarians and liberals is found in Stephen Mulhall and Adam Swift, *Liberals and Communitarians* (Oxford: Blackwell Publishers, 1992).

5. Michael Walzer, *Spheres of Justice* (New York: Basic Books, 1982); *Interpretation and Social Criticism* (Cambridge, Mass.: Harvard University Press, 1987).

6. Etzioni, *The New Golden Rule,* 241.

7. Etzioni, *The New Golden Rule,* 244.

8. Etzioni, *The New Golden Rule,* xviii–xx, 241–4, 249–50.

9. Hume, "Of the Origin of Government," 40.

10. Etzioni draws important implications in a wide array or areas, including, for example, the regulation of privacy, the application of individual rights, the development of local institutions, and safety regulations. See Etzioni, *The New Golden Rule*, 28–33, 53–6, 154–5.

11. To be clear, the central task of *The New Golden Rule* is not defending a moral sense, or a source of value that issues values that are compelling in and of themselves. On the whole, Etzioni is more concerned with showing why any good society must reconcile values that are in tension, specifically autonomy and moral order. It is only in the final chapter that something like a moral sense is invoked as a source of final justification for social values. Still, the moral sense plays an important argumentative role in the final chapter. See, for instance, *The New Golden Rule*, 217–8, 241–4. Also, the moral sense understood as a source of social values that are compelling in and of themselves is distinct from what Etzioni calls the "moral voice," which is a source of moral motivation akin to conscience, which in its inner sense reflects an individual's moral beliefs and in its external sense refers to the moral exhortation or chiding that comes from others, especially those to whom one has affective attachments. See *The New Golden Rule*, 119–26.

12. Charles Taylor, *Sources of the Self: The Making of Modern Identity* (Cambridge, Mass.: Harvard University Press, 1989), 72–3, and 53–90 more generally.

13. John Rawls, "Justice as Fairness: Political not Metaphysical," in *Collected Papers*, ed. Samuel Freeman (Cambridge, Mass.: Harvard University Press, 1999), 388–9; Rawls, "The Law of Peoples," *Collected Papers*, 530–3; Rawls, *Political Liberalism* (New York: Columbia University Press, 1993), 8–15; on the absence of a "flat opposition or contradiction" between liberal and communitarian views, see Stephen Mulhall and Adam Swift, *Liberals and Communitarians*, 160–4.

14. Richard Rorty, *Contingency, Irony, and Solidarity*, (Cambridge: Cambridge University Press, 1989), xv. Also see Judith Shklar, *Ordinary Vices* (Cambridge, Mass.: Harvard University Press, 1984), 7–44; and "The Liberalism of Fear," in *Liberalism and the Moral Life*, ed. Nancy Rosenblum, (Cambridge, Mass.: Harvard University Press, 1989), 28–30.

15. Michael Walzer, *Just and Unjust Wars* (New York: Basic Books, 1977), xv.

16. Judith Jarvis Thompson, *The Realm of Rights* (Cambridge, Mass.: Harvard University Press, 1990), 1–33.

17. Thompson, *The Realm of Rights*, 17.

18. Etzioni, *The New Golden Rule*, 222, 227, 231, 241; see generally 218–44.

19. Nancy Rosenblum, *Membership and Morals: The Personal Uses of Pluralism in America* (Princeton, N.J.: Princeton University Press, 1998), 87–94.

20. Etzioni, *The New Golden Rule*, 241.

21. Intense dissatisfaction with the view that makes moral values simply a matter of common sense drove the development of the two dominant strains of contemporary moral theory, the one founded in Bentham's utilitarianism and the other in Kant's deontological moral theory.

22. Jeremy Bentham, *The Principles of Morals and Legislation* (Buffalo, N.Y.: Prometheus Books, 1988; first published, 1781), 17. Bentham is explicitly referring to those who base morality on the principle of sympathy in this comment, but he likens this to founding morality on the moral sense, common sense, or the law of nature; see 17 n. 1.

23. Immanuel Kant, *Grounding for the Metaphysics of Morals*, trans. James W. Ellington, (Indianapolis, Ind.: Hackett Publishing, 1993; first published, 1785), 3 (section 390).

24. For a similar example about lying, see Etzioni, *The New Golden Rule*, 242.

25. Etzioni, *The New Golden Rule*, 4–5, 34.

26. Etzioni, *The New Golden Rule*, 12.

27. Etzioni, *The New Golden Rule*, xvi.

28. This is why Aristotle, who in a Machiavellian mode gives advice to tyrants, also argues that the best course for tyrannies is to become less tyrannical; Aristotle, *The Politics*, trans. Carnes Lord (Chicago: Chicago University Press, 1984), book 5, ch. 10, 167–73.

29. Hume, "Of the First Principles of Government," in *Essays, Moral, Political*, 33.

30. John Winthrop, "A Model of Christian Charity," *Old South Leaflets No. 207*, (Boston, 1916), 7–21. Andrew Delbanco calls this speech "the first great communitarian statement in American literature"; see Delbanco, *The Puritan Ordeal* (Cambridge, Mass.: Harvard University Press, 1989), 74.

31. Winthrop, "Model of Christian Charity," 7.

32. Winthrop, "Model of Christian Charity," 8.

33. Winthrop, "Model of Christian Charity," 20.

34. John Locke, *Second Treatise of Government*, ed. Peter Laslett (Cambridge: Cambridge University Press, 1967), 302 (para. 50).

35. Locke, *Second Treatise*, 269 (para. 4).

36. Locke, *Second Treatise*, 297 (para. 42).

37. Locke, *Second Treatise*, 301 (para. 48).

38. Locke, *Second Treatise*, 297 (para. 41).

39. Locke, *Second Treatise*, 284 (para. 21).

40. Judith Shklar, "The Liberalism of Fear," 36.

41. I do not mean to argue that this has in fact happened in the United States, only that this may be the long-term consequence of widening inequality. See, for instance, Alan Wolfe, *One Nation After All* (New York: Viking Penguin, 1998), 195–207; also Robert H. Frank and Philip J. Cook, *The Winner-Take-All Society* (New York: The Free Press, 1995).

42. John Rawls, *A Theory of Justice* (Cambridge, Mass.: The Belknap Press of Harvard University), 107, and 105–7. Rawls notes that the difference principle "provides an interpretation of fraternity" but does not justify the difference principle in terms of fraternity.

43. For a more full and precise account of how the ideal of individuality can serve as the basis for social unity, see Samuel H. Beer, "Liberty and Union: Walt Whitman's Idea of the Nation," *Political Theory* 12(3) (August 1984): 373.

44. I would like to thank Peter Berkowitz and Sarah Gibbons for their helpful comments on this chapter.

13

Toward an International Human Rights (and Responsibilities) Regime: Some Obstacles

Daniel A. Bell

In chapter eight of *The New Golden Rule*, Amitai Etzioni argues for the need to "find a set of worldwide moral foundations that could undergird judgments of the values of various particular societies."[1] He notes that the aspiration to affirm a set of global values also informs the Universal Declaration of Human Rights (UDHR) and similar documents but argues that "the trouble with this approach is that the United Nations Charter, international law, and various declarations—in which the globalists find the values they seek to build on—are not widely affirmed."[2] In response, Etzioni suggests several original ideas for improving the international rights regime so that it would reflect more meaningful agreement on global values. The problem, however, is that the attempt to implement some of these ideas may prove to be ineffective if not counterproductive. In this chapter, I discuss (briefly) three issues that need to be resolved before we can feel confident about the prospects of achieving a truly universal human rights regime.

THE PERILS OF INCLUSIVE DIALOGUES

Etzioni notes that international documents such as the UDHR are not widely affirmed primarily "because of the ways these documents have been formulated. Typically, they are neither the reflection of a truly democratic process in the international bodies or in the countries represented in them, nor do they reflect the result of a worldwide moral dialogue." Etzioni argues that "such resolutions would command more respect if they reflected the work of a properly representative world parliament or a global tribunal." Even that, however, would not be sufficient: "Before we can expect to see global mores that have the compelling power of those of various societies, the citizens of the world will have to engage in worldwide moral dialogues."[3]

In other words, only the inclusion of diverse participants from a wide range of Western and non-Western societies can ensure that the agreed-upon global norms reflect truly universal global aspirations. Anything less, by implication, translates into an attempt by a minority of voices to promote their particular values under the spurious banner of universalism.

While I agree with this diagnosis of the problem, Etzioni's suggestion for "global megalogues" including elites and ordinary citizens from diverse societies would likely be difficult to implement. It may well be true that "technological developments have made such global megalogues possible."[4] But the main obstacle such dialogues face is getting participants to agree on more than vague aspirations and empty platitudes. Put simply: the more inclusive the deliberations, the more difficult it will be to arrive at any politically meaningful resolutions.

Addressing this problem by limiting participation, however, would raise its own set of problems. One might reasonably argue that a representative sample of leaders and citizens from around the world, if the sample is kept small enough, would be able to reach agreement on the global values that are supposed to guide and constrain policymakers. But this leads to a number of questions: Should the dialogue involve political leaders, diplomats, international lawyers, leaders of religious traditions, academics, representatives of nongovernmental organizations, ordinary citizens, or a combination of these? How many from each group? How many from each country? If the outcomes of these deliberations are meant to command international legitimacy—that is, to trump the decisions of national political leaders—there will be endless disputes over the right way to select "representative" participants.

APPEALING TO FOUNDATIONAL VALUES

A small set of crucial rights is valued, at least in theory, by all governments in the contemporary world. The most obvious are the prohibitions against slavery, genocide, murder, torture, prolonged arbitrary detention, and systematic racial discrimination. These rights have become part of international customary law,[5] and they are not contested in the public rhetoric of the international arena. Of course, many gross human rights violations occur "off the record," and human rights groups such as Amnesty International have the task of exposing the gap between public allegiance to rights and the sad reality of ongoing abuse. This is largely practical work, however. Theoreticians can contribute with suggestions for rendering more meaningful and expanding this rather thin list of rights.

Etzioni contributes to the debate in the following way. He notes that this thin list of human rights represents nothing more than an empirical consensus between different parties. As a result, "it embraces only a few values, such as condemning murder, theft, and rape. And even here we are on unsure grounds."[6] Thus he suggests that we engage in the previously described global moral dialogues, which would "advance the articulation of a core—rather than a thin list—of globally shared values." Such dialogue would not simply consist of a search for de facto common ground that avoids condemning other societies on the basis of one's own moral values. Instead, Etzioni says that he "deliberately refer[s] to laying moral claims."[7] Participants in the global dialogue should not be afraid to raise their cross-cultural moral voices and to lay moral claims on other societies by appealing to their own controversial moral beliefs. Quite the opposite: they are actively encouraged to do so. If people bring "strong substantive values to the nascent worldwide dialogue . . . [then a] . . . much stronger global core of shared values"[8] is likely to evolve. In effect, Etzioni is arguing that the key to a truly international human rights regime is for each side to attempt to persuade the other that their own strongly held moral convictions have universal validity.

But what if some people fail to be persuaded? Etzioni imagines a dialogue where the West "criticizes China for its violation of human rights. And China should be viewed as equally legitimate when it criticizes American society for its neglect of filial duties."[9] One can imagine other possibilities. A committed Muslim points to the "loose" sexual morality in Western societies, arguing for the worldwide criminalization of homosexuality. A farmer in India notes the decadent use of resources in Western countries and argues for a radical redistribution of global wealth. A Thai Buddhist committed to the doctrine of nonviolence condemns the use of the death penalty in the United States. A devout Catholic in the United States objects to the widespread practice of abortion in China. What is the likely outcome of this "dialogue," where people criticize what they take to be the moral failings of other societies on the basis of their own strongly held views? Tempers flare, positions harden, and the quest for global values is dealt a severe setback.

A contrasting suggestion for expanding the current "thin" list of universal human rights is put forward by Charles Taylor. Like Etzioni, Taylor imagines a cross-cultural dialogue between representatives of different traditions. Rather than argue for the universal validity of their views, however, he suggests that participants should allow for the possibility that their own beliefs may be mistaken. This way, participants can learn from each other's "moral universe." There will come a point, however, when differences cannot be reconciled. Taylor explicitly recognizes that different groups, countries, religious communities, and civilizations hold incompatible fundamental views on theology, metaphysics, and human nature. In response, Taylor argues that a "genuine, unforced consensus" on human rights norms is possible only if we allow for disagreement on the ultimate justifications of those norms. Instead of defending contested foundational values when we encounter points of resistance (and thus condemning the values we do not like in other societies), we should try to abstract from those beliefs for the purpose of working out an "overlapping consensus" of human rights norms. As Taylor puts it, "we would agree on the norms while disagreeing on why they were the right norms, and we would be content to live in this consensus, undisturbed by the differences of profound underlying belief."[10]

Contra Taylor, it may not be realistic to expect that people will be willing to abstract from the values they care deeply about during the course of a global dialogue on human rights. But this approach arguably holds more promise than Etzioni's "global megalogue," where each participant deliberately lays moral claims on members of other societies on the basis of their own controversial moral beliefs. Participants in multicultural dialogues need to identify areas of common ground rather than get bogged down by areas of difference. It is far easier to undermine than to build up trust between members of different societies, and the best way to undermine trust is to invoke contested foundational values. In short, those concerned with the quest for a truly global human rights regime should suppress, rather than encourage, the tendency to condemn different values in different societies on the basis of their own "strong substantive values."

RESPONSIBILITIES: THEIR USE AND ABUSE

Many critics of the current "international" human rights regime, particularly in the non-Western world, have argued that the language of rights may not always be ideal for protecting the substantive human interests underlying human rights. For one thing, the term *rights* might sometimes have pejorative connotations in some societies, even among dissident intellectuals. Secondly, the language of rights seems to lend itself to the model of an individual exclusively concerned with seeking protection against an intrusive state. In the modern world, however, individuals also need to be concerned about abuses by corporations and other nongovernmental entities. Thirdly, relatively communitarian societies in East Asia and elsewhere often resort to nonjudicial remedies, such as informal negotiations and public education, for the purpose of securing vital human interests. Resorting to legally enforceable rights can sometimes undermine traditional (and effective) modes of conflict resolution. This is not to suggest that the language of rights should be entirely displaced in the quest for global values, but it might need to be complemented by the language of duties and virtues.[11] The important point is to agree on the need to secure vital human interests. The choice of rhetoric depends only on practical concerns of effectiveness. Dogmatic emphasis on rights can be unhelpful, even counterproductive.

These sorts of considerations converge with Etzioni's argument that rights need to be balanced with responsibilities. In the U.S. context, Etzioni has argued that an overemphasis on individual rights has led to unintended consequences, such as justifying the neglect of social responsibilities and weakening all appeals to rights by devaluing the really important ones. In response, he has argued for "a *temporary* moratorium on the minting of *new* rights."[12] At the international level, Etzioni has argued for an Asian sense of responsibility to combine with the Western notion of rights. This may be an admirable aim, but once again the implementation is fraught with potential difficulties.

Consider the attempt by a group of former heads of state to formulate "A Universal Declaration of Human Responsibilities," which was published in the spring 1998 issue of *The Responsive Community*. This declaration aims to complement the UDHR, but its probable effect will be to dilute it. Most of the declaration consists of vacuous moralizing. Article 3 is not atypical: "Everyone has the responsibility to promote good and avoid evil in all things." Such platitudes are not necessarily harmful, but they might serve to draw attention away from the really important rights that do need to be enforced.

The more serious problem is that some sections of the declaration would be politically dangerous if they were taken seriously. Consider Article 14: "The freedom of the media is to inform the public and to criticize institutions of society and governmental actions, which is essential for a just society, must be used with responsibility and discretion. Freedom of the media carries a special responsibility for accurate and truthful reporting. Sensational reporting that degrades the human person or dignity must at all times be avoided." It is interesting to note that the group of former heads of state includes Singapore's Senior Minister Lee Kuan Yew, who is still a dominant figure on the Singaporean political scene (not to mention the world stage). In Singapore, Lee has often advanced similar arguments about the need for "responsible" journalism that "at all times" avoids "sensational reporting that degrades the human person or dignity." The result? Singaporean newspapers have been completely defanged. The *Straits Times*—once an admirably critical and well-respected source of news—has degenerated into the official cheerleader for the government's policies.[13]

Needless to say, I do not mean to imply that Etzioni himself endorses these abuses of the language of responsibility (or that publishing a document in *The Responsive Community* is necessarily an endorsement of all that it says). And these criticisms are not meant to undermine the general point that there is a need to complement the language of rights in the quest for global values. But those who want to inject the language of responsibility into the international human rights regime should be aware that there are serious risks associated with trying to implement this desideratum in the real world.

THINK LOCALLY, ACT GLOBALLY

It is my sincere hope that these obstacles to a truly international human rights (and responsibilities) regime can be overcome. Meanwhile, however, how should we respond to those who question the universality of contested values? What do we say to people from other cultures who question moral truths we take to be self-evident on the grounds that local constraints or cultural mores render them inapplicable in their own societies? One response is to argue for the universality of one's own moral values. One should note the moral failings of other societies on this basis, with the hope that others will eventually come around to one's own viewpoint. I have tried to show that (notwithstanding the best intentions) this response is likely to poison the debate. The opposite reaction—the relativist response—is to conclude that both viewpoints are equally valid, refrain from criticism of "the other," and leave it at that. This response runs the risk of endorsing self-serving statements by authoritarian rulers who distort local cultural norms for their own dubious purposes.

Another response—perhaps it can be termed "culturally sensitive communitarianism"—is to refrain from judgment until one has learned enough about the other culture so as to be in a better position to make sound moral judgments.[14] This means allowing for the possibility of justifiable moral differences, particularly when these are endorsed by both government officials and social critics. Consider the case of Dr. Sulak Sivaraksa, a leading pro-democracy activist in Thailand and a nominee for the Nobel peace prize. In 1991, the Thai ruler, General Suchinda, pressed charges against Sulak for lèse-majesté—derogatory remarks directed at the royal family— and for defaming him (the general) in a speech given at Thammasat University in Thailand. Fearing for his life, Sulak fled the country but returned in 1992 to face charges after the Suchinda government had fallen. In court, Sulak did not deny that he had attacked the "dictator" Suchinda, but he did deny the charge of lèse-majesté, referring to the many services he had performed for the royal family. Sulak explains:

> I did not . . . stake my ground on an absolute right to free speech. My defense against the charge of lese majeste was my innocence of the charge; my defense was my loyalty to the King and the Royal Family and, where I discussed the use of the charge of lese majeste in current Siamese political practice, it was to highlight abuse and to point to the ways in which abuse might undermine the monarchy, rather than to defend any theoretical right to commit this action. I am not affirming, nor would I affirm, a right to commit lese majeste. This aspect of the case is particularly concerned with my being Siamese and belonging to the Siamese cultural tradition.[15]

In other words, Sulak aimed to persuade fellow citizens that the dominant political system should be replaced with an alternative, relatively democratic political structure. But he made it explicit that this did not mean advocating the removal of the existing constraint on direct criticism of the Thai king. Perhaps Sulak, like many Thais, would feel deeply offended, if not personally harmed, by an attack on the king. In such a case—where a constraint on the freedom of speech is endorsed by both defenders and critics of the prevailing political system—it seems to me that there is a strong presumption in favor of respecting this deviation from absolute, "American-style" freedom of speech.

Of course, local knowledge does not necessarily lead to an endorsement of the status quo. Sometimes, the foreign critic will be appalled by the gap between the official rhetoric and the reality. Consider, for example, the fact that the value of "communitarianism," identified as "community over self," has been identified as one of Singapore's four core values in a presidential address to Parliament. The government argues, with substantial social support, that Singaporeans place special emphasis on the value of community. As Senior Minister Lee Kuan Yew put it, Singaporeans have "little doubt that a society with communitarian values where the interests of society take precedence over that of the individual suits them better than the individualism of America."[16]

Yet the same government does not hide the fact that it also makes life difficult for Singaporeans who aim to enter the political arena on the side of opposition parties. Between 1971 and 1993, according to Attorney General Chan Sek Keong, eleven opposition politicians have been made bankrupt (and hence ineligible to run in elections). Whether intended or not, such actions send the message that politics is a dangerous game for those who haven't been anointed by the top leadership of the ruling party. As the Singaporean journalist Cherian George put it, one can hardly blame people for ignoring their social and political obligations "when they hear so many cautionary tales: Of Singaporeans whose careers came to a premature end after they voiced dissent; of critics who found themselves under investigation; of individuals who were detained without trial even though they seemed not to pose any real threat; of tapped phones and opened letters. . . . The moral of these stories: In Singapore, better to mind your own business, make money, and leave politics to the politicians."[17] Put positively, if the aim is to secure attachment to the community at large, then implementing genuinely competitive elections, including the freedom to run for the opposition without fear of retaliation, is an essential first step.

This might seem like a strange reason to value democracy. From a U.S. perspective, for example, competitive elections may be valued primarily as a means of limiting the power of the state or preventing any one person or group from having absolute power over the rest. This kind of justification, however, will not resonate as much in a context that prioritizes the moral language of community.[18] Even social critics in Singapore, for example, defend democracy on the grounds that it is essential for building up a sense of national community.[19] Foreign critics can, and should, lend support to this argument for opposing authoritarian rule in Singapore.[20] Local knowledge, however, is essential.

This is not to imply that social critics can readily engage with the ways of another culture. Culturally sensitive communitarianism can be demanding. It often requires learning another language and familiarization with the specific examples and argumentative strategies that another culture uses in everyday moral and political debate. It requires an open mind that does not foreclose the possibility of revising one's political ideals. There is, however, no other path to effective and morally justified cross-cultural criticism.

NOTES

I'd like to thank Amitai Etzioni and Edward Lehman for their helpful comments on an earlier version of this chapter.

1. Amitai Etzioni, *The New Golden Rule: Community and Morality in a Democratic Society* (New York: Basic Books, 1996), 235.

2. Etzioni, *The New Golden Rule*, 236.

3. Etzioni, *The New Golden Rule*, 236.

4. Etzioni, *The New Golden Rule*, 236.

5. See Oscar Schacter, *International Law in Theory and Practice* (Dordrecht, The Netherlands: Martinus Nijhoff Publishers, 1991), 337–8.

6. Etzioni, *The New Golden Rule*, 235.

7. Etzioni, *The New Golden Rule*, 237.

8. Etzioni, *The New Golden Rule*, 241.

9. Etzioni, *The New Golden Rule*, 240.

10. Charles Taylor, "Conditions of an Unforced Consensus on Human Rights," in *The East Asian Challenge for Human Rights*, ed. Joanne R. Bauer and Daniel A. Bell (New York: Cambridge University Press, 1999), 124.

11. But for an argument that international human rights standards already (and sufficiently) incorporate references to notions of individual duties and responsibilities, see International Council on Human Rights Policy, *Taking Duties Seriously: Individual Duties in International Human Rights Law* (Versoix, Switzerland: International Council on Human Rights Policy, 1999).

12. Etzioni, *The New Golden Rule*, 42.

13. The *Straits Times* has recently begun to print more critical pieces, though opposition figures continue to be presented in a negative light.

14. I develop this argument in *East Meets West: Human Rights and Democracy in East Asia* (Princeton, N.J.: Princeton University Press, 2000), esp. part I.

15. Quoted in Joanne R. Bauer and Daniel A. Bell, "Introduction," in *The East Asian Challenge for Human Rights*, 14.

16. Quoted in the *International Herald Tribune*, November 9–10, 1991.

17. *Straits Times* (Singapore), July 11, 1993.

18. This is not to deny that the moral language of community is also present in the United States. As the authors of *Habits of the Heart* note, however, the "second language" of community is buried beneath the dominant individualistic understandings; see Robert N. Bellah, Richard Madsen, William M. Sullivan, Ann Swidler, and Steven M. Tipton, *Habits of the Heart: Individualism and Commitment in American Life* (Berkeley: University of California Press, 1985).

19. See Chee Soon Juan, *Dare to Change: An Alternative Vision for Singapore* (Singapore: The Singapore Democratic Party, 1994), ch. 1.

20. See my article, "A Communitarian Critique of Authoritarianism: The Case of Singapore," *Political Theory* 25(1) (February 1997): 6–32.

Epilogue

Amitai Etzioni

Communitarian thinking has been much enriched by the fine collection of chapters that Ed Lehman has assembled here so diligently, edited carefully, and introduced so well. I am also much indebted to his longtime partner, Bunnie Lehman, for the excellent commentary she has often made on my works (including this epilogue) as well as on chapters in this volume. In the following pages I first provide a brief overview of what I consider to be the essential points of responsive communitarian thinking (as distinct from Asian and several other forms of communitarian thought) based on the discussion provided in *The New Golden Rule (NGR)*. I then focus on select issues raised by the chapters assembled here, rather than responding to each issue.

Many of the points I make are difficult to defend without repeating arguments made in some 300 pages of the *NGR*, which of course cannot be done. I hence must assume that those who find some of the points I make here to be unsupported will in fairness turn to the *NGR* and its detailed arguments before rejecting them.

OVERVIEW

While philosophers often seek to establish the extent to which they can derive a position from one core principle, responsive communitarians advocate a balance among not fully compatible values and societal needs, as the basis of our conception of the good society. Therefore, the fundamental issue we face should not be framed as the importance of community, or of the social realm, or the embeddedness of the individual, but as a quest for a carefully crafted *balance between autonomy (often equated with liberty) and social order*, between individual rights and social responsibilities. This quest for balance distinguishes responsive communitarianism not merely

219

from individualistic philosophies but also from nostalgia for early communities, Asian communitarianism, and fundamentalism.

Furthermore, responsive communitarians take the position that the issue is not one of recognizing particularistic social responsibilities owed to one's communities as opposed to universal individual rights. Instead, we recognize that one can both respect the claim that all people have certain *universal individual rights and* that they have *layered particularistic social responsibilities* to the specific communities of which they are members, such as their families and their immediate communities, as well as more encompassing communities.

Responsive communitarians put the basic communitarian position into a contingent, *historical context*. Rather than viewing the issues at hand merely in general and abstract terms, such as "people are social" and "societies need social formulations of the good," responsive communitarians point out that some societies lose their communitarian balance in an individualistic direction (as especially indicated by Robert Bellah and his associates)[1] while other societies are excessively communal (not to be confused with authoritarian or totalitarian states), as has been recognized in criticisms of Japan. Hence, societies that strive to reach the ideal communitarian balance of autonomy and order may approach it from very divergent starting points and must move in rather different directions to achieve the same balance. Thus, while some will need to become less communal, others need to become more so. Here too, the subtext is to delineate the difference between responsive communitarians and other communitarians prone to authoritarian and theocratic interpretations.[2]

In seeking a model of society that reduces the inevitable tension between autonomy and order, responsive communitarians point to the importance of a social order that relies *on mores (or social norms) largely enforced by the moral voice*. These mores are accepted as truly legitimate and internalized, rather than resting primarily on the coercive power of the state. In effect, reliance on the state is the earmark of theocracies and other forms of authoritarian and totalitarian governments that seek to foster values by force. Similar issues arise when democratic societies attempt to largely use the law to make people more virtuous (for instance, by banning divorce), under the pressure of right wing or religious groups. (As I see it, it matters less if the law either precedes or follows the evolution of shared norms, as long as it does not stray too far from them.)

To put it differently, the more a society can rely on shared mores as its basis for social order, the lower the conflict between order and autonomy, and the more communitarian the society. One key role of the moral voice is to change preferences so as to bring them more in line with shared values than they would be otherwise.

Shared mores need not be treated as given; they can be changed but mainly through moral dialogues rather than reasoned deliberations. (To prevent moral dialogues from deteriorating into culture wars, rules of engagement of the kind formulated by James Hunter and Deborah Tannen need to be applied.)[3] Reasoned deliberations deal in facts and logic, are rational, "cool," and engage minds. To recast mores additionally requires tapping into values that have affective elements and entails not merely reasoning but also nonrational processes, such as persuasion and leadership. (It is telling that advocates of reasoned deliberations ignore or abhor these two last concepts.)[4]

The mores of a community, whether traditional (and passed down from generation to generation) or newly recast, *must be morally evaluated*. Consensus is not a sufficient criterion to determine their moral standing. Communities are not the final arbiters of the worth of their values. (Cf. Michael Sandel and Michael Walzer.)[5]

It is further implied that *we need and can evaluate the moral values of communities other than ours*, a position that is called postcultural relativism.

The toughest question responsive communitarians face is which are the correct criteria for judging values or "cultures?" Constitutionalism provides a partial answer; if a local culture violates our Constitution for instance, we tend to disapprove.[6] Pluralism, that defines some values as beyond the pale, also provides a partial solution, as Isaiah Berlin has argued.[7] But ultimately, cross-cultural dialogues are expected to foster shared values whose virtues people of divergent backgrounds will recognize (a deontological position).[8]

Therefore, one should consider the concept of a *good society* (one that lives up to shared conceptions of virtue) rather than merely a civil society. For instance, a good society will promote some voluntary associations over others rather than treat all as equally good, as the conception of civil society tends to.[9] Indeed, as William R. Lund, in this volume and elsewhere,[10] correctly points out, my concept of the good society violates the liberal notion that the ways of life of all citizens are morally equal.

Closely related is the notion of *community of communities*, or as Philip Selznick addresses this question, a unity of unities.

This position contrasts both with notions of assimilation (or of the melting pot) on the one hand and of unbounded diversity on the other. It relies on layered loyalties, according to which people have some commitments to their own communities and some to overarching ones. It allows for pluralism as long as it does not break out of some unifying bonds and values. This invokes the image of a mosaic that is composed of pieces that differ in color and size but are held together by a shared frame (which itself can be recast).[11]

Communitarians have been charged with suppressing conflict in the name of cultural conformity and consensus. Actually, we recognize that *conflicts within communitarian societies* take place, but they take a special form: *a combination of attempting to preserve the encompassing community while seeking to adjust the distribution of power and assets among the members*. That is, members of a community who are not content face three basic choices, somewhat like a married couple: leave, acquiesce, or try to change the relationship without destroying it. Only the final option is fully compatible with a communitarian position.

A new concept of the self as enriched *and* constrained by community, one whose autonomy demands close communal ties *and* is threatened by them when they become excessive. This is in contrast to the view of the self as freestanding, as well as being "situated," embedded, or implicated in the social.[12] The concept draws on the works of George Herbert Mead as well as Dennis Wrong's concept of the oversocialized (and by implication undersocialized) concept of the person.[13]

Far from being abstract, unlike many of their predecessors, responsive communitarians have engaged in numerous policy matters and have contributed to the development of scores of *specific policies*. A few examples follow.

a. Family policies: The concept of peer marriage (where fathers have the same rights and responsibilities as mothers);[14] super vows (what is now called "covenant marriage");[15] and support for parents at home, flextime, and part-time work.[16]

b. Character education: Focus on the experiences schools generate rather than merely on curriculum, and on the school as a total environment. A new program on sex education. Plans for community schools, open year round.[17]

c. Crime: It takes a village to prevent a crime. For instance, through measures such as community policing, crime watch, community patrols, and reintegrative justice.[18]

d. New balances for specific rights and the common good (especially public safety and health) such as mandatory drug tests but only of those who directly have the lives of others in their hands.[19]

e. A view of privacy based directly on the Fourth Amendment.[20] By referring to unreasonable searches, the Fourth Amendment clearly recognizes that there are reasonable ones, in which privacy is set aside to serve compelling community needs. The Fourth Amendment further defines a process for sorting out which searches are reasonable, in most circumstances by requiring a court warrant.[21]

RESPONSES TO ISSUES RAISED IN THIS VOLUME

In the following discussion of the chapters included in this volume, which by necessity focuses on select points rather than on all the many points raised, I move from the more immediate community to the larger society and finally to the cross-societal level.

Communities Defined

A key concept for this discussion is the term *community*. Several critics have argued that the concept of community is so ill defined that it has no identifiable designation. Robert Booth Fowler, who wrote the book *The Dance with Community*, showed that the term is used in six different and rather incompatible ways.[22] Colin Bell and Howard Newby state that "There has never been a theory of community, nor even a satisfactory definition of what community is."[23]

The following definition seems to me quite workable: Community is a combination of two elements: a) A web of affect-laden relationships among a group of individuals, relationships that often crisscross and reinforce one another (rather than merely one-on-one or chainlike individual relationships); and b) A measure of commitment to a set of shared values, norms, and meanings, and a shared history and identity—in short, to a particular culture.[24]

This definition does not rule out conflict or make any assumption about its level, but it does suggest that such a social entity includes the necessary ingredients (bonds and shared values) to contain conflict within manageable limits. Moreover, the definition indicates that communities need not be territorial. Indeed, there are many ethnic, professional, gay, and other communities that are geographically dispersed; that is, members of these communities reside among nonmembers. (Often, these communities are centered around particular institutions, such as places of worship, bars, or social clubs.)

The observation that social entities that meet the previously mentioned two defining criteria can be identified and that they resemble those entities most people informally refer to as "communities" does not mean that such social units are *good* in the normative sense.

Benjamin D. Zablocki raises the question of whether communities can be restored in postmodern life, reversing some predetermined historical trends that have seemed to reduce them, and whether such reversal is desirable. As I see it, like all historical comparisons, one's conclusion greatly depends on the baseline one chooses. If one uses 1900 or even 1950 as one's baseline, one is likely to find that by the year 2000 communities thinned out (although in the process also became less authoritarian). However, whether the same trend can be documented for the last twenty years is much less clear. The fact that some thirty-two million Americans have chosen in recent years to move into residential communities (which critics call planned or gated communities) should give some pause to those who presume that communities are continuing to die out.[25] However, the mere fact that communities exist leaves unanswered the question whether communities are necessarily good (in the moral sense) social entities.

In evaluating communities, a great deal depends on the kind of values embodied (discussed later), the kind of polity that evolves, and the extent to which such communities are total institutions (versus a single element of the social realm in which a person lives). I agree with Zablocki that all communities have, by their very nature, an inherent serious normative defect: exclusion. All communities draw distinctions between members and nonmembers, and most treat nonmembers worse than members. (Rare exceptions are some religious orders that administer to the sick and poor.) Exclusivity arises out of one of the two defining elements of community, specifically bonds. There are severe limits to the number of people any one person can bond with. Moreover, bonding is much more achievable with people who are similar in social background and perspective than with those whose social attributes are different. Finally, turnover must be limited if bonds are to solidify.

The fact that communities exclude is normatively troubling to the point that several critics regard communities negatively merely on this ground and prefer to limit social relations to those based on universal criteria, especially individual achievements.

Indeed, if we treat one and all as unique persons, we avoid community-based exclusivity. (Consistent champions of this approach reject treating legal and illegal immigrants differently, or members of our national community differently from those of other communities.)

However, as I see it, a society that seeks complete elimination of exclusivity will grossly neglect the profound human need for social bonds. Hence, in what is a key example of the general point that the quest for perfect societies undermines a basic human need, communitarians must settle for an imperfect world in which the very profound human need for community is stated and the criteria for exclusion are strictly limited.

Given this background, while a good society would allow communities to maintain some limitations on membership, it would at the same time greatly restrict the criteria that communities may use to enforce such exclusivity. The criteria for exclusion cannot be race, ethnic origins, religion, sexual orientation, or a whole host of other criteria based on ascribed status. The bonds of good communities, it follows, are based on an affinity whose nature remains to be defined.

Finally, Zablocki suggests that reconstituted communities (fostered as antidotes to excessive modernism, somewhat like reconstituted families) would be either "toothless communities of discourse," that rely on (what I call) the moral voice and hence will have a minimal social effect, or *enforce* mores, which will be difficult and authoritarian. In contrast, I suggest, that informal social control within communities (including peer groups, gangs, militias) is often very powerful.[26] This is largely an empirical question that requires a comprehensive secondary analysis of existing data (what some people call mega-analysis), yet to be undertaken.

Paul Lichterman's well-taken observation should be integrated into this analysis of what constitutes a community. I agree with him that it is incorrect to view community membership as a zero-sum game, if by that one means that membership in one community precludes membership in others. Lichterman is also convincing when he observes that community borders are "permeable" and people can have mixed loyalties and not merely layered ones (which I focused on). However, none of these observations obviates the inescapable choice that people face in specific given situations. Thus a person who acts as a member of community *x* in situation *y*—for example, votes in line with the expectations of a gay community of which he is a member rather than in line with his coworkers—excludes the other community. (A person may in the same act come under the influence of two or more communities, but as a rule will not be equally affected by all.) In short, the fact that community borders are quite a bit "softer" than they might first seem does not deny their existence, social import, or the normative dilemma they pose.

The Value of Bonds, Their Limits, and the Communitarian Self

The idea that people ought to relate to one another by bonds of affection rather than merely as instrumental means is so widely established that it barely needs discussing. From Immanuel Kant to Karl Marx, many consider the dominance of the instrumental orientation a major threat to human well-being. Others have drawn on empirical research to document that people are social creatures and require bonding with others. It would thus at first seem that bonds are beneficial, period.

Actually, this emphasis on the benefits of bonding reflects the fact that these matters are often discussed within a Western context, in which bonding is believed to have declined over the last centuries. This presents a one-sided picture. More attention should be paid to the opposite condition, in which bonding is excessive. The reference here is not to hierarchy, power relations, or oppressive legal or moral codes. Reference is instead to communities in which bonds, even those among peers, are highly restrictive, preventing proper development of self, cramping individuality, spontaneity, and creativity, a condition many associate with several Asian societies.

In fact, tightly knit bonds and not just frayed ones are incompatible with basic human needs. Responsive communitarians hold that social bonds are indispensable for human beings but only if they remain rather slack. A good society is one in which strong communal bonds are balanced by similarly powerful safeguards for the self. Such a society is not simply communal, but—like two taut stays of a mast that keep it erect—firmly upholds both social ties and autonomy. It further follows that different societies may need to move in opposite directions to approach the same desired point of balance. Some need to shore up their weakened social bonds; others—to loosen them.

In this context, Dennis Wrong raises several important issues that he is uniquely qualified to address. I hope to return to them in a much more extensive treatment of a subject that communitarians often touch or presume to have dealt with, but which actually requires much more study, namely, the nature of the communitarian self. The starting point for any such development is the *properly socialized person*, clearly a concept implicit in Wrong's work, even if he does not use the same phrase.

Such a person avoids the dangers of conformism, has a clear sense of individuality and identity, and does not suffer from a deficient innovative capacity or an inability to function autonomously. The absence of these attributes characterizes what Wrong called the oversocialized self. Moreover, the properly socialized person does not suffer the consequences of being undersocialized, for example, an inability to form wholesome relations with others, failure to internalize the community's basic values, and behaviors that are impulsive, self-centered, exploitative, or perhaps even indicative of mental instability. The ability to reason and make rational choices—that liberal theory assumes people command naturally—actually exists only among people who are properly socialized and are members of viable communities but not absorbed by them.

We need to know much more about the qualities of such persons and how to develop and nurture them. Such people, one must stress, do not treat their social milieu mainly as a constraint, although all social environments have such an element.

In short, the communitarian self is both fostered and impeded by the communities of which it is an integral member. And the communitarian self always experiences a measure of tension, subject to the push and pull of various, not fully harmonized, expectations and from the never fully socialized inner self. These points are merely initial down payments for the development of the communitarian conception of the self, a path Wrong has helped blaze and, one hopes, will extend.

The Community of Communities

The essence of my argument regarding community of communities has two parts: (a) Society is not composed of millions of individual citizens but of various communities (as well as some "free-floating" individuals), each of which has some measure of bonds and shared values. (b) Community particularism is not incompatible with societal unity as long as certain society-wide bonds and shared values are respected.[27]

Tom Tyler and Robert Boeckmann convincingly demonstrate that people in a community do not so much seek moral consensus with all members but only with some. Communities can be based on mutual respect among such groups and on moral pluralism, rather than on shared substantive values and mores. I agree up to a point; indeed chapter seven of the *NGR*, "Pluralism within Unity," supports pluralism. However, Tyler and Boeckmann and I do differ on one critical point. I contend that if several groups of people hold different substantive values but *share* none they will not make one solid, lasting community.[28]

The reason I advance this proposition is that, as I have argued in the *NGR*, to keep pluralism within some bounds—if we are to avoid civil wars a la Bosnia—members of one group in a community need to share more than self-respect with members of other groups in the same community. At the same time, such groups can share merely a few core values rather than require an extensive and encompassing consensus. In effect, that is one major difference between responsive communitarians (who favor sharing a limited set of values) and social conservatives (who seek adherence to many more shared values and detailed norms). Thus, while communitarians favor a delicate balance between autonomy and social order, social conservatives, for instance the religious right, seek to define what people drink (i.e., no alcohol), what music they listen to (i.e., no rock and roll), when they have sex and with whom, how often they pray and to whom, who their proper marriage partners are (i.e., same faith marriages), the proper division of labor within the household, and much more.[29]

Wilson Carey McWilliams's important essay advances this subject, usually flagged under concepts such as melting pot, diversity, multiculturalism, and shared values. The following lines reiterate several of what I consider McWilliams's most important points, as a way of indicating my agreement with him.

First of all, McWilliams argues persuasively that there is a strong U.S. tendency to be suspicious of society as a community, as a body that can foster substantive values among the members, rather than merely respect for their differences and procedures for resolving specific issues (e.g., voting in Congress). McWilliams further points out that in order to maintain a cohesive society, more than megalogues (society-wide dialogues composed of many local dialogues pieced together by the media and national, regional and other cross-community meetings of thousands of voluntary associations) are needed. This is especially true in an age where individualism dominates and society is viewed as a tool for private purposes.

McWilliams's examination of the role of the Constitution here is especially telling. He sees it as largely protecting pluralism from excessive pressure to expand the realm of unity (although—as he notes—this role of the Constitution may have declined throughout our history). Gradually, society-wide (national) norms (e.g., those concerning civil rights) have taken priority over state and local ones in some important areas. At the same time, McWilliams is right when he observes that communities are weakened by the Constitution because it eases exit, allowing members who are pressured to conform to move elsewhere quite readily.

Most importantly, McWilliams brings the examination of communities into the era of globalization when he points out that newly enhanced economic forces further undermine communities' ability to govern themselves and to influence their members. He concludes that fostering sustainable communities in the future will require the protection and support of the society (and national government). Here he is way ahead of the curve because the current fashion is to look at the balance between local and national power from the opposite direction: transferring, through devolution and other devices, social missions from the national society to local communities.

Globalism's effects on local communities and the national society is a topic that deserves much more attention by communitarians.

Accounting for Autonomy, Social Order, and Balance

As I see it, I have taken two rather original positions in *NGR*. One concerns the combination of universal rights (including liberty or more broadly autonomy) with particularistic responsibilities (and social order). Liberals focus on rights; social conservatives focus on social responsibilities. My thesis that these two core values can be combined is relatively easy to illustrate. Ask yourself why a loyal member of a kibbutz, a citizen of small town America, or a faculty member of a campus community could not also command the right to free speech? True, the social order of the community may at some point clash with this right, as when hate speech occurs. But the fact that there is some tension between autonomy and order does not invalidate either (there is tension between any two values we hold) and leads to my analysis of the conditions under which these tensions can be reduced (for instance, work on convincing people not to engage in hate speech) and to the need for balance rather than domination by either core value.[30]

My second position, which combines deontological justification with functionalist analysis, demands a more complex defense. The notion that certain truths are self-evident is not readily accepted by our relativist age. The same holds for the notion that reason follows revelation rather than the other way around. Thomas Kohler states that "nothing is self-evident" and "the truth of a proposition is evident only to a person who has already weighed the relevant evidence." This may be true for science but not for moral, spiritual, or religious values. Kohler, who takes a religious position, may wish to note that if nothing is self-evident, neither is God. (Attempts to prove the existence of God by theological "evidence" have convinced only those who are already in awe of the Lord.)

We are not as far apart here as it first seems. While I have no doubt that history teaches us that people who are religious can conduct themselves in very evil ways (way beyond violating both autonomy and social order), and that people who are not religious can be quite ethical (way beyond respecting the core communitarian virtues), I do accept that religion can be a major source of the values undergirding the good society. For me, the source of virtue is less critical than the observation that all value systems need some incontestable, self-evident, anchoring point.

I agree with Kohler that my positions concern religion, if one means by that, questions of ultimate value, what Talcott Parsons called other-worldly matters. But these are matters not subject to empirical evaluation. Kohler, however, regrets that despite the fact that I recognize the importance of ultimate values I do not take the essential next step and anchor them in a bona fide religion.

Nicos Mouzelis draws on an example from the *NGR* concerning a daughter in a hypothetical traditional society who is being compelled into marriage to benefit her family. He questions whether the value of personal autonomy is self-evident here. He suggests that in this situation personal autonomy may be irrelevant and that what we consider "sacrifice" may be viewed as virtuous for promoting family or group well-being and solidarity, which are higher values. In this instance, Mouzelis does not necessarily contradict my position for, as I note in *NGR*: "Given that we recognize multiple virtues, which cannot be all fully adhered to at the same time, we must work out conflicts among them, and even sacrifice a measure of some for the sake of the other."[31]

I suggest an empirical test to resolve our differences, relying on two observations that can be quite readily tested. First, if there are girls who feel ennobled under the given conditions (and all others who sacrifice autonomy out of conformity), they will be found in traditional villages in which there has been limited or no exposure to communications explaining the value of autonomy. As I have argued in the *NGR*, people do not hear their inner self unless aided by open and inclusive dialogues, which are not available in these villages.

Second, there is reason to suspect that while people in such conditions often yield to social pressure, they do not truly accept such arrangements as their preferred choice. Rather, they understand that their autonomy is being violated even if they go along for pragmatic or principled reasons. This is demonstrated by both passive and active resistance, expressed in whatever forms are available in the given culture.

Let me put it more strongly: if the evidence were to show that young girls truly eagerly married old men because they think this is a noble act, that widows jump content into their husbands' funeral pyres, then I will consider my position scientifically invalidated. (Note that as I have pointed out elsewhere,[32] the evidence that violating autonomy is hurtful to the individual and hence not truly acceptable may be indirect, for instance a high rate of suicides and psychosomatic illness, rather than open disapproval.) In short, the difference between Mouzelis's and my views on this matter needs to be settled through additional empirical research.

William R. Lund, recognizing the novelty of my position, fears that my functionalist analysis of autonomy's merit for society leads us down the road to a consequentialist position and in turn to relativistic positions. This is true *only* if one does not accept the primacy of the deontological position. As I see it, we first realize that we value autonomy over coercion (unless we see compelling reasons to forgo free choice in a given area, like speeding near schools) and then note that a society functions better if it makes considerable room for autonomy. In short, functional accounts are secondary.

Lund is correct in pointing out that the twin core virtues do not necessarily provide satisfactory guidance on specific moral issues such as abortion and the balance between responsibility to children and career interests. They take us part of the way; for instance, in urging those who oppose abortion to rely on suasion rather than on violence. However, I certainly do not suggest that the moral code of a good society is exhausted by the two core virtues I have highlighted.

Lund's rich analysis also questions the role of political authority, procedures, and law in a good (communitarian) society. I find it difficult to deal with these issues without repeating much of what I have said in chapter four ("Sharing Core Values") and chapter five ("The Moral Voice") of the *NGR*. But briefly, the main realm of the good society is neither political nor private, but social. One can thus argue for "substantive," although of course limited, authority of parents over children, educators over their charges, and leaders of voluntary associations over their members, without dealing with the state at all. Involving the state (or the law) is an indication that the society is not as good as it could be, although no society can be fully persuasive.

Similarly, while differences of interest and opinions among members of the community sometimes can and need be settled by a vote, majoritarianism has well-known problems. A community is better off when it curbs the need for such procedures by engaging in dialogues that lead to a shared commitment to new moral directions. A comparison of prohibition (in which such sharing of new moral commitments was lacking) to recent campaigns that seek to convince people to not let friends drive drunk is illuminating in this respect.

Finally, Lund is correct that from the viewpoint of the good society—unlike that of a civil (liberal) one—people are not all equal in moral standing. Civil society proponents are basically not only nonjudgmental but also nondiscriminatory. All members can define their own concept of the good; no socially shared definitions are appreciated. Typically, all voluntary associations are equally "functional." From the perspective of the good society, people are "ranked." Those who treat their spouses as equals are more highly regarded than those who do not; those who do community service, more than those who avoid it; those who attend to their children, more than those who neglect them. (Reference is to behavior the society considers good, whether or not they are codified in laws.)

J. Russell Muirhead correctly notes that, unlike other communitarians, I do not hold that the community should be the final arbiter of values but that assessing values requires higher criteria. This leads to the question—what are these higher criteria?

Here Muirhead's chapter, in effect, raises an interesting issue, which to my knowledge has not been previously explored: What is the relationship between the moral sense and the deontological position? As I see it, these are rather distinct positions. The moral sense, as the term is used by James Q. Wilson, by many sociobiologists, and most recently by Francis Fukuyama, refers to a biological source of values. Given that we all share the same basic biology, it is suggested that we should espouse common values.[33]

While I do, once, mention approvingly this position, the one I follow is rather different and falls into a major philosophical camp, called deontology. Its core claim is that certain moral causes speak to us in compelling terms. It does not ask where these values come from but takes it as its starting point the assumption that these values address us without filters. This does not mean that they are exempted from examination but that they first present themselves and only later do we study them. We do not reach them through some kind of utilitarian or consequentialist analysis. We realize that truth telling is morally superior to lying (with the exception of some limited conditions, when so-called white lies are called for, defined as those that truly benefit others, is a case in point).

Those who are accustomed to other forms of justifying ethical positions tend to reject the deontological position as arbitrary. They should note the enormously powerful, important role the concept of self-evident truths—deontological par excellence—has had and of course still has in our Constitution and all that is based on it. Given that Muirhead's chapter deals with the moral sense rather than with deontology, much that he has to say I find both valid and beside my point. (By the way, neither concept should be confused with "common sense," one of Muirhead's favorite terms.)

Hans Joas points to a major criticism leveled against standard communitarianism: that the theory assumes a relatively strong set of shared values. In a fragmented society, Joas suggests, the moral voice cannot work because it will inevitably be a conflicted voice. A major goal of *NGR* was to permit responsive communitarianism to transcend this liability. My aim has been not only to clarify our understanding of the status of value consensus in seemingly fragmented societies but also to suggest ways to overcome cultural relativism and conflict in an effective and authentic manner.

Let me begin by noting that reliance on the moral voice is not a zero-sum game. A community successfully exercises its moral voice when it manages to assert a core of shared values. The fact that a community may allow all other (non-core) values to vary does not diminish the potential importance of its moral voice (see *NGR*, chapter seven).

In chapter eight of the *NGR* I tried to address a rather different and possibly more serious problem than the one raised by Joas: even in a highly consensual community, the standard communitarian position drives one to cultural relativism because it implies that the community is the ultimate arbiter of that which is right and wrong. Both others and myself have pointed out that this is a morally untenable position; just think of a community in which one and all agree to lynch all foreigners who enter. I hence drew on the deontological position.

Joas's principal aim is to compare how Jurgen Habermas and I attempt to overcome cultural relativism and mitigate conflict. In fact, Joas suggests that the two of us are not so far apart as it first seems. As I see it, the abiding difference between Habermas and me is not that he prefers rights-talk while I prefer moral dialogues, but that Habermas is a proceduralist and rationalist while I favor moral dialogues that can affirm substantive values and draw on nonrational processes such as persuasion. To be sure, both Habermas and I are concerned with the ways one evaluates the results of the give and take we each are advocating. However, Habermas stresses the importance of following proper rules; if these are heeded, in the ethical realm, then the outcomes are moral. I suggest that ultimately such outcomes must be examined to establish whether or not they are compatible with self-evident moral truths that speak to all of us, specifically our commitment to a well-crafted balance between autonomy and social order.

In his effort to build a bridge between Habermas's position and mine, Joas draws skillfully on the American pragmatists. While it is to be commended for theoretical acuity, Joas's effort is not completely successful. He recognizes the need to defend this philosophical tradition against the charge that its followers subscribe to situational ethics, a form of relativism. And Joas succeeds more than others in his attempt to rescue the pragmatists from this conundrum but, in the final analysis, pragmatism remains a situational ethics. It may set some limits on that which is considered morally sound (as pluralists like Isaiah Berlin also do) but ultimately it rejects the kind of deontological, self-evident moral truths I draw on. Indeed, Joas is right when he implies that Habermas and pragmatism require the presumption that society is fully fragmented. But is this a reasonable assumption?

Toward the end of Joas's chapter his position (which builds on Habermas's) and mine do come closer together. We agree that it is not theoretically necessary (although it has often been historically correct) to argue that liberals tend to be universalists (in the sense that they claim the same rights for all people and do not focus on particularistic commitments such as to special values of one's community) while communitarians tended to be particularistic (concerned with the commitments to one's community rather than with universal rights). I certainly agree that these two philosophies are not totally antithetical and can up to a point be combined. For instance, one is able to respect everyone's right to free speech and still believe that charity begins at home; or oppose "unwarranted seizures" of property by the government and continue to maintain that one has special responsibilities for one's family and community. However, any effort to bridge proceduralism and deontology that does not cede priority to the latter will, in my view, ultimately fail.

Cross-Cultural Moral Judgment

In the *NGR*, I argue in favor of cross-national dialogues (in contrast to cultural relativism) that result in laying moral claims on one another. These should gradually lead us to a worldwide shared core of values, including both Western ideas of human rights and East Asian (as well as Muslim and Jewish) ideas of social responsibility. Daniel A. Bell argues that this approach is ineffectual if not dangerous.

Bell holds that worldwide dialogues will not lead to substantive, meaningful agreements. However, recent agreements about such matters as land mines, protection of whales, child labor, sex slaves, and nuclear testing, suggest that shared mores do arise. The fact that these agreements are not universal and are at best partially implemented does not belie the fact that we have *begun* to develop global mores. We are beginning as a world community to recognize certain behaviors are unethical. Moreover, there is some movement to heed some of these mores. And when force is employed, as in Kosovo, it makes a difference whether it is based on shared understanding or strictly on brute power.

Bell further argues, in line with Tyler and Boeckmann, that people who have conflicting basic values may still agree to support specific policies. This may well be true, but I suggest that such pragmatic agreements have less staying power and will be less closely heeded than those backed up by shared values.

Bell correctly points out that one major attempt to formulate a Universal Declaration of Human Responsibilities (which would be added to the Universal Declaration of Human Rights, and would make for the kind of East–West shared understanding that I favor) ran into trouble. Indeed, some of the statements made by the campaigns of such a declaration reflect some fairly authoritarian views.[34] I would argue, though, that if we give up on such a crucial project just because first attempts are defective, we cannot move forward. After all, even the first formulations of the U.S. Constitution required quite a bit of amending.

Shalom Schwartz and Anat Bardi provide evidence of great relevance to the issue of whether or not we might be able to develop a worldwide shared understanding of moral issues. Drawing on three different samples, they report that there is already considerable agreement on several rather important values, what they call pancultural norms. Their list of shared values, is much "thicker" than I believed—good news indeed. The fact that autonomy, understood as self-direction, has very wide support is greatly encouraging for those of us who seek worldwide shared moral understandings.

Social order scores much less well in Schwartz and Bardi's analysis for reasons that may deserve further exploration. One possible explanation is that in the societies studied social order is rather high if not excessive. Hence it is treated just the way people of Seattle treat rain; rather less kindly than those of Nevada.

Schwartz and Bardi also find that what is considered balanced varies a great deal from society to society. One must take into account that these findings concern many societies in which the dialogues that I argue are required for people to favor the communitarian balance have not taken place (or have taken place in rather truncated ways), because these are authoritarian societies. It would be helpful to repeat the kind of study Schwartz and Bardi undertook after such dialogues take place, even if only between two nations.

Joel Rosenthal rightly observes that my focus has been on moral issues and factors and not on the role of power (a valid criticism made about other communitarians as well). Unfortunately, he seems to think that my position is some kind of Gandhiism, which holds that one can and should rely only on the moral voice to move the world. (The mirror image of this viewpoint is that of realpolitik, which maintains moral claims are but public relations gestures used by powers to justify their actions.) My position is highlighted by my discussion of the law, which of course is ultimately coercive. I argue that (a) moral claims have a measure of power of their own and (b) the efficacy of other kinds of power (such as economic and police) depends on whether or not they are backed by moral claims that are themselves accepted by those subject to the powers. As I see it, this is the reason why tyrannies such as the Nazi and Communist states have been relegated to the dustbins of history, while democracies continue to have a strong appeal and—power. But I never suggested that moral causes suffice to move the world or to order the universe or even one community. I do hold that the more a social order can rely on moral persuasion, the less coercive it will be and the less coercive it will seem to the members of the communities involved.

IN CONCLUSION

These chapters in toto (as well as papers published in a special issue of *The Responsive Community*,[35] only two of which, those by Lund and Bell, overlap with papers published here), greatly advance communitarian theory and research. They are chock full of ideas and findings that demonstrate, beyond reasonable doubt, the richness of the subject as well as the profound differences between responsive communitarian thinking and other forms of communitarian thinking, and liberal and social conservative thought. To the extent that the *NGR* helped launch and sustain this fine scholarship, it more than justified itself.

Most important to me is an emerging worldview that encompasses communities, national societies, and even a budding world community. It is one in which autonomy and order are carefully balanced; in which individual rights are respected and social responsibilities are willingly assumed; in which the moral voice plays a much greater role than the coercive state[36]; and in which we all recognize that underneath our various cultural backgrounds there are some core virtues we view as compelling, and indeed as self-evident.

NOTES

1. Robert N. Bellah et al., *Habits of the Heart: Individualism and Commitment in American Life* (Berkeley: University of California Press, 1985).

2. For more discussion on this topic, see chapters one and two of *The New Golden Rule: Community and Morality in a Democratic Society* (New York: Basic Books, 1996).

3. James Davison Hunter, *Culture Wars: The Struggle to Define America* (New York: Basic Books, 1991); James Davison Hunter, *Before the Shooting Begins: Searching for Democracy in America's Culture War* (New York: Free Press, 1994); Deborah Tannen, *The Argument Culture: Moving from Debate to Dialogue* (New York: Random House, 1998).

4. For more discussion on this topic, see chapters three and four of *The New Golden Rule*.

5. Michael J. Sandel, in Bill Moyers, *A World of Ideas II* (New York: Doubleday, 1990), 155; Michael Walzer, *Thick and Thin: Moral Argument at Home and Abroad* (Notre Dame, Ind.: University of Notre Dame Press, 1994).

6. Sanford Levinson, *Constitutional Faith* (Princeton, N.J.: Princeton University Press, 1988).

7. Sir Isaiah Berlin, *Four Essays on Liberty* (London: Oxford University Press, 1969). See also William A. Galston, *Liberal Purposes: Goods, Virtues, and Diversity in the Liberal State* (Cambridge: Cambridge University Press, 1991).

8. For more discussion on this topic, see chapter eight of *The New Golden Rule*.

9. Nancy Rosenblum's new book speaks particularly to this issue. See Nancy L. Rosenblum, *Membership and Morals: The Personal Uses of Pluralism in America* (Princeton, N.J.: Princeton University Press, 1998).

10. William R. Lund, "Taking Autonomy Seriously," *The Responsive Community* 9(1) (Winter 1998/1999): 10–22.

11. For more discussion on this topic, see chapter seven of *The New Golden Rule*.

12. Sandel, in *A World of Ideas II*, 155; Walzer, *Thick and Thin*.

13. Dennis Wrong, "The Oversocialized Conception of Man in Modern Sociology," *American Sociological Review* 26 (April 1961): 183–93.

14. Pepper Schwartz, *Peer Marriage: How Love between Equals Really Works* (New York: Free Press, 1994).

15. Amitai Etzioni and Peter Rubin, *Opportuning Virtue: Lessons of the Louisiana Covenant Marriage Law*, A Communitarian Report, (Washington, D.C.: Communitarian Network, 1997).

16. Jean Bethke Elshtain et al., *A Communitarian Position Paper on the Family* (Washington, D.C.: The Communitarian Network, 1993).

17. Amitai Etzioni, *The Spirit of Community* (New York: Simon and Schuster, 1993), ch. 3; Carolyn Denham and Amitai Etzioni, *Character Building for a Democratic, Civil Society* (Washington, D.C.: The Communitarian Network, 1997).

18. David R. Karp, ed. *Community Justice: An Emerging Field* (Lanham, Md.: Rowman and Littlefield, 1998).

19. *The Responsive Communitarian Platform: Rights and Responsibilities* (Washington, D.C.: The Communitarian Network, 1997); Etzioni, *The Spirit of Community*, ch. 6.

20. Amitai Etzioni, "A Contemporary Conception of Privacy," *The Limits of Privacy* (New York: Basic Books, 1999), 183–215.

21. Etzioni, "A Contemporary Conception."

22. Robert Booth Fowler, *The Dance with Community* (Lawrence: University Press of Kansas, 1991), 142.

23. Colin Bell and Howard Newby, eds., *The Sociology of Community: A Selection of Readings* (London: Frank Cass, 1974), xiii.

24. Etzioni, *The New Golden Rule*, 127.

25. Daniel A. Bell, "Residential Community Associations: Community or Disunity?" *The Responsive Community* 5(4) (Fall 1995): 26. According to Bell, "the number may exceed 50 million by the year 2000."

26. See for instance, Tom R. Tyler and Robert Boeckmann's article in this volume and Robert J. Sampson, Stephen W. Raudenbush, and Felton Earls, "Neighborhoods and Violent Crime: A Multilevel Study of Collective Efficacy," *Science* 277 (August 15, 1997): 918–24.

27. Etzioni, *The New Golden Rule*, ch. 4.

28. It should be further noted that Tyler and Boeckmann's comment that the U.S. society historically emphasized moral pluralism is a rather contested one. For every scholar who agrees with Tyler and Boeckmann's liberal position (liberal in the political science terms not the Humphrey-Cuomo kind of liberals), there is one who believes that the U.S. genius is found on shared republican (small *r*) civic virtues. For an example of the argument that the United States is a Lockean nation, see especially Louis Hartz, *The Liberal Tradition in America: An Interpretation of American Political Thought since the Revolution* (New York: Harcourt, Brace, 1955). In response to Hartz, see, among others, J. G. A. Pocock, *The Machiavellian Movement: Florentine Political Thought and the Atlantic Political Tradition* (Princeton, N.J.: Princeton University Press, 1975); Isaac Kramnick, *Republicanism and Bourgeois Radicalism: Political Ideology in Late Eighteenth Century England and America* (Ithaca, N.Y.: Cornell University Press, 1990); and Rogers M. Smith, "Beyond Tocqueville, Myrdal, and Hartz: The Multiple Traditions in America," *American Political Science Review* 87(3) (September 1993): 549–66.

29. Amitai Etzioni and Robert P. George, "Virtue and the State: A Dialogue between a Communitarian and a Social Conservative," *The Responsive Community* 9(2) (Spring 1999): 54–66.

30. For more discussion, see Etzioni, *The New Golden Rule*, ch. 8.

31. Etzioni, *The New Golden Rule*, 245.

32. Amitai Etzioni, *The Active Society: A Theory of Societal and Political Processes* (London: Collier-Macmillan, 1968).

33. Francis Fukuyama, *The Great Disruption: Human Nature and the Reconstitution of Social Order* (New York: Free Press, 1999); James Q. Wilson, *The Moral Sense* (New York: Free Press, 1993).

34. "An R.C. Document: A Universal Declaration of Human Responsibilities," *The Responsive Community* 8(2) (Spring 1998): 71–7.

35. *The Responsive Community* 9(1) (Winter 1998/1999).

36. Edward W. Lehman, in his essay, "From Compliance to Community," *The Responsive Community* 9(1) (Winter 1998/1999), 38–47, and in his prologue to this book has already revealed that I have been pursuing this trend since the publication of my first academic book, *A Comparative Analysis of Complex Organizations* (Glencoe, Ill.: The Free Press, 1961).

Index

achievement: as a value type, 158–61, 164,
  165, 166, 172–75
Ackerman, Bruce, 38
action: communicative, 38; social, 47–51
active society, xxi–xxii
African American environmental group,
  136–37
alienation, xii, xix, xxii, xxiv, 2, 32, 77,
  186
Amish, 82
Amos, 77
Anderson, Benedict, 33
Arendt, Hannah, 52
Aristotle, 26, 44, 45, 58, 64, 111
Aron, Raymond, 31
Asian communitarianism, 214, 217, 220,
  225
authoritarianism, 4, 25, 26, 78, 125,
  143, 149, 216, 220, 224, 232, 233
authority: formal-procedural vs.
  substantive-purposive, 12–14, 16, 17,
  21n35; legitimacy vs. morality of, 93,
  96; obedience to, 94; procedural basis
  of legitimacy of, 93–95
autonomy, xii, xviii, xxii, 1, 2, 4, 6–10,
  17–19, 60, 160, 172–75, 197, 200–
  201; balance and tension with order,
  xii, xiv, 1, 5–10, 13, 20n18, 25–34,
  57–61, 65, 77–79, 143–51, 155–56,
  172, 176–79, 185, 189–91, 194,
  201–208, 209n11, 214–15, 219–22,
  226–34; threats to, 10–17

Banfield, Edward, 27
Bardi, Anat, xiv, 232–33
Barres, Maurice, 32
Bauman, Zygmunt, 32–33
Beck, Ulrich, 145
Bell, Colin, 222
Bell, Daniel A., x, xv, 232, 233
Bellah, Robert N., 220
Bendix, Reinhard, xxivn3
benevolence: as a value type, 158–61,
  163–67, 169–70, 172–75, 176–79,
  181n14
Bennett, William, 27
Bentham, Jeremy, 198, 209n21
Berlin, Isaiah, 8, 31, 32, 221, 231
Bernstein, Richard, 40, 43
Blakely, Edward J., 81
Boeckmann, Robert, xiii, 226, 232, 235n28
bonds, social, xiii, 76, 91–102, 105–7,
  126–28, 133–38, 221, 226; affective,
  xxii, 203, 206, 207
bases for exclusivity, 74, 79–84, 103,
  223–24; value and limits of, 224–25

237

Bork, Robert, 27
boundaries, social, 74–75, 79, 103, 106,
    127–33, 137–38; interpenetrating and
    mutually constitutive, xiv, 127;
    permeable, xiv, 127, 131–33, 224
Bourne, Randolph, 111
Boyte, Harry, 131
Bruderhof, 80
Buber, Martin, xxi, 15
Burke, Edmund, 62

Calvin, John, 77
Chan Sek Keong, 217
character education: communitarian
    policies for, 222
Chesterton, G. K., 112
civil society, 32, 61, 108, 116, 131, 133–
    38, 140n16, 221
Clinton, William Jefferson, 28, 30, 34
cohousing movement, 81
common good, xiii, 1–19, 27, 67–69
communes, 79–84
communitarian vs. libertarian, and
    moderate liberal approaches to, 19n3
communitarian societies, 19, 26, 58, 134–
    138, 214, 221. *See also* good society
community (ies), xiii–xiv, 25–26, 30–34,
    45, 46, 57–59, 61–69, 111, 113,
    125–38, 143, 145, 146, 155, 188–89,
    193, 203, 206, 217, 219–22, 224–27;
    definition of, xiii, 18, 71, 72, 85, 90,
    137, 222–24; desirability or value of,
    xiii, 32–33, 71–76, 84–86, 89, 223–
    224; feasibility of, xiii, 71–76, 84–86;
    formation and maintenance of, 71–
    76; gated, 81–82; motivations to
    participate in, xiii, 89–108; "old" vs.
    "new," 75–76; psychological founda-
    tions, xiii, 96–108. *See also* commu-
    nity of communities
community of communities, xiii–xiv, 27,
    32–33, 111, 115, 119, 120, 125–36,
    221, 226–27
complex organizations, xvii–xxi;
    comparative analysis of, xviii–xxi;
    typology of goals, xix–xx

compliance, xii, xvii, xviii–xxi, xxiii–xxiv,
    91, 186; coercive, xix, xx, xxii, 185–
    186, 233; deterrence and, 92–93;
    normative, xix–xxii, 186; social
    normative, xxi, xxiii; utilitarian, xix–
    xx, xxii
Comte, Auguste, 23, 152n10
conformity: as value type, 157–61, 164–
    66, 169–70, 172–75, 177–79
Confraternity of the Holy Spirit, 77
consensus, xiii, xv, 5, 12, 34, 40, 43, 59,
    64, 90–108, 143, 155, 157, 167–70,
    178, 213, 226
consequentialism, 9, 15, 22n42, 229, 230.
    See also functionalism
Constitution, U.S., 97. 113–15, 117,
    133–34, 221, 230, 232; Bill of
    Rights, 114, 118, 130; First Amend-
    ment, 120; Fourth Amendment, 114,
    118, 222; Second Amendment,
    112n27
constitutionalism, 5, 50, 135, 196, 221
convention, social, 197–98
crime: communitarian policies to combat,
    222
cultural relativism. *See* relativism
culture(s), xxii–xxiii, 50, 78, 113, 114,
    116, 117, 127, 145, 147–51, 155–79,
    215, 217, 221, 223; culture wars, xii–
    xiii, xxiii, 1, 128, 180, 220; post-
    cultural value pattern, 163–67, 169–
    75, 232–33

deliberations: nonrational elements, xxiii;
    rational, reasoned, xii–xiii, 38–42,
    51–52, 220–21. *See also* dialogues
democracy, democratic institutions, xvii,
    1, 4, 5, 13, 13, 38, 40, 50, 78, 112,
    113, 116, 118–20, 126, 127–38,
    148–50, 196, 211, 216, 224, 233
deontological position, 3, 9, 50, 209n21,
    221, 227–32
desires: first and second order, 7–8
Dewey, John, 38, 39, 40, 42, 46–47,
    55n53, 116, 119, 187

dialogues: of conviction, xii, 48; cross-cultural, global, 188–91, 211–17, 221, 232–33; inclusive, perils of, 211–17; moral, xii–xiv, xxi–xxiii, 1, 38, 50–52, 58–59, 96–97, 135, 143, 155–56, 185–91, 196, 212, 220, 231; procedural, 38–49, 93–95, 96–102, 125–27, 135, 143, 178–79, 196, 231. *See also* deliberations; megalogues

discourse theory, 37, 38–42, 51–52; critiques of, 43–46

discourses, formal. *See* dialogues, procedural

discursive legitimation, 38

diversity. *See* pluralism

Durkheim, Émile, xviii, 23, 39, 43, 128

Dworkin, Gerald, 6

Dworkin, Ronald, 4, 16, 17, 19n3

Emerson, Ralph Waldo, 112–13

Essenes, 77

ethics, discourse in, xii–xiii, 42–46. *See also* dialogues, procedural

Etzioni, Amitai, ix, xi–xxiv, 1–19, 23–33, 37–38, 51–52, 57–65, 67–69, 71–72, 75–76, 80, 86, 89–92, 95–97, 100, 107–8, 111–20, 125–38, 143–46, 150–51, 155–57, 160, 170, 175–79, 185–91, 193–94, 196–201, 211–17

Eurocentrism, 148–50

evolutionary universals, xiv, 150

family: communitarian policies for, 222

Flache, Andreas, 72

Flanagan, Joseph, 63

Flathman, Richard, 12

Ford, Richard, 32

Fowler, Robert Booth, 222

Frankfurt, Harry, 7

free-rider problem, 74–75

Freud, Sigmund, 27

Friedan, Betty, 29

Fukuyama, Francis, 230

functionalism, xii, 2, 8–19, 171, 177, 227–30; requirements for ordering pancultural value hierarchy, 171–75; teleological, 146, 151n7

fundamentalism, 190, 220

Gandhi, Mohandas K. (Mahatma), xiv, 186, 187–88, 189

Gellner, Ernest, 31, 146

Geneva (Calvin's), 77

George, Cherian, 217

global community. *See* community of communities

"golden rule": compared to "golden mean," 26–27; perspective, 143–44; self-evidence of, 143–45, 150–51

good society, xii, xxii,1, 3, 6, 58, 89, 90, 93, 96–98, 105, 107, 111, 185, 186, 201, 208, 209n11, 219, 224, 229; contrasted to civil society, 221, 229–30. *See also* communitarian societies

Goren, Arthur A., 78

Granovetter, Mark, 72

Günther, Klaus, 42

Habermas, Jurgen, xiii, 37–46, 51–52, 95, 231

Harrington, Michael, 31

Havel, Václav, 63

Hawthorne, Nathaniel, 86

hedonism: as a value type, 158–61, 164–66, 170, 172–75

Heidegger, Martin, 64

Hirschman, Albert O., 115

historical context, xiv, 3, 75, 76–79, 175, 220; and macrocomparative, evolutionist perspective, xiv, 145–51, 152n10

Hobbes, Thomas, 23, 24

Holmes, Stephen, 33

Homans, George, 72

Honesty Markets, 83–84

Honneth, Axel, 40

Horkheimer, Max, 41

human consciousness: levels of, 59, 62–65

human nature, 7, 9, 24, 27, 46–47, 59, 60, 171, 188; competing conceptions, 23–25. *See also* self, conceptions of

human rights: international, universal regime, xv, 196, 211–17. *See also* rights, individual

Hume, David, 194
Hunter, James Davison, 220
Hutcheson, Francis, 9

identification, 91, 103–5
identity politics, 25, 32, 33, 111, 117, 118, 125, 130, 226
individualism, individuality, xiv, 1, 9, 12, 74–75, 207–8, 227; American, xii, 112, 120; expressive, xiii, 32,58, 68; revolt against, 23
individualistic philosophies, xi, xii, 3, 31–32, 125, 126, 209n21, 220; egalitarian liberalism, xii, 2, 6, 16; liberalism, xiii, xiv, 1, 16, 24, 31–32, 51, 57, 127, 193–94, 202, 206, 207, 227, 231–32; libertarianism, 25; moderate liberalism, 1, 6, 17
inequality, xiv, 18, 34, 128, 186, 194–95, 201, 203, 204, 206, 221
interpenetration, sociocultural, 147–48
inverting symbiosis, 8
involvement: in Etzioni's organization theory, xviii, xix

James, William, 46
Jefferson, Thomas, 21n29
Joas, Hans, xii–xiii, xv, 230–32
Jonah, 77
juridification, 37

Kallen, Horace, 33
Kant, Immanuel, 9, 47, 49, 55n59, 193, 198, 199, 209n21, 225
Kanter, Rosabeth M., 80
Kehillah movement, 77–78
kibbutzim, 80
Kierkegaard, Søren, 59
King, Martin Luther, Jr., xiv, 186, 197, 188
Kohler, Thomas C., xii, xv, 228
Kolakowski, Laszek, 31

Lapham, Lewis, 116
Lasch, Christopher, 26
law, legal regulations, xii, 14, 17, 18, 28, 37, 40, 41, 45, 46, 50, 91, 92, 95,

113, 115, 118, 134, 135, 137, 211, 212, 229–30, 233
layered loyalties, xxiii, 134, 221; vs. evolving and interpenetrating loyalties, xiv, 127, 131–33, 138; vs. mixed loyalties, 224
leadership, 221
Lee Kuan Yew, 215, 217
Lehman, Edward W., x, 186, 219
Lehman, Ethna (Bunnie), x, 219
Lemann, Nicholas, 34
lesbian and gay activist group, 129–30, 131, 132
Lewinsky, Monica, 28, 30
liberalism. *See* individualistic philosophies
liberties, negative vs. positive, 7–8, 12, 15, 16, 114
liberty. *See* autonomy
Lichterman, Paul, xiii, xiv, 224
Liddy, G. Gordon, 18
Lincoln, Abraham, 112
Lipset, Seymour Martin, xxivn3
Locke, John, 23, 111, 193, 195, 204–5, 207
Lonergan, Bernard, 62
Lukes, Stephen, 30
Lund, William R., xii, xv, 221, 229, 233

Macpherson, C. B., 31
Macy, Michael W., 72
Madison, James, 4, 113
Magnes, Judah L., 78
Mansfield, Harvey, 114
Marx, Karl, xviii, 23, 147, 152n14, 225
Maslow, Abraham, 73
McCarthy, Joseph, 29
McNeill, William H., 149
McWilliams, Wilson Carey, xiii, xv, 226–27
Mead, George Herbert, 25, 38, 46–47, 52, 222
megalogues, xiii–xiv, 119, 212, 227
Milgram, Stanley, 94
Mitchell, Gregory, 94, 97
modernization, Chinese route, 149–50
moral consensus. *See* consensus
moral dialogues. *See* dialogues, moral

moral judgments, 58–65, 194–200; cross-cultural, global, xiv, 3, 179, 211, 212, 213, 216, 217, 232–33
Moral Rearmament, 77
moral relativism. *See* relativism
moral sense, xii, xiv, 5, 9–11, 14–19, 21n29, 193, 194–95, 197–200, 201, 209n11; compared to deontological position, 230
moral voice, xii, xxi–xxiv, 26, 27, 37, 57, 64, 179, 186, 189, 209n11, 220, 229, 231, 234
morality in society, judgments of, xiii, 91–102
moralization, 37
mores, 211, 215, 220–21, 226, 230. *See also* norms
mosaic metaphor, xiii, 111, 112, 113, 128, 134, 221
Mouzelis, Nicos, xiv, 228–29
multiculturalism. *See* identity politics
Muirhead, J. Russell, xiv, xv, 230

new communitarianism, xi–xv, xvii. *See also* responsive communitarianism
Newby, Howard, 222
Niebuhr, Reinhold, 187
Nineveh, 77
norms, 27–29, 40, 42, 43, 47, 60, 62, 102, 172–75, 212, 213, 220–21, 223, 226, 227; democratic, xiii, 211; distinguished from values, 43–44, 49–50; sieve of norms, 48

order, xiv, xxii, 4, 6, 90, 92, 143, 160, 167, 172–75, 197; 1950s and 1960s as baselines for, xii, 2, 26–30, 31–32; organic vs. liberal accounts of, 195, 201–8; "thick" vs. "thin," xiv, 116, 125; as a value, 194–95, 201–8

Paris Communes (1848 and 1968), 77
Parsons, Talcott, xiv, xviii, 150
participation in communities, voluntary, 90, 96–102, 104, 106
particularism, xiv, 5, 37, 50, 147, 189, 190, 226, 231–32

Peirce, Charles S., 38, 53n14
Pelikan, Jaroslav, 190
person, conception of. *See* self, conception of
personhood, xiii, 58–61
persuasion, xii, xxiii, 4, 221
Phillips, Derek, 26
Plato, 4, 12
pluralism, xiii, 32, 91, 93, 94, 97, 101, 104, 111–14, 136, 221, 226, 231, 235n28; communitarian, 125–38
politics. *See* power, political
postcultural relativism. *See* postrelativism
postrelativism, xiv, 185–91
power, xii, xiv, xvii–xxiv, 185–86, 188–91, 221, 232; economic, 186; political, xiii–xv, xxi, 11, 14, 138, 185–86, 188, 189, 200, 203, 205, 207; of principle, 186–87; typology of, xviii–xix; as a value type, 158–61, 164–66, 170, 172–75
pragmatism, 38, 41, 42, 45, 46–50, 73, 82, 231, 232
pride, 91, 102
privacy, 21, 209n10; communitarian policies regarding, 222
proceduralism. *See* dialogues, procedural
Promise Keepers, 83–84
psychoanalytic theory, 27–28

rationalization, process of, 74
Rawls, John, 3, 19n3, 38, 195, 206
Reagan, Ronald, 34
Reich, Robert, 116
relativism, xii, xiv, 5, 50, 117, 143–51, 155, 216, 229, 230, 231, 232; postmodern, 145–46, 150–51
religion, xiii, 2, 41, 61, 66–67, 79, 80–81, 147–48, 228; success of strict, 73, 80, 112, 190, 197; and valuing and the common good, 67–69
respect, 91, 102–3, 108, 226
responsibilities, social, xi, xii, xv, 214–20; "curl back" toward greater, 2, 27, 30. *See also* order
responsive communitarianism, xi, 14, 219–22, 225, 226. *See also* new communitarianism

Ricoeur, Paul, 48, 55n59
Riesman, David, 31
rights, individual, xi, xii, xv, 4, 6, 17, 19, 112, 113, 115, 117, 125; communitarian policies to balance with the common good, 222; and majority rule, 4–6, 111, 229, 230; universal human, 1, 17, 211–17, 220. *See also* autonomy
Rosenthal, Joel H., xiv, xv, 233
Rousseau, Jean Jacques, 24
Royce, Josiah, 111, 112

sacred, linguistification of, 39, 41
Sadagraha, 188
Sandel, Michael J., 3, 24, 221
Satyagraha, 188
Scheler, Max, 55n59
Schwartz, Shalom H., xiv, 232–33
security: as a value type, 158–61, 163–67, 170, 172–75, 177–79
Seel, Martin, 51
self, conceptions of, 16, 17–18, 25, 221; communitarian, 221–22, 225–26; oversocialized, xii, 25, 222, 225; properly socialized, 225; under-socialized, 222
self-direction: as a value type, 157–61, 163–67, 169–70, 172–75, 176–79
Selznick, Philip, xxivn3, 221
Shaftsbury, Lord, 9
Shakers, 80
Simmel, Georg, 74
Smilie, John, 114, 115
Smith, Adam, 23
Snyder, Mary Gale, 81
social conservatism, xi, xii, 1, 2, 3, 28, 29, 30–31, 125, 194, 226, 227
social order. *See* order
social structure, xvii, xviii, xxi, xxii, 174, 185, 188; consensus formation, xxii
socialism: compared to communitarianism, 30–31, 33
specific greater communities, 131–33, 137–38. *See also* community of communities

Stalin, Joseph, 29
Stark, Andrew, 81
status judgments, as bases for defining relationships, xiii, 102–7
Stengel, Richard, 81
stimulation: as a value type, 158–61, 164, 165, 166, 172–75
subsidiarity, principle of, 60, 69n13
Suchinda, General, 216
Sulak Sivaraksa, Dr., 216
Supreme Court, U.S., 94, 95, 97, 115, 120; reactions to abortion decisions of, 94, 95, 97
survey, three-sample sixty-two-nation study of values, 160–79

Tannen, Deborah, 220
Taylor, Charles, 9, 41, 54n34, 54n40, 213–14
teleological approach, xii, 1, 3, 7, 16, 17; compared to consequentialism, 22n42
Ten Commandment societies, 83–84
Tocqueville, Alexis de, 112, 113, 119, 129
totalitarianism, 63, 220
tradition: as a value type, 158–61, 164, 165, 166, 172–75
trust, 73, 105; intersocietal, xv
Tyler, Tom R., xiii, 92, 94, 97, 226, 232, 235n28

Universal Declaration of Human Responsibilities, 215, 232
Universal Declaration of Human Rights, 211, 232
universalism, 4, 33, 42, 44, 45, 48–49, 50, 189–90, 212, 223, 231–32; moral, xiii, 38, 46–50, 156; as a value type, 158–61, 163, 164, 165, 166, 169–70, 172–75
urban ecumenical association, 132–33

"value pluralism" compared to "moral universalism," 38, 46–50
value types, 157–79

values, xiii, xv, 11–12, 15, 16, 28, 29, 33, 37–40, 43–46, 49–52, 57–65, 67–69, 90–108, 115, 133–37, 140n17, 143–51, 155, 160, 163, 166, 167, 171, 178, 189–90, 193–208, 220–22, 223–24, 225, 226–32; core, xiv, 12, 27–29, 68, 99–107, 134–37, 155–79, 193, 194, 197, 226, 227–32; foundational, 212–14; genesis of, 39, 40, 43, 50; global, xv, 5, 9, 212–17; postmaterialist, 3; relations and order of, 65–67; self-evident, morally compelling, 143–45, 150–51, 156, 177–78, 194–95, 197–200, 202, 228–29, 231, 234; shared, xxii, 60, 68, 125–27, 155, 167, 177, 213–21, 226, 230; "thick" vs. "thin" core, 176–79; ultimate, 228

virtues, 4, 7, 8, 9, 10, 14, 16, 60, 65, 67, 115, 221, 228

Wallerstein, Immanuel, 147
Walzer, Michael, 20n13, 196, 221
Weber, Max, xvii, xviii, 31, 73, 74
Wellmer, Albrecht, 42
Wilson, James, 21n29
Wilson, James Q., 9, 21, 230
Winthrop, John, 195, 202–4, 205, 206, 207
Wolfe, Alan, 33
world system, 147
Wright, Robert, 9
Wrong, Dennis H., xii, xv, 222, 225–26

Zablocki, Benjamin D., xiii, 223–24

About the Contributors

Anat Bardi has recently completed her doctorate in the department of psychology at the Hebrew University of Jerusalem. She is currently a postdoctoral fellow at the University of California, Berkeley. She studies values, in particular values in cross-cultural perspective, and relations of values to everyday life.

Daniel A. Bell is a professor in the department of philosophy at the University of Hong Kong. He has also taught at the University of Singapore and was a Visiting Rockefeller Fellow at the University Center for Human Values, Princeton University. He is the author of *East Meets West: Human Rights and Democracy in East Asia* and *Communitarianism and Its Critics*, coauthor of *Towards Illiberal Democracy in East Asia*, and coeditor of *The East Asian Challenge for Human Rights*.

Robert Boeckmann is an assistant professor in the department of psychology, Flinders University in Australia. His research is concerned with retributive justice and the punishment of wrongdoing. He is the coauthor of *Social Justice in a Diverse Society*.

Amitai Etzioni is university professor and the director of the Center for Communitarian Policy Studies at George Washington University. He is the author of nineteen books, most recently *The Limits of Privacy*. He served as senior advisor to the White House from 1979 to 1980 and as president of the American Sociological Association from 1994 to 1995. He founded and was the first president (1989 to 1990) of the International Society for the Advancement of Socio-Economics. He is the editor of *The Responsive Community: Rights and Responsibilities*, a communitarian quarterly.

Hans Joas is a professor of sociology at the Free University of Berlin and, beginning in fall 2000, also at the University of Chicago as a member of the Committee on Social Thought. His main interests are in social theory, the sociology of war, and comparative studies of Germany and the United States. His books include *Social Action and Human Nature, Pragmatism and Social Theory, The Creativity of Action,* and *The Genesis of Values.* He has recently completed *War and Values,* which was published in Germany.

Thomas C. Kohler is professor of law at Boston College, where he writes and teaches in the areas of domestic and comparative labor and employment law as well as in the theory and structures of civil society. His appointments include serving as a member of the Council on Civil Society (jointly supported by the Institute for American Values and the University of Chicago Divinity School), on the Institute's Council on Families, and as an advisor to the American Council of Learned Societies. He has been a fellow of the German-Marshall Fund of the United States, Fulbright Visiting Professor at the University of Frankfurt, and a visiting faculty member at the Columbia University Graduate School of Business.

Edward W. Lehman is a professor of sociology at New York University. His research interests include political sociology, cultural sociology, and sociological theory. He is the author of *Coordinating Health Care: Explorations in Interorganizational Relations, Political Society: A Macrosociology of Politics,* and *The Viable Polity.* He is coeditor (with Amitai Etzioni) of *A Sociological Reader in Complex Organizations.* His present scholarly interests deal with issues of symbols, culture, and agency. He is currently book review editor of *The Responsive Community.*

Paul Lichterman is assistant professor of sociology at the University of Wisconsin, Madison. He writes about political and civic commitment in America. His book, *The Search for Political Community,* probes the everyday world of grassroots activists. His current research examines how religious volunteer groups get involved in their communities and the factors that allow them to promote civic renewal in a time of shrinking government.

William R. Lund is a professor of political science at the University of Idaho. His research has focused on Hobbes's political theory and on issues raised by the liberal/communitarian debate. His publications include articles in such journals as *History of Political Thought, Political Research Quarterly,* and *Social Theory and Practice.* His current project focuses on the relationship between liberal theory and the problems of income inequality and civil society.

Wilson Carey McWilliams is professor of political science at Rutgers University. His most recent book is *Beyond the Politics of Disappointment? American Elections 1980–1998.* His earlier, *The Idea of Fraternity in America,* won the National Historical Society Prize in 1973. A winner of the John Witherspoon Award for Distinguished Service to the Humanities, he is a frequent contributor to *Commonweal* and other journals of opinion.

Nicos Mouzelis is professor in the department of sociology at the London School of Economics and Political Science. He is a leading sociological theorist and political analyst. His books include *Early Parliamentarianism and Late Industrialization in the Balkans and Latin America*, *Post-Marxist Alternatives: The Construction of Social Orders*, *Back to Sociological Theory: The Construction of Social Orders*, and *Sociological Theory: What Went Wrong?*

J. Russell Muirhead is an assistant professor in the department of government at Harvard University. He has previously taught at Williams College. His interests focus on contemporary political theory and American political thought. He is currently completing a book, *Just Work*, which is forthcoming from Harvard University Press.

Joel H. Rosenthal is the president of the Carnegie Council on Ethics and International Affairs in New York City. In addition to several articles on ethics and U.S. foreign policy, he is the author of the book *Righteous Realists*, editor of *Ethics and International Affairs: A Reader*, and editor of the journal *Ethics and International Affairs*. He has also served as adjunct professor in the department of politics at New York University.

Shalom H. Schwartz is the Leon and Clara Sznajderman professor of psychology at the Hebrew University of Jerusalem where he has taught since 1979. He previously taught for twelve years in the department of sociology of the University of Wisconsin, Madison. His most recent work has focused on the nature of human values. He coordinates an international project that studies the content and structure of value systems and the antecedents and consequences of individual differences in value priorities. This research, conducted in more than sixty nations, has provided the basis for identifying dimensions of value culture on which societies can be compared.

Tom R. Tyler is a professor of psychology at New York University. He previously taught at the University of California, Berkeley. His research is concerned with social justice and the dynamics of authority in groups. He is the author of *Why People Obey the Law* and coauthor of *The Social Psychology of Procedural Justice* and *Social Justice in a Diverse Society*.

Dennis H. Wrong is a professor emeritus of sociology at New York University where he taught for more than thirty years. His books include *Power: Its Forms, Bases and Use*, *The Problem of Order: What Unites and Divides Us*, and, most recently, *The Modern Condition: Essays at Century's End*. He is a frequent contributor to *The Times Literary Supplement*, *The New York Times Book Review*, *The New Republic*, and *Dissent*, where he is an editor. He was the first editor of *Contemporary Sociology: An International Journal of Review*.

Benjamin D. Zablocki is professor of sociology at Rutgers University. He has also taught at the University of California at Berkeley, California Institute of Technology, and Columbia University. He is the author of *The Joyful Community* and *Alienation and Charisma* and the soon to be published *Misunderstanding Cults*. He is currently doing research on the long-term effects of peer influence.